W9-ASL-533

Books by John Bowle

MAN THROUGH THE AGES

HENRY VIII

HENRY VIII

DA332
B6
1965

HENRY VIII

A BIOGRAPHY

JOHN BOWLE

WITH ILLUSTRATIONS

LITTLE, BROWN AND COMPANY
Boston   Toronto

AUG 1965

100042

COPYRIGHT © 1964 BY JOHN BOWLE

ALL RIGHTS RESERVED. NO PART OF THIS BOOK MAY BE REPRO-
DUCED IN ANY FORM WITHOUT PERMISSION IN WRITING FROM THE
PUBLISHER, EXCEPT BY A REVIEWER WHO MAY QUOTE BRIEF PAS-
SAGES IN A REVIEW TO BE PRINTED IN A MAGAZINE OR NEWSPAPER.

LIBRARY OF CONGRESS CATALOG CARD NO. 65-15237

FIRST AMERICAN EDITION

PRINTED IN THE UNITED STATES OF AMERICA

942.05?
B68

PREFACE

✦

'Read until you can hear them talking', G. M. Young used to say; and when you hear them how vivid and pungent seems their speech, coming out of rural England before the Industrial Revolution struck it, and while the heart of the country beat still in the south.

This biography portrays Henry VIII against a background of Tudor England in its European setting, and that society in all its crude vigour still lives in the ample sources which form a panorama of the age: no dialogue has been invented, it is all there. Anyone used to modern clichés may be glad to recall how the old English spoke their minds, the commons as articulate as their masters.

Henry VIII was a tyrant, but a splendid and able prince. Academics who believe in administration and the mordant phrase may seek to belittle him, but fashions change and each age admires its own image; hence, perhaps, the cult of that common bureaucrat of genius, Thomas Cromwell. Rather, one discerns a great king, mediaeval, or 'early modern'; much rooted in the past, though touched with the new learning and fashions.

In writing this book, I have owed much to the advice and encouragement of Dr A. L. Rowse, whose *Tudor Cornwall* includes so detailed a picture of the West Country in Henry's day, whose understanding of the king reflects a deep knowledge of sixteenth century minds, and whose eye for county as well as court history is so sympathetic and penetrating. I have also to thank Mr Wyndham Ketton-Cremer for reading part of the script, and for his advice; and Mr Charles Furth, of Allen and Unwin, whose experienced hand has cut back some genealogical thickets and pruned some hardy ramblers.

In the congenial but exacting tasks of research and transcription, my principal obligation is to Mr John Quentin Davies, scholar of Gonville and Caius College, Cambridge, who has given much time and energy to the work. I am grateful, also, to the Trustees of the Rockefeller Foundation, who invited me to the Villa Serbelloni at Bellagio, Italy, and enabled me to complete the book in superb surroundings, as well as to my hosts there—Mr and Mrs John Marshall. Mr E. V. Quinn, Librarian of Balliol College, Oxford, and Mr G. A. Webb, assistant Librarian at All Souls, have greatly helped me over many months; and I would again like to thank Mrs Barbara Phillips for typing a script whose affinities were more with the late mediaeval handwriting of the conservatives of early Tudor times than with the italic script then coming into fashion.

JOHN BOWLE

Oxford. December 1963

And there swaggers the Shade of a straddling King,
  plumed, sworded, with sensual face,
And, lo, too, that of his Minister, at a bold,
  self-centred pace:
Sheer in the sun they pass; and thereupon
  all is still,
Save the mindless fountain tinkling on with thin
  enfeebled will.

THOMAS HARDY
A Spellbound Palace (Hampton Court)

CONTENTS

❖

ILLUSTRATIONS

✿

INTRODUCTION

THERE are times in history ripe for change, when, deliberately or by improvisation, adepts in power transform society. Among such realists Henry VIII stands pre-eminent in the history of the English speaking world. Directly, with cold calculation and bull-headed obstinacy, and, indirectly, through the policies of agents whom he broke, he cut the knot of the future. A strict Catholic, he destroyed the power of the Papacy in England and consolidated a sovereign state; he was the founder of the British navy, and he secured the Tudor dynasty and their descendants on the throne. He remains, of all the English kings, the most ruthless, the most versatile, and the most terrifying. It is this vigour and opportunist realism, focusing the life and force of his people, and not the variety of his wives, that sets him apart, and makes his reign more decisive than that of any monarch before him, save Alfred and William the Conqueror.

He has come down in British and American popular tradition as an elderly, bluebeard tyrant, with a comic touch singularly unsuited to the sinister facts of his career and to the terror he inspired.[1] Yet, compared with other rulers in the sixteenth century—an Ivan the Dread in Muscovy, a Selim the Grim in the Turkish Empire, or Shah Abbas of Persia—his rule was humane, his executions sporadic: he never killed anyone with his own hand, used poison, or ordered such a massacre as that of St Bartholomew in Paris; and his passions were, at least, conventional.

So important a ruler has attracted able biographers. In particular A. F. Pollard's *Henry VIII*, first published in 1902, remains a masterpiece, a 'splendidly executed portrait (not a Holbein, but neither a Sargent—perhaps a Winterhalter)';[2] J. S. Brewer's study, collected from his earlier prefaces to the *Letters & Papers of Henry VIII*, is judicious and penetrating, though it deals only with the years up to 1530. But since

---

[1] The best-selling Francis Hackett compares him to a 'plum pudding' and heads five chapters with the names of his wives. (*Henry the Eighth*, p. 513.) Charles Laughton's famous film of *Henry VIII* confirmed this genial but erroneous impression.

[2] G. R. Elton. *Henry VIII*, An Essay in Revision. 1962, p. 4.

these books appeared, more information has become available and the angle from which events were then regarded has changed; since Edwardian days, too, the stark realities of war and dictatorship, of ideological conflict and persecution, have been borne in on two generations; religious controversies have ceased to command such intense concern, and psychology has given much behaviour a new look. Many Victorians and Edwardians read into history the liberal ideas of their own time or treated it as a pageant: modern historians tend to make a more objective, disillusioned appraisal of how policy and institutions in fact worked out and were improvised. While the economic interpretation of history can be overstressed for times when questions of religion, and even honour, counted for so much, the tensions which prematurely aged those at the centre of Tudor power can be paralleled by the stress of our age, so that the hectic and precarious is more intelligible than it was half a century ago. Moreover, the Tudor flair for brute essentials was plain in their language, earthy and rural even in the idiom of the court; and the clumsy double-talk, which enwrapped and hinted at the meaning of ambassadors and agents, has its subtle nuance.

If we look back to what seems the miniature stage of Tudor England, the assumptions of men's lives seem alien, but the motives, manœuvres, and objectives constant, and the predicaments familiar. Often, a flash of sympathy will span the centuries; an English envoy will term a pompous ambassador 'Summer will be green' because of his platitudes; Pope Julius II complains that the Emperor Maximilian duns him for money 'to spend on hunting chamois', and the victorious English after Flodden are surprised at the excellence of the Scots ale.

Today, when the famous are indelibly recorded in print, radio and television, and masses of material demand research, the tasks and opportunities of historians have changed. It is worth taking a long look at events now fallen into the perspective of time, for which the evidence, if still controversial, is relatively manageable. The characters are neither inarticulate through illiteracy or barriers of time and language, nor overarticulate in vindicating themselves. And the personality of Henry VIII—'this enormous man', writes Sir Winston Churchill, 'was the nightmare of his advisers'—has lost none of its interest.

He was a prince of versatile accomplishments, an instinctive, ruthless artist in power; in later years, a tyrant, 'subject', says his first biographer, 'to more obloquies than any since the worst Roman Emperors' times'.[1] As Sir Walter Ralegh put it in the Preface to his *History of the*

---

[1] Edward, Lord Herbert of Cherbury, *The Life and Reign of King Henry VIII*, together with a history of those times. 1649.

World: 'Now, for King Henry the Eighth, if all the pictures and patterns of a merciless prince were lost to the world, they might again be painted to the life out of the story of this King. For, how many servants did he advance in haste and with the change of his fancy ruined again, no man knowing for what offence? To how many others, of more desert, gave he abundant flowers from which to gather honey, and in the end of harvest burnt them in the hive? How many wives did he cut off, and cast off, as his fancy and his affection changed? How many Princes of the blood (whereof some of them for age could hardly crawl towards the block), with a world of others of all degrees, did he execute?'[1]

Yet this coldly formidable king could blunder, improvise, and neglect business; sometimes an 'inspired opportunist, making the most of other men's help in a given situation, rather than a creative statesman',[2] he depended on an audience and upon women; he needed, it seems, reassurance. Lavishly generous on occasion, he was ungrateful and mean over and above the demands of policy; he was, in fact, as Baskerville well puts it, *'faux bonhomme'.*[3] The enigmatic personality of Henry VIII will keep its secret; but psychologically as well as politically, he attracts, and will long command, the attention of historians and of a great public throughout the English speaking world.

For in spite of modern efforts to belittle his importance, the fact is that Henry VIII generally had the last word. He disliked 'London business', when it interfered with the racket of sport and company in which he moved, but he never too long allowed his ministers to exploit him; in the end he exploited them, and any institutions to hand. He could take his ease and let Wolsey or Thomas Cromwell do the work, but a twitch on the line could bring their careers to nothing. It was the king's furious determination to have his will which drove through the break with Rome; the revolution was not due to the sudden, electric consequence of men reading the Bible in Tudor translations, though that splendid prose, soaking in over the years, was to consolidate the *fait accompli;* it was due to a brutal and ruthless royal initiative, all the more implacable because the king's monumental egotism and complacency made it inconceivable to him that he could be wrong. 'A good Catholic,' wrote Macaulay, 'he preferred to be his own Pope.'

Modern totalitarian brain-washings and executions have shown how much determined rulers can achieve, and how, save for very exceptional men, most people can be forced by enough arbitrary power to

---

[1] Pp. viii-ix.
[2] Elton, op. cit., p. 17.
[3] Geoffrey Baskerville, *English Monks and the Suppression of the Monasteries,* 1937, p. 12.

toe the line. Even in times when 'salvation', or the lack of it, meant the
difference between an eternity in Heaven or Hell, there were relatively
few martyrs. The number of victims, though sensationalized by the
propaganda of both sides, was not large for the population. Most citizens kept their mouths shut and kept their property, or used the ideological conflict for their own ends. It was the king's will, working,
tactically, through Thomas Cromwell, that changed the future of
England, and most men made the best of it.

If both Protestant and Catholic versions of the 'Reformation' or
'Protestant Schism' no longer colour the modern view of Henry's
nationalization of the Church, other *idées reçues* must also go by the
board. Historians, for example, both of Catholic Right and Socialist
Left, have grossly overestimated the importance of the dissolution of
the monasteries. They were already on their way out; their charity a
drop in the bucket of the distress being aggravated by a creeping European inflation, gradually increased by the flooding in of silver from the
new world. It has been well said that 'the silvermines of Peru destroyed
long in advance the extremist legends beloved alike by Fabian and
Catholic propagandists'.[1]

Again, the rural populace were not evicted by capitalist sheep farmers on a scale at all comparable to that caused by the enclosures of the
eighteenth century. This belief, derived by socialist historians from
Tudor preachers, has had to go; the main Tudor social disruptions and
unemployment came from inflation, and that creates gainers as well as
losers.

It was the class already on the make by the later fifteenth century
who now muscled in on an expanding society; in the law, in trade, in
administration and war. They were younger sons of Welsh gentry, like
the Herberts; of Dorset wine merchants and members of Parliament,
like the Russells; of a sergeant at arms in the City, like the Pagets; of a
yeoman of the wardrobe, like the Cecils; of a blacksmith and brewer,
like Thomas Cromwell. And this class produced not only the ancestors
of the high Tudor aristocracy, but their dependent lawyers, bailiffs,
auditors and men of business who founded families of middling and
minor gentry. Along with their patrons, these people formed the establishment which the Tudors consolidated and on which their power was
based. All, indeed, comes back to the Crown, which hastened a transformation socially and economically ripe.

The egotist who carried it through, still, as the older historians believed, its mainspring, looks less mysterious to modern eyes than he did

[1] A. G. Dickens, *Thomas Cromwell and the English Reformation*, p. 182.

to the Victorians. He was not, as for those who 'idealized' their Protestant hero, an Argus-eyed Carlylean or Nietzschian figure. Nor was he the syphilitic which a disproved medical diagnosis once depicted him; he remained physically vigorous, a 'grand gross figure', as Stubbs called him, gigantic in build and gargantuan in appetite, until, clear-minded to the end, he died of an occluded sinus in his leg, due to gout. He was what his heredity and circumstances made him; at once a dynamo of energy and will, yet lazy, exhibitionist, easily bored, spoilt, and cold; subject to appalling rages, when, like some Byzantine emperors, he must have had 'that wild beast look'. What else could he be, given his high Plantagenet blood, his essential loneliness, his regal pride, the setting of his life? But he came also from sharp Welsh adventurers; brave, vigilant, avid for power, with a grasp of essentials, like his father. He was the greatest builder of all the English kings, and the greatest patron of learning; extravagant in the Rabelaisian exuberance of the time, but as shrewd a man of business as anyone. He remained the sovereign who could make or break: he was England.

Psychologically, as well as politically, Henry was consistent; from his adolescence a cunning realist; never, as Pollard thought him, a political innocent. The flamboyant gusto of his youth won him a popularity which the cruelties of his prime never dispelled, for he seemed to the people what a king ought to be. Yet his athletic, omnivorous aspect masked subtle sensibility; talent in verse and music; connoisseurship in architecture and decoration; more, it seems, than in women, for few of his apprehensive wives appear particularly attractive. And when splendid youth and brilliant maturity gave way to stertorous middle age, the will of steel and impersonal cruelty of one who felt himself, since youth, the embodiment of the state, were never eroded. He always retained the realism of his father and of Elizabeth I, the daughter who was most like him; 'although I may not be a lion', she said, 'I am a lion's cub, and I have a lion's heart'.

Too many historians have portrayed Henry VIII as a monster, either of good or of evil. Both the eloquent Protestant genius of Froude, who created a father-figure for the Reformation, and the detestation of Catholic writers, provoked by the rift he made in Christendom, must give place to a cooler appraisal of an intelligible character in an intelligible situation.

For Henry VIII was born to the summit of power in hard precarious times, to which the battered and wary faces even of the successful bear witness. Conscious that his dynasty and people depended upon his sole cunning and will to foresee and master circumstance and chance, he used his subjects with instinctive and successful opportunism. He paid the price in the demoralization which always affects the wielders and the victims of arbitrary power. What other fate could he have but to become seasoned, carapaced and corrupted in the egotism that alone could master the demands of his royal predicament?

HENRY VIII

CHAPTER I

PRELUDE TO POWER

◼

O N June 28, 1491, in the height of summer, at the royal manor of
Greenwich, where the ships went down the Thames to the sea
and the air came fresh with the tang of pitch and the cry of gulls, a
third child and second son was born to Henry VII, the first Tudor
monarch of England, and to his queen, the Lady Elizabeth of York,
daughter of Edward IV. The prince, baptized Henry, was to live to his
fifty-sixth year, a long life for that time, and to found a modern state, a
national church and the British navy.

Henry VII had won the throne by conquest. His hereditary claim
was weak, for the Tudors came of obscure origins. They derived from
a certain Meredith-ap-Theodore, or Tudor, steward to the Bishop of
Bangor in North Wales. A forebear, Tudor-ap-Goronwy, had fought
for Edward III; and the family, like other Welsh gentry, claimed descent from Cadwalladr. They owned land at Bangor and Plas Penmynydd on Angelsey, and their arms were gules, a chevron between
three closed helmets—'the steel helmet of fair Tudor'—*Helm ddur hil i
Dudur deg*.[1] Their standard was a dun cow on a yellow field.

Meredith had killed a man and fled out of Wales; his son, Owen, had
to seek his fortune in England and he transformed the prospects of his
line. As clerk to the wardrobe of the Lady Katherine of France, Queen
Dowager of the great Henry V, he fascinated his mistress. They were
married in secret, and when, in 1437, the affair came to light, the Queen
Dowager retired to Bermondsey Abbey; Owen Tudor to Newgate
prison. Pardoned, he fought for the Lancastrians, and died, defiant,
under the Yorkist axe. The two sons born of the marriage thus combined with their Welsh blood the high, tainted, lineage of the Valois:

---

[1] *Archaeologia Cambrensis*, 1st Series, IV, pp. 267 ff. At Plas Penmynydd tombs of
collaterals are extant. One of them had been Forester of Snowdon, and drowned in a
bog:

> ... of excess of mead it happened.
> Senseless loss the black pool caused
> By covering the dread lion.
> (3rd Series, XV, 292-3.)

Henry VI acknowledged his half-brothers and created Edmund Earl of Richmond; Jasper Earl of Pembroke.

Edmund Tudor of Richmond took the next decisive step to greatness. He married the Lady Margaret Beaufort, daughter and heiress of John Beaufort, Duke of Somerset, grandson of John of Gaunt, Duke of Lancaster, by his mistress Katherine Swynford. 'Time honoured Lancaster', fifth son of Edward III, came of the blood royal of England; when the Beauforts had been legitimized, their claim to the throne had been officially barred, but it had descended to the Lady Margaret Beaufort. And Edmund Tudor's posthumous son was called Henry of Richmond, after his glamorous Lancastrian descent—for, as the Welsh bard put it, his mother came of 'the first stock of the Lancastrian race'. According to Bacon, Henry VI, in a lucid interval, had remarked: 'This is the lad that shall possess quietly what we now strive for'; and as Henry VII, Richmond was to found the ablest dynasty in English history.[1]

II

'*For God's sake,*' said Shakespeare's *Richard II*, '*let us sit upon the ground,*

'*And tell sad stories of the deaths of Kings,*

  How some have been deposed, some slain in war . . .

  All murdered.'[2]

The Tudor outsider had benefited from these crimes, for the Lancastrian Henry IV, who had ousted Richard II, had founded a fated line. His son, the dour and martial Henry V, had died of camp fever, still young; his grandson, Henry VI, had founded Eton and King's College, Cambridge, at eighteen, but he had been politically incompetent;[3] 'mute as a calf', he had been knocked on the head in the Tower (when gnawing a cutlet) at the orders of his Yorkist cousin, Edward IV, on whose command also the young Prince of Wales had been executed after the battle of Tewkesbury.

Edward IV, who represented the Yorkist branch of the Plantagenets, had revived the monarchy, but he had died in 1483, still only forty. And then the Yorkists, too, had committed dynastic suicide; for Richard of Gloucester, the king's brother, had 'occupied' the throne, and had probably murdered his nephews, the young Edward V and the

---

[1] See Pedigree A (at end).

[2] Act II, sc. I, 155 ff.

[3] Henry VII tried to get him canonized, but Julius II said he had to draw the line somewhere between saints and imbeciles.

Duke of York, last seen shooting and playing in the garden of the Tower in July, 1483. Certainly by August they were dead; 'suddenly lapped up', according to More, 'among the clothes . . . the feather bed and pllows hard unto their mouthes that within a while smored (smothered) and styfled, their breath failing, they gave up to God their innocent soules'.[1]

The rumour of this crime had weakened Richard III's position, and his policy had been thwarted by the death of his own son. Thus the Yorkist male line had been cut off, and their claims had descended to Elizabeth of York, daughter of Edward IV. And by now the Lancastrian claim, too, had devolved, through his mother, on Richmond, who had taken refuge in Brittany. Already forced by the agents of Richard III to move into Anjou, he had to strike soon or die.

III

In 1483 Henry Tudor of Richmond tried to land near Poole Harbour. He was driven off by the embattled men of Dorset, and Richard III soon executed his fellow conspirator, the Duke of Buckingham, in the market place at Salisbury; but Richard's position remained precarious. As an informant wrote to Sir William Stonor from London, well summing up the times: 'Every man doubts other. On Friday last was the lord Chamberlaine hedded soon apone noon. On Monday last was at Westminster great plenty of harnessed men. . . . The Lord Archbishop of York, the Bishop of Ely (Morton) are yet in the Tower . . . for Foster, he is in hold and mew for his life. Mastres Chore is in prison; what shall happen her I know not. And Jhesu preserve you.'[2]

In August 1485 Henry Tudor, now twenty-eight, tried again, and this time he succeeded. With a power of 1,800 French mercenaries and

---

[1] Sir Thomas More, *History of the Kyng Rycharde the Thirde*. See also Lawrence E. Tanner and Professor W. Wright, *Recent Investigations regarding the fate of the Princes in the Tower*. *Archaeologia*, LXXXIV, 1935. What were thought to be the remains of the Princes, buried deep under a staircase of the White Tower, were discovered in 1674 and, by order of Charles II, placed in an urn in Henry VII's Chapel in Westminster Abbey. In 1933 the urn was opened, and the bones found to be those of two boys of appropriate ages, 12–13 and 9–10. There were traces of suffocation on the elder boy, and Professor Wright then considered that, on evidence 'more conclusive than could, considering everything, have reasonably been expected', the bones were those of the Princes. If they were, 'by no possibility could either, or both, have been still alive on August 22, 1485, the date of Henry's accession': if they were not, 'the fact remains,' writes Professor Jacob, 'that [the princes] disappeared from view while Richard was on the throne. . . . Their uncle had declared them bastards and could hardly have afforded to keep them alive.' *The Fifteenth Century*, pp. 624–5. *Oxford History of England*, VI, 1960.

[2] Stonor Papers, ed. C. C. Kingsford. Camden Society, Third Series, XXX, p. 161.

a handful of supporters he landed at Milford Haven in South Wales; they moved swiftly through the hills on Shrewsbury, where substantial Welsh forces joined the dragon standard of Cadwalladr. As he advanced into the midlands across the August countryside, Richmond was making one more desperate throw in the dynastic vendetta of the Wars of the Roses, which had long convulsed the royal house and the high nobility. Nine-tenths of the populace, cultivating their rural holdings and the manor fields, thought such affairs 'king's games', a nuisance of endemic warfare among aristocrats in the plate armour still depicted on their tombs and brasses. But to the participants and their gangs battles were deadly and victories precarious: executions followed each battle, 'some hanged, some headed'.

Richard III, an able if criminal ruler, regarded his rival with contempt: 'Henry Tydder' he called him, 'an unknown Welshman, whose father I never knew nor him personally saw'. But on August 22, 1485, on Bosworth Field in Leicestershire, Richard died fighting like the wild boar of his cognizance. Offered a swift horse to convey him away, he remarked that he would make an end of all battles or else finish his life, closed his helmet, and made at Richmond himself, to be hacked to death after he had killed his enemy's standard bearer. The king's mutilated corpse was thrown over a horse and carried stark naked from the field, hair sweeping the ground. The 'crown of ornament'—not of course the authentic crown, unsuitable for battle—was found under a hawthorn bush and placed on Henry of Richmond's head.

Though few contemporaries expected his regime to last, the history of England had taken a decisive turn. The direct Plantagenet line was finished; though insecure until the end of the century, Henry VII consolidated his success. The ancient powers of the crown, the mainspring of government, were still in hand, though too often in abeyance since the fourteenth century: Henry VII brought them to bear on a potentially vigorous realm, now climbing out of the decline which had come in with the Black Death and the disruption of the old order of the high Middle Ages. Already, the economy had been reviving in the 'seventies, and only the misfortunes and the crimes of the Yorkist house had masked recovery.

Moreover, Henry Tudor, Earl of Richmond, had learnt in exile and diplomacy to keep his own council and to handle men: he could hold aloof and inspire fear, and he became the greatest architect of the Tudor fortunes. Without the sheer blood lust of his contemporaries, he had a sardonic wit; telling rebellious Irish chieftains that they 'would crown apes at last'. He 'understood the Latin' and could use fine clothes, jewels

and ceremony for political effect; he added a superb chapel to Westminster Abbey and although 'traditional reports that Henry VII left
treasure worth £1,300,000 or £1,800,000 . . . appear to be quite un-
founded. . . . He may have left to his successor a valuable accumulation
of jewels and plate equivalent to something like two years' gross yield
of the permanent revenues.'[1] No great fortune, but solvency.

On September 3, 1485, he entered London in triumph (*laetenter*,
rejoicing, not *latenter*, 'furtively', as misread) and dedicated his banners
in St Paul's: the banner of St George, the red dragon of Cadwalladr on
a green and white field, and, for his family, a dun cow on yellow tar-
tern.[2] By October 30, he was crowned with an ancient ritual that had
come down from the Confessor, enriched by fashionable Burgundian
ceremony; presented to the people as the 'rightful and undoubted inheritor by the laws of God and man to the crown and royal dignity of
England'. 'Will ye, sirs,' asked the Archbishop, 'at this time give your
wills and assents to the same?' . . . Whereupon the people [said] with
a great voice, 'Ye! Ye! Ye! So be hit. King Henry! King Henry!'[3]

A methodical realist had won the throne. After asserting his right to
the crown by sole conquest and meeting his first Parliament, and not
before, Henry VII fulfilled his oath, taken in Brittany two years earlier,
to marry the Lady Elizabeth, daughter of Edward IV, representative of
the Yorkist line; a ceremony that, to the annoyance of the king, won
more popular applause than the coronation. It was followed by a banquet which included jellied lampreys and perch, mutton royal richly
garnished, peacock, 'conys (rabbits) of high grece', sturgeon with fen-
nel and larks 'engryled', and which ended with 'marchpayne royall'
and 'castells of jelly in templewise made'.[4]

IV

The infant Prince Henry and future Henry VIII was the second son of
this dynastic marriage. He thus inherited both Lancastrian and Yorkist
blood and took after that 'big carnal man', his pleasure-loving, magnificent and able grandfather, Edward IV; he certainly inherited his fine
physique from his mother, Edward's daughter, Elizabeth of York, a tall
fair-haired princess with blue eyes. Henry VII was a wiry lightweight
who died of bronchitis at fifty-two.

[1] B. P. Wolffe, 'Henry VII's Land Revenues and Chamber Finance,' *E.H.R.*, April
1964, p. 254.
[2] J. D. Mackie, *The Earlier Tudors*, Oxford, 1951. p. 54.
[3] *Rutland Papers*. ed. W. Jerdan. Camden, 1842, p. 13.
[4] *A Relation of the Island of England*, ed. C. A. Sneyd. Camden, 1847, note 79. pp. 114-15.

Prince Henry's upbringing, as a second son and Duke of York, was
strictly orthodox and conservative, influenced by his affectionate and
devout grandmother, the Lady Margaret Beaufort, Dowager of Richmond, from whom his Lancastrian strain derived. But it is most unlikely, as Herbert suggests, and other historians have repeated, that he
was meant to be Archbishop of Canterbury, for the only evidence
comes from Paolo Sarpi's casual remark, made long after, that 'Henry
was destined by his father to be archbishop and so made to attend his
studies from boyhood'.[1] Like Prince Arthur, his elder brother, he
would have been made to attend to them anyway.

Arthur, Prince of Wales, four years his senior, was a delicate handsome boy without his younger brother's stamina; the elder sister, the
wild and spirited Margaret, married James IV of Scotland, and became
grandmother of Mary Queen of Scots, and so of the Stuart kings of
England. By her second marriage to Archibald Douglas, Earl of Angus,
she also became ancestress of Lord Darnley, who by his marriage to
Mary Queen of Scots fathered James I of England. Mary, the other
sister, became briefly Queen of France, then Duchess of Suffolk.
Edmund, the youngest brother, died an infant.

The royal children grew up amid luxury and ceremonial; the official
seat of government was still the palace of Westminster, a royal residence since the days of Edward the Confessor. Here, in a warren of
mediaeval buildings, government was carried on and justice administered. In the centre of the private apartments lay the splendid Painted
Chamber, embellished by Henry III with murals of the Confessor's
coronation and battle pieces of the Old Testament, done in gold, silver,
scarlet and blue. Here Henry VII slept in a great bed prepared with
extraordinary precaution and ceremonial.[2]

This historic setting was the official background of Henry's youth.
With the Thames, then much wider, running beneath its windows, the
old palace was damp and insanitary, liable to flood and fog; its site
remains the official centre of the government of England.

---

[1] *History of the Council of Trent*, Vol. 3, p. 25, quoted by Lord Herbert of Cherbury.
Op. cit.

[2] See Neville Williams, *The Royal Residences of Great Britain*. Barrie and Rockcliff,
London, 1960, to which this chapter is indebted.

'It took ten attendants to make the bed . . . the groom stood at the foot of the bed
holding a torch, the yeoman lined up, four on each side. One of them searched the
straw with a dagger to see "that there be no untruth therein". The straw was then
covered with a length of canvas and on top of it went the feather bed . . .' On top of
the blankets went an ermine coverlet and the tucking in was complicated. Each yeoman
then made the sign of the Cross upon the place where his hands had touched the bed
and kissed the spot. Op cit., p. 19.

The other official residence in London was the Tower, the fortress built by William the Conqueror to overawe the city; here were the Mint and the Crown Jewels, and from it the sovereign set out for the coronation. Its grim past was apparent from the heavy Norman architecture of the main keep; from the armouries, where Henry VIII's gigantic armour may still be seen; and from the echoing, dank corridors and the traitor's gate. Henry VII still used it; his wife died there; and when three years after his accession, in 1512, the palace of Westminster was gutted by fire, Henry VIII went to live there in temporary quarters and put up the half-timbered 'King's House', still extant. But he did not often reside there, and, after Wolsey's fall, he took over York Place, Wolsey's great palace, which became Whitehall, the main London palace of the Tudors and Stuarts.

But the King's children were not much in London; the country palaces were healthier. Windsor, superbly commanding the curve of the Thames, had long been famous. Here Edward III had founded the Order of the Garter, and Edward IV had begun St George's Chapel, that masterpiece of late mediaeval architecture. Henry VII had continued the work and dedicated it; his son was to install an elaborate carved royal closet from which his queens would watch services and ceremonial, and rebuild the main entrance, now the Henry VIII gate. But Henry VII generally preferred the more comfortable palaces of Richmond and Greenwich; the former up river near Kew, the latter down river near the sea.

Richmond was originally the palace of Sheen, where Edward III had spent his declining, disreputable years, and where Richard II had lived with Anne of Bohemia, his first queen. Wild with grief at her death, he had demolished much of the building, but the Lancastrians had rebuilt it, and added a monastery. In 1498, when Prince Henry was still a child, it had been burnt down, and his father had erected an elaborate renaissance palace, naming it Richmond, after his own original title.

It was, however, at Eltham, in Kent, near Greenwich, that Henry spent most of his childhood. Here stood a moated, mediaeval house, the scene of much Plantagenet splendour, recently reconditioned; it stood in a deer park, and, as Henry VIII, he made it the most comfortable of the royal residences.

Such was the background of Henry's youth; Greenwich, where he was born, and Eltham, where he was brought up, would have held his earliest memories; then Richmond, where his father spent much of the year and was to die; then, for great formal occasions, Windsor, the Tower, and the Palace of Westminster, under the great bulk of the Abbey.

V

Henry emerged from infancy to childhood among the oaks of Eltham and by the ships and the river at Greenwich: and he was subjected to the full rigour of scholastic and renaissance learning. His earliest portrait depicts a horribly precocious child, alert and observant, with a tight little mouth—all too like the monarch in his prime. He proved a good linguist, fluent in French and Latin and competent in Spanish and Italian: he was keen on mathematics, and a talented musician. He had a delicate, rather high voice; when the king was nearly fifty, an observer who described his daughter, the Lady Mary, reported that she had 'a voice more manlike, for a woman, than he [had] for a man'.[1] He learnt to play the lute, the organ and the recorder, and, though he did not, as was formerly believed, compose *O Lord Maker of All Things*, the work of an Elizabethan, he composed masses, now lost, and a song for the lute:

> *For my pastance*
> *Hunt sing and dance*
> *My hart is set;*
> *All goodly sport*
> *For my comfort,*
> *Who shall me let?*

He is depicted, in his battered decline, playing the harp in a rather plaintive manner.

He grew up to take music for granted: the court orchestra included trombones, sackbuts and five bagpipers, and seventy-nine singers in the Chapel Royal recruited from all over England; six choristers always travelled with the household to sing mass, and the king installed elaborate organs in his palaces.

As these intellectual abilities developed, Henry also showed a vigorous, practical side. He was fascinated by the design of ships, as well as by architecture, and he would concoct medicines for his own use; a plaster 'designed to heal ulcers without pain', and an unguent 'devised by his Majesty at Greenwich to cool inflammation to take away the itch'; in his mature age, he invented 'The King's Grace's oyntment made at St James's to coole and dry and comfort the Member'.[2] There

[1] L. and P. Vol. XVI, p. 586.

[2] *Horace Walpole's Correspondence with the Rev. William Cole*, ed. W. S. Lewis and A. D. Wallace, New Haven, 1937, p. 332. 'Another to the same purpose,' writes Horace Walpole, 'was devised at Cawoode. Was not that an episcopal palace? How devoutly was the Head of the Church employed!'

was 'no necessary kind of knowledge from King's degree to carters', it was rumoured, 'but he had an honest sight of it'.

By the age of nine, Henry was demanding a piece from Erasmus' pen, and his Latin became admirable: 'there cometh no letters from any other prince unto his Holiness (Pope Leo X) to be exhibited in the Consistory', Cardinal Bainbridge wrote in 1513, 'that be judged more elegantly written than they be'. And when, as theologian, Henry came to set about Luther, he could meet that scurrilous controversialist with effect. Amid the pomp and glitter, the parade of chivalry and war which so much appealed to Henry's exhibitionist, extrovert side, he early displayed, and always maintained, a versatile, hard ability.

He was brought up to splendour. At Woodstock, in 1494, when he was only three, his father decided to 'doube his ijde son Knyght of the Bath, and after to creat hym duc of York'. So, that October, the child was brought from Eltham to the palace of Westminster for the elaborate ceremony, with 'joustes roiall, ... great honour and triumph of great estates'. The Duke of Buckingham placed a spur against his right heel, and the king dubbed him knight and 'set him upon the table'. Next day, Sir William Sandys carried him in before the queen, the king's mother, and the assembled Court, to be created Duke of York, with a gift of a thousand pounds a year. It was a significant title, reviving and emphasizing his Yorkist descent, and ever since, the sovereign's second son has borne it.

As Henry, Duke of York, stared in wonder round the glittering assembly, the trumpets blared and the York heralds, in blue and tawney, proclaimed '*Largesse de Tréshault, puissant, et excellent prince, secound filz de nostre seigneur, duc de Yorc, Lieutenant General de D'irlonde, Counte Marishall, Marishall d'Engleterre et gardien des Cinque Portz, Largesse par Troys Fois!*'[1]

Outside Westminster Hall followed days of elaborate tournaments. 'Then should you have seen the great riders', wrote an observer, 'the well-doing horses ... what gambadys and jangling of bells and glistering of spangels', and 'especially among others the Lord Abergavenny had a small black horse which in mounting so high above ground did marvels'.

The knights emerged out of the great hall in fantastic mediaeval panoplies—horses 'trapped with green velvet and white damasc, enramplished with red roses', or with cloth of gold bordered with black velvet embroidered with golden letters. Many spears were 'well

---

[1] *Letters and Papers of Richard III and Henry VII*, Rolls Series, ed. James Gairdner, 1861. Vol. I. Appendix A, p. 394.

broken', though Rowland de Vielleville's 'hors would not cope', and
ran only five courses instead of six, and some were in 'jeopardy to have
been unsaddled'. Henry's elder sister, the Princess Margaret, presented
the prizes: a ruby ring to John Peche, another to a 'valiant esquire,
Thomas Brandon.'

The pageant of this 'noble and triumphant company' may have
coloured the earliest memories of a child who already faced the fullest
publicity. But it was only on state occasions that the king's children
came to Westminster; and Henry's childhood was spent mainly at
Eltham; first, under the charge of his nurse, Ann Luke; then under a
formidable number of tutors. One was Friar Bernard André of
Toulouse, tutor to the Prince of Wales, a blind historian and humanist,
who, in his *Life of Henry VII up to 1497*, had glorified King Arthur as
the ancestor of the Tudor dynasty: for 'under Henry VII, the foreign
poets at Court had no compunction in accepting his existence'.[1]
Another, Giles d'Ewes, or Du Guez, a French grammarian who dab-
bled in alchemy, survived to instruct the Princess Mary, for whom he
wrote *An Introduction for to Lerne to Rede, to Pronounce and to Speke French
Trewly*, dedicated to Henry VIII. John Skelton, the East Anglian poet
laureate to Henry VII, called 'beastly' by Pope, and since better appreciated,[2] was probably the most forceful personality. 'The honor of
England,' he wrote, 'I learned [taught] to spell.'

This flamboyant figure must, indeed, have had his impact on the
small household; he would hardly have confined himself to the pompous sentiments expressed in his Latin poem on Henry's creation as
Duke of York. But Skelton only attended Henry when the boy was
being taught to spell and 'sit at meat seemly'; he was removed, though
not from Court, after Henry became Prince of Wales. Skelton did,
however, give him some advice in his *Mirror for a Prince*, though it was
not followed, for he advised Henry 'to pick out a wife for himself and
love her alone'.

The young Henry, Duke of York, was described in 1499 by Erasmus,
who visited Eltham with Sir Thomas More. 'In the midst' (of his
attendants), he wrote, 'stood Prince Henry, now nine years old, and
having already something of royalty in his demeanour.' More presented the child with 'a writing', but Erasmus had nothing prepared;
Henry, perhaps already determined to get full value, sent him a note at

---

[1] Professor Denys Hay, *Polydore Vergil*, Renaissance Historian and Man of Letters,
p. 158.
[2] See E. M. Forster's vastly entertaining lecture in *Two Cheers for Democracy*, pp. 145–61.
Arnold, 1960.

dinner, 'challenging something' from his pen. So Erasmus obliged with a poem which took three days to write.

VI

In October 1501, Henry played a leading part in the marriage of his fourteen-year-old brother, Prince Arthur, to Catherine of Aragon. At sixteen, Catherine was a beauty; she had grey eyes, golden brown hair and a fresh complexion, though, in the way of some southern women, she was early to lose her looks. She was also highly educated, elegant, a good dancer. She had arrived at Plymouth after a dangerous voyage, and had been acclaimed in the West. From Exeter, by easy stages, she come up through Honiton, Crewkerne, Sherborne, Shaftesbury and Amesbury, then, over the chalk downs, by Andover and Basingstoke, to Chertsey and Lambeth. The wedding was the climax of long, tortuous, and complex negotiations, and the officials planned the ceremony with meticulous care.[1]

The river swarmed with the state barges of the royalties, bishops and magnates, as young Henry rode to St George's Fields, to bring the Spanish princess to the palace of the Bishop of London. At the wedding itself, it was again Henry who conducted her from the bishop's palace to the west door of St Paul's, while the bells of London rang out and trumpeters blew fanfares as the pair entered the cathedral. Here Prince Arthur was waiting for his bride; slowly he led her to the high altar, between the great Gothic pillars hung with tapestry, past the 'hault place', specially constructed, from which King Henry VII and his queen privately watched the wedding. When the bridegroom left the church separately for the palace, to make ready to receive his bride, 'as the custom of England is', it was Henry, a great boy already taller than the slender white-clad bridegroom, and who had 'stared his wide eyed unblinking stare throughout the service',[2] who led Catherine through the choir, down the long nave to the west door, and so to the bishop's great gate. As they entered, a conduit 'pompously devised to run diverse sortes of good wine' began to spout, and the whole city gave itself over to a magnificent orgy. Arthur and Catherine then proceeded to

[1] *Letters and Papers of Richard III and Henry VII*, vol. I. Arrangements for the Reception of Katherine of Aragon, pp. 404–7. The English were already efficient organizers of pageantry; everything was thought out, including a place for the principals secretly to resort to 'for such casualties as may fall during high mass'; Westminster Hall had new rushes and glass, the great 'bruge' [bridge] at Westminster was 'amended', and the King's heraldic beasts and arms repainted and renewed.

[2] Garrett Mattingly, *Catherine of Aragon*, Cape, 1950 edition, p. 38.

Baynard's Castle by Lombard Hill, that day specially sanded and grav-
elled 'for the horses more surely to kepe thaim silf upright', and there
they were publicly and boisterously bedded, according to the custom
of the day.

What happened, or did not happen, that night, and during the
months in the castle at Ludlow to which the young people were dispatched, was fateful for England. When, years later, Henry discovered
that he had gravely sinned by marrying his brother's widow, the whole
evidence was closely examined. The boy Arthur boasted, it seems, that
he 'has been six miles into Spain', but Catherine always maintained
that she came to Henry a virgin, and that he knew it perfectly well.

Unaware of the tragic future, the young people danced; and the boy
Henry threw off his formal surcoat and leapt and pirouetted with the
rest. He was always to be a great dancer, even in middle age, when he
danced in yellow silk with queen Anne Boleyn on the evening after
the announcement of Catherine of Aragon's death.

The marriage of Catherine to Arthur had been a landmark in the
Tudor dynasty's success. Their whole policy had been to secure the
succession and extend their power; by the turn of the century the
Spanish ambassador, da Puebla, had informed Ferdinand of Aragon
and Naples and Isabella of Castile that, in a notoriously turbulent
realm, all was at last 'purged and clean, so that not a doubtful drop of
royal blood remains in the kingdom, save the true blood of the King
and Queen, and above all that of the Lord Prince Arthur'. The assurance had, perhaps, secured the alliance.

But in April 1502, after the rejoicing and pageantry in London, dire
news arrived from Ludlow, where the young Prince and Princess of
Wales had spent the winter, showing the flag on the Welsh border.
Prince Arthur was dead, stricken with the sweating sickness, or acute
influenza, for which Tudor medicine had no remedy; 'a malign vapour
which proceeded from the constitution of the air'. The whole policy
seemed in ruins; the princess was not even with child.

But the event marked a turning point in Henry's life; he became
heir apparent, and Duke of Cornwall; in the following year, Prince of
Wales and Earl of Chester. He also early lost his mother: in February
1503, Queen Elizabeth died of puerperal fever in the Tower and, three
years later, Henry could write, on the death of the King-Archduke
Philip of Castile and Austria, 'never since the death of my dearest
mother, hath there come more hateful intelligence'.

From set fair, the prospects of the dynasty had now become precarious. The king's health was already notoriously bad; Henry, now

1. Henry VIII. Portrait in the hall of Trinity College, Cambridge
(Reproduced by permission of the Master and Fellows of Trinity College, Cambridge)

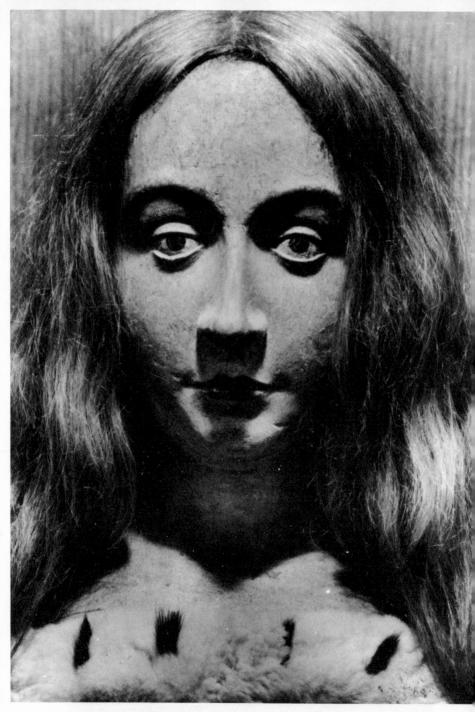

2. Funeral effigy of Queen Elizabeth of York in Westminster Abbey
(photo: Eric de Mare)

the only surviving son, was not of age, and there were 'moles' at work. Disquieting reports came in from the king's spies: important people were remarking that 'the King's Grace was but a weak man and sickly'; what would happen were he to 'depart'? The Duke of Buckingham, the only surviving Duke, was being canvassed for the succession, and 'none of them spoke up for my Lord Prince'; subordinates were saying 'they had good [strong] holds to resort to' from which they could make their peace, 'howsoever the world turn'.

Beneath the glitter, luxury and privilege, there was danger. Henry must already have remembered the year of crisis, 1497, when he was six and the queen had taken him for refuge to the Tower; and how the Scots had threatened the border, and the Cornishmen, led by a gigantic blacksmith, had marched across the length of England into Kent and only been defeated by the king's forces at Blackheath. How, too, that autumn, the Yorkist Pretender, Perkin Warbeck, had tried to raise the West Country and fled from his company at Taunton—'tooke no leave nor license of them'—and been rounded up in sanctuary at Beaulieu Abbey. Henry's father, standing in the new window of the cathedral treasurer's house at Exeter, had seen the rebels, bareheaded, with halters round their necks, begging for pardon and crying 'God save the King!'

Perhaps the memory of these vicissitudes, early in mind, gave the boy a wary sense of danger; when, in after years, he smelt rebellion, he always knew how to handle it and his political grasp was instinctive.

Not only was the old king's health precarious; bubonic plague, carried by fleas from black rats, attacked all classes; Henry, when king, always took extreme precautions to avoid it, moving about in the country when it raged in London. What more could a generation do who seriously recommended, as the latest remedy against plague, treacle and vinegar diluted, fasting, 'for you and yours', five mornings running, and solemnly advised each other 'ne use ne baths, ne sweate too much, for all these openeth the pores of the body and maketh the venemous aires to enter'?

Without the amiable Queen Elizabeth, the court may well have been a gloomier place: the king had always 'kept his distance' and the queen had had no political influence; his mother 'heard little'. Henry VII became more enmeshed in dynastic projects and accumulating money, piling up the savings his son was to inherit—'a great miser'. the Venetian ambassador wrote, 'but a man of vast ability, who had accumulated so much gold that he was supposed to have more than well nigh all the other kings in Christendom'.

VII

The dynasts, playing their game of power, did not bat an eyelid for bereavement. No sooner was Arthur dead, than Ferdinand and Isabella pounced upon Prince Henry for Catherine. But their daughter was now in the English king's hands, and Henry VII proposed, blandly, after the queen's demise, to marry her himself: he was only in his late 'forties. The Spaniards countered by withholding the unpaid portion of Catherine's dowry and demanding the return of the rest. After haggling, Henry VII conceded their point, and, in June 1503, young Henry and Catherine were formally betrothed, an arrangement sanctioned, the following year, by a dispensation from Rome. But Isabella died, and Castile did not devolve, as planned, on her son, the Infante Don Juan, for he, too, was dead—enervated, it was rumoured, by his premature marriage to the Archduchess Margaret of Austria. It came to the Infanta Juana, whose marriage to Archduke Philip the Handsome of Austria and Burgundy had been the reinsurance for the link between the Netherlands and Spain.

Henry VII turned even this to account: Philip and Juana, avid to seize Castile from Ferdinand at once, risked the January gales in the Channel, and were forced to take refuge at Melcombe Regis, now part of Weymouth; they were taken to Wolferton, the Trenchards' house, and brought up, along with John Russell as interpreter, to Court at Windsor, an occasion which made the fortunes of the Russell family. Henry received them with full honour, and, hardily enough, proposed himself to marry Don Juan's widow, Margaret, while young Henry and his sister Mary married Eleanore and Charles of Ghent,[1] the visitor's children. When Philip and his consort proceeded to Spain, Henry VII had scored a diplomatic success.

But within three months, Philip too was dead; Juana, always neurotic, now became crazy, traipsing about Spain with her husband's coffin, or sleeping on the floor in her castle of Tordesillas. Undeterred, Henry VII, refused by Margaret, now tried to marry mad Juana herself, and so get his claws into Castile, and he pressed on with the betrothal of Charles of Ghent, now Prince of Castile, to Mary.

This tortuous scheming affected young Henry's betrothal to Catherine; for Ferdinand, furious at successive attempts to disrupt his kingdom by depriving him of control of Castile, had begun to look askance at Catherine's English marriage. So on June 27, 1504, just before he was fourteen, young Henry formally renounced the contract;

---

[1] Afterwards the Emperor Charles V (1519-55), see Pedigree B (at end).

Ferdinand married a French princess, and Catherine was left in neglect, even penury.

Henry was now adolescent; soon boisterous enough, at sixteen, to insult a French courtier who complimented him on his archery by saying his shot was 'good for a Frenchman', but kept from contact with his contemporaries, mewed up with tutors, his comings and goings supervised. The old king, whom Bacon compares with Louis XI of France, created fear and suspicion; he made too many notes in his own hand, 'especially touching persons'; and when his monkey, set on by one of the officials, tore his principal notebook to pieces, the courtiers, who 'liked not these pensive accounts', were 'tickled with the sport'.[1]

He had never been particularly indulgent to his wife, for he loathed his Yorkist relatives, and though he showed a proper paternal affection to his children, he had always been careful that they should not be too popular. It was from this atmosphere that in April 1509 Prince Henry was released by his father's death.

VIII

Slowly the five great horses, hung with black, drew the old king's chariot to St Paul's. The funeral procession was splendid, bishops and abbots to the right; great lords and barons to the left. Sir Davie Owen bore the steel helmet with a golden crown; Sir Thomas Fynes a rich armour embroidered with the arms of England; the king's spear was covered in black velvet, his battle axe borne head down.

On May 10 his body was taken to Westminster in an illuminated hearse, and, while the choir sang *libera me, domine*, there interred; the Lord Chamberlain and the great officials breaking their wands of office and casting them into the grave.

Careful in life, Henry VII had been lavish in death. Big sums had been assigned: £5,000 for the chapel at Westminster; an endowment to complete the splendid King's College chapel at Cambridge; 10,000 masses endowed in honour of the Trinity, the Five Wounds of Christ, the Five Joys of Our Lady, the Nine Orders of Angels; £2,000 for repairs to highways and bridges from Richmond to Southwark and from Greenwich to Canterbury. Torregiano, the famous Italian sculptor, was to carve his effigy, a superb monument.

[1] Francis Bacon, *History of the Reign of Henry VII*, ed. J. R. Lumby, Oxford University Press, 1876, p. 218. Written after the author's disgrace, this masterpiece is full of anecdote and insight.

CHAPTER II

GLORIOUS MORNING

§

The new king, Henry VIII, at once withdrew from Richmond to
the Tower. Now the focus of the life of England, he had much
business 'in the continuance of that Royal Authority which should
never die'. A general pardon was proclaimed, save for murder, felony
and treason, and the inner ring of the Council were reappointed, with
Warham, Archbishop of Canterbury, Chancellor; Fox, Bishop of
Winchester, Lord Privy Seal. They feared 'lest such abundance of
riches . . . the King was now possessed of should move his young years
into a riotous forgetting of himself', so they 'gate him to be present
with them to acquaint him with the politique government of the realm,
with which at first he could not endure to be much troubled'.[1]

They were able men. Warham, whose melancholy, weather-beaten
countenance looks from his portrait so sardonically, was a Wykehamist
lawyer from New College, ordained in his forties; the fine panelling
still in the College Hall was his gift. He had been Master of the Rolls,
and on many commercial and diplomatic missions abroad; a pliant,
sceptical character, frugal, and with no interest in sport—he 'only read'
—he was a munificent patron, who was to die with only £30 in hand,
remarking—'*sat est viatici* (enough for my funeral)'.

Fox came of yeoman origin in Lincolnshire, and was probably at
Magdalen, Oxford; he founded Corpus Christi College there. A
veteran of Bosworth, he was a good organizer and man of business, and
had taken the responsibility of baptizing his royal master.[2] The lay members of the inner Council were hard-bitten soldiers; Thomas Howard,
Earl of Surrey, was the son of the first Howard Duke of Norfolk, who
had been killed, on the wrong side, at Bosworth—

> *Jack o' Norfolk, be not too bold,*
> *For Dykon, thy maister, is bought and sold.*

[1] Stow, Annals, p. 486.
[2] He was probably the inventor of the famous dilemma termed Morton's fork, attributed to Archbishop Morton, on which the victims of taxation were impaled. If they
came to his office well dressed, they could obviously afford to pay; if meanly dressed, they
must be misers.

An East Anglian magnate, his roots were at Thetford and Framling-
ham, and he had worked back into favour after three years in the
Tower; since 1501, he had been Lord Treasurer, an example to other
great nobles, but with estates only partially restored. He had seen much
service against the Scots and in diplomacy; in his late 'sixties he was
experienced, reliable, astute.[1] George Talbot, fourth Earl of Shrewsbury, Lord Steward and Chamberlain of the Exchequer, was a soldier
of more limited horizons, experienced in asserting the royal authority
and in mustering the forces of the countryside. Sir Edward Poynings, a
Kentish squire, remained Lord Warden of the Cinque Ports; as Lord
Deputy, he had subjected the Irish in the Pale to the English Crown and
Parliament by laws which were to last until the late eighteenth century.
Sir Thomas Lovell, a Norfolk lawyer, was President; the secretary,
Thomas Ruthal, newly appointed Bishop of Durham, was a reliable
administrator, and succeeded Fox as Lord Privy Seal.

Continuity was thus maintained. But the old king's taxation had
been savage, and Sir Richard Empson and Edmund Dudley, his most
unpopular officials, were at once sent to the Tower 'to quiet men's
minds'.[2] When, as Bacon puts it, the Council had 'meddled too much
with *meum* and *tuum*', they had feathered their own nests: they were
now thrown into the Tower for 'usurped jurisdiction' and attainted for
'constructive treason'.

The son of a Towcester 'sieve maker', Empson had been Speaker of
the House of Commons and an executor of the old king's will; Dudley
was more aristocratic (though his enemies said his father had been a
carpenter at Lewes); he, too, had been Speaker and had made his way
by the law. Both had lived in close touch with the City. Empson, it
was alleged, seeing the old king would die, had 'resolved to seize the
government for himself'; Dudley had 'summoned knights to repair to
him with all their power'. Justified precautions were termed conspiracy; the following August, both were executed while the court
were junketting at Windsor; not before Dudley had tried to propitiate

---

[1] According to Camden, when he was asked after Bosworth how he had dared bear
arms on behalf of Richard III, he had replied 'He was my crowned King, and if the Parliamentary authority of England set the Crown upon a stock, I would fight for that stock.
And as I fought for him, I will fight for you, when you are established by the said authority'. *Remains Concerning Britain*, ed. 1870, p. 294, quoted in J. D. Mackie, *The Earlier
Tudors*, Oxford 1951, p. 12.

[2] Stow, p. 487. Their most detested subordinate, 'Baptist Grimald, the most cruell
wretch of them all, went to Westminster and there registered himself a Sanctuary.' Others,
perpetrators of false inquests, were put in the pillory and sent to Newgate, where they
'died for very shame'. The English were not yet docile tax payers.

the king by his 'Tree of Commonwealth', vindicating monarchy, written
in the Tower, from which he had attempted to escape.[1]

This sacrifice of newly rich scapegoats may not have been at the new
king's command; but it foreshadows Henry VIII's later technique—the
sudden blow, the trumped-up charge, the eye on public opinion: the
whole episode, as Elton well writes, 'carries all the stigmata of political
motive, sickening self-righteousness, and drastic success which mark
later occasions in the reign when others, whose services had become
inconvenient . . . found themselves in the same unhappy position'.[2]

The Dudleys, however, were soon reinstated; the heir became Lord
Lisle, then Earl of Warwick and Duke of Northumberland; dominated
England under the dying Edward VI, tried to oust the dynasty and
perished at the block: the brilliant grandson, Lord Robert, afterwards
Earl of Leicester, nearly married Elizabeth I.

II

As spring broadened into the summer of 1509, there was bustle and
excitement while plans went forward for the Coronation. In May,
Archbishop Warham was inviting Erasmus to spend the rest of his life
in England and offering free living and 150 nobles down; Lord Mountjoy, too, was writing of 'Henricus Octavus or rather Octavius', alluding
to Augustus and the return of the Age of Gold; all England, he alleged,
was 'in ecstacies'.

For obvious reasons, Henry was keen to conclude his interrupted
marriage to Catherine of Aragon. His father, on his death bed, had
expressly commanded it, and Ferdinand, too, was now determined at
last to clinch the affair. On the first rumour of the old king's death, he
had written to Fuensaldo, his resident 'orator' in England, that the
French would stop the marriage if they could; it would, indeed, be a
sin for Henry to back out, and Dom Manuel of Portugal, who had
married Catherine's sisters Isabell and Mary, in succession, had numerous offspring.[3] The Pope had given a dispensation; Ferdinand was even
willing to pay up the rest of the dowry, and conclude the betrothal of
his grandson, Charles of Castile, to Henry's sister, the Lady Mary:

---

[1] His elaborate will, after complex provisions for his family, leaves a good legacy to
'Will Thikpenny, that took payn with me in the Towr'. Two other servants involved
in his attempted escape, must not, he begs, be penalized. Of other bequests, he remarks 'I
pay all these folks to be helping and friendly to my wife and children'. He left £50 for
'poor priests at Oxford' to sing for the souls of his parents, himself and his successive wives.
[2] *Henry VIII*, op. cit, p.9.
[3] L. & P. I. p. 20.

200,000 crowns were dispatched, not, for fear of delay, in cash by sea, or overland (for the French might impound it), but through Italian bankers in bonds and bills of exchange.

Henry had in fact anticipated him: on June 11, less than two months after his accession, he privately married Catherine in the palace at Greenwich. To make the union impeccable, Henry was formally asked, 'Most Illustrious Prince, is it your will to fulfill the Treaty of Marriage, and, as the Pope has dispensed with the marriage [to Arthur], to take the Princess who is here present as your lawful wife?' As Henry was afterwards to find, everything was in order.

On June 24, 1509, the Coronation was celebrated with great magnificence in Westminster Abbey. Two days before, Henry had been served in the Tower at dinner by the courtiers chosen to be Knights of the Bath, carrying dishes 'in token that they shall never bear none after that day'. Vast quantities of cloth in scarlet and red, white and green (the Tudor colours), had been ordered; the entire Households of the king and queen were marshalled, including the king's old nurse, Ann Luke, who attended as one of the queen's chamberwomen. The Households included the king's yeoman brewer; his yeoman of the bottles and of the mouth; his groom at the bar. The staffs of buttery, confectionery, spicery, saucery, and scalding-house had their places; the yeomen of the stirrup and the litter and the chariots; the yeoman farrier, the sergeant of the carriage, the groom of the hackneys. There were William Norris, Master of the king's hawks; the leashmen for the greyhounds; the clerk of the aviary; Mr Peter, Marshal of the trumpets; Bertram Brewer, minstrel; John Porth, Keeper of the Books; then the pages of the chamber—Henry Kemyas, Peter Champion, John Copenger, Noel Loveday—good English names; even 'Phyppe, Keeper of Merton, the king's fool'. The cost, for the king's Household, was over £1,749; for the queen's, over £1,536.

On the eve of their midsummer Coronation, Henry and Catherine rode through London to Westminster. The city was hung with arras and festooned with decorations, the goldsmiths' stalls in Old Change resplendent with girls in white, waving branches of white may. The young king's amiable and princely bearing was much admired: he wore crimson velvet furred with ermine, and shone with rubies and emeralds, diamonds and great pearls; he rode a charger with trappings of damask gold under a canopy borne by the Barons of the Cinque Ports. Behind rode the bearers of his hat and cloak, their mounts trapped with silver cloth under a web of green and gold; the Master of the king's Horse shimmered in tissue embroidered with golden roses. Then came nine 'children of honour' in blue velvet and fleurs de Lys, their horses trapped with the coats of all the king's dominions, actual or claimed—England and France; Gascony and Guienne; Normandy, Anjou, Cornwall, Wales and Ireland.

The queen was borne in a litter between two white palfreys; she wore white satin and her hair 'of very great length, beautiful and goodly to behold', hung down her back under a coronet: her Household followed, in appropriate splendour, and, that night, the royalties slept in the Palace of Westminster.

Next day, after the ancient ritual of the Coronation (the 'common people' cut up and stole the cloth laid down for a carpet), there was an enormous banquet: 'what should I speak,' writes Hall, 'of the sumptuous, fine and delicate meates' . . . the 'clean handling', the 'plentiful abundance'?[1] It began, with a fanfare of trumpets, when the Dukes of Buckingham and Shrewsbury rode in on their coursers before the first service; it culminated when Sir Robert Dymmocke, the king's Hereditary Champion, armed at all points and wearing a great plume of ostrich feathers, rode his stallion the length of Westminster Hall into the presence of the king. 'Who are you?' demanded Garter King at Arms: 'Sir,' boomed Dymmocke, through his vizor, 'the place that I come from is not material.'

The Heralds proclaimed silence for the portentous figure, and the Champion defied anyone to deny the king's right to his royal inheritance. 'I, Sir Robert Dymmocke,' he roared, 'offer my glove to fight the quarrel.' He repeated the defiance in other parts of the Hall; each time he flung down the gauntlet. He then repaired to the king's presence, demanding drink; Henry sent him wine in a gold cup, and Dymmocke claimed not only the cup but its cover; 'this given, he rode out of the Hall with the said cup and cover as his own'.

The Coronation was too much for Henry's grandmother, Margaret Beaufort, Dowager Countess of Richmond, who died a few days after it, but the young monarchs and the Court gave themselves over to a riot of summer feasts, tournaments, hunting, dancing, gambling and dressing up: 'The King's Majesty,' wrote one observer, 'is young and cares for nothing but hunting and girls.' He was a splendid youth; at eighteen his face had a feminine beauty, with pink and white cheeks, cherubic above the thick neck. He was already over six foot, and, as he

[1] Edward Hall. *The Union of the Two Noble and Illustre Famielies of Lancastre and Yorke . . . proceeding to the reign of the high and prudent Prince King Henry the Eyght: 1550.* Edition here quoted *Henry VIII*, by Edward Hall, ed. Charles Whibley, 2 vols., London, 1904, pp. 7–11.

matured, his measurements—apparent from successive suits of armour
—were to become formidable: like Bismarck's, perhaps, the more so
when combined with a highish voice. At twenty-three, he was six foot
two, 42 inches round the chest, 35 round the waist: at fifty, his chest
would be 57 inches and his waist 54. Yet he was no mere hearty exhibitionist if he could also enjoy reading Thomas Aquinas; he had all the
Plantagenet passion and pride, and a great 'laff', but the dazzling boy
was already a cold-hearted politique.

At present, Henry was mad about games and tournaments, and tired
out everyone with his pent up vitality, compensating for lost time in
adolescence. New contests came into fashion. Besides the traditional
'running at the ring' and jousting, the courtiers went in for single com-
bats on foot 'in imitation of Amadis and Lanzilote and other knights of
olden times of which so much is written in books'. They called the new
sport 'Barriers': behind a waist-high obstacle, to prevent wrestling, the
combatants in breastplates and special helmets cast blunt seven-foot
lances, then fought with two handed swords, giving twelve strokes
apiece. Gentlemen, it was said, 'passed the summer in disports', but in
May and June hunting and hawking were not yet in season; so they
were encouraged to play 'Barriers' to 'eschew idleness'. In Greenwich
park, on a white shield hanging on a tree, the competitors would in-
scribe their names—they were 'most of them' now literate—ready to
face all comers with casting spear and target, or with 'your bastard
sword', the point and edge 'rebated'.[1] Many young men excelled in
these sports, but among them all 'the most assiduous *and the most interested* was the King'.[2]

In the evenings there were elaborate 'disguisings', and the king
would burst into the queen's apartments, conspicuously incognito; she
would express appropriate alarm, astonishment and relief. Catherine
spent much of her early married life telling Henry how marvellous he
was, and begging him to be more careful.

III

The Government, meanwhile, smoothly consolidated the régime. The
king confirmed Ruthal in his appointment to the great bishopric of
Durham, the better to settle the North, where rumours of mild discontent continued. 'My Lord of Buckingham,' grumbled Northumberland's servants, 'should be Protector of England'; and Northumberland

---

[1] L. and P. I. p. 284.
[2] Spanish Calendar, II, 45 (author's italics).

'should have all from Trent North and have Berwick and the Marches';
if he 'had not room in the North as his father had, all should not long be
well'. These rumours were insignificant, but 'good it is', Lord Darcy,
Warden of the Marches, concluded to Fox, 'to have a good eye'.

Henry VII had early formed the Yeoman Archers and Arquebusiers
of the Bodyguard: his son now created and aristocratic Horseguard
called the Spears; all fifty had to provide a 'demilance and a custrel',
two archers and three horses; they drew high pay, promised to settle
for their victuals in cash, and were not to be absent for more than four
days; 'which ordinance continued not long, the charges were too
great'.[1]

On January 21, 1512, Henry met his first Parliament. King and Lords
assembled in the queen's chamber at Westminster, and he entered the
Abbey with a great train borne behind him and 'supported in the
midst'. Arriving at the Chair, he sat, glittering and enthroned, next the
altar, then swept through the throng into the Parliament Chamber,
where he donned his Cap of Estate. He was taking over a mediaeval
Council, intermittently 'attendant', selected and authorized by the
monarch. An inner ring of under a dozen dealt with routine business;
eleven to twenty with judicial work; twenty to fifty with ceremonial
occasions.

This fluctuating Council dealt with a vast range of business, from the
highest policy decisions at home and abroad to local disorders and cor-
ruptions; its functions were economic and social as much as political. In
the last two years of the old century, for example, it had dealt with the
aftermath of the most serious rebellion of the reign; with renewing the
Treaty of Etaples (and its subsidy) with the new French King Louis
XII; with tricky negotiations over the ambitious dynastic marriage of
Prince Arthur to Catherine of Aragon. But it was also concerned with
outrages by local officials in Purbeck in Dorset; with how the bailiff
and sub-bailiff of Wareham had extorted twenty-four sheep from the
parson of Steeple, confiscated ten gold crowns and forty shillings from
a coffer washed up at Kimmeridge, 'rewarding the pore man never a
farthing for the finding'. They had abetted smuggling cargoes of raw
wool out of Studland and Lulworth, and when a French ship was
wrecked 'off the foreland of St Aldem', impounded gear worth £40
which the crew could have saved; they had seized wrecks 'fallen often
times by fortune of tempest on the coast', and even filched gulls eggs
from the cliffs of the Clavell property at Tyneham and taken bribes
from the Prior of Holme for leave to hunt; and, when reported, they

[1] Stow, p. 487.

had embezzled' the document.[1] Innumerable complaints of this kind came up among major policy decisions.

The Council, transmitting the power of the king, was the mainspring of order, and its Proclamations had the force of law. A new 'Star Chamber', so-called from the decorations of the ceiling under which it sat, had developed from the Council, and it brought new backing to the courts of common law, often terrorized by magnates, with their archers and pikemen, as, in earlier times, had been the Council itself. The disorders it had helped to put down are familiar: 'whosoever shall live at Paston,' wrote John Paston in mid-fifteenth century Norfolk, 'will have need to know how to defend himself'; in 1469 the Duke of Norfolk had besieged the Paston castle at Caister with 3,000 men, and it was only through their London influence that the Pastons won through. Estate jumping, abduction of heiresses, casual brigandage—leaving the 'carreyn in the bush with throte y-corven'—were endemic evils which Henry VII had striven, successfully, to stamp out. When Sir William Say, for example, had threatened the 'affraying of the peace' at Hertford Quarter Sessions, Henry VII had commanded him 'in straitest wise' to 'forebear to be there', and to do nothing 'privately or openly repugnant to the equitie of our laws or the rupture of our . . . Peas' at 'his uttermost peril'.[2]

Compared with this protean Council, which in part realized the ideas of Fortescue's *Governance of England*, written under Edward IV, the importance of Parliament was intermittent. It was summoned, if and when the king wanted it, to enhance prestige, to endorse policy, to consent to taxation, and to legislate for specific problems. It was already the highest court in the realm; 'the roots of Parliament's two modern pillars—control of taxation and the supremacy of Parliamentary legislation— had taken hold, although the institution was still 'mediaeval'.[3] It was still of course mainly a background to the executive power of the Crown.

The Council relied far more upon the local justices, appointed by the Commission of the Peace. The collaboration of these six to seven hundred J.P.s was essential; they controlled the shire and hundred courts; the courts of township, parish and manor; indeed the local gentry, even more than the nobility, were to dominate local affairs until the nineteenth century. This habit of self-government had mediaeval origins, but it

[1] Letters and Papers of Richard III and Henry VII. Op. cit., Vol. II.

[2] Ellis, *Original Letters*, I, p. 40.

[3] G. R. Elton, *England under the Tudors*, London, 1959, p. 67. q.v. for the best short account.

first became settled under the Tudors, who exploited and even over-burdened these natural allies: 'The J.P., if not born, certainly came of age under the Tudors, who saw in his office the ideal instrument for their purposes.'[1]

The Tudors depended upon this establishment, which ramified wide and deep over the country, since they had no standing army, though they had an artillery train and built up a navy. They could raise forces, in emergency, by 'Commissions of Array', empowering local magnates to embody archers and pikemen, available since all able bodied men had to keep proficient to defend their neighbourhood. The king could also summon 'trusty, well beloved', and battle-worthy subjects directly; as when, in 1495, the old king had commanded Sir Gilbert Talbot to raise four score horsemen 'defensibly arrayed', with as many spears and demi-lances as he could, and the rest archers and bills; and again, in the greater crisis of 1497, had 'heartily prayed' him to bring 'six score tall men on horseback to Woodstock'.[2]

IV

Young Henry's married bliss was now blighted by disappointment. In November 1509, he had told Ferdinand that 'Her Serene Highness, the Queen, our dearest consort, with the favour of heaven, has conceived ... a living child and is right heavy therewith', but, by May, Catherine had to write that her daughter had been still-born. She begged her father, pathetically, 'not to be angry'; it was the will of God, and she hoped to propitiate Him by giving one of her richest headdresses to the Franciscans.

Christmas had been kept at Richmond (the plague was abroad in London): then, in the spring, the Court was at Greenwich, where the king's amusements continued. On May Day 1510 'His Grace, being young and willing not to be idle, rose very early to fetch in the may and green boughs, himself fresh and richly apparelled, and clothed all his knights and gentlemen in white satin ... and went every man with his bow and arrows shooting in the wood, and so returned to Court, every man with a green bough in the cap'. There was an undercurrent of clowning; one virtuoso who shot well balanced on one foot, the other on his chest, was nicknamed 'foot-in-bosom'. There were many 'feats of prowess and great strength'.

In July and August the Court were at Windsor in the lush Thames valley overlooking the curving river and the great park. Here Henry's

---

[1] S. T. Bindoff, *Tudor England*, Pelican, 1950, p. 56. A good short general survey.
[2] Ellis, op. cit., I, I, pp. 21 and 33.

feats recall those of Pantagruel; shooting, wrestling, casting the bar; feasting, drinking; singing, playing the recorder, making ballets. He also studied history and theology; wrote verse; debated questions of courteous love.

In the autumn the Court moved to Greenwich, with its brisker air, then back to Richmond: the queen was again with child, and on January 1, 1512, a prince was born. He was christened Henry, with tremendous rejoicings in Court and City, high dynastic hopes; but by February 22nd, he was dead. The king made no outward mourning: the queen was prostrated.

That year, most of the Palace of Westminster was burnt out, and not, says Stow, 're-edified; only the Great Hall [of William Rufus] with the offices near adjoining were kept in good reparation, and served as afore'.[1]

Henry enjoyed the elaborate royal tennis then fashionable, with nets, gallery, penthouse and complicated scoring. His fair skin, it was observed, glowed through his silk shirt as he slogged with the racquet down the echoing court

Set now on his war with France, he was also shooting regularly at the new butts at Tothill Fields: he always had an eye for an archer, and Sir John Trevelyan sent two of his best Cornishmen to show their skill. 'When the King shot in Tothill,' wrote his representative, 'I spoke twice to the King's Grace for your servants. "Let me see them," he said, and I called them unto the King and Knot shot before him . . . my Lord Treasurer [Surrey] said good words of you and them.'[2] Henry took them both into his own service.

V

The realm which Henry had inherited was a miniature economy; prosperous, in the main self-sufficient. Save for wine, spices and silks, the English did not then depend on imports; stringent laws forbade the export of bullion, and much wealth in gold and silver was hoarded up in plate and in the shrines of the great religious foundations.

Most of the people were countrymen. Apart from the manufacture of cloth, tin mining in Cornwall, small scale lead mining in Mendip, and coal mining in the north, there were no major industries: London, a seaport and already one of the biggest cities of Europe, alone could compare with the towns of the Low Countries, the Rhineland and Northern Italy; Bristol, York and Norwich were the only other major

---

[1] *A Survey of London* (1598), Everyman, 1929, p. 146.
[2] *Trevelyan Papers*, Part III. Camden, 1872, p. 10.

towns. The country north of the Trent was still wild and sparsely populated, the Welsh and Scottish borders harried and insecure: even in the Midlands and the South there was a vast acreage of 'waste'. A relatively small area of 'champion' and meadow—Polydore Vergil noticed 'most delectable valleys'—sustained the villages clustered about their often ancient churches and the market towns about their abbeys, minsters and cathedrals, as at Romsey, Salisbury, Norwich, York and Wells. 'The population', wrote a Venetian observer, of England, 'does not bear any proportion to her fertility and riches',[1] and agriculture was limited to what was 'required for the consumption of the people'. Riding from Dover to London and then to Oxford, he noticed how few people there were.

The primeval oak forest and its tangled underwood, the heaths of Norfolk and Surrey, the moors of the West Country and the North, the chalk downs with their flint and springy turf, the swamps and fens made by rivers with broken banks and weeds uncut, had not changed greatly since the Anglo-Saxons had tamed the valleys and made their settlements. Great forests were preserved for the chase by the king and nobility, who also fenced off deer parks to make easier hunting. Henry was passionately addicted to hunting, and his visits and progresses were arranged accordingly. Squires and lesser gentry, their interests bounded by their neighbourhood, by their marriages of convenience adding acre to acre, by their endowments of local piety, by quarter sessions and the price of wool, were equally concerned with hawks and hounds, with the harts and fallow deer. Game, birds and fish stocked the larders of the rich and the well to do; in summer one could

> '*Se the dere draw to the dale*
> *And leave the hilles hee;*
> *And shadow him in the leves green*
> *Under the green-wode tree*'.

This hinterland provided great store of timber for houses, wagons and ships; timber-framed farms and cottages were the rule, along with wattle and daub and thatch, save in the Cotswolds, Purbeck, and the Peak district, where stone was easily come by. As in primeval North America, it was easier to build in wood; most town houses were timbered until brick came in from the Low Countries in Tudor times,[2] a

---

[1] *A Relation of the Island of England*, op. cit.

[2] But when Professor Bindoff writes 'England's woodlands *served a more valuable purpose*' (Italics mine) 'than that of *providing her Kings and Nobles with their favourite recreation*' (Bindoff, op. cit., p. 10), he reflects modern prejudice against the aristocracy and 'blood sports', not the feelings of sixteenth century Englishmen.

development of which Henry was a pioneer. Only the great stone keeps and battlements, as at Corfe and Ludlow, Rochester and War-wick, stood out, like the abbeys, reminders of an obsolescent world; already, some of them, adapted to the new amenities of chimneys and glass.

As the king well understood, the vital export was cloth, made up from vast flocks of sheep, the greatest wealth of the kingdom. Already, men complained, they were eating up the subsistence of the small yeo-men and driving the villagers off the land. Aubrey, looking back to Tudor times, remarks 'the destroying of petty mannors began in Henry VII's [time] to be now common; whereby the meane people live lawlesse, nobody to govern them':[1] a shepherd and his dog, or a milkmaid could manage land that 'upon arable employed the hands of several score of labourers'. This dislocation has been exaggerated, but there may have been eight million sheep to a population of under three million people.

The cloth export had long superseded that of raw wool, so important in the twelfth and thirteenth centuries: the main market was in the Netherlands, in particular in Antwerp, and export was monopolised by the great Corporation of Merchant Adventurers of London, whose business had long outstripped that of the old wool merchants of the Staple of Calais. The concern to find 'vent' for the cloth in Flanders pushed Henry's foreign policy predominantly towards the Empire, not France; and during the Wars of Religion, which disrupted relations with Spain, the English were to look to the Levant, to Muscovy and Iran, even to the markets of the Far East by the supposed North West Passage through the Canadian Arctic.

The cloth was manufactured in rudimentary factories—Jack of New-bury's the most famous—and by village weavers and spinsters, who delivered piece-work to travelling merchants, so that the trade ramified through the countryside. The bleating flocks, the sheep-bells on the downs, symbolized the raw material; the chimes of elaborate steeples in the Cotswolds and East Anglia the wealth brought by the finished cloth.

This predominant trade greatly contributed to the prosperity of London, with which the king was, in general, careful to keep on good terms. It was already a cosmopolitan city, with its close contacts with the Netherlands and the Baltic, and its great market for the fisheries of the North Sea. On their broad, tidal river, London and Westminster must then have resembled Amsterdam, the Thames being the principal

---

[1] *Brief Lives and other Selected Writings by John Aubrey*, ed. Anthony Powell, Cresset Press, 1949, p. 5.

means of transport, even for the great, with their liveried watermen.
By the 'thirties the Tudor palace of Whitehall, like a great rambling
brick built Cambridge college, looked out over the water, gardens and
orchards sloping to the water-steps, where the royal barges rode the
tide. The City under Elizabeth I has been exactly described by Stow,[1]
whose survey is retrospective, but the poem doubtfully attributed to
Dunbar, in the early sixteenth century, best recalls it.

> '*Soveraign of cities, seemliest in sight,*
> *Of high renoun, riches and royaltye.*'

The poet particularly celebrates the river,

> '*Where many a swan doth swymme with wyngis fair;*
> *Where many a barge doth saile and row with are;*
> *Where many a ship doth rest with top-royall.*
> *O, towne of townes! patrone and not compare,*
> *London, thou art the flour of Cities all.*'

This world of rich traders and civic luxury; of apprenticeship and
accounts; of mob riot, public executions and pestilence, contrasts with
the still mediaeval households of the great territorial magnates, now
better under control, but still keeping up an elaborate, often insolvent,
grandeur. In these vast households the lord dined at high table, with
over four hundred at a session, in their degrees. The Earl of Northumberland had his great salt cellar before him, his manchet (white) bread
set 'couched' to it, and the carving knives (there were no forks) 'laid
down fair, the points to it', beneath the trenchers, similarly disposed.[2]
The magnates rode about the country with their trumpeters and liveried
men at arms, and their households still served the sons of the gentry,
to whom they were 'good lords', as schools of manners, horsemanship
and war. They had immense social prestige; sport and what reading was
done were still mediaeval. Romances, as Ranke observes, were now
first printed, but their content was traditional, unlike the new, realistic
writings of Erasmus, More and their circle.[3] Yet the great nobles were
not independent princes, as often on the continent: 'These English
noblemen', it was observed, 'are nothing more than rich gentlemen in
possession of a great quantity of land belonging to the crown'. Save in

---

[1] *A Survey of London* (1598), op. cit.

[2] Rutland Papers, note 60, pp. 98–9.

[3] Roger Ascham complained in 1570 that 'in our Forefather's Time . . . few books were
read in our Tongue, saving certain books of chevalrie,' and cited the *Morte D'Arthur*, 'the
whole pleasure of which book standith in two special points, in open manslaughter and
bold bawdry'. (The Schoolmaster, p. 80.)

3. Henry VIII at the age of 35. From a miniature
(Reproduced by permission of the Syndics, Fitzwilliam Museum, Cambridge)

Catherine of Aragon with a monkey. From a miniature
(Reproduced by permission of is Grace the Duke of Buccleuch)

ANNA BOLINA VXOR ·   HENRI · OCTA

4. Anne Boleyn
   (Reproduced by permission of the National Portrait Gallery)

exceptional areas, such as Durham, the king's writ ran everywhere; he had, in theory, owned all the land since the Conquest, save that the Church owned nearly a third of it.

Since Anglo-Saxon piety, in the reign of Ethelwulf in the ninth century, had saddled England with 'Rome Scot', now 'Peter's Pence', gigantic possessions had been accumulating to the Benedictine, Carthusian and Cistercian foundations: they were 'more like baronial palaces than religious houses' and possessed enormous riches; even 'unicorn's horns of extraordinary size'.[1] If, it was said, the Abbot of Glastonbury bedded the Abbess of Shaftesbury, their offspring would be the richest landowner in England. This predominance looked overwhelming, but, like the over-mighty magnates, the mediaeval church was becoming obsolete.

The urban middle classes already appeared, to an Italian, to be reserved in family life; hard on the children. As, again, Aubrey remembered even of the Elizabethans, conventional parents were 'so austere and grave' that the child might 'perfectly loathe' the sight of them. 'Gentlemen of thirty or forty years old' would 'stand as mutes and fools bareheaded before their parents, and the daughters, grown women, would stand at the cupboard side during the whole time of their proud mother's visit'.[2]

At the Sheriff's banquet in London, the Italians observed that the English seemed glumly and conventionally silent as they ate their way through the courses. The visitors even thought, from their reserve, that they were either the most 'discrete lovers in the world' or incapable of love. The women, on the other hand, the Italians had cause to consider, were violent in their passions.

Family life, they thought, in comparison, doubtless, with the fervent affections of Mediterranean peoples, were sacrificed to getting on in the world. By eight or nine, boys were sent out to hard service in strange households (the cult of the boarding preparatory school persists). They were sent, it was alleged, to 'learn better manners'. Snobbery was already intense, and the common people docile to the rich, though apt for riot, for the country was swarming with thieves, 'taken up by dozens, like birds in a covey, especially in London'.[3] And the murmur of conventional piety was already familiar: the middle classes 'reciting in Church verse by verse, in a low voice after the manner of Churchmen'.

[1] Relation, p. 29.
[2] Aubrey, op. cit., p. 11.
[3] Relation, op. cit., p. 36.

These already puritanical characteristics were offset by lusty vigour and insularity: 'He looks like an Englishman', they would say of a handsome foreigner—'*che àp pare un Inglese*'.[1] Even respectable women would go to taverns, and many of the English, if offered wine, would prefer beer 'in great quantities'. There was a convention of hearty hospitality, though they would 'sooner give six ducats to entertain a person than to assist him in any distress'. Few cared for learning; a lay-man who read books was called a 'clerk'; and there were no injuries that could be committed against the lower orders that might not be atoned for by money. There was a great pursuit of rich widows—through plague, sweating sickness, and malaria there were many. As a nation, the English were very conservative; if the king changed an old rule, they would think he was going to take away their lives: but, already predominant, was the eye for the main chance, the tropistic drive for money and advancement; the dogged endurance which made English soldiers the terror of their neighbours.

VI

In the realm which Henry inherited the feudal order was thus breaking down into the class divisions of more modern times. An illiterate peasantry still provided the manpower for agriculture, stock farming, and, on occasion, for war, while the fisheries were a training ground for merchant seamen and piracy.[2] Upon this basis, the great territorial magnates still appeared to dominate the countryside as they were expected to do.

But a third class had long been coming up; the 'new men', gentry and bourgeois, whose interests coincided with those of the Crown. The already formidable power of the early modern state, as established by the abler Plantagenets and their administrators, came thus to be re-vived and reinforced after its decline during the wars of the Roses and after the emergencies of the reign of Edward IV and Henry VII. Under Henry VIII, this social change was to intensify, and to underlie the king-worship and cult of sovereignty that at once developed mediaeval precedents and became something new, when the sovereign power, the '*maiestas*', of the dynastic nation state, first stood out, alone, an accom-plished fact, justified in its own right.

---

[1] Op. cit., p. 20.

[2] 'Poole in the early fifteenth century, under the leadership of the redoubtable Henry Pay, became notorious for its pirate squadrons. So also did Fowey, whose mariners, "the gallants of Fowey" roved the whole Channel.' J. A. Williamson, *The English Channel*, 143.

But the monarchy was still 'early modern', ruling in the main through the Household. The Council officials, the inner ring who had executive power, being appointed solely by the king, had no permanent bureaucratic status. In the 'thirties, after his break with Rome, Henry would claim an independent 'Empire', and rule the realm as a national commonwealth through an organization which came to exist more independently of the royal estate. But this momentous transformation was made by consent, reviving institutions already there, without sheer despotism; and it coincided with the strategic transformation of the island from a country on the fringe of a continent which looked to the Mediterranean, to one commanding the sea routes of the oceanic world. At present both domestic administration and foreign policy remained conservative.

CHAPTER III

FOREIGN ADVENTURE

❖

THE European power politics which confronted the eighteen-year-old Henry VIII were simple in brute essentials, if complex and changing in appearance: the great dynasties of Valois and Habsburg, competing to dominate the continent, were making Italy their main battleground. The French kings ruled the most compact and heavily populated territories in the west; for Henry, they were the traditional enemy. Since Brittany had been united with France, they threatened the English trade routes to Bordeaux, the Iberian peninsula and the Mediterranean. The Habsburgs, on the other hand, controlled the Low Countries, long linked commercially with England, for the Habsburg Holy Roman Emperor-elect, Maximilian, had married Mary of Burgundy, heiress of Charles the Bold, whose richest dominions were in Flanders. When, as already observed, their son the Archduke Philip had married the Infanta Juana of Spain, daughter of Ferdinand of Aragon and Isabella of Castile, and sister of Henry's own queen, the rich Habsburg-Burgundian inheritance had become united with the reversion of the Spanish crowns, and with the Spanish dominions in Italy, the Western Mediterranean and the Caribbean.[1] This tentacular dynasty, which extended from Vienna and Innsbruck to the Low Countries, the Iberian peninsula and the New World, could thus challenge the formidable armies of France. The Spaniards were to be incongruously and disastrously involved in the Netherlands; the treasure, won by Cortes and Pizarro in Mexico and Peru, to be poured out on European battlefields; and Charles V (Charles of Ghent), the heir of Philip and Juana and Maximilian, to be hampered in the main Habsburg duty to keep Germany in order and defend central Europe and the Mediterranean from the Ottoman Turks.

The new dynasty in England, like the Baltic monarchies, was creeping up in the scale of power; but it was not yet strong enough for more than wary diplomacy and limited intervention; designed, in so far as consistent motives are discernible, to prevent any overwhelming

[1] See Pedigree B.

hostile coalition, and win what could be got out of a contest of giants. Henry, in the first flush of youth, was spoiling to cut a figure on the continent, and saw the contest in personal terms. Compared with the august dynasties of Valois and Habsburg, his own family, in spite of its distaff Plantagenet and Valois blood, was *parvenu*: he had no army to compare with the professional forces on the continent; he had wealth and the nucleus of a navy, but less than three million subjects. Further, the French maintained their old connection with the Scots, always poised to exploit the troubles of England. Yet Henry was determined to make himself felt: his first attempt was a fiasco; his second made more sense.

II

Since the capture of the Duke Ludovico Sforza of Milan nine years before, the French had intermittently controlled Milan, and in May 1509, in collaboration with Ferdinand, Maximilian and the Pope, they routed the Venetians at Agnadello. This victory now so alarmed their allies, that Pope Julius II was able to form a Holy League with Ferdinand and Venice against them.

Henry at once seized his chance: he was naturally drawn into the Habsburg-Spanish coalition, and saw himself as the defender of Holy Church and heir to the traditional English claim on the French throne. When Stile, his envoy in Spain, warned him that his father-in-law was only 'aferd for his realm of Napulys', and cared nothing for English interests, such advice did not appeal. Henry early determined to join the coalition. Stow puts the matter crisply: 'The French King made sharp war upon Pope July, and the King of England wrote to the French King that he should leave off.'

In September 1509, Henry snubbed the French envoy, the corpulent Abbot of Fécamp, who had commended his desire for 'peace' expressed in a routine letter to the French king. The young king rounded on him: 'Who wrote that letter?' he demanded. 'I ask peace from the King of France who dare not look at me!' Next day Henry went tilting, but the abbot found no place among the official spectators; it was plain, reported the Venetian envoy, hopefully, that the king 'held the French King in small account'. Henry also curtly demanded the subsidy paid his father: 'My father is me,' he told the Frenchman, 'and I am my father, so I choose to have it.'

But Henry's elderly advisers opposed warlike adventures. 'The Councillors,' wrote de Villaragut, the Spanish envoy, anxious to draw Henry in against the French, in May 1510, were 'very different from the King; slow in concluding anything and caused him much disgust'. So he told Durham and Winchester, separately, that they both ought to be Cardinals. At once both begged him to speak to the king, without, of course, mentioning that they knew of the proposal, and Henry, when tackled, 'thought it a necessary thing'. Neither became Cardinals, but business was expedited; had he not, reported the envoy, 'excited in the bishops the desire to be created cardinals', the treaty would have been further delayed.

Henry was, indeed, rightly suspicious of his Council, who were all bribed by the French. He scarcely knew, he told de Villaragut, indiscreetly, whom to trust, for the French got to know of his designs and 'countermined' them. He could trust Fox best. 'Do you confide in him?' asked the Spaniard. 'Yes,' said the king, 'at my risk. Here in England they think he is a *fox*, and such is his name.'

Astutely, the Venetians, too, fanned Henry's ambition. The French king, they said, was 'elate and haughty'; he 'wanted to be monarch of the whole world'. What more glorious than to rescue Venice, long the guardian of Christendom on the Adriatic, and join the emperor in humbling French haughtiness? Henry might even conquer France, like Henry V. The king instructed Bainbridge at Rome to approach the pope.

Julius II, that fiery Genoese, had succeeded the notorious Roderigo Borgia, Alexander VI, in 1503. He, also, after Agnadello, had seen enough of the French in Italy; so he 'absolved' the Venetians for a large sum, and, in the spring of 1510, sent Henry a 'Golden Rose'; it symbolized the flowers which preceded the Saviour's Passion and a military alliance.

The king's concern with Venice was at least more realistic than his aspirations in France. If Venice was ruined, or the French cut the Atlantic trade routes, English and Flemish interests were concerned. Venetian cargoes of spices, malmsey wine and sugar 'candy' from Candia in Crete, still came into Southampton, Antwerp and Bruges; the spices were already undercut by Portuguese imports direct from India, but the Flanders galleys took back English wool and Flemish cloth.[1] By the autumn of 1511, the English had joined the Holy League, now reinforced by Ferdinand (confirmed in his possession of Naples) and by a Swiss army: Julius II even took the field himself.

Henry was now entering political quicksands, for his allies were out solely for what they could get. But he was already contracting with Hans Popenruyter of Malines for 24 Serpentines and 24 Courtaulx,

[1] C. S. P. Venetian. I. 852.

great guns over seven feet long; he had even specified their badges and names. And if these warlike preparations were not relished by Warham and Fox, they were much to the mind of a rising plebeian careerist, who was now to dominate the king's affairs.

III

Thomas Wolsey, that superb prelate, in whom the power of the mediaeval church culminated and collapsed, came from East Anglia. His father was a butcher and grazier of Ipswich, and Skelton, a Norfolk man, harps on his 'greasy genealogy', though such origins were not unusual among the princes of the Church.

Born in 1472 or 3, and ordained priest in St Peter's Church at Marlborough, 1498, Wolsey had been Fellow and Bursar of Magdalen College, Oxford, and Master of the still flourishing Collegiate School. He was forced, it seems, to resign his Fellowship for spending too much on Magdalen tower—'worse things', writes Pollard, 'have been done by bursars in recent times'—but he owed his start to his college. For at the school he had taught the younger sons of the Marquis of Dorset. Invited to spend Christmas with that magnate, young Wolsey had obtained the living of Limington, near Ilchester, Somerset. Here, says Aubrey, he had 'committed some debauchery—I thinke drunke (no doubt he was of a high rough spirit)'—and been put in the stocks at Hinton St George. 'Sir Amyas Paulet was so bold as to set the schoolmaster by the feet . . . which was never forgiven or forgotten.'[1] But he was soon chaplain to Archbishop Deane of Canterbury; then to Sir Richard Nanfan, Deputy Governor of Calais; by February 1509, Wolsey was Dean of Lincoln, with substantial benefices in Kent and Devon, and a chaplain to the king.

He was also, already, a family man. He had taken up with the 'daughter of one Lark', innkeeper at Thetford in his native East Anglia; Skelton runs on about 'lusty Lark'. And by her he already had two bastards: for the boy, Thomas Wynter, who developed into an easygoing, travelled, man of taste, with beautiful handwriting, he provided two rectories, four archdeaconries and the deanery of Wells; the daughter was accommodated at Shaftesbury Abbey as a nun. He was to settle his mistress in life by marriage to a gentleman called Legh, and her brother, who ended up Master of Trinity Hall, Cambridge, became Wolsey's confessor. All was thus kept in the family. Wolsey, the last and greatest prelate in England, was one of those who found the Church the only way to power, and who formed 'a celibate civil

[1] Stow, p. 497.

service, unaccustomed to the surgical operations of the late Roman Empire'.[1]

The French war now made him, as the king's divorce was to break him. As almoner and member of the Council (1509), he fascinated the young king, who shirked business, but admired brilliance, energy and wit. Wolsey was an adroit flatterer: 'Loth would we be,' he could write, 'that your Grace being so expert in archery, the Emperor should have more strings to his bow than yours.' He hunted and danced; he lived in fabulous splendour, a tireless politician and diplomat, in a blaze of ambition and pride, 'the first great cleric', it was remembered, 'in England that ever wore silk for his uppermost vestment'.[2] As Chancellor and Legate he was virtually to rule England for seventeen years, until his European ambitions brought failure and the deadly displeasure of his master, whom he had made to look a fool: for 'Henry's devotion to the favourite of the moment was complete. . . . When trust ceased it ceased at a blow.'[3] Warham was against foreign adventures; it was Fox, overwhelmed with business and anxious to attend to his diocese, who gladly brought Wolsey forward, and who launched his great career as the organizer of Henry's first continental war; 'the victualling of the army', says Herbert, 'was remitted to Wolsey, not without a sarcasm to his birth.'

By June, 1512, 12,000 men, commanded by Thomas Grey, the new marquis of Dorset, elder brother to Wolsey's former pupils, embarked from Southampton under the king's own eye. They filled him with unjustifiable pride: 'We believe,' he wrote, 'that never, its numbers considered, has there been seen a finer army . . . We believe that by the grace of God this our army will acquit itself right nobly.'[4]

Following a plan concerted with Ferdinand, the English were convoyed to Fuentarrabia, near Hendaye. But Ferdinand, 'that ancient and politic prince', merely used them to mask his annexation of Navarre: prepared, in the tradition of their country, for the last (Hundred Years') war, the English faced novel continental formations of pikemen and arquebusiers. With negligible artillery, and blocked by French guns and cavalry in Bayonne, they sweltered through the summer, looking across the bay of St Jean de Luz. 'Their victaile was muche part Garlike, and the Englishmen did eate of the Garlike with all meates, and drank hote wynes in the hote wether, and did eate all the hote frutes that they

---

[1] Pollard, p. 305.
[2] Herbert of Cherbury, op. cit.
[3] G. R. Elton, op. cit.
[4] *The Letters of King Henry VIII*, ed. M. St Clare Byrne. Cassell, 1936, p. 16.

could gette, which caused the bloudde so to boyle in their bellies that there fell sick three thousande of the flixe.'[1] So that autumn they mutinied, and told Dorset that they 'would abide after Michaelmas for no man'. A demoralized expedition, 'glad that they had deported out of such a country', crawled back to England. The king swore to hang those responsible.

IV

In 1513, Henry and Wolsey launched a much more serious and successful attack across the Straits of Dover; they beat the French in Picardy at Guinegate, Thérouanne and Tournai; more important that year the English routed the Scots at Flodden.

The new expedition was based on Calais, but masked by an offensive off Brittany. Here the English ships risked the fierce rocks and tides of the Breton coast, and the French had swift Rhodes galleys with superior fire power, brought up from patrolling the Barbary coast. They could 'drown' small craft with their oars. 'Now is the day come,' said the Spanish auxiliaries, when they saw them, 'that we shall fain go to the hospital.' 'Because I had no rails to my deck,' reported one commander, 'I coiled a cable round the deck breast up, and so hang'd, upon the cable, mattresses and such bedding as I had within board . . . setting out my pikes and fighting sails ready for the encounter.' Sir Edward Howard, the Lord Admiral, Surrey's second son, himself boarded a galley off Whitesands Bay, and was thrust 'with morris pikes' into the sea.

The attack on Brest had failed; on one ship only fifty-six out of a hundred and seventy-five men returned. Ferdinand even said maliciously, he was 'grieved' that Spanish sailors had been there. But the French may well have been distracted from interfering in the Straits of Dover; by May, 16,000 English troops were in Calais. The Merchant Adventurers in London had been warned that 'six men o'war out of Dieppe' were lying in wait for the artillery from Antwerp, but by the end of June, Henry himself, with 11,000 men, and many of his nobles, had crossed the Channel. And already Wolsey, as Royal Almoner, had as large a household as Fox.

Before he left England, the young king had committed his first dynastic murder. 'The White Rose', Edmund de la Pole, Duke of Suffolk, had been extradited from Flanders in 1505, and since held captive. He was the Yorkist claimant to the throne, so Henry, as a precaution, had him killed, and the dukedom of Suffolk, with its high

[1] Hall, op. cit., I, p. 46.

connotations, was soon conferred on the king's favourite, Sir Charles Brandon, an upstart in the eyes of the royal relations and the old nobility.

Henry's entourage was enormous—not exactly professional by the standards of Henry V. He had his own aristocratic Spears; the entire Chapel and Wardrobe; twenty-nine grooms and pages, and, it seems, a young mistress dressed as one, as well as heralds, pursuivants, trumpeters. By the end of June, two days after the king's twenty-second birthday, this circus descended on Calais, and Henry, for the first time, had set foot on the continent. Soon, at archery with the Spears, he surpassed them all. More importantly for the campaign, Wolsey had provided complete harness for over 13,000 men, and twelve heavy guns known as the Twelve Apostles. These 'bumbardells' which could fire a 260 lb shot for 80 lb of powder, and could only be fired five times a day,[1] were drawn by 24 Flemish mares apiece. Further, 8,000 'Almayn' [German] mercenaries joined the army; they were given a banner in the Tudor colours, and three had to be hanged at once for desecrating a church.

The rain, normal to campaigns in Flanders and Picardy in July, now closed in: Henry had to muster the army in a fog and Winchester was kicked by a mule; but the infantry, slogging through the mud, managed to besiege Thérouanne. Here, near the camp, Henry received a well-worn but important European figure.

Romantic, tricky, discredited but august, the Emperor Maximilian still symbolized the old Burgundian feud against France, and his appearance heartened the mercenary troops, 'Osterreich!' shouted the Germans, and the Flemings, 'Bourgoynge!' Between the lines of English infantry, white coats edged with green, Henry rode forward to meet him in the rain, his great bay stallion jingling with golden bells. Then came fourteen pages, their scarlet mantles trimmed with green; bagpipes and flutes skirled and shrilled as the boys tossed silver horsebells among the Germans. In armour over cloth of gold, a shaggy, redfeather hat tilted above his jewelled cap, Henry, now red-bearded, towered over them all. 'The King of England,' wrote one of the Germans, who liked that sort of thing, 'is a very proper man: he seemed intelligent, with a jolly look, and talked to people in a friendly, knowledgable way.'[2]

---

[1] L. and P., I, I, p. 785. 'Curtows' fired a 60 lb. shot for 40 lb., forty times a day 'Lizards' 12 lb. for 14 lb. thirty-seven times.

[2] *Of the honourable and sumptuous reception and friendly courtesy shown by the King of England to the Emperor Maximilian.*

Old enough to be Henry's grandfather, Maximilian behaved with impeccable charm; he refused to spread his own banner; even offered, for his expenses, to serve under the banner of St George. Pollard describes this flattery as 'serving as a private', a phrase better suited to the Boer war than to the conventions of sixteenth-century chivalry, but the ironic diplomatic gesture pleased the young king.[1]

Maximilian also gave him sound tactical advice: 'Turwin', as the English called Thérouanne, was highly vulnerable, and the flower of the French army was trying to relieve it. Why not cross the Lys beyond the town and cut them off?

The manoeuvre accomplished, the guns opened up: on August 16th, at Guinegate, the French, under orders to avoid battle, bolted from the trap. In this skirmish or 'Battle of Spurs', the Ducs d'Orléans and Longueville and the famous, elderly Bayard, were all taken. Sweating in his armour, Henry had won the first action of his first campaign.

A week later Thérouanne surrendered; the garrison marching out, bag and baggage, colours furled. 'Madame,' wrote an observer to Margaret of Savoy, Regent of the Netherlands, the emperor's daughter, in Brussels, *'vous ne veistes oncques si gorgias que le roy d'Angleterre et son armée.'*[2] Queen Catherine, too, rejoiced in the victory: 'I think that with the company of the emperor,' she told Wolsey, 'his Grace shall not adventure himself as much as I was afeard of before'; Maximilian, she hoped, could now be 'taken for another man that he was before thought'.

The combined armies now advanced further into France. They passed Lille, 'a place having much the appearance of an island in the middle of a marsh', and laid siege to the rich and well-fortified city of Tournai. 'We ordered our artillery,' Henry boasted to the Duke of Milan, 'to be disposed for the assault. We greeted the inhabitants thereof with some shots, and conceded them, at their request, a two-day truce for the negotiation of a surrender.'[3] *'Que ne vous rendrez'*, sang the courtiers, *'povres Théourneoys?'* By September 25, king and emperor entered the

---

[1] The unhappy phrase, so much out of period, has been repeated by other historians. 'Ten days later,' wrote Byrne, 'the penniless Emperor Maximilian joined him to *serve as a private in return for* [sic] *a hundred crowns a day* (op. cit., p. 17.) Pollard also gives Maximilian no credit for the subsequent victory. But Karl Brandi, in his celebrated biography of Charles V, goes to the other extreme: he describes Henry as merely 'at the head of well paid German troops'. It was Maximilian, he says, 'who won the day at Guinegate on August 16, 1513'. (*The Emperor Charles V*, trans. C. V. Wedgwood, Cape, 1939, p. 51.)

[2] 'You have never seen anything quite so splendid as the King of England and his army.'

[3] Byrne, op. cit., p. 20.

city in a torchlight procession, all the bells ringing, and were presented with the keys and six barrels of burgundy.

V

To crown all, much greater news arrived from England. At Flodden Field a total victory had been won over the Scots. James IV had early threatened to invade England, if Henry attacked the French, and, on August 12th, Henry, writing from camp, had defied him. 'Such imagined quarrels,' he had written, 'causeless devised to break with us, contrary to your promise, all honour and kindness, we cannot greatly marvel, considering the ancient accustomed manners of your progenitors, which kept never longer faith nor promise than pleased them. . . . As you do unto us and our realm, he had concluded, 'so it shall be re-marked and acquitted hereafter, by the help of our lord God and patron saint, St George.'[1]

But before this defiance could have reached him, the Scots king was dead. In July the English government had made its dispositions: the aged, indomitable Surrey had left London with 500 picked men and concentrated the power of the North at Newcastle-upon-Tyne, whither his artillery had been dispatched. Queen Catherine, left Regent, had faced the crisis with spirit, 'horrible besy at making standards, banners and badges'.

James IV had sold his gold plate, 'eaten off pewter', and raised 40,000 men: he had crossed the Tweed with a powerful train of guns, sacked the dilapidated castle at Norham in the diocese of Durham, and drawn up on Flodden Edge. With 22,000 men, Surrey had advanced to meet him, and offered battle 'between 12 and 3 in the afternoon, upon sufficient notice from them at eight or nine in the morning'. But James had not been drawn, so the English, without beer for four days, had advanced 'to go between the Scots and Scotland', and, on September 9th, this threat had dislodged the enemy. The Scots had then craftily fired their 'filthey straw', and moved back, parallel, under the smoke screen, along Brankstone ridge. But their five great clumps of spearmen had botched the change of direction and their artillery had got stuck. The Scots knights still stood intact, but the English gunfire and arrowstorm had galled the unarmoured Highlanders; so the whole Scots army had come down the hill, in unwonted silence, *en masse*, 'after the Almayn fashion'.

It was a fatal decision, formation had been lost; the Scots were sur-rounded and in the ensuing carnage James IV and his bastard son,

[1] Byrne, op. cit., p. 18.

Alexander, the twenty-year old archbishop of St Andrews, had both perished within a yard of the English standard.[1] The bishops of the Isles and Caithness, the abbots of Inchaffney and Kilwinning; the earls of Montrose, Crawford, Argyle and Lennox, together with most of the Scots nobility, had been massacred: for fifteen hundred English, eleven or twelve thousand Scots had fallen. The victors had left king, bishops and nobles naked on the field, while local borderers plundered both sides, and the English slaked their four days' thirst in Scots ale. They would never have believed it so good, they said, 'had it not been tasted . . . by our folks'.

'This victory,' wrote Ruthal of Durham to Wolsey, 'hath been the most happy that can be remembered. All believe that it hath been wrought by St Cuthbert, who never suffered injury to be done to his church.' Fortunately the Scots had offended the Saint by plundering Norham, or they might have done much more harm: 'my folks,' he concluded, 'under St Cuthbert's banner have brought home the King's banner, his sword and his *qwyschys* (cuisses).' Queen Catherine, announcing the victory, reminded Henry to thank God for it: 'Your Grace,' she wrote, 'shall see how I keep my promises, sending (in exchange) for your banners, a King's coat.' It was an intimate trophy, the Scots king's cloak:[2] Henry showed it with pride to Maximilian.

In October he complained to Leo X, Medici, whose election, at thirty-seven, after the death of Julius II, had 'mortified' the older cardinals 'not so much for the loss of the Papacy as for the green age of the new Pope',[3] about the state of the Scots Church.[4] The Scots bishops had actually fought in secular garb, and the Metropolitan See of St Andrews, he suggested, might now be subordinated to the Metropolitan Archbishopric of York: God was clearly fighting for the Holy League. Henry also forbade his sister, Margaret, the widowed Queen of Scots, to remove the infant James to the Outer Isles, and Surrey was restored to the Dukedom of Norfolk, forfeited by his father.

This great victory removed the Scots menace for years; now, with the capture of Tournai behind him, Henry negotiated an ephemeral treaty at Lille. He engaged to invade France next spring, with the

---

[1] *Articles of the bataille betwix the King of Scots and therl of Surrey in Brankstone feld* (L. and P., I, II, 1002 A). The young Archbishop, who had been a pupil of Erasmus, was extremely short-sighted, so he had not much chance.

[2] *Paludamentum*, perhaps here translatable as 'plaid'.

[3] L. and P., I, I, p. 770.

[4] This was nothing new. In 1509 the Archbishop of Glasgow had applied to Julius II for a licence to decontaminate the churches, churchyards and 'ecclesiastical places' in the diocese with holy water, if defiled *sanguinis vel semenis effusione*.

emperor and Ferdinand, and renewed his father's pledge of his younger sister, the Lady Mary, to their grandson, Charles of Castile. That autumn as the mist drew in over Picardy and Flanders, the English withdrew through towns to be familiar to their descendants—Lille and 'Ipres, Dixmew, Newporte and Donkirke', and the city fathers of Tournai ordered the *métiers* of the town to return their banners, brought out for the surrender, to be locked up again in the town hall. Not all the Tournois had been impressed by the concourse of the great: another order, in October, had forbidden them to 'sing or utter libels, ballads or otherwise, against Princes and Kings'. At home, that September, the people of Devizes, also representatively indifferent to great affairs, had been entirely preoccupied, Sir William Hungerford told the Council, with strife over the election of a mayor. John Taylor, clerk of Parliament, concluding his account of the adventure—the first large scale English invasion of Picardy and Flanders since the Hundred Years' War—reflected, rightly, that far too much English money, 'which greatly excells foreign coinage in value', had been disbursed. And, indeed, the cost had been enormous; in the first three years of the reign, despite the extravagance of the court, annual expenditure had not exceeded £65,000; by 1512, it was £286,000, and by 1513, nearly £700,000. By the next year, Henry and Wolsey had run through the limited capital in cash accumulated by Henry VII; though Wolsey soon cut this war expenditure (by 1516 it was back to £78,000), the reserves had gone.

VI

Henry had revelled in the expensive triumph; during the festivities arranged by Margaret of Savoy in Brussels, he had 'performed wonders, leaping like a stag'. All pointed to further success; the Swiss mercenaries in Wolsey's pay had captured Dijon, and the French in Italy had been heavily defeated by a large Swiss expedition under another cardinal, the cardinal of Sion, who had even restored the Sforza to Milan. But a more experienced diplomatist might have expected the sequel: no sooner had the treaty of Lille been agreed, than the two old foxes, Ferdinand and Maximilian, began negotiating with the French, a move made easier by the death of Julius II, the mainspring of the Holy League, and the accession of Leo X. Writing to his grandson, Charles of Castile, in September, Maximilian still called the French *'anchiens et encoires naturelz ennemis de nostre maison de Bourgogne'*,[1] but

---

[1] 'Old and still natural enemies of our Burgundian House.'

his immediate over-riding objective coincided with that of Ferdinand —to obtain an Italian kingdom for their common grandson, Ferdinand of Austria, Charles' younger brother.

Henry thus found himself double crossed. Reconciled to the Holy See, and tempted by the prospect of a favourable compromise in Italy, Louis XII agreed that young Ferdinand should marry the Princess Renée of France, who would bring with her all the French rights in Italy; both grandfathers would see Ferdinand settled, and the marriage of Charles of Castile to the Lady Mary would be shelved. In March, 1514, Stile was writing in bewilderment from Spain that 'all policy and craft be here used more for thayre awne security . . . than for any natural love or kindness to thayre fryndes. . . . It passeth my pore understandyng, and, it please your Grace, wants other better lerneyd than I am for to understand thaym.'

But Henry and Wolsey still held strong cards, and they now outmanoeuvred their allies. Since England had proved much the most dangerous enemy, the French soon came to terms, and Louis XII, now a widower at 52, was pledged to marry the Lady Mary, who was seventeen. By August 1514, the *volteface* had been executed: Henry retained Tournai; the 'pension' accorded by the French to his father was doubled, and, by October, the reluctant Tudor princess was Queen of France.

These arrangements were blessed by Leo X; they promoted, he said, the peace of Europe. They might even lead to a crusade against the Ottoman Turks, now, under Selim the Grim, in train to overrun Syria, Egypt and much of Arabia, and to take over from the last Abbasid the Sunni Caliphate of Islam.[1] In Italy a precarious balance of power had thus been restored; and England had won a new prestige, with Scotland cowed, and a firmer foothold on the continent.

The main architect of this success had been Wolsey, who now got his reward. Already Dean of Lincoln and York, he attained the bishopric of Lincoln, with which, *in commendam*, he held Tournai; and when, in July 1514, Cardinal Archbishop Bainbridge died in Rome, Wolsey was consecrated Archbishop of York. Vast prospects now opened before him: he determined to be cardinal; he meant to be pope.

Henry, too, cherished wider ambitions. He still retained the medi-

---

[1] The mirage of a crusade took various forms: in April 1514, a rumour reached Venice from Lisbon that two caravels from Calicut with pepper, ginger, and sandalwood, had brought an ambassador from Prester John, 'bearing a letter in Chaldean', praying the King of Portugal to send a fleet to be equipped by him, make a landing from the Red Sea, and liberate Palestine. The letter, the Venetian envoy commented, 'reads like one of St Paul's epistles'.

aeval and impracticable hope that, one day, if the French were at a disadvantage, he might regain what he held to be his rights in France. He was long, also, to use them as a form of blackmail: 'We went more roundly to our matters,' he told Wolsey, describing a talk with the captive duc de Longueville about his sister's projected French marriage, 'in as much as I said to him ... if your master considered what heritance he withholdeth from me, and what good my amity may do to help the matter in Italy, I think he will not greatly stick at it.' (He referred to a yearly subsidy of 100,000 crowns.) 'This furthermore,' he had continued, 'I said to the Duke, surely I cannot see how the amity made for years can no longer endure than the payment.'[1] After all, if he were slack in demanding recompense for his inheritance, he had told Longueville, his subjects would murmur at it; already a shrewd and characteristic touch.

No longer the gull of Aragonese and Venetian diplomacy, but with the Straits firmly held and a continental nuisance value, Henry was learning to exploit his power. And that, he knew, would depend on a project on which he had long determined—a stronger fleet.

[1] Byrne, op. cit., p. 23.

CHAPTER IV

OCEANIC HORIZONS

T HROUGHOUT his long reign, Henry VIII was to take a personal and expert interest in the navy; in the ships, the dockyards, and the forts of the main harbours throughout the realm. The old king had made the first dry dock at Portsmouth, and left him two 'great' ships, *Regent* and *Sovereign*, and Henry at once developed the fleet: 'in naval policy, from his accession . . . he was an alert and original thinker. His early councillors showed no interest in the fleet . . . the growth of the Navy, in principle and in detail, was the king's own work. At the end he had an efficient naval staff, but it was his own creation.'[1]

He had inherited seven major fighting ships, with auxiliaries; already, says Hall, they 'skowered' the Channel between Dover and Portsmouth; by 1512, on the eve of the French war, Henry had caused 'all his good ships and galleys to be rigged and prepared with all manner of ordnance meet for ships of war'. He had appointed the commanders; mustered soldiers at Blackheath; personally supervised the expedition against Fuentarrabia. That year he had also commissioned another 'great' ship 'such as was never before seen in England'; it was to be named *Henry Grace à Dieu*, or the *Great Harry*.

Early in 1513 Henry had personally commanded Sir Edward Howard, the Lord Admiral, soon destined to perish, to 'send word how every ship did sail'.[2] Howard had reported from *Mary Rose* on each one of them, as they had sailed past him off the North Foreland into the Downs: 'I called for pen and ink to mark [the] ships,' he had written, 'for they came all by me to an anchor.' First, after *Mary Rose*, came *Sovereign*: 'Sir,' he had reported, 'she is the noblest ship of sail at this hour that I trow be in Christendom. A ship of a hundred tons will not sooner come about than she.' Then came 'the *Nicholas*, the *Leonard* of Dartmouth, then the *George*, then the *Harry of Hampton*, then the *Anne*, then the *Nicholas Montrygo* called the *Sancho de Garra*, then the *Catherine*, then the *Mary*, . . . Sir one after another'.

[1] J. A. Williamson, *The English Channel*. Collins, 1959, p. 166.
[2] Ellis, op. cit., Series II, Vol. I, p. 215.

The *Catherine*, he had thought 'overladen with ordnance, beside her having tops which are big enough for a ship of eight or nine hundred tons', but 'in Christendom', he concluded, 'out of one realm was never seen such a fleet'. And morale was high: 'I saw never poor men so in courage to be doing as your men be.' Further, the ships of Bristol were with him, 'I assure your Grace gorgeas ships for their burden.' But the fleet needed supplies: 'Sir, for God's sake haste your Council to send me down our victuals, for, if we shall lie long, the common voice will run that we lie and keep in the Downs, and do no good but spend money and victuals, and so the noise will run to our shames.' Sir Edward Howard had got his way, as already recorded: 'when the wind served the navy royal of England weighed anchor and made sail into Britaine (Brittany)'. They had tried to assault Brest, but after a ship 'ran on a blind rock', the commanders concluded that they needed 'lodesmen' to take soundings, and only blockaded the port. Henry was invited to come in person to share the expected victory, a project wisely vetoed by the Council. The sequel off Whitesands Bay, in which Sir Edward Howard was 'thrust by morris pikes into the sea', has already been described; and how, by keeping the French busy, the navy contributed to the land victories of 1513.

II

The building of new ships went on. In April 1514, the king paid for 'seven banners of linen cloth and buckram, painted with divers arms to be delivered to Sir Thomas Wyndham and divided among the ships',[1] and for a streamer fifty-one yards long for the *Henry Grace à Dieu*.

The need was now urgent; the Norman and Breton seamen were experienced and bold; they could attack the Spanish colonies in the new world, unhampered by any commitments to the Emperor or to Spain, and they had long been exploiting the Newfoundland fisheries. Moreover, when, in 1515, Francis I came to the French throne, he began to build a large naval base at Le Havre. The French frequently raided the Channel coasts, and the English retaliated in kind.

By the end of 1514, the 1,000 ton *Henry Grace à Dieu* was 'hallowed' and launched: she was a heavily gunned carrack, designed probably for the new tactics of sinking the enemy by gunfire rather than by boarding; but she proved unseaworthy, and her timber was unseasoned, so that she never saw much action. Eight years after, on the eve of re-

[1] L. and P., I, I, p. 750.

newed war with France, she was at Northfleet, needing to have a dock made for her at Erith, 'to caulk and search her under water'.

In 1515, considering Portsmouth too vulnerable, Henry founded new royal dockyards at Deptford and Woolwich in the estuary of the Thames. By the autumn of 1515, he had a great new galley, the *Virgin Mary*, driven by six score oars and carrying a thousand men. She had 207 small guns, 70 of copper and the rest iron, and the king himself acted as Master; he wore 'a sailor's coat and trousers of frieze cloth of gold; he had on a thick chain of which five links and three plates were of gold, with *Dieu et mon Droit*', from which hung a 'large whistle with which he whistled almost as loud as a trumpet or clarionet'.

The fleet was now divided between Portsmouth and the Thames estuary. With growing experience, mistakes in material and design were rectified, and when, in the 'thirties and 'forties, Henry was defying the pope and both the major continental powers, much monastic wealth was spent on fortifying the coast. And as early at 1514, he had sanctioned a guild of pilots to be formed at Deptford for the better navigation of the Thames estuary; by 1546 it had become the Corporation of Trinity House, still in charge of buoys and lighthouses around the British Isles.

III

The merchants of London, Southampton, Plymouth and Bristol, meanwhile, were slowly becoming aware of the shift to Atlantic trade routes which was to transform England from an island on the periphery of the Mediterranean world to one commanding a great oceanic trade with the Americas, India and the Far East.

In 1492, a year after Henry was born, Columbus had planted the standards of Spain on Guadahani in the Bahamas and renamed it San Salvador. Five years later, John Cabot out of Bristol had discovered Nova Scotia and sighted Newfoundland; next year he had sailed along the American coast, perhaps as far as Chesapeake Bay. There had been other ventures from Bristol, encouraged by Henry VII, and Sebastian Cabot had explored the fringe of Arctic Canada for the North West Passage, returning in the year of Henry VIII's accession.

Those tentative contacts had little impressed England. But the great Portuguese discovery of the route to India and the Far East, which followed their exploration of Madeira, Cape Verde, and the West Coast of Africa, quite outclassed any English enterprise. Two years after Bosworth, Vasco da Gama had circumnavigated the Cape and entered the Indian ocean, the first European to outflank the great land empires of the East; by 1511, two years after Henry VIII's accession, the Portuguese had broken the Arab domination of the Indian Ocean, established themselves under Albuquerque in India, and taken over Malacca, a springboard to the spice islands of Indonesia and beyond.

In 1513, when Henry had been invading Picardy, set on mediaeval objectives, Balboa was claiming the Pacific or 'South Sea' for Spain, and by 1523, more than half a century before Drake, Magellan's expedition had first discovered the Philippines and circumnavigated the world. In the early 'twenties, Cortes was conquering Mexico, and, in the 'thirties, Pizarro taking over the Inca Empire of Peru; and Jacques Cartier of St Malo was exploring the St Lawrence, while Henry was preoccupied with European power politics and Anne Boleyn. 'The English,' writes Dr Rowse, 'were the most backward of the significant peoples along the Atlantic littoral on the fairway to the New World.'[1]

Yet, if Henry VIII, like his subjects, was little concerned with exploration, his care of the fleet and of the existing trade with Bordeaux the Iberian peninsula and the Baltic encouraged the seamanship and navigation on which the Elizabethan expansion was based. Court circles were now at least aware of the new lands. More's *Utopia* is based on rumours of them—'Ralph Hithloday' with his black sunburned face, who described it, was a 'portugal born'; and in 1517 John Rastell, More's brother-in-law, a London lawyer, tried to colonize Newfoundland, with Henry's approval. He never got beyond Ireland, where his crew put him ashore, returning themselves to London; but the fiasco did not prevent him writing the first 'English description of America',[2] though he never set eyes on it. It was a country

> *so large of rome*
> *Much larger than all Christendome.*

A pity, he thought, that it had not been colonized by the English.

> *... What an honorable thynge*
> *Both to the realme and to the Kynge,*
> *To have his domynyon extendynge*
> *Which the noble Kynge of late memory*
> *The most wyse prynce the VII Henry*
> *Causyd first to be founde.*[3]

[1] *The Expansion of Elizabethan England.* Macmillan, 1955, p. 158.
[2] Rowse, op. cit., p. 166, citing J. A. Williamson. *The Voyages of the Cabots and the Discovery of North America*, pp. 89, 90.
[3] Quoted by A. L. Rowse, ibid., p. 166.

Yet although contacts were made with Brazil and West Africa, the old ties with Spain were still far more important. Henry gave a charter to his merchants in Andalusia and religious hatred was still reserved for Muslims. In 1515 the king licensed the collection of alms for Christian captives at Tunis, merchant crews in irons on bread and water; it was meritorious, he declared, 'to redeem the said Christen prysonners oute of th' ondes of the said Infideles'.

Henry was mainly interested in the Navy for European power politics and for defence. His realm lay athwart the Imperial communications between Flanders and Germany and the Iberian peninsula and the Mediterranean; he was always concerned with the cloth trade with Flanders and the trade with the Baltic. With his bridgehead at Calais 'keeping the Channel', Henry's best diplomatic asset was not his money, though that was important, but his fleet. If the French, too, profited by the Gascon trade, the traditional feud with France had been worsened by the French threat from Le Havre and the Breton ports. So, if Henry was probably little aware of the profound revolution in his country's strategic and economic position which the original Portuguese and Spanish discoveries were to bring about, his immediate concern with the Navy and with the security of what became his sovereign 'Empire', helped consolidate the base from which the Elizabethan and Jacobean expansion was to spring.

Certainly it was Henry who first gave continuity, organization, and protection to the building yards and dockyards of the fleet; and he created a permanent Navy Board, some of whose personnel served into the reign of Elizabeth I.

IV

The king's extrovert, energetic character thus found expression in a practical interest other than tournaments, hunting and war. His work for the navy was decisive, not merely in its immediate context, but in the far wider vistas of the future, in which Europeans were to dominate the planet, founding great empires and new nations across the oceans. Had anyone been able to contemplate the entire world during Henry's day, many events might have appeared much more decisive than the fortunes of an island off the Western European coast. In Muscovy, Ivan IV, when he died in 1514, had consolidated the nucleus of a great continental power; he had married into the Imperial family of Byzantium and was calling himself 'Tsar' (Caesar), using the blazon of the double headed eagle and claiming to be heir to the empire of Eastern Christendom. In 1533 his grandson, Ivan V, began the reign that lasted until 1584 and richly earned him the title of 'the Terrible', consolidating the basis of a massive state. Or, again, the Turkish conquests in Asia and the Levant, the fall of Rhodes in 1522, and the threat to Central Europe after the defeat of the Hungarians in 1526, might have appeared much more important; or the great victories won by Babur over the Afghans at Panipat in 1525 and, in the next year, over the Rajputs at Khanua, which won him, and his Mughal descendants, the empire of India. And in the Far East the Chinese Ming emperors were ruling the greatest population in the world.

Yet, in the perspective of time, all these great events were to prove less important than the oceanic enterprise of the descendants of the Tudor English, who were to make an empire and commonwealth in the Americas, India, Africa and Australia, carrying Western ways of government, industry and science over the face of the world. But Henry and Wolsey were immediately and inescapably concerned with the power struggle between Valois and Habsburgs, still centring on Italy; with how to exploit and to reinsure.

CHAPTER V

THE CARDINAL OF YORK

❖

THE French alliance, concluded in August 1514, did not last long. On December 31 the gallant but decrepit Louis XII expired, a martyr, it was said, to dynastic duty. His nephew Francis Duc d'Angoulême, who succeeded him, was to keep Europe in turmoil for years; '*ce grand gaillard*', the old King had said, '*gâtera tout*'.[1] Francis I was a tall and brilliant prince, whose hand-writing, unlike the crabbed script of Charles V or the unvaried, slogging style of Henry VIII, shows a Renaissance flourish and clarity. At twenty-two he was insatiable in love, politics and war; 'the monarchy of Christendom,' he declared, 'shall rest under the banner of France as it used to do'. If his nose was porcine and his legs too thin, he was the mirror of fashion, and he disposed of a power which dwarfed Henry's insular realm. On February 13, 1515, in white and cloth of silver, curveting on a barbary horse outside his canopy of state, the new King of France entered his great city of Paris to the thunder of bells.

In April the English Treaty was renewed, but the Lady Mary, now Dowager of France, had deprived her brother of a dynastic card. During her brief marriage to Louis XII, the young *Reine Blanche*, with her fashionable golden pallor, had been the toast of Paris; Francis himself, holding the crown over her head at the coronation, had been attracted and she had told her brother she 'felt afeard'. Faced with the advances of the new king, and once more with the old dynastic marriage to Charles of Castile, with his adenoidal look and Habsburg chin, she was now determined to follow her own inclination. And in such matters, Tudors knew their own minds. Charles Brandon, the recently created Duke of Suffolk, and long boon companion to the King, was the son of a plain esquire, the standard bearer at Bosworth, killed by Richard III himself. But he was high in favour; one of the handsomest men at court, with a spade beard, much admired. Suffolk had won great prestige at 'Barriers' during the coronation festivities, for the French had set on a colossal German to challenge him, and, for some

[1] 'This great fellow will spoil everything.'

time, odds were even. At last Suffolk struck him with the butt end of his spear, till he staggered; they then both took a breather, and fought again, 'when the Duke so pommelled the German about the head' that blood gushed from his nose; 'which being done', the German was 'secretly conveyed away'.

When Suffolk again arrived in Paris to renew the alliance, arrange the Queen Dowager's return to England and reclaim her dowry, she spoke out: 'You are come,' she said, 'to 'tice me home, that I may be married [to the Archduke Charles] in Flanders.' As she afterwards told her brother, she 'put my Lord Suffolk in choice whether he would accomplish marriage within four days, or else he would never have enjoyed me'.

Suffolk capitulated. 'To be plain with you,' he told Wolsey, 'I married her heartily, and have lain with her, in so far as in me lies, that she be with child.'

Soon, glad to deprive Henry of a diplomatic asset, Francis I was enquiring publicly whether Suffolk was to marry the king's sister; Suffolk denied all, but the Court buzzed. 'I were like to be ondon,' he wrote to Wolsey, 'if the matter should come to the knollag of the Kynge me masster.' He would 'rather a died', he asserted, than that Henry should be 'miscontent'; 'Me nown good Lord,' he concluded, simply, . . . 'help.' Under stress of anxiety, his spelling became more than usually peculiar. 'Me lord,' he wrote, 'Sche and I bouth rymyttis this mattar holle to your dysskras: tresting ye in hall hast possebbyll wye schall her from you some good tydyngns. . . .'[1]

Wolsey advised him to secure the dowry, jewels and plate at once, and so pacify the King; and the dowager queen declared she had 'in a manner enforced Lord Suffolk' and 'done it for her own mind'. She had only married Louis XII, she reminded her brother, on condition that, should he die, she might 'do as she did list'.

Henry had tolerated the affair and, indeed, may have conferred a dukedom on Suffolk with 'that future development already decided upon',[2] and admitted the accomplished fact. But his sister had to refund her entire dowry, and repay expenses up to £24,000; for years the

---

[1] 'My lord, she and I both remit this matter wholly to your discretion, trusting that in all possible haste, we shall have good tidings from you.'

'Of the three greatest noblemen of the time,' writes Brewer, 'the Duke of Suffolk, the Duke of Buckingham and the Marquis of Dorset, it would be hard to say which was the most illiterate. Perhaps the spelling of the Duke of Suffolk is the most tortuous and ingeniously perverse. Doubtless it was phonetic.'

[2] Polydore Vergil, *Anglica Historia*, ed. with a translation by Denys Hay, Camden, LXXV, 1950, p. 223. Stow says Henry had 'meant Suffolk to have her, but a better offer came in the way'.

diplomats were to haggle over the jewels and the money. But on May 13th, the young dowager of France married Suffolk in full state, and her husband continued a powerful intimate of the king.[1] But the new Duchess of Suffolk was out of the dynastic market, though her granddaughter, Lady Jane Grey, was to expiate on the block her inheritance of Tudor blood,

Henry's flighty elder sister Margaret, Dowager of Scotland as widow of James IV, had also remarried; this time to Archibald Douglas, Earl of Angus. Scotland was in chaos, for 'every Scotsman', as Brewer writes, 'from sire to sire inheriting blood which cried aloud for vengeance . . . with his keen appetite and canine sagacity for strife, was only too ready to share in the fray'. 'There was never so mekill myschefe,' wrote Lord Dacre from the English border, 'robbry, spoiling and vengence in Scotland that there is nowe, without hope of remedye; which I pray our Lord God to continewe.'[2]

The confusion which neutralized the Scots was an opportunity for the French. In conjunction with plans to invade Italy, Francis I now sent John Stewart, Duke of Albany, cousin and heir to the child-king, into Western Scotland. 'He will not,' said Wolsey, 'desist until he has compassed the death of the queen and the infant king in order to make himself master of that realm.' Early in 1515, Queen Margaret wrote to her brother, in the Scots idiom, 'God send I was such a woman that I might go with my bairn in myn arms, I trow I should not be long fra you.' Albany was made Regent by the Scots Parliament and virtually kidnapped James V.

By the autumn of 1515, with Dacres' assistance, Margaret escaped to Northumberland, 'physically and mentally sick lest the life of her son James should be put in danger'.[3] Here, in England, she bore a daughter to Lord Angus, Lady Margaret Douglas, afterwards Countess of Lennox. She was to be the mother of Lord Darnley, from whose marriage with Mary Queen of Scots, herself Margaret's granddaughter by her marriage to James IV, came the royal Stuaart line. In the spring of 1516, complaining of sciatica from the northern climate, Margaret came south to the English Court at Greenwich, where she revelled in the un-

---

[1] 'The motto on a label appended to the Duke's lance in the picture of Mary and him at Strawberry Hill,' writes Ellis (I. 123), 'indicates at least his knowledge of the world . . .

> *Cloth of gold do not despise*
> *Though thou be matched with cloth of frize* (freize)
> *Cloth of frize be not too bold,*
> *Though thou be matched with cloth of gold.'*

[2] Ellis, I, I, p. 93.
[3] Polydore Vergil, p. 241.

accustomed luxury, and 'could not take her eyes off' the sumptuous
dresses provided by the king. Henry and both his sisters were reunited
in a round of tournaments, feasts, and masquerades, but both in France
and Scotland their dynastic marriages had hardly achieved success.

II

These set-backs were followed by unexpected, swift and mortifying
triumphs by Francis I in Italy. In alliance now with the Venetians, who
disliked the pro-imperialist Swiss presence in Milan supporting the
Sforza duke, he had crossed the Cottian Alps by the pass of Argentière,
south-east of Grenoble, with the loss of only a few knights and guns,
bypassed a strong Swiss garrison at Susa, and arrived at Saluzzo, whence
he had advanced north east on Milan. Then, on September 13/14, 1515,
he had utterly defeated the Swiss at Marignano. It was regarded as a
great victory of the old knightly order over professional mercenaries;
a resounding European event. The day was, in fact, won by the French-
employed condottiers, Trivulzio, who used the irrigation canals to
flood the meadows and break up the Swiss phalanx, but the defeat ended
the Swiss supremacy and the attempt of the Federation to play one side
off against another in major power politics.[1]

Henry had entirely miscalculated; he had told the Venetian ambassador that the French King was much too afraid of him to cross the
Alps, and refused at first to believe the news. The Swiss were still
thought the best troops in Europe, and had despised the French feuda-
tories, whom they called 'armoured hares'; they had thus attacked the
French camp without proper preparation—like *sangliers eschauffés*, said
Francis I, 'infuriated boars'—and they had met total defeat. Ferdinand of
Aragon voiced the fears of France's enemies when he wrote 'the manner
in which the battle was lost gave him more concern than the loss of
Milan': the invincible Swiss could not now be relied on.

Francis I had thus turned the Sforzas out of Milan, and frustrated the
policy of the Holy League. He had also scored heavily over the English,
still nominally his allies; he had won great personal renown; mastered
Northern Italy, and arranged that Henry's sister should be driven from
Scotland. King and cardinal cast about for revenge by means short of
war, and they threw good money after bad. In May 1515, before

[1] By the treaty of Freiburg in the following year the French gained virtual monopoly
of recruiting in the cantons; the Swiss gave up control of the Simplon, though they kept
control of the St Gotthard, the Lukmanier and the St Bernardino passes. They also retained
Lugano and part of its lake, and part of Maggiore, and they still controlled the passes of
the Valtellina and so of the Stelvio, Splugen and Maloja, but their strength became
defensive: Swiss neutrality had begun.

Marignano, they had sent 100,000 gold crowns to Antwerp to pay the Swiss; now Sir Richard Wingfield, their ambassador to Maximilian, was instructed to suborn him to lead 30,000 German and Swiss mercenaries against the French in Italy during the following spring. Wingfield was a courtly old gentleman, who complained that Maximilian had led him such a dance that he had 'white hairs gotten in the snowy mountains of Germany, which have the power to make all hares and partridges that abide among them turn white,' and Wolsey now re-enforced and undercut him by sending his own brilliant secretary, Richard Pace, to Zurich, to hire the Swiss. An Oxford humanist who had started life as a musician to Bishop Langton of Winchester, and who became Dean of St Paul's and of Salisbury, Pace found his senior colleague dilatory and pompous; 'summer will be green' he called him, because of his statements of the obvious. When exhausted by diplomacy, Pace would retire to Konstanz on the Bodensee, where, 'in a public bath,' he wrote '*de Fructu qui ex doctrina percipitur*', reflecting, among more serious topics, on the notable thirst of the citizens.

In March 1516, Maximilian came down over the Brenner and advanced on Milan; he had a good chance to take it, but, bribed, or short of funds, decamped, through Verona, back to Innsbruck.

These notorious manoeuvres made the French more dangerous, and Henry's position had been further weakened by the death of Ferdinand near Granada in January 1516. Long ailing, he had shortened his life, Stile reported, by 'always, in fair weather and in foul, labouring in hunting and hawking', and had 'left no manner of treasure'. His grandson, Charles of Castile, now succeeded to his realms of Aragon and Naples and was forced, in order to take them over, further to conciliate the French. In August 1516, he confirmed his peace with Francis I at Noyon and even undertook to marry the infant daughter of the French king. Henry declared it a scandalous alliance, as the bridegroom was seventeen and the princess not yet one year old; and indeed it was reported that Charles would never 'abide the time', particularly as his ministers had 'suffered him to enter *ludum veneris*'.

Henry of course had continued his round of noisy gaieties. In Garter robes and crimson cap, he much impressed Pasqualigo, the Venetian envoy: he dined alone, served with august ceremony, or he went a-Maying, dressed, like his guards, in green, while the damsels of the Court, who eclipsed the Queen, rode on white palfreys.

What sort of legs, he had asked Pasqualigo in 1515, had the French King? 'I replied spare; whereupon he opened the front of his doublet and placing his hand on his thigh said, "Look here, *I* have a good calf to *my* leg."' Crashing down the lists, Henry would capsize his opponents, horse and all. That January 1516, running at the ring with Suffolk and nine others, he wore a wreath of green satin embroidered with pomegranates, symbolizing both fertility and the Queen's parents' capture of Granada: behind were great pavilions with romantic names—Flowerdelyce, Whytte Hart, Harpe, Greyhound, Lebard's Hed, Estereche Fether. In the evenings there were elaborate masques and dancing.

Wolsey was well content to see his master so engaged. In 1515 he had attained his ambition to be a cardinal and was already immensely rich: he now ousted Warham from the Lord Chancellorship, while his collaborater, Ruthal, succeeded Fox as Lord Privy Seal. With the retirement of these veterans of the previous reign, Wolsey, under the king, now combined the supreme power in church and state.

The cardinal and his master cast about to redeem the set back to their adventure into the Holy League. They could at least put Charles under one obligation through their sea power and their money; for in spite of the treaty of Noyon, Charles could not risk travel through French territories. But he had to go to Spain, and was still in 1517 chafing at Middelburgh on Walcheren, pledging his own credit and even that of the Knights of the Golden Fleece. Henry sent him 20,000 gold nobles in cash and arranged credits in Antwerp to finance the voyage.[1]

So, early in September, Charles sailed from Flushing. His pampered court had not enjoyed their stay on Walcheren: 'the whole country', complained Cuthbert Tunstall, the English envoy, later Bishop of London and Durham, to Erasmus, 'is below the level of the sea, two paces at high tide, and, but for the dams, it would break in upon the inhabitants in the midst of their feastings . . . they say there is no other way of escaping these inconveniences save by draining hogsheads'.

The voyage proved horrible: off Winchelsea the vessel containing the King's horses and apparel was burnt out and all lost; the ships were forced by a gale to put into Plymouth Roads, then becalmed in the Bay of Biscay. When at last they sighted Spain, the pilots thought they were off Galicia when they were off Asturias, and they landed on a cruel coast: the ships had to put back north without even landing the courtiers' beds. There were rumours of plague, the food was appalling and the inhabitants intolerably arrogant.

Yet Charles took over his inheritance. He was ruler now of all Spain and of the Spanish possessions in Italy and of his Burgundian Flemish territories, and heir to the entire Habsburg lands in Central Europe. He would not be easy to manage.

[1] C. S. P. Spanish, II, 256.

Maximilian, moreover, having accepted English subsidies on the pretext of coming to Flanders to dissuade his grandson from his commitments to the French, had also joined the treaty of Noyon. He had neatly summed up the situation with the remark to his grandson, 'You are about to cheat the French and I the English—or at least I shall do my best.'

Yet so great was Wolsey's ingenuity that he managed to turn this apparent line up of the great continental powers to his advantage by taking the initiative for a 'universal peace.' He repeated the manoeuvre executed in 1514, and made overtures to the French. There was much talk of a pacification of the European powers leading to a Crusade; the Turks were fast encroaching on central Europe and the Levant, and in March, at Cambrai, Maximilian, Francis and Charles had engaged to collaborate.

The English had more limited objectives: Tournai had already become a liability; the governor had told Wolsey that he doubted if he could hold it; and if he lost the town and escaped, he would be 'hayned and distayned within the reyam (realm) as birds do to a nowl': even the salary of £4 a year paid to the tipstaff of the privy watchword was in arrears.

Moreover, Henry now at last had a child; an important dynastic card. On February 18, 1516, at Greenwich, Catherine had borne him a daughter, who had survived to a tragic destiny. The princess was christened Mary, and Henry had displayed her to courtiers and ambassadors with delight: 'by the Grace of God,' he said, 'a son will follow.'

The child early showed a fixation on clergymen. When, aged two, she saw Dionysius Memo, an Italian friar, she 'called out in English, "Priest", "Priest",' and he was 'obliged to play with her'. As heiress to the throne she was given a great household, and on October 5, 1518, betrothed by proxy to the infant Dauphin of France. A treaty had been signed ceding Tournai in return for 600,000 crowns and a large pension for the cardinal; Francis had undertaken not to support Albany, and to meet Henry near Calais the next year. These arrangements were a sequel to a resounding treaty of universal peace between France, the Empire, the Papacy and England; the Scandinavian states, Hungary and Portugal were included. Wolsey now seemed the architect of a European peace.

III

The cardinal was now, virtually, ruler of England, the last great mediaeval prelate to be Lord Chancellor, and in 1518, as Papal Legate *a latere*, he was confirmed as a European prince of the universal Church. His entertainments were splendid: when the French delegates arrived in London that October to celebrate the betrothal of Mary to the Dauphin ('these gentlemen of France', said the English, 'are very fresh') he gave a sumptuous supper, writes the admiring Hall, 'the like of which I fancy was never given by Cleopatra or Caligula; the whole banqueting hall being decorated with huge vases of gold and silver, that I fancied myself in the tower of Chosroes'. As the king was present, guests were even provided with bowls of ducats and dice. They needed the money, for Henry would draw £1,000 for gambling at a time, more than £25,000 in our values.

The feasting was fantastic; beeves and muttons, porkers and fat hogs; capons and chickens by the dozen; six salmon, fifteen swans, four peacocks, fifty-four dozen larks; lashings of butter; green ginger, marmalades, quinces; gallons of cream and 'frumenty'. The infant Princess Mary, already in cloth of gold, wore a black cap, blazing with jewels, and was betrothed with a minute ring.

Henry much appreciated this diplomatic triumph; a treaty of international importance had been ratified in England: 'in the memory of the oldest inhabitant, no occasion like it had happened'. Fox told the cardinal, perhaps sincerely, 'it was the best deed ever done for England, and, next to the King, the praise of it is due to you!' The Archduke Charles was called 'a cookoo' for missing the princess's hand.

These high policies were less appreciated by the populace, who detested Wolsey's cosmopolitan arrogance; his apparent domination of the King was particularly resented. The year before, his spies had reported the tavern gossip at Swineshead in Lincolnshire: 'that it was a wonder to see how the king is ordered nowadays; for the cardinal and the Duke of Suffolk, which the king hath brought up out of nought, do rule him in all things as they list; whether it be by necromancy witchcraft or policy, no man knoweth'.[1] 'Symond Magus,' it was said, 'ascended also by arte magyke.' Imbecile rumours were current among the unemployed: that December Thomas Hykkes had said, 'Wolsey would put all the beggers in a barn and brenne em up'; but the king, shocked, had explained he could hardly consent without consulting the Archbishop of Canterbury, and Warham had refused to agree unless Wolsey was 'set in a pulpit and burnt with them'.

But Wolsey tried to turn even discontent to account. In 1517 riots broke out in London against the foreign merchants and craftsmen from Flanders, France, Italy and the Baltic, whose techniques surpassed those

[1] L. and P, II, I, 2733.

of the English, and who monopolized the most lucrative trades. Incited by a preacher at Paul's Cross, and led by a disillusioned broker, John Lincoln, a mob of apprentices and roughs used the May Day holiday to wreck and loot the foreign quarters and overrun the city. So bad was the riot, known as 'Evil May day', that the Lieutenant of the Tower fired his guns to intimidate the mob, and the riot was only quelled when Suffolk and Surrey brought in harnessed soldiers.

Lincoln and the ringleaders were hanged, drawn and quartered and their remains gibbetted; hundreds of the mob were rounded up. But the cardinal, who had fortified his house at York Place, staged a remarkable scene. Henry came up from Richmond, where he had remained through the disturbance confining himself to threats, to Westminster Hall. Here, in full state, with Queen Catherine, his two sisters, dowagers of Scotland and France, Wolsey, his Council, Lord Mayor and Aldermen and nobility ranged about him, the young king sat beneath his canopy of state.

Down the long hall came a miserable procession, 400 'poor younglings and old false knaves and a plain woman, in tattered shirts, halters about their necks, all along, one after the other'; they fell on their knees before the royalties and the government, 'Mercy!' they cried, 'Mercy!'

Then the cardinal, too, fell on his knees before the king. Henry remained adamant, even when the three queens added their supplications; only when Wolsey, weeping, pledged himself for the good behaviour of the prisoners, the king was seen to relent. He accorded the mob their lives: whereat the whole crew 'took the halters from their necks and danced and sang'. So Wolsey dealt with the symptoms, not the cause, and the king doubtless got more credit with his people than the cardinal.

Henry must have sensed the cardinal's unpopularity, and how much those who had business with him disliked him. Petitioners and courtiers said they would rather be ordered to Rome than approach the cardinal, who, walking in the park, would 'suffer no suiter to come near but commanded them as far off as a man could shoot an arrow'. 'If ye be not content to tarry my leisure,' he would say, 'depart when ye will.'

But the king approved Wolsey's personal splendour, expected in that age. 'His upper vesture,' writes Cavendish, his gentleman usher, in a vivid, admiring account, 'was all of scarlet, or else of fine crimson taffeta, or crimson satin engrained . . . with a black velvet tippet of sables about his neck, holding in his hand an orange, filled with a sponge of vinegar or other confection against pestilent airs. This he most commonly held to his nose . . . when he was pestered by many suitors. And before him were borne the broad seal of England and the cardinal's hat.'[1] It was embroidered 'T.C.—Thomas Cardinal': he was like a 'glorious peacock—gloriosum pastophorum'.[2] 'On masters before,' cried his gentlemen, 'and make room for my Lord.' Four footmen in black and scarlet with pole axes went before him. He dined alone, like the king, under a cloth of state, his guests and vast household at their own tables about him. As Cardinal Legate as well as Archbishop of York, he had two crosses carried by the tallest priests he could find: he needed both, said his enemies, such were his sins. He was brilliant and convivial, and knew just how to take his master. He would present Henry with a jewel and insinuate a new notion as the king handled it. According to Cavendish, Henry's confidence was well-placed: 'In my judgement,' he writes, 'I never saw the realm in better obedience and quiet than it was in the time of his authority, nor justice better administered . . . the realm had then abundant riches, whereof the King was most inestimably furnished, and called them the Golden World',[3] a shallow judgment in view of popular discontent.

Today the limitations of Wolsey's foreign and economic policy are patent, and clearly he never understood finance. Only his work as Lord Chancellor was to last: influenced by the Roman Law predominant on the continent, he strengthened equity jurisdiction by creating case law; for he 'would do right to all manner of people, poor and rich, after the laws of the realm'. He also extended the power of Star Chamber, bringing riot, forgery, contempt of court, and packed juries under its authority.

His control of the church was absolute. As Legate he could override all other jurisdictions and set the Convocations of York and Canterbury aside. He intended to make wide reforms, but he had no time. This 'bold, bad man', as Shakespeare called him,[4] was immensely able, versatile, astute, but he took on more than anyone could manage. Why did Henry, now coming to his full powers, tolerate the gossip that asked 'was there no King in England?'; the unprecedented concentration of secular and clerical power; the monstrous display? First, doubtless, as Elton puts it, because 'this very puzzling king . . . often relied on others for ideas'. He took after Edward IV; had too much company, hunting, music, talk, women, to attend to; in modern

---

[1] *The Negotiations of Thomas Woolsey, the great Cardinal, containing his life and death, etc.*, by George Cavendish, 1641. Definitive edition, *The Life of Cardinal Wolsey*, ed. John Holmes, 1852.

[2] Polydore Vergil, op. cit., p. 267.

[3] Cavendish, op. cit., p. 7.

[4] *Henry VIII*, Act II, sc. II, 44.

terms, he naturally liked the contents of his in-tray summarized and those of his out-tray drafted. This service Wolsey arranged through the secretaries Pace and Knight,[1] who were subordinate to him; he earned all the rope he was given. Yet the king regarded him, always, as an instrument: 'Neither Wolsey nor anyone else ever held [Henry] in the hollow of his hand.'[2]

In 1518, the king wrote to Wolsey, telling him not to overwork, 'Myne owne good Cardinale,' he said, 'take some pastime and comfort to the intent *that you may longer endure to serve us* . . . surely you have so substantially ordered our matter both on this side of the sea and beyond that in mine opinion little or nothing can be added . . . written with the hand of your loving master. Henry R.'[3]

IV

The king liked to have cheerful faces round him and saw to it that his immediate entourage were very well paid. The pages of the King's Chamber got as much as £100 a year—'during pleasure'; the Master of the Minstrels £53, on the same condition. Ralph Blagge, the King's Remembrancer, got £55.17.4 for life; Margaret Bryan, governess to the infant Princess Mary, £50 for life; Sir Thomas Guildford, who held more important offices, was paid £40 for life as Master of the Horse; Squires of the Body had £33.6.8, and the Chief Surgeon the not very generous fee of £26.13.4 for life, though he doubtless had other occasions to augment it. The Armourer, Jasper de Watte, had £20, and Jasper Worseley, who kept the lions in the Tower, £18.5.0, while the appropriately named Tosso, the 'Tumbler', had £12.3.4, the same as the master carpenter. All these provisions were for life, though the Overseer of the King's Gardens had only 8d a day during pleasure, less than the plumber (12d a day) but a halfpenny more than the Master of the Barge (dp). Richard Pinson, printer, seems hardly used with £4 a year for life; he had to print Tudor spelling. The contrast is marked between the large salary of the well-born pages and the good ones of the master minstrel and the governess, and the wages of the artisans. Tudor Society was firmly stratified in its 'degrees'.

---

[1] *William Knight*, 1476–1547, educated at Winchester and New College, Oxford, he had been employed in 1512 on an embassy to Spain, and in that year made Dean of Newark. In 1514–15, on embassy to Flanders and royal Chaplain; in 1526 he became a Secretary to the King. On embassy to Venice and Rome, 1527–8, and to Paris. Ambassador to the Emperor, 1532. Bishop of Bath and Wells, 1541.

[2] G. R. Elton, *The Tudor Revolution in Government*, C.U.P. 1953, pp. 67 ff, q.v. for a penetrating analysis.

[3] *Letters of Henry VIII*, op. cit., p. 28. Italics mine.

Henry seems to have become restive in 1519, and instructed Wolsey to draw up a *Remembrance* on how policy and administration could be controlled directly by the king himself. He demanded regular quarterly payments into the Privy Purse, and duplicate quarterly audits, one for his own perusal, the other for the official concerned. They were to cover the wardrobe, the artillery, the ships, the armoury, the stables, the buildings. 'Henry the King pleasured is,' it is recorded, 'that the Chancellor of England and his judges of the same shall quarterly make report on the administration of justice and the whole state of the realm'; he was also pleasured that the whole Household be 'put in honorable substanciall and profitable ordre without dilay'.[1] This initiative had little immediate result, if it led to the reforming ordinances of Eltham in 1526; only the unremitting drive of a Henry VII would have achieved such efficiency and the cardinal hardly wished to place power too directly in the royal hands.

But the *Remembrance* of 1519 is most revealing on general policy,[2] for Henry the king is concerned with wider issues; with 'how the lands of Ireland may be reduced and brought to good order and obeyssance'; with 'how the commodities of the realm may be imployed to the most profit, and how the idle people of the land may be put in occupation', as well as with how 'to devise for the maintenance of the frontiers and the fortification of the same'. 'Henry the Kynge,' it notes, 'hath commanded that the shippes, tackling and all other habilyments . . . shall be renewed.'

And in a final *Pryvie Remembrance*, it is further recorded 'That the King's Grace do desire to put himself in strength . . . for the royal crown and succession'—a very revealing preoccupation. Here, in fact, the main programme for the following years is foreshadowed; Ireland, unemployment, the strengthening of the defences and the fleet; and putting oneself in strength for the succession might mean anything, from executing potential claimants to taking a new wife.

[1] Elton, op. cit., pp. 37–8.
[2] British Museum. Ms. Tt. B.1. fo. 192 ff.

CHAPTER VI

THEOLOGICAL WARFARE

◘

Henry's versatile mind had always been fascinated by the theological problems then deemed crucial to salvation, and he early encouraged the Christian humanists who were applying Greek scholarship to the textual criticism of the Bible. In court circles the new learning had become fashionable; Thomas Linacre of All Souls, who became one of the king's doctors and founded the Royal College of Physicians in 1518, had translated Galen and won his reputation as a humanist. Erasmus, known to the king since childhood, now had a European fame, 'a giant figure in the history of ideas. He is the intellectual hero of the sixteenth century.' He included, as he once wrote, the King of England among his 'disciples'.[1] And though Erasmus too long lived precariously and died defeated, his influence on Henry was lasting, and contributed to make him, within the limits of an orthodox Thomist education, a vigorous reformer and a munificent patron of the learning suited to train up men not only for Church but for State.

Erasmus, indeed, wrote for an elite of laymen, to which, intellectually, the king belonged; and when Henry attacked the Church, he intended, though defence and a financial crisis crippled his intention, to reinvigorate and redeploy its power. 'All his life Henry VIII remained an enthusiast for learning',[2] except that, fortunately for one in his position, he never had an original theological idea.

To the old Catholic establishment the new learning was less attractive: it roused some generally sleeping dogs which the mediaeval Church had kennelled or let lie. Heresies, long endemic, but confined to esoteric monkish circles or to chiliastic revolutionaries who exploited economic discontent, began to break out in strident clamour. They often reflected the temperamental distrust of the northern peoples for the Mediterranean hierarchy and image worship which had come down from the Roman Empire, already Christian before its decline. Hence, in

---

[1] H. R. Trevor-Roper, *Historical Essays*, Macmillan, 1957, p. 35, q.v. for a penetrating estimate.
[2] Op. cit., p. 79.

part, the Protestant and Catholic schism, comparable in bitterness to the Sunni and Shi'ah division of Islam.

In this disruption, Henry VIII, like Gustav Erikson Vasa of Sweden, with whom he had affinities, played a decisive part. But the Anglican secession was only one aspect of a movement which long convulsed Western Europe, as the Protestant 'Reformation' and Catholic 'Counter-Reformation' infused dynastic power politics with new venom. These ideological tortures, burnings and massacres re-enacted the conflicts between Arian and Catholic converts among the barbarians amid the ruins of the Roman Empire, and the destruction of the Albigensians in the Midi by the French barons of the north. They were mainly occasioned by laymen, exploiting or deluded by abstractions which they travestied but for which they would often die.

When Henry was a young king, the humanists had not yet been overwhelmed by the fanatics, and Erasmus was coming to his full celebrity with the popular *Adagia* and *Praise of Folly*, or *Encomium Moriae*, written under More's roof in 1511, and with the *Enchiridion Militis Christiani*, the *Manual of a Christian Soldier*, now becoming a best seller. Sir Thomas More was already high in favour with the king, as was John Colet, Dean of St Paul's, who had studied in Italy and France; and William Lily, whom Colet appointed High Master of St Paul's School, his new foundation, had travelled in Palestine and lived in Rhodes and Florence. Henry would converse and argue with these cosmopolitan scholars 'with remarkable courtesy and unruffled temper', and would even read St Thomas and Duns Scotus before a discussion.

In spite of this patronage, by the great bishops as well as the king, the condition of independent men of the new learning was often abject. It was only through Warham, Fox and Fisher, Bishop of Rochester and Chancellor of Cambridge, that even Erasmus had then been able to exist.[1] Yet discounting the obvious tetchiness and sensibility which

[1] In August 1511, Erasmus wrote 'from his chamber over the water' at Queens' College, Cambridge, complaining that his sparse audiences had 'nothing to give'. The beer and wine were undrinkable and he would be glad, he said, of a skin of Greek wine, not too sweet. In October, still lecturing on Greek grammar to a small attendance, he wanted to come to London, but dared not, for the plague; he would come up when the frost cleared it. He attempted, on behalf of Colet, to find an undermaster for St Paul's school, and got a response which shows how little the academic type has changed. To teach boys, said Erasmus, was pleasing to Christ; it was much more logical, the Cambridge dons told him, to go into a monastery for obviously that would please Christ more. After all, you then forsook the world; much more correct to be useless. And anyway—and here the real argument emerged—'who would be a schoolmaster that could live in any other way?' Erasmus could not find a competent amanuensis. '*O Academiam!*' he ecxlaimed. And in February, the next year, a bishop said that Colet's new-fangled school was nothing but a 'school of idolatory'. L. and P., I, I, 848, 63; 961, 986.

made him 'difficult'—for he noticed, as others did not, the 'lower layers
of the rushes' which lay for years 'harbouring the leakage of dogs and
men', the ale droppings and the scraps, and felt the draughts through
the oiled linen in the casements—he saw to the root of the evils of the
times. What better than his comment on the Church's attitude to the
power politics and wars of which he and his kind were the helpless
spectators?

> '*O theologos elingues*
> *O mutos episcopos,*
> *Qui tales rerum humanarum*
> *pestes taciti spectant!*'[1]

II

Henry was early a humanist, critical of the conservative monks, but
also a fierce enemy of heresy; and heresy in England had a long pedigree. Wycliffe's doctrines had inspired the Lollards, and even the
Bohemian Huss, whose teachings had caught on in terms of the old
Czech-German conflict. Tunstall, reporting on Luther, at once related
his ideas to the 'opinions of boheme'. English laymen, too, were apt to
apply common sense to the mysteries of the cosmopolitan Church; like
the Scandinavians, they had never liked a celibate priesthood, and resented the claim of the clergy to act as intermediaries with the Almighty.
Like Henry, the English were orthodox, but often anti-clerical; with
a perennial grievance, too, against a Church which owned so large a
part of the wealth of England and which, as in Germany, paid a heavy
tribute to an alien power. With the rise of the urban middle class,
insularity and provincialism became more articulate.

Scattered heretical opinion among the lower orders was, of course,
regarded by king and hierarchy with contempt, and the main sub-
version came from a handful of clerics in the universities and in London;
but popular heresy was creeping in; it had never died out since the time
of the Lollards. In 1489, for example, two years before Henry's birth,
a certain Stephen Swallow was roundly denying transubstantiation:
'for XXX years he had believed and taught that in the sacrament of the
altar remaineth the substance of material bread, and likewise in wine
after consecration. And that Christ is not in the same sacrament in his
own bodily presence.' Swallow would not turn from the said heresies
'for noon exortation'.[2] Again, two years after Henry's accession,

---

[1] 'Oh tongueless theologians, oh dumb bishops, who regard such plagues of human
life in silence.' See also More's *Utopia* on this theme. L. and P., I, I, 1548.
[2] *The Reign of Henry VII from Contemporary Sources*, p. 236.

Christopher Gribbell, aged twenty-two, was examined on his parent's beliefs. They had taught him, he said, that confession, pilgrimage, sacraments, images, were 'vain': the boy had not realized how wrong his parents were until his eyes had been opened by a Master Ive. His younger brother John, less intellectual, also admitted that they had taught him these things, though 'he gave no heed to it'. On the evidence of her two sons, good Archbishop Warham had Agnes Gribbell burnt as a heretic.

Such cases, over the years, made the clergy unpopular. In 1512, too, Parliament, rectifying an ancient grievance, had provisionally deprived clerical murderers of benefit of clergy.

As an Erasmian reformer, Henry, too, disliked the secular pretensions of the clergy, and he had the Tudor feel for the shifts of opinion. And when, in 1514, an appalling scandal occurred, he intervened, he sensed the legal powers of the Crown over the Church. It was Richard Hunne's use of the antique weapon of *Praemunire*, with disastrous consequences to himself, that made the king realize its power.[1]

Hunne was a wealthy merchant tailor, who on the death of his infant son, refused to give the parish priest his fee, the linen garment in which the child had been baptized. 'Richard,' says Polydore, 'for his part, denied that anything was due to him, since it had not been the infant's property. The quarrel grew so hot between them that they both went to law . . . the priest being accused by Richard of offending against that terrible law of *praemunire*.'

Under the 'terrible law'—a statute of Edward III of 1351 against interference by the Pope with English benefices—Hunne sued out a writ from the King's Bench against the priest for having cited him before a court sanctioned by a foreign power. A litigious man, who could well have afforded to allow the priest his perquisite, Hunne talked loudly of his case, 'being high minded and set on the glory of victory which he hoped to have had of the *praemunire*, whereof he much boasted . . .'

The Bishop of London now became alarmed. He instructed Dr Horsey, his Chancellor, to prosecute Hunne for heresy; after examination, Hunne was imprisoned in the Lollard's Tower of St Paul's to await trial, and there he was found, hanged. Dr Horsey declared that

---

[1] 'The terrible writ of *praemunire*,' writes Powicke, 'under whose threat the Reformation was carried through, had its humble beginnings as a method of procedure against elusive persons who defied the jurisdiction of the royal courts in cases where Papal claims to provision had affected royal rights . . . gradually the statutes of *Praemunire* were interpreted to justify action against the exercise of foreign or private jurisdiction without the royal consent.' Sir Maurice Powicke, *The Reformation in England*. Oxford, 1961, p. 15.

the accused had committed suicide, overcome with guilt; but this the coroner's jury refused to admit. He had been found, says Hall, 'hanged with a fair countenance . . . without any staring, gaping or frowning. Also without any drivelling or spurging in any place of his body.'[1] The noose had not even been really tight, and his neck had been broken first.

Nor was it in character that so prosperous and sanguine a man should have killed himself before being convicted, even if he had owned a Wycliffite Bible in English, and *unum Librum vocatus le Pocolipps* (Apocalypse) and remarked 'poor men and ideotts have the Trowth of holy scripture more than a thousand prelates and clerks of the school'.[2]

Dr Horsey's jailer, or 'sumner', then absconded, but he was caught, and under 'pain and durance' he confessed to an amateurish murder, clumsily covered up; Horsey was taken into custody.[3] The bishop was now thoroughly alarmed; he could not, he told Wolsey, expect justice for his chancellor from any London jury, 'so set were they on heretical depravity', and he hit on a swift, horrible, expedient. He prosecuted Hunne's corpse for heresy; convicted it, and had it burnt, four days before Christmas, in the murk of a London December.

These proceedings had roused violent popular indignation, and two bills were brought forward in Parliament to vindicate Hunne. They were thwarted by clerical influence; and, by April 1515, prorogation of Parliament stopped further proceedings.

Such was the macabre *cause célèbre* which roused Henry to intervene, for he sensed hostility to his royal rights in the clergy's swift moves to prevent action on *praemunire*. With the king's connivance, Dr Standish, who had supported the Act rescinding benefit of clergy, raised the question of the royal rights; then, summoned before convocation, appealed to the monarch. Henry now convened a great assembly at Blackfriars, and declared the clergy concerned, cited to appear by Standish, guilty under *praemunire* for supporting the pope's jurisdiction against the king's law.

Only after Wolsey, on his knees before king, Council and both Houses of Parliament, had made a partial submission, did Henry allow

---

[1] Hall, op. cit., p. 130.

[2] E. H. R. July, 1963, pp. 530-1, q.v.

[3] H. A. L. Fisher in *The Political History of England*, Vol. V, p. 209, writes: 'It seems probable, though far from certain, that Hunne, conscious of midnight scripture readings and forbidden books . . . put an end to his life.' Mackie, on the other hand, thinks it 'quite possible that they did Hunne to death, tried to make the death look like a suicide, and failing to do this pleaded instruction by Horsey, who may have suggested that they need not be too gentle with the recalcitrant prisoner'. (*The Earlier Tudors*, p. 292 n.) The evidence collected by Arthur Ogle in his *The Tragedy of the Lollard's Tower* (Pen-in-hand, 1949) seems conclusive for deliberate murder.

the affair to lapse. Thus the case of Richard Hunne had left an indelible impression; Hall, for example, says Fisher, reflected much London opinion that 'a black murder had been committed under ecclesiastical sanction . . . .' when he 'stamped the force of this indignant conviction upon the pages of his gorgeous chronicle'.[1] It had also led Henry, as his hard eyes travelled round the scared assembly, to sense what the writ of *praemunire* might effect. He had smelt new power.

III

Late in 1517, in all the press of business, the king developed a new hobby: he began writing a book. The occasion was the uproar on the continent created when Martin Luther, on October 31st of that year, had nailed his ninety-five theses against the sale of Papal Indulgences to the door of the Castle Church of Wittenberg. Henry was indignant at Luther's arguments, but sensed, also, his own chance to assert that loyalty to the pope which had brought him a Golden Rose from Julius II, and which might now bring him the title he had long coveted. Were not the monarchs of Spain 'Most Catholic', and those of France 'Most Christian' kings?

The crisis which gave him his opening had been occasioned by a European portent, a German religious genius of great power. Martin Luther, now in his late thirties, came of Saxon peasant stock, the son of a foreman in a copper mine in Thuringia who rose to be overseer; his parents were 'worthy little people thick-set amd the colour of dried herrings'.[2]

Brilliantly talented and destined for the law, Luther had become an Augustinian friar; by 1516, Professor-Doctor and local Visitor of his Order. Like St Augustine, he was obsessed with the utter bondage of mankind to original sin, a view encouraged by a study of that introspective mystic, Tauler: the ways of God were ungraspable and unfollowable—*unbegreiflich und unausforschlich*; further, His 'all powerfulness, combined with his eternal fore-knowledge, absolutely and inevitably dispose(d) of the idea of reason acting freely within us': indeed, reason was a 'harlot eaten up with the itch'. In face of this conviction, coloured with fantasies of demons and hell fire, Luther, had proclaimed with the force of literary genius his doctrine of justification by faith. Man could be saved only by Grace, and the Pauline-Augustinian dualism, flesh warring against spirit, could only be resolved when the sinner flung himself, in abject humility and contrition, at the feet of a

[1] H. A. L. Fisher, op. cit., p. 210.
[2] See F. Funck-Brentano, *Luther*, Cape, 1936, p. 20.

sustaining God. Luther repudiated all human intermediaries, priest or pope.

The resulting tumult in Germany coincided with a momentous political change: for in January, 1519, the Emperor Maximilian died. After desperate briberies and intrigues, in which Henry and Wolsey played their part, Maximilian's grandson, Charles, already King of Spain and inheritor of vast Habsburg and Burgundian possessions, was elected emperor as Charles V.

He was at once confronted with the new upheaval in Germany; Luther, in 1520 alone, poured out three pamphlets; on the *Liberty of a Christian Man*, *To the Nobility of the German Nation*, and *On the Babylonish Capacity of the Church of Christ*. He was to render the Bible into moving, simple, prose which went straight to the hearts and heads of his compatriots, and to compose the religious battle hymn, '*Ein Feste Burg ist unser Gott*', the '*Marseillaise of the Reformation*'. Henry had an opponent of tireless force.

In the field of mundane controversy Luther was also redoubtable. He called his opponents swine and jackasses, bawled for the expulsion of the Jews, and detested the Latin races as predatory foreigners—Welsch. It made him ill, he declared, to observe the sale of indulgences for building St Peter's at Rome. *So bald das Geld im Kasten klingt*, he mocked, *Die Seele aus dem Fegfeuer springt*.[1]

His literary and theological genius and his flair for gross controversy, operating in the context of religious disturbance already described, was beginning to set off a European revolution, in particular north of the Alps, going far beyond the Erasmian reforms which Henry had countenanced; what had appeared another monkish quarrel was to become political dynamite in the cities and princely courts of Germany, along the Baltic, in Scandinavia and in Switzerland. And by 1520 the Lutheran movement was dividing Germany into the Catholic areas of Austria, Bavaria, Wurtemburg and the Rhineland, and the mainly Lutheran territories of Saxony, Hesse, the North German plain and Brandenburg, a division reflected by the Catholic League of Ratisbon and the Protestant Leagues of Torgau and Schmalkalden. Outside Germany, Riga, Reval and Dorpat went Lutheran—at Riga in 1524 they threw the statue of the Virgin into the Dvina: and the Teutonic knights took the occasion to plunder bishoprics and set up their own Duchy under the King of Poland; their Grand Master, a Hohenzollern, became Lutheran by 1525. In Denmark, by the mid-twenties, following the exile of Christian II, Frederick I turned Lutheran; in Sweden, as will be

[1] As soon as the money chinks in the box, the soul leaps out of the fire of Purgatory.

apparent, Gustavus Vasa I was to play a part not unlike Henry VIII,
and already in Switzerland, by 1518, Zwingli was expounding the
scriptures in Zurich, and by 1528 Berne was to be Protestant.
Lutheranism was also to spread in Bohemia, Slovakia, and Hungary.

Henry observed the beginnings of the disorder in Germany with
disgust. Passionately interested in theology, and trained in Thomism,
he studied dubious ideas with horror and mobilized the Thomist arguments against them. And when, early in 1521, Luther defied the emperor and the assembled forces of German Catholicism, clerical and
lay, at Worms, Henry was shocked to get Tunstall's report.

On January 29th Tunstall had written to Wolsey giving the facts—
mainly in cypher—as he saw them. 'The people of Almayn,' he said,
'be so minded to Luther, whose opinions be condemned by the Pope,
that, rather than he should be by the Pope's authority oppressed . . .
[they] would spend a hundred thousand of their lives.' Luther had
burned the Papal Decretals before the citizens and university of Wittenberg; printed his own declaration 'in the Dotch [German] tonge', and
sent it about the country; Tunstall enclosed a Latin version of the
appalling document 'to the intent that ye may see it and burn it when
ye have done': the booksellers ought not to import or translate it, 'lest
thereby might ensue great trouble to the realm and Church of England;
as is now here'. All Luther's books, he reported, where 'in the Dotch
tonge' and in every man's hand that could read, and in Hungarian as
well. 'The beginning of all this,' he continued, 'has been because of the
great sum of money that yearly goith to Rome for annates,[1] which the
country would be rid of, and the benefices be given by the Pope to such
persons as do serve at Rome, unlerned as cooks and grooms, and not to
the virtuous and lerned men of the country, as they say.' The Pope, he
declared, must stop this practice, or 'lose the total obeissance of
Almayn'.

Tunstall also described Luther's theological views, and concluded,
'they say the[re] is moch moo strange opinions . . . nere to the opinions
of boheme'; as for Luther's *De Babylonica Captivitate Ecclesiae*, he
prayed that God would 'kep that boke out of Englond'. But Luther
had strong popular support, and the papal nuncio had been warned not
to meddle with him. Luther even wanted to go and reform Italy—a
popular move—and had offered the emperor a hundred thousand men.
And although Charles V—like a virtuous prince, 'would not harken',
he had observed that Luther had 'many great clerks to hold with him on
certain points . . . whereof the Pope will not hear, but stondith to his

---

[1] A year's revenue of an appointment, paid when taking it up.

sentences of condemnation'. Tunstall understood that the new emperor would 'execute the Pope's bull and graunt bann imperiale' for confiscation of the goods of those who maintained Luther or held with his opinions.[1]

By April, Henry was himself reading the *De Babylonica Captivitate*, and 'dispraising' it, alarmed, like Tunstall, at the infiltration of Lutheran ideas into England. That year Archbishop Warham, too, wrote to Wolsey from Knole in Kent, complaining that Oxford university was badly infected with Lutheran heresy. 'It is a sorrowful thing,' he wrote, 'to see how greedily inconstant men, and especially inexpert youth, falleth to new doctrines, be they never so pestilent. . . . Pity it were that through the lewdness of one or two cankered members, which I have understood have seduced the young, the whole university should run into the infamy of so heinous a crime.' A good Oxford man, he said that Cambridge, though claiming to be undefiled, was thought to be the original occasion of the fall of Oxford. But Warham, a humane person, thought it best not to summon the culprits to London; rather to play down the scandal: 'it is thought the less brute [noise] the better.'[2]

Against this background, Henry now completed his book, the *Assertio Septem Sacramentorum adversus Martinus Lutherus*.[3] He probably wrote much of it himself—'Mountjoy,' says Fisher, 'told Erasmus that Henry was the real author . . . and there is nothing intrinsically improbable in the statement',[4] though the book was revised by professionals, in particular Sir Thomas More, who was soon himself to attack the reformer as 'lowsy Luther'. The king already had the reputation of a 'sharpe wit'—'this the Great learned man Erasmus well knew'[5]—and mobilized the usual apparatus of scholastic argument and Latin cliché, asserting the orthodox position. Henry may have missed the point of Luther's arguments, but in such conflict no argument was really possible, merely assertion. Luther had attacked the basis of Catholic Christendom, the validity of the priesthood and the supremacy of Rome. Henry, in spite of More's advice, entirely vindicated its authority. 'All the faithful,' he wrote, 'honour and acknowledge the

[1] Charles Sturge, *Cuthbert Tunstall*, London, 1938, Appendix X, pp. 360–2.

[2] Ellis I (Series III), pp. 239–42.

[3] The title page of the edition of 1521 has a crude woodcut of Mutius Scaevola holding his right hand in the burning coals after his unsuccessful attempt to assassinate Lars Porsenna, the Etruscan King, who, told that there were three hundred Romans equally resolute, came to terms. On the reverse, it is stated that anyone reading or listening to the book would get ten indulgences for their sins—a sound way of promoting sales. The presentation copy was laid up as a rarity in the Vatican.

[4] *Political History of England*, p. 235.

[5] Strype. Ecc: Mem: I. 34.

sacred Roman See for their mother and supreme'[1]—a statement which
later might have caused him embarrassment had he been capable of it.
Indeed, he was to accuse More, the very man who had warned him, of
provoking him to put a sword in the pope's hand to fight against himself. For the rest, the monarch scornfully abused the reformer in conventional style: who was he, a 'single insignificant friar, *fraterculus,
doctorculus, sanctulus, eruditulus*', to 'challenge the majestic tribunal of the
saints, the Fathers and the Popes'? Henry also, ironically enough,
attacked Luther's loose view on matrimony: 'whom God have joined,
let no man,' he quoted, 'put asunder ... who does not tremble when he
considers how to deal with his wife?'; and he denounced Luther in well-
worn Latin phrases which look no less threadbare in translation—'he
belches out of the filthy mouth of the hellish wolf those foul inveigh-
ings', and the like. In private he was even more vicious, describing
Luther to Charles V as 'this weed, this dilapidated, sick and evil-
minded sheep'.[2]

That autumn of 1521 the magnificent copy of the royal work, shown
to the king by Wolsey before it was dispatched, was presented to Leo X
in Rome, the English ambassador giving a broad hint that his master
had styled himself 'the very defender of the Catholic Faith of Christ's
Church which (title) he had truly deserved of the Holy See'. The ailing
connoisseur pope affected greatly to admire the book and arranged a
more formal presentation before the consistory of cardinals: he then declared that Henry had displayed eloquence and wisdom in confuting
'this terrible monster', and thanked God for raising up such a prince to
defend Holy Church.

And soon Henry's main objective was achieved. After various titles
had been discussed, including 'Most Orthodox' and even 'Angelic'
king, the decision was made for the king's own choice—*Defensor Fidei*,
Defender of the Faith, a title which the sovereigns of England have
since retained.

[1] See E. Doernberg, *Henry VIII and Luther*, an account of their personal relations, 1961,
p. 21.
[2] Doernberg, op. cit.: 'Vocabulary of this kind was the normal tool of controversy, and
not a Lutheran monopoly. In fact it would have been surprising if either Henry VIII or
Luther had conducted the controversy in the modern manner, formulating their attack
or their rejoinder ... with deliberate and exquisite courtesy in order to make it devastating.'
He cites (p. 32) the titles of the booklets exchanged between Luther and Emser in 1520–1.
I. Emser against the Unchristian Book of Martin Luther, Augustinian, to the German
Nobility. II. Luther to the Sheep of Leipzig. III. To the Bull of Wittenberg. IV. In reply
to the Sheep's Answer. V. Answer to the Wittenburg's Bull's furious Rejoinder. VI.
Reply to the Super-Christian, Super-Spiritual, Super-Artful Book of Sheep Emser of
Leipzig.

So, in February 1522, there arrived at Greenwich a magnificent legation, headed by Wolsey and the Papal ambassador. Henry advanced to meet them at his chamber door, 'as though they had both come from Rome'. After fulsome compliments to the royal person, 'so formed and figured in shape and stature . . . which signified the pleasure of our Lord God', the cardinal presented the Papal Bull declaring the king's new title, which was proclaimed. The whole glittering entourage of courtiers and ecclesiastics then proceeded to high mass, while trumpets blared and 'shalmes and saggebuttes' played in honour of the king's new style. Thus, Hall concludes, 'his Highness went to dinner'.

IV

There was a less dignified sequel. Luther was not the man to allow any opponent the last word, and set himself to give worse than he had got. 'It is of little consequence,' he wrote, 'if I despise and bite some earthly King considering that he did not hesitate to blaspheme against the King in Heaven and commit sacrilege with his poisonous lies. The Lord judges the nations in righteousness. Amen.' In another context, he wrote, 'From now on I will no longer deal gently with slanderers and liars. My preaching and writing has reached a limit.' He could stand no more.

Luther alleged that the book was not Henry's own work, but written by Dr Edward Lee. 'I expect the King,' he wrote, 'gave one or two ells of homespun to that good for nothing, who cut himself out a cape and then trimmed it with lining. N.B. I'll give him some bells to trim it with!' He then called Henry a liar, 'who in his pamphlet raves like a strumpet in a tantrum': it was clear, too, that the Tudor was not of royal blood; 'if,' he declared, 'a King of England arrogates to himself the right to spew out impudent falsehoods, he gives me the right to stuff them back down his throat . . . with his filth he sullies the crown of my own King who is Christ.'[2]

Henry now reproached Luther's patron, the Elector of Saxony, for encouraging a 'wretched monk who dared to throw filth in his face', and Sir Thomas More was commissioned to write a scurrilous counterblast under the pseudonym *Rossaeus*. Bishop Fisher of Rochester, too, issued a lengthy refutation. Henry also brought pressure on Erasmus who, with the usual miscalculation of a liberal mind, had hoped to remain aloof from the spate of degraded controversy he had helped to

[1] Cited in Doernberg, op. cit., p. 33.
[2] Quoted in Funck-Brentano, op. cit., p. 175.

release. His masterpiece on Free Will was to be the sequel, in which, at last, he came out against Luther. Henry himself continued the controversy on similar lines.[1]

More immediately, the gross polemics went echoing on—just as in an even more tedious idiom, Marx was to fulminate against Bauer; Engels against Dühring: the ideological 'positions', too, were adapted to the shifts of power politics, Luther making up to Henry and putting the blame on Wolsey; Henry seeking Luther's support for his divorce in vain. In the end they remained at cross purposes and, indeed, in 1523 a satirist who had written in the manner of Brant's *Narrenschiff* (*Ship of Fools*), wrote a pamphlet in German on the king's behalf, entitled *Whether the King of England or Luther is a liar*.

[1] He insisted that the polemics were his: 'Although ye fayne yourself to thinke this boke not my own . . . yet it is well known for mine, and I for mine avow it.' *Ellis*, III, II, p. 134.

CHAPTER VII

THE EUROPEAN DYNASTS

I N 1519 Henry had remarked to the Venetian ambassador '*Domine Orator*, we wish all potentates to content themselves with their own territories; we are satisfied with this island of ours', and the Venetian had been much impressed. 'He is the best-dressed sovereign in the world,' he reported, 'his robes are the richest and most superb that can be imagined, and he puts on new clothes every holiday.' The king also, he said, had a good head for business; when his favourites were in debt to the Florentine bankers in London, whom he himself had helped to finance, he would intervene to postpone their paying interest, then take a rake off for securing them respite, as well as interest from the bankers for himself. This manoeuvre the Venetian naturally admired.

But Henry was now out for bigger, political, game, and assessing new shifts of power outside his island; the more so as the Scots had again got into a 'rere broilerie' and their feuds were as usual giving the king's enemies their chance.

The death of the Emperor Maximilian in January, as already recorded, had caused a political crisis in Europe, a fever of intrigue and bribery for the succession. Henry, though tempted to become a candidate, in the end mainly tried to thwart the candidature of Francis I: the election of Charles V, in June 1519, changed the face of continental politics and enhanced the mighty contest between Habsburg and Valois which was to dominate the scene for the rest of Henry's life and to which English policy had to be accommodated. His own claims to the empire had never been serious, and Wolsey told Pace he was 'right glad the King had not obtained the same', seeing how much Charles' backers paid to get it for him: 850,000 florins, of which 543,000 had been put up by the Fugger bankers of Augsburg and 143,000 by the Welsers, secured in the mines of Tyrol and on the revenues of military orders in Spain.[1]

Of the two contenders, Charles V was the more formidable, if French resources were more compact; the Habsburg Austrian inheri-

[1] See the *New Cambridge Modern History*, pp. 338–9.

tance was handed over to Charles' brother Ferdinand in 1522,[1] but he
closely collaborated with the Emperor elect, who controlled Spain and
its expanding American colonies, as well as Naples and Sardinia.
Charles V now became at least titular ruler of divided Germany, and
had always been hereditary lord of the Netherlands, ruled by his aunt,
Margaret of Austria, and vital to English trade; while he was also
brother-in-law of the kings of Denmark, Hungary and Portugal.
Henry was tempted to leave the French alliance and combine with this
gigantic, if ill-co-ordinated, power to revive his ancestral claims to the
French crown; Wolsey, whose one fixed objective was the interest of
the papacy and his own succession to it, was also veering the same way,
if still with an eye on the French.

But by the Treaty of London of 1518 Henry was due to confer with
the French king; together, Francis had told him they could 'give laws
to Christendom'; elaborate preparations had been going on for a
spectacular meeting in France and Henry had again been growing a
red-gold beard. But Queen Catherine, in spite of the Cardinal, had
long worked for a prior meeting with Charles V, and this, by a narrow
margin, she achieved; the English court had already left Greenwich
and the Kentish ports were seething with preparations, when the stolid,
observant, young emperor-elect paid a hurried, but important, visit to
his aunt and uncle of England.

By Whitsun the court had arrived at Canterbury; Henry was impatient to leave for France and the navy was standing by in the straits.
Then, on the evening of May 26, 1520, the imperial ships came into
Dover to the salute of the beflagged fleet: 'the mighty ordinaunce . . .',
says Hall, 'broke out by force of fyre . . . marvellous was the noyse of
the gonnes. . . . Thus landed the Emperour Charles under the clothe
of his estate of the Black Eagle all splayed on riche clothe of golde.'[2]
That night he slept in Dover Castle; and when Henry appeared next
morning, Charles V actually descended the steps to meet him: the
English were delighted with the 'benign manner of so high a prince'.
The imperial and royal cavalcade rode over the downs to Canterbury
to the acclamations of the populace, who detested the French.

Officially, of course, Henry's policy was to mediate between the two
sides; peace was always, he said, his objective; then a crusade against the
Turk. But the flattery which Charles V liberally applied soon ingrati-
ated him with his uncle; and Catherine felt all the arrogant protective-
ness of her house: she was, after all, the eldest survivor of the family of

---

[1] Eight years later, when Charles V was crowned, he became King of the Romans.
[2] I, p. 188.

Ferdinand and Isabella, saluted, as such, with elaborate deference by the secular head of Christendom. Wolsey, moreover, was given a pension of 7,000 ducats by the emperor who promised him his help when the papal election occurred.

There was a private family conference, in which both sides sounded out the other; Henry must have agreed to walk warily with the French, for another conference was arranged at Gravelines, along the dune-fringed coast near Dunkirk, to be held after the meeting with Francis I. More important, the idea was mooted that Charles V might marry the Princess Mary, now aged seven and pledged to the Dauphin of France. The imperial marriage, it was thought, would be a more splendid prospect for England. It was with a better opinion of his young but calculating nephew that Henry crossed to France for the meeting with the French king.

II

The Field of Cloth of Gold—not of *the* Cloth of Gold, as often written —provided a surfeit of Northern Renaissance ostentation; all was meticulously organized, with strict precautions against a clash of the arrogant kings. Henry's retinue numbered over four and a half thousand and the queen's was proportionate; they brought more than three thousand horses and vast quantities of gear, including an image of Our Lady in a great leather case; the largest pavilion, of wood, canvas and glass, was over three hundred feet square.

Both sides advanced slowly to a prepared schedule. Henry moved from Calais to Guynes; Francis from Montreuil to Ardres. They were now about two leagues apart, and on June 2, 1520, Wolsey rode over on a mule with crimson trappings and golden stirrups. He wore full Cardinal's robes, *velours sur velours cramoisy figuré*, under a rochet of fine linen, and the great red, tasselled hat. Next day, the Archbishop of Sens returned the visit, to be received with 'great noise of artillery and music'.

All was now set for a meeting of the monarchs themselves. On Thursday, June 7th, at exactly the same time, both began to move, the guns firing a salute to let each know that the other was on the way. The French procession was superb, 'with all the rustlers and gallants of the French Court'. First came the Provost Marshal to clear the vast camp 'on pain of the halter' (Henry's equivalent had 'made scurrage' for the king's security): then, preceded by arquebusiers, their weapons chased with gold, rode the Marshals of France, all shining in cloth of gold, followed by two hundred gentlemen in gold and crimson. Next, with their professional swing to the beating drums, came the Swiss Guards; after them, the woodwind and the brass; then the king's chamberlains in cloth of gold and silver, *eschiquestez et escarlatiez*; and now, flashing with jewellery, the Constable of France, bearing before the king a drawn sword.

Francis I himself, 'merry of cheer, brown coloured, great eyes', rode a charger covered with gold filigré. He was sheathed in a 'cassock' of cloth of gold under a jewelled mantle, and accompanied by his Council and the princes of the blood; this cavalcade was followed by the famous Archers of the Guard. As for Henry's and the cardinal's entourage, they defeated even the eye-witness's eager pen; as Shakespeare was to write,

> . . . Today the French
> *All clinquant, all in gold, like heathen gods,*
> *Shone down the English; and to-morrow they*
> *Made Britain India: every man that stood*
> *Show'd like a mine.*[1]

Slowly the processions converged upon the small pavilion (cloth of gold again, and 'spread with carpets of new turkey making'), where the futile summit was to take place.

Both kings arrived on time, each on a small eminence: they halted; the music stopped; they regarded each other. There was another burst of music; silence again, and suddenly, both spurred forward; thrice they embraced on horseback; then, dismounted, embraced again. Accompanied only by the cardinal and the Admiral of France, they vanished into the little golden tent.

English officials now 'ran with great pots of wine to the French; "French and English", they pledged one another, "good friends"!' But many suspicious islanders held aloof.

That Sunday Henry rode over to Ardres to call on the Queen of France; a fountain spouted claret and white wine; even silver cups were provided—*chose singulière*. He wore a double mantle of cloth of gold, flashing with precious stones, and a headdress of *toille d'or*: he was 'entirely at ease . . . *honnête, hault et droit*; rather fat, with a red beard large enough to be very becoming'. Francis, meanwhile, had been paying his respects to the English queen at Guynes: both monarchs were thus hostages for each other. As they took their leave, to the synchronized minute, the guns again fired a salute. Returning, they met and embraced, asking 'What cheer?' But they never officially exchanged visits; and when Francis broke protocol and appeared inform-

[1] *Henry VIII*, Act I, sc. I, ll. 18–22.

ally in Henry's quarters, his advisers were horrified: '*Mon Maître,*' one said, '*vous êtes fol d'avoir faict ce que vous avez faict.*'[1]

There was only one moment of real tension. Henry suddenly laid a heavy hand on the French king's neck: 'Come,' he said, 'you shall wrestle with me.' Francis instinctively took up the challenge and the two tall monarchs closed together on the spot. With an expert twist, the Frenchman threw the majesty of England, who landed on his back; Henry, now in cold anger, challenged him again, and it was only through swift intervention of the courtiers that this curious form of diplomacy was called off.

Elaborate jousts were now organized. Two 'Trees of Honour' were set up, 'the one called Aubespine and the other Framboister, which is in English hawthorn, which was Henry, and the Raspis Bery for Francis after the signification of the French'. They were 'artificially wrought and intertwined', 34 feet high and 120 feet round, and both kings' shields were hung on them, in token of challenge. Both monarchs, too, broke spears valiantly: on his second course Henry gave the Sire de Grandville such a stroke that he broke his tilting helmet, and the king had to wait three courses, but 'never devisored nor breathed till he had run his five': he ran 'course after course', writes Hall, 'and lost none, but ever more he broke his spear and so nobly ended the joustes royall'. The kings also fought selected challengers so hard at Barriers that sparks were struck from their armour.

They thus got up good appetites. Three menus planned for Henry's own table, all of which began with soup, included in the first service, cygnets, 'carpet of venison', pike, heron, pies of pears, custard and fruit; in the second, kid, sturgeon, peacock, quails, baked venison and tarts; in the third, pheasant, egrets, 'roo reversed' (kid), 'German haggis', and oranges. The chef was called Merryman, an artist who evidently disregarded the 'beefs, muttons, veales and hogges' available in gargantuan quantity for the rest of the entourage. 'Hyprocras' (spiced wine) 'was the chief drink of plenty.'

The populace soon got wind of these orgies. In Breughelesque crowds, the peasants of Picardy and West Flanders flocked to the camp; conduits ran wine all round the clock, and soon, 'for drunkeness', they lay in 'routes and heaps'.

But no knights of the empire, it was observed, had come in to accept the challenges. The emperor was deeply suspicious, and as soon as Henry and the cardinal were free, they hastened, early in July, to

[1] *Memoires* of Fleuranges, quoted in Rutland Papers. Ed. W. Jerdan. Camden Society, 1842, pp. 28–48, q.v. for a full account.

meet him, as arranged, near Gravelines. Next day, Charles and Henry rode back to Calais, where a banqueting house was erected 'upon the masts of a ship like a theatre'. The canvas was painted with sun, moon and stars; there were images of wicker, says Stowe, covered with canvas representing men of strange nations, and round the central mast were platforms for organs and musicians. A gale blew it all down, put out the torches, 'dashed' the rich chairs. Undeterred, Henry, and other 'lusty maskers', appeared at the emperor's lodgings, dancing and revelling in black velvet, cloth of gold and crimson cloaks. Wolsey, meanwhile, reaffirmed with the imperial advisers the defensive alliance tentatively made at Canterbury, and arranged to meet them the following year.[1]

In the autumn of 1520, the prospects for the alliance looked favourably. Charles V was once more badly needed in Spain; and the Germans demanded that he settle 'Almayn' and Luther, then lead them to the plunder of Italy. Both monarchs needed each other; Wolsey, in particular, ambitious to be Pope, was keeping well in both with Leo X and the emperor. There was 'no man', it was reported, 'on the face of the earth that his Holiness so much detested as Wolsey', but he needed English support; moreover, Leo X's health was already precarious; should he die, not only the Emperor would want a Pope of his own making, but the French king would be 'ready to spend a million écus d'or, though it was as hard for the French to find them as for Charles V to find a good cardinal for pope'.

Events now pushed Charles V further into the English alliance. That summer a rebellion broke out in Spain, and the French seemed likely to seize their chance for another invasion of Italy. Henry, as yet unprepared for war, urged Francis I to keep the peace; officially, he remained a mediator. But the French started unofficial war in Navarre, along the upper Rhine, and in the Low Countries: early in 1521 Wolsey wrote to his master 'In this controversy . . . it shall be marvellous great praise and honour to your grace so by your high wisdom and authority to pass between them and stay them both, that ye be not by their contention and variance brought into war.'

In fact the decision was taken: under cover of mediation on English territory at Calais, Wolsey was to arrange a truce, during which Charles V could once more go by sea to settle Spain, while Henry looked after the Low Countries. Henry himself was already making a 'device' whereby the combined ships of England and the Empire could destroy the French fleet—'a high and great enterprise'.

[1] Rutland Papers, pp. 49–57.

III

In view of these commitments, Henry now decided to secure his dynastic position at home. When planning war, he was particularly dangerous, and before his first expedition to France, as already recorded, he had killed Edmund de la Pole, Earl of Suffolk, long held captive by his father. And now his prospects of an heir were less promising: in July 1518, Pace had informed Wolsey from Woodstock that 'The Queen did meet with his Grace at his chamber door, and showed unto him, for his welcome home, her belly something great, declaring openly that she was quick with child.' The King had been delighted, and declared that as soon as he had spoken within, 'we should all be merry';[1] but Catherine had again miscarried. The Lady Mary was still his only legitimate descendant, and Henry Fitzroy, his son by the beautiful Elizabeth Blunt, was only two.[2]

Henry decided that the most obvious candidate for the succession among the great magnates had to die. Edward Stafford, Duke of Buckingham, High Constable of England, was descended from Thomas of Woodstock, Duke of Gloucester, sixth son of Edward III; his father, as before mentioned, had been executed by Richard III in the market place at Salisbury; his mother, Catherine Woodville, had been sister to Edward IV's Queen. His family connections remified among the highest nobility, and he was on terms of intimate *faux bonhomie* with the King; rich enough to gamble for immense stakes, as 'lost to my Lord of Suffolk since coming to the King, £51'; to the same 'at shooting, £31'; 'lost at dice to my Lord of Suffolk and the Frenchman, £76.1.4', as well as 'lost to my brother of Wiltshire and Lord Montague, £40; . . . lost at dice to my Lord Montague at Syssiter, £15'.[3]

Buckingham had a great estate at Thornley in Gloucestershire: superstitious and *dévot*, he had, in youth, showered largesse, great and small, on West Country churches, in particular in Somerset.[4] He was genuinely

---

[1] State Papers of King Henry VIII, I, pp. 1–2.

[2] Elizabeth Blunt was the daughter of a Shropshire landowner, considered the 'mistress piece of her time', and a lady-in-waiting to Queen Catherine. In 1518 Francis I had characteristically remarked, 'My good brother of England has no son, because, although young and handsome, he keeps an old and deformed wife': that year, Henry showed it was not his fault that there was no prince. He was twenty-seven, 'Bess Blunt' was eighteen, and in 1519 she retired to the Priory of St Lawrence Blackmore in Essex, to bear him a son. The child was well provided for, but Mistress Blunt remained merely the 'mother of the king's son', and Wolsey married her off to a well-to-do gentleman called Tailbois. (See W. S. Childe Pemberton. *Elizabeth Blunt and Henry VIII*. London, 1913.) Unfairly enough, the cardinal was afterwards accused of 'encouraging our young gentlewomen to become concubines by the well-marrying of Bess Blunt'.

[3] L. and P., III, p. 499.

[4] 'oblation to St Joseph of Arimathaea at Glastonbury, 6s 8d: to an idiot of the Abbey of

shocked by the upstart Wolsey, on whose shoes, it seems, he had once deliberately spilt water when holding a basin for the king to wash his hands.

Henry's mind had long been poisoned by the cardinal against this arrogant magnate and, in the spring of 1521, Wolsey arranged the frame-up. His agents contacted Charles Knyvet, the duke's former surveyor, who desired to enter the service of the king; once established, Knyvet declared, he could provide sensational evidence—'then woll I speke, by Saint Mary, for it toucheth the king indeed'. 'So, if it please your Worship,' wrote the cardinal's man, 'of likelihood some great matter is this, else is Chas: a marvellous simple and insolent [ignorant] body.' Wolsey smelt treason and interviewed Knyvet at once, while Robert Gilbert, the duke's chancellor, and his chaplain, John Dela-court, also turned informers: Gilbert declared that not only had his master said 'my lord Cardinal is the King's bawd, showing him what women were most wholesome, and best of complexion', but that in 'his fumes and displeasures' he had railed against the king himself.

Henry at once examined the evidence: it confirmed his suspicions and he struck. Summoned unexpectedly to Windsor, Buckingham found his 'spirit so much troubled' that at breakfast 'his meat would not downe';[1] sick with fear, he went by his splendidly upholstered barge to Westminster, and landed at Wolsey's palace; as he came up the watersteps, however, he was told that unfortunately the cardinal was indisposed. 'Well,' said the duke, with a show of heartiness, 'yet will I drink of my lord's wine or I pass.' So with formal but gloomy courtesy a gentleman of the household conducted him to the cellar; but when the duke perceived 'that no cheer to him was made', he 'changed colour' and departed to his barge.[2]

In May 1521, a London jury, including the Lord Mayor, Sir Robert Brudenell, and Sir Thomas Boleyn, found a retrospective indictment. In 1511, the duke had 'imagined and compassed the death of the King'; in 1512, he had sent his chaplain from Thornely to Hinton Charter-house, where a Father Nicholas Hopkins 'pretended to have knowledge of future events', and the obliging Carthusian had bade him tell the duke that 'he should have all' and advise him to make himself liked

---

Glastonbury 20d.' He would highly reward 'a Fleming at Westminster bringing certain images', and, in the years before his downfall, give charity to 'a fool of Sir Edward Wadham', and to 'a servant of the Anchorite at Marlborough'.

[1] Hackett, letting his imagination rip, says: 'He cantered up to London without appre-hension.' *Henry the Eighth*, p. 183.

[2] See Hall, I, p. 222.

('obtain the love of the community'). Again, in 1513, before the king went to France, the Father was asked how the war would turn out, and whether James of Scotland (another claimant to the succession) would enter England? And Father Nicholas had replied, among other things, that 'the king would have no issue male of his body'. The next February, after Norfolk and Suffolk had been made dukes, Buckingham had, tactlessly, remarked there were now two new dukes created in England, but that if anything but good should happen to the king, he was next in succession to the Crown. Then, in April 1516, Buckingham had himself gone to Hinton Charterhouse and put treasonable questions to Father Nicholas: he had taken his own prospective greatness seriously; confessed that he 'lacked grace', and might, therefore, 'speed badly'; for the present, he had decided, he ought to wait. But the Father had got an annuity of £6 for a tun of wine, and as much as £20 for 'carrying of water to the Priory'; there had been £3 for Father Nicholas himself. In 1519, too, Buckingham's accounts show 'to my ghostly father at Hinton, 100/-'.

In secular circles, also, the duke had not been idle; by presents of rich apparel he had curried favour with the king's guards and re-marked, at large, 'all the King's father did was wrong and he had always been dissatisfied with everything the King did'; the nobles should 'break their minds' for few were contented, they were 'so unkindly handled'.

He was now unkindly handled himself: writs were issued on the indictment for a panel of his peers. Buckingham was arraigned in Westminster Hall, and Norfolk, now seventy-eight and father-in-law to Buckingham's son, conducted the case. He was supported by Suffolk, the Marquis of Dorset, seven Earls and twelve Barons: all were terrified of the king. 'Sir Edward, Duke of Buckingham,' in-toned the Clerk of the Council, 'Hold up they hand! Thou art indicted of high treason.' 'It is false and untrue,' retorted Buckingham, 'and con-spired and forged to bring me to my death.'

But the farce soon ended with a put-up question: 'What say you,' Norfolk asked Suffolk, 'of Sir Edward, Duke of Buckingham, touching of High Treason?' 'He is guilty,' Suffolk replied and the others acqui-esced. Buckingham made a reverence, and paused, sweating, it is said, in the silence. As Norfolk passed the whole ghastly sentence upon him, the old man was seen to weep. The duke pulled himself together. 'Me lord of Norfolk,' he replied, 'you have said as a traitor should be said unto, but I was never none. But, me lord, I nothing malign you for what you have done to me.' Both understood the compulsion which pre-determined the verdict: 'The Eternal God,' he concluded, 'forgive you for my death, as I do.'

When rowed away to the Tower through the summer weather, Buckingham refused to sit on the splendid cushions and carpets of his ducal barge. 'When I went to Westminster,' he said, 'I was Duke of Buckingham; now I am but Edward Bohun, the most caitiff in the world.' He died by the axe, and the people said 'God forgive him, he was a proud prince'. The king had killed the greatest magnate in the country: 'If the lion knew his strength,' Sir Thomas More commented, 'it were hard for any man to rule him.'

IV

Having taken these precautions at home, the king felt confident that Wolsey would play his hand well in diplomacy. The mediation between both sides at Calais, in August 1521, now developed into a two-sided meeting at Bruges, where the Cardinal was magnificently received. A mile outside the city Charles V himself, who, that spring, had been faced with the appalling problem of Luther at the Diet of Worms, came to meet him, and they rode together into the *grande place* where seething crowds watched them dismount. As Chancellor, Wolsey brought with him the Great Seal of England, for he was empowered to conclude a marriage treaty between the Princess Mary and the emperor.

Bruges was packed to capacity, the banners of the Guilds displayed; Flemish hospitality was lavish, every lodging furnished with 'fuel, bread, beer, wine, beeves, muttons, veals, lambs, venison and, all manner of dainty viands as well in fishes and flesh . . . with no lack of spices and banquetting dishes'. The late summer foliage overhung the canals; the bells rang out.

Wolsey was negotiating, as he told the king, 'sometimes with sharp winds, sometime in pleasant manner'; he reported how 'coldly and discretely' Charles V behaved, 'pondering and regarding' the affair. He had come to Wolsey's lodgings 'familiarly', with his aunt, the Archduchess Margaret, and 'my lady had demanded' that Henry 'make the declaration against France at once', though Charles would be content to postpone it until he had come to England *en route* for Spain. He had also agreed to 'respite' the Lady Mary's 'tradaction' for their marriage till she were of perfect age—she was not yet ten. He would, moreover, accept her dowry of £80,000, though he had demanded a million of ducats, 'showing how much was offered with the daughter of

Portugal'. In return she would get a settlement 'assessed most part on these Low Countries and the residue in semblable (similar) lands in Spain', which would be 'larger than any dower that was ever assigned to any daughter of England'.[1] Moreover, the large amounts already owing from Charles would be deducted from the £80,000, 'which shall diminish the sum for the most part thereof'. They had then all resorted to St James's Church for mass; Charles V had, indeed, been most generous, entertaining the English 'in such delicate plentious and sumptuous manner as I never heard or saw the like'.

Henry was delighted with the cardinal's diplomacy, the more so as news had arrived that the French had been driven from Milan, and he told Pace that he could not see how his affairs could have been better handled, though the post was so slow that they had thought the letters were being intercepted. And when Wolsey, bitten presumably by mosquitoes, found the late summer climate of Bruges oppressive, the king urged him to 'set apart all business'. The king's 'contentment with all your acts', Pace insisted from Guildford, 'cannot be so well painted with a pen as it is imprinted in my heart'; indeed, Henry had said that he was under the greatest obligation to God for giving him such a chaplain.

In due course, by November 1521, a treaty was signed which arranged for a joint invasion of France. For Wolsey's part, he had, he thought, got a genuine guarantee from Charles V that he would help to make him Pope.

This question was now becoming actual. Leo X, long in poor health, did not dare so much as to hunt in the campagna without a heavy escort, and was stepping up the recruitment of the famous Swiss guards, whose blue and yellow uniforms, designed by Michelangelo, are still familiar in the approaches to St Peter's and the Vatican. He was concerned at Luther's virulent attacks and apprehensive because the Emperor had even interviewed 'one who would not be well received even in hell'. In early December 1521, two months after he had commended Henry's book, and made him Defender of the Faith, Leo X died, aged only forty-five.

Anxious for money, Charles V and his aunt, Duchess Margaret, promised the English great things. In mid-December she wrote to Wolsey promising to urge her nephew to procure his 'exaltation': with informal flattery the emperor even wrote himself, 'I suppose you have heard of the death of the Pope. You remember the conversation we formerly had, and I shall gladly do what I can for you.' He kept Wolsey

[1] State Papers of King Henry VIII, 1830, I, pp. 39 ff.

guessing by wishing he were nearer Rome and that the time was not so short.[1]

Henry, too, earnestly desired that Wolsey should be elected, and said that he had dispatched Pace to Rome 'as if he had sent his very heart', while Wolsey insisted that, of course he wanted the Papacy for no other purpose than to 'exalt their Majesties'. And he went on setting his master against the French and their deceits.

But the emperor's ambassador, de Mesa, considered the affair extremely tricky; he advised Henry to write two letters, one backing Wolsey, and in case Wolsey had no chance, another backing the favourite, Cardinal Giulio dei Medici. But Wolsey seemed as 'cheerful as if he had been elected Pope'; he would mount an expedition against the French; then against the Infidel and go on it himself. Henry swore that the election 'should not be lost for want of 100,000 ducats';[2] and Duchess Margaret told Wolsey 'all goes well, in as much as our dispatches arrive in time'. But all the Habsburgs in fact cared about was money to pay the Swiss.

As the Conclave assembled to elect the new Pope, Rome was ominously quiet, full of soldiers and guns. Among the predominantly Italian Cardinals 'there could not' it was reported, 'be so much hatred among so many devils in hell'; the outcome was uncertain, save that whoever was elected would be poor, for Leo X, the great Medici art patron and rebuilder of St Peter's, had died heavily in debt.

The Conclave was painful and prolonged. The 500 Swiss guards were thought to favour Medici, and remained in occupation, saying the Conclave must be held in the usual place. 'Here,' wrote Pace, 'is *summa licentia* in saying evil . . . and in all languages—*haec est Romana libertas.*'[3] The cardinals demanded that the doors of the Sistine Chapel, in which they were confined, be opened, such was the filth; but their request was refused and their 'meat diminished'. Into January 1522 the scrutinies went on: Wolsey, of course, had no chance, nor did the emperor mean him to; no one on the spot thought 'the cardinal of St Cecilia' a strong candidate and he only got seven votes in the fifth and twelfth scrutinies. His friend, Cardinal Campeggio, afterwards alleged that his relative youth had disqualified him, and claimed to have urged that on his own 'personal impression' Wolsey was nearer sixty than fifty, but that he had not been able to prove it to the satisfaction of the Conclave.

[1] L. and P., III, II, 1877.
[2] L. and P., III, II, 1884.
[3] This is Roman liberty.

In the event, an aged pope was elected, a Dutchman, Adrian Floren-
tius of Utrecht, formerly tutor to Charles V. He had been Bishop of
Tortosa, since 1516 Grand Inquisitor of Aragon and since 1520 virtual
viceroy of Spain. So severe had the Italian imbroglio become (Cardinal
Grimaldi even retired with a troubled conscience) that, under imperial
pressure, the Conclave had elected an outsider: 'the schoolmaster of the
Emperor', said Francis I, 'has been elected Pope'.

Adrian VI, at sixty-three, was a stop-gap appointment; he was said
to be mean, but the most pious of the cardinals: he seemed reluctant
to take up his great office, though pressed to do so, as the cardinals were
plundering the palace. He remained simple in his tastes—talked exactly
as he had when only Dean of Louvain; the imperial ambassador reported that he wanted to take a house in Rome, with a small garden
attached: why on earth should he do this when God had given him the
finest palace in the city? He seemed easily imposed upon; *Muerto de
miedo del Collegio*—deadly afraid of the College of Cardinals. If the
Curia had been inspired by the Holy Ghost when they elected him,
the inspiration soon flagged.

V

Wolsey was realist enough to be less disillusioned than his agents in
Rome when he heard of Adrian's election; and Charles V compensated
him heavily out of the revenues of Spanish bishoprics. Adrian himself
wrote to Henry VIII from Spain that his election was 'an honour which
he had not only never solicited but never wished for[1] . . . I write to
you', wrote this good but ineffectual man, to the Defender of the Faith,
'. . . that I may express my affection for you on account of your zeal for
the peace of Christendom. I ask you to join with the Emperor-elect for
the purpose of preserving peace.' Adrian was himself incapable of taking
control, delaying to come to Rome from Spain and not sending anyone with authority to take charge.

Francis I that winter was enjoying the chase at St Germain, where
Henry's protégé, the young Sir William Fitzwilliam, afterwards Lord
Admiral, Earl of Southampton, and owner of Cowdray Park, Mid-
hurst, 'found him at dinner talking about hunting'. 'Sir,' said Fitzwilliam, 'your grace doth as the King, your brother doth, for when he
has been a hunting, and hath had good sport, he will talk thereof three
of four hours after': and, indeed, the French king continued on the subject till the end of the meal. He then said he had never liked the duke of

[1] L. and P., III, II, 2018.

Buckingham and always thought he would come to a bad end—hadn't he always said so, he asked his mother? And the dowager queen suggested that the young duc d'Orléans should be sent to Henry's court, 'to learn to shoot and speak the language'.[1] But, back in England, Henry was 'laughing much', saying that the French king had gained little honour and less profit that year.

Yet Wolsey and his master had one anxiety: the risk of allowing, or not allowing, the normal collection of the vintage from Bordeaux on the eve of war with France. 'No man,' wrote Wolsey, in 1521, 'can more groundly consider the politique governaunce of your said realm, ne more assuredly look for the preservation thereof than yee yourself.'[2] In a tone of objectivity, which anticipates a modern Foreign Office assessment and which confounds anyone who thinks Wolsey's statesmanship inept, the Cardinal depicted the situation and suggested action. In the shifting diplomatic situation, in which a façade of amity was being kept over the war being planned, Wolsey found it hard to recommend whether or not to allow the ships to sail. The question, he informed the king, was whether, 'foreseeing the dangers, damages (and losses . . . that might ensue for your Navy)' in this 'suspect and casual time', they should resort to Bordeaux for the vintage at all. To forbid them to sail would be most unpopular, and annoy the French, who might stop the substantial pension they still paid the king (and of course Wolsey, though he did not say so). On the other hand, the risks were great, although in the cardinal's 'pore opinion', the French king was already much harassed and the Chancellor of France, who had just dined alone with Wolsey, had promised to forbid any Frenchman, on pain of death, to seize English ships. Further, Wolsey had arranged that no ship over 100 or 120 tons was to go, and those that went were not to consort together. Thus, he said, 'the great ships of your Realm shall be in safety'. And the French ships, of course, might be encouraged to bring the wine instead. This, after all, would augment the custom dues and 'relieve Flanders and the emperor's countries with wine, whereof during the (anticipated) war they shall be destitute'; it would also get the French and Breton ships into Henry's power. But the safety of the herring fleet had to be considered; the French were already 'taking hulks, and also the Easterling hulks owing to the enmity of the merchants of Danske and them'. On balance, Wolsey recommended a quick collection of the early vintage.

Rumours of the coming war were now running in the Low Coun-

---

[1] L. and P., III, II, 2049.
[2] Strype, *Ecclesiastical Memorials*, Vol. I, 1721, pp. 29, 30–3.

tries. The scholar Nicholar Darington, driven from Paris to Louvain by the threat of it, complained not only that the Belgians ate too much butter—*felicitatem teutonicorum*—but that travel was disrupted. Though Luther seemed quiet at the moment, it was thought certain that the Emperor would visit England soon. Young Charles himself was reported by Wingfield, with satisfaction, to be in gallant form at a tourney at Brussels, in which he broke more spears than any other, and 'sported himself like a prince that will be called a patron of horsemen'.

In February Henry had promised to guard the Low Countries 'like the apple of his eye', and the queen, still interested in hawking, was asking her nephew to send two falcons, one for water fowl, the other for herons. On March 20th Charles himself wrote to Wolsey thanking him for the great pains he has taken: 'I have found by experience,' he said, 'that the common affairs of England and myself succeed best wherever you are,' and added, in a postscript in his own hand, 'I beg you to continue your good efforts, of the value of which I am fully sensible.' He addressed Wolsey as *'Legat primate et Lieutenant General d'Angleterre'*. A week later Wolsey told the King that Charles had unexpectedly advanced the date of his visit, and now 'desired to keep Easter in England'. This move, he told Henry, was simply to force their hands in declaring war against France, and insisted that Charles' arrival be deferred; otherwise they would have to 'labour in Holy Week', which 'were not convenient for princes, nor for meaner personages'.

VI

When it came, on May 22, 1522, Charles V's second visit far eclipsed the first, which had been relatively informal. The young emperor-elect, again determined to unbend, was received by Wolsey at Dover; they embraced and rode up to the castle together. Henry, according to plan, pretended to arrive on impulse 'that it might appear to the Emperor that his coming was of his own mind and affection'; he then took his guest on board his best warship, the *Henry Grace à Dieu*; they were rowed round the harbour to all the great ships, and Charles declared he had never before seen ships so armed.

Both monarchs,

> *Alter Germanis lux*
> *Alter clara Britannis,*[1]

[1] One the light of Germany, the other of Britain.

then rode by Canterbury, Rochester, Gravesend and Greenwich to London, where Charles asked the queen's blessing 'as is the fashion of Spain between aunt and nephew'. This time he only looked on at the jousting, while Henry, as usual, was breaking spears, but he held his own at tennis, when he partnered the king against the Prince of Orange and the Markgraf of Brandenburg, for the game ended 'even hands on both sides, after six games fully played'.

The emperor had brought at least 1,000 persons with him, half of those originally proposed. They included the dukes of Alva and Cleves, the Bishop of Córdoba, the Count Egmont, and George, 'bastard of Austria', squire of the Chamber; there were also doctors, surgeons, an organist and a '*souffleur d'orghanes*'; 'ung maystre Keux (cook), *ung patissier, ung potegier, ung saucier*'. The emperor-elect always cared a great deal about food.

The pageants laid on by the Easterlings resident in London were lavish, heraldic and complex, with fantastic hangings and decorations and garlands of May flowers.

Long Prosperitie, ran one doggerel, with an Anglo-Saxon rhythm,

> *To Charles and Hen(e)ry; princes most puissant,*
> *The one of Faith, th'other of Church, chosen defendent.*

Four tuns of beer a day were provided for the imperial entourage, Gascon and Rhenish laid on in advance along the route: indeed, the resources of the wine merchants and taverns of London were over-taxed. The Flemish and German magnates, in particular, were used to doing themselves well, and needed 'young vele, grene ges', kid, lamb, and 'Daryols custard baked in crust'. The 'Countie van Nassoo' had a Dutch appetite, and expected, for 'ys lyvery nyghtly', not only man-chets of the best white bread and wafers, but apples, caraway seeds and pistachio nuts; a gallon of Rhine wine, a gallon each of white and red Bordeaux, and one of spiced hypocras.[1] In case he felt faint in the night, he had two loaves and two gallons of beer in his bedroom. Indeed, as grand Chamberlain, he set high standards:[2] no wonder that the order went out to the local clergy and gentry *en route* to provide trout, carp, 'roasting eels', and fresh salmon; or that letters were directed to lords,

---

[1] Rutland Papers, p. 98.

[2] His daily official allowance at home included, besides routine quantities of beef and mutton, and 'half a veal', quails and partridges in season, '*toutes sortes de bonnes herbs*'; oranges, lemons and olives. On fish days, his daily allowance included eight pairs of large soles, two dozen small ones, a salmon, turbot, two dozen plaice, '*des crabbes, des mussells*', vast quantities of cream and butter and 300 eggs. The English were evidently worried at what even they had to live up to.

both spiritual and temporal, 'for fishing their ponds for dainties'. The Court, moreover, was so short of beds that extra ones were requisitioned from Richmond palace and even the Tower.

All, however, passed off successfully. Charles admired the Chapel of Henry VII, and the size of Westminster Hall; both royalties were nearly mobbed by the populace, trying to touch them; they both went hunting in Richmond Park, then down to Hampton Court and Windsor, where the emperor, in garter mantle, occupied his own stall in St George's Chapel, and both sovereigns took the sacrament and swore amity. A play was put on in which a symbolic horse (whether human or not is unclear) represented the French king and was tamed.

Hunting as they went, they came to Winchester, preceded by twenty tuns of Gascon wine and seven vats of Rhenish: 'item', the anxious officials noted, 'speke to the bere brewers of Portsmouth and Winton; speke to the brewers of Salisbury'. Through Bishop's Waltham, they arrived at Southampton, where Charles departed with his own fleet for Spain, loaded with promises, gifts, and a great deal of English money. All was set for the second invasion of France.

CHAPTER VIII

A HABSBURG TRIUMPH

H ENRY once told Charles V, in a moment of candour, that unlike his cousin of France, he had to reckon with danger both from the north and west; Wales was no serious problem to the Tudors, but he always had Scotland and Ireland on his mind. In spite of his apparently bluff, and often violent, personality, Henry was always extremely cunning. His policy towards Scotland was consistent; he tried to unite the two kingdoms by diplomacy; only in the last extremity, by force: in Ireland he refused to attempt either conquest or plantation, long leaving the island to be governed by the greatest of the aristocracy, the earls of Kildare, and then limiting his own attempt to impose a direct settlement.

When Henry VII had married his daughter Margaret to James IV of Scotland, whose death at Flodden and its sequel have already been described, he had hoped to bring Scotland into his dynastic net. But the Regent Margaret had married Archibald Douglas, Earl of Angus, and fled into England, while the Duke of Albany, with French backing, had virtually kidnapped the infant James V: in spite of Flodden, there was again danger of a Scots attack. Henry had then complained to Francis I, that Albany had ousted Margaret 'contrary to the testament and last wishes of the King, her late husband, who had willed that she should have the ordering and rule',[1] and since the Anglo-French rapprochment, Francis had kept Albany out of Scotland. Margaret and Angus had thus regained power; but, by 1521, Margaret's temperament (inherited by her granddaughter, Mary Queen of Scots) had again spoiled her brother's policy; she now wanted to be rid of Angus. Then, in December 1521, Albany had returned, removed the young king from Stirling, where he had been 'well at ease', to the 'wyndy and unpleasant Castle and rock of Edinburgh', and won round Margaret herself, 'with fair words'. Implored to remember 'whereof she was come and of what House', and warned of scandal, she had remained 'mekill inclinet to the pleasure of the said Duc'; indeed, it had

---

[1] Byrne, op. cit., p. 263.

5. Margaret Tudor, Queen of Scotland. Portrait by Daniel Mytens in Holyrood
    House
    (Reproduced by gracious permission of H.M. The Queen)

6. Thomas Cromwell, Earl of Essex
    (Reproduced by permission of the Bodleian Library, Oxford)

been reported that there was 'marvellous great intelligence' between them, 'all the day as much of the night', and they did not care who knew it; in fact, the pro-English Bishop of Dunkeld would testify they were 'over tender'.[1] Dacre, the able Warden of the Marches, had even warned Wolsey that the young king might be destroyed and the king's sister marry the 'Frenchman'; and Henry had accused Albany of the 'dishonourable and damnable abusing of our sister, inciting and stirring her to be divorced from her lawful husband (to what corrupt and God knoweth). We cannot,' he wrote, 'be contented with your said arrival, ne yet take your being there in good part.'[2]

That December, however, Margaret had caught smallpox. 'I assure you,' she had told Wolsey, 'I and he shall never foregather'; she could not write herself, for her hands and whole body were 'so full of the smalle pockes that I much noder writ, nor syt, nor skantlie speke'.[3]

Albany, for long 'like a fox in a hole', had again left Scotland.

It was in this context that Henry launched his war on France. Sporadic warfare continued: in the autumn of 1523, Surrey ravaged the border and burnt Jedburgh, and Albany's last attempt failed. He landed at Dumbarton with French troops and guns and advanced as far as Wark on the Tweed; but confronted with an army led by Surrey, he fled—'ran away', as Skelton elegantly put it, '*with a hey dog, hey!*' In the following year he left Scotland for good, and in July, under English auspices, James V, now twelve, assumed nominal power. Once his young nephew was 'out of danger and peril of the said Duke', and the Scots were . . . 'disposed to live in good rest', Henry, wrote the cardinal, he would now make them 'such benign and gracious answers as should be for their weal'. And by the summer of 1524, the king was able to play the benevolent uncle to young James direct, referring to the tender regard he bore to his person, life and estate, and recalling how he had urged him to take over the government. He spoke of the boy's reported 'fresh wit and great towardness of wisdom', and assured him that 'one of the principal things he cared for on earth' was his security, 'being so nighly conjoined unto us in proximity of blood'. The English interest was thus to predominate in Scotland during the second French war; Henry was able to prevent that traditional stab in the back.

---

[1] Ellis, Series II, Vol. I, p. 285.
[2] Byrne, op. cit., p. 265.
[3] L. and P., III, II, 2725.

II

One of the king's main items of the *Remembrance* of 1519, it will be recalled, had been 'how the lands of Ireland could be brought into order and obedience'. The problem had taxed his father, for the island had hatched successive Yorkist conspiracies and had long been ruled by the great Geraldine Earl of Kildare, of the Anglo-Norman creation, known to the Irish as *Garret Mór*. In 1494 Henry VII had sent Sir Edward Poynings to reorganize the English Pale from Dundalk, through Louth and Meath to Dublin and the Wicklow mountains, and to bridle the Dublin–Leinster Irish Parliament, subjected by 'Poynings' Law' to the veto of the king and Council in London.

Henry VII had 'resumed' all royal rights, and forbidden, but not suppressed, such favourite Anglo-Irish war cries as '*Butler aboo!*' In 1596 Poynings had been recalled: rule had reverted to the overmighty subject, Kildare, who, with English firearms, had conducted his own 'wars of magnificence' in pursuit of ancient vendettas, and lived in a strange Gaelic-Renaissance splendour in his castle at Maynooth, dominating the Dublin Pale. In 1513, a few days before Flodden, *Garret Mór* had been shot in a skirmish with the neighbouring O'Mores; but his son *Garret Oge*, had succeeded him, and was still ruling Ireland, after a fashion.[1]

The Renaissance part of the culture was exotic; even the great Anglo-Norman families—Kildare Geraldines, Desmond Geraldines, Ormonde Butlers—had long gone predominantly Irish, and the lesser chieftains were absorbed in traditional feuds. Their clans and septs were numerous and pugnacious, still more pastoral than agricultural, moving with their herds according to the seasons; neglecting their hay and corn harvests often rotted with the damp. The Irish wore 'glibs'—matted hair over their eyes—and mantles of Bronze age cut; cattle raiding was endemic, and they attached their ploughs to their animals' tails. They were, in fact, in a state of arrested development, a 'run down' heroic age, in a world of their own, amid the peat smoke, the rain, the soft Atlantic air. They lived in hovels with their animals; promiscuous, illiterate, superstitious, but with the charm, wit, loquacity, grand manners and gregariousness of their kind: 'time,' writes Dr Rowse, 'had rather stood still for Ireland, as it is apt to do for Celts.'[2]

This slatternly picturesque and poverty-stricken world formed the background to the grandeur of Maynooth, of the O'Brien, the O'Neill, the MacWilliam and the rest, with their wolfhounds and bards, saffron

---

[1] See E. Curtis, *A History of Mediaeval Ireland*, and *A History of Ireland* (Methuen), pp. 156 ff. for 'Poyning's Law'.

[2] *The Expansion of Elizabethan England*, Macmillan, 1955, p. 117.

robes and tartans, their *'Kerne'* dartsmen and bowmen, their *Gallóglach*—Norse axemen from the Hebrides, the *Inse gall*—and their mercenary *Redshanks* from Argyll and the Western Isles.

Into this casual and unpredictable world had marched the armoured, methodical, English, accustomed to centralized government and settled parishes, with a shrewd eye for business and exploitation. It was a clash of alien epochs, incompatible worlds. Even the Irish Church was untouched by Erasmian influences, and the chroniclers still called the king in London the 'King of the Saxons'. Beyond the Pale, the country was unmapped and untamed.

Henry, with his second French war in mind, now had to reckon with this background. He had early declared that 'none of his progenitors were so resolved to reduce that disordered land to good government than he was', but he still harboured illusions. 'We and our Council,' he wrote to the new Lord Lieutenant, Thomas, Earl of Surrey, Norfolk's son, in 1520, 'think and verily believe that in case circumspect and politic ways be used, ye shall . . . bring them to further obedience. . . . Which thing must as yet be practised in sober ways, politic drafts and aimiable persuasions, founded in law and reason (rather) than by rigorous dealing, comminations or other enforcement by strength or violence.'[1] Surrey, who already knew his Ireland, made a better judgment. 'After my poor opinion,' he wrote, 'this land shall never be brought to good order and due subjection but only by conquest.' In 1521 he wrote that, given enough men, he could subdue it.

Already a cold realist, for all his ferocity, Henry was too cautious to put his foot in that bog. His immediate concern was the coming French war, and he needed Surrey elsewhere: for the present, he left Ireland to Kildare, *Garret Oge*. Externally quiescent, it remained a problem shelved.

III

So, by May 1522, when the English heralds were giving formal defiance to the French and Charles V was still in England, the affairs of Scotland and Ireland, though hardly satisfactory, were not a major menace; nor, during the second war against France, were they to become so.

In July, Surrey burnt Morlaix in the Cherbourg peninsula, an adventure in which Sir John Russell lost an eye; he harried Brest; by August he was ravaging Artois and the country round Boulogne, but he was

---

[1] A. L. Rowse, op. cit., p. 96. Quoting from C. Maxwell, *Irish History from Contemporary Sources, 1509–1610*, pp. 105–6.

back in England that winter, when he succeeded his father as Lord Treasurer, a position he was to hold until the last months of the reign. The major assault was planned for the following year; Thomas Grey, Marquis of Dorset, writing to his right trusty and well-beloved Sir John Trevelyan in Cornwall to send him 'iii or fore good archers or mo', told him that the king 'our sovereign Lord' was 'utterly determined . . . to take his viage into the partes of France'.[1]

The estimates for the war made in that year were formidable. The land army of 26,000 English foot, to cross into Flanders; 4,000 Almain foot at 6d a day, and 8,000 horsemen at 8 florins a month, along with the cost of wagons, and 'carriage of ordnance', would cost, in all, £292,689 6s 4d. Add to this £47,460 for forces against Scotland, and over £28,000 for the navy and the 'sea army', as well as 'conduct money' to get it to the ships, and the total worked out at £372,404.[2] The victualling of 3,000 men at sea for eight weeks was reckoned at 750 quarters of wheat, 140 pipes of beer, 600 oxen, with 'bay salt', and 18,000 barrels of salt fish, while the land army was expected to consume 7,000 pipes of beer in four weeks.

Henry was also spending lavishly on building and repairs at home. £3,000 for Newhall, £3,000 for Bridewell, £500 on Greenwich, £300 at Windsor: 124 coats for the Yeomen of the Guard came to £300. The combined civil and war expenses led to taxation which rendered the government unpopular; by 1524 to the first climb down by the king before hostile opinion since his accession. The blame was, of course, put on the cardinal.

Neither in London nor the country were foreign campaigns popular, save among the magnates and gallants of the Court and the caterers who profited. When John Brode of Shaftesbury in Dorset called John Williams a vagabond and a thief, Williams retorted that he had served King Henry in the wars. 'Ah Sir,' Brode answered, using 'unfitting words', 'have ye been with Master Henry King? A noble act ye did there! Ye spent away my money and other men's!'[3] This remark was representative, and when, in April, 1523, Wolsey, set to finance the French war, went down to the House of Commons in the fifth Parliament of the reign summoned for the first time since the cardinal had taken full control, and demanded the then monstrous levy of four shillings in the pound on the value of lands and goods, there were pungent things said.

[1] Trevelyan Papers, op. cit., III, Camden Society, 1872, p. 11.
[2] L. and P., III, II, 2745.
[3] L. and P., III, I, 1165.

Wolsey explained that the king 'in his honour' could no longer suffer the bad faith of the French king, who had withheld the payments for Tournai and 'Tirwin', and sent Albany into Scotland. He thought that no less than 'VIII C. M. pounds' (£800,000—a colossal sum) would be needed and exhorted the Commons to aid their prince.[1] When the Speaker, Sir Thomas More, urged that, of duty, men ought to pay the four shillings in the pound, members objected that there was not so much money out of the king's hands in the whole realm; though five men were well monied, five thousand more were not; and 'gentlemen of landes' had not the fifth part of their estates in coin; it was the same with merchants, clothiers, farmers and retailers. They produced baffling statistics; 'if all the coin were in the King's hands,' they concluded, 'how should men live?'

Wolsey, says Hall, 'currishly answered' that he would rather have his tongue plucked out of his head with a pair of pincers than to move the king to take less, and cited the sumptuous buildings, rich apparel and 'fat feasts' now fashionable. But the Commons 'greatly grudged'; said that affluence was good for trade and not 'prodigal'; and objected to Wolsey's coming down to the House in full state. More told them to 'receive him in all his pomp, with his maces, his pillars, his poleaxes, his crosses and his great seal, too', but treat him for what he was, an intruding stranger. So the Commons received the cardinal in what he termed 'a marvellous obstinate silence'. He had to retire. There followed weighty speeches on the costs and risks of invading France; in the end, two shillings in the pound, not four, were conceded, and, that autumn, local magnates all over the country set about collecting the money.[2]

The grand strategy to which the loan was to contribute was ambitious and far-flung: as before, the decisive theatre in the Habsburg-Valois contest was Italy, already menaced by the Turkish advance, and where the pope, Venice, Florence and Genoa were now in league with the emperor against the French.[3] But the Spaniards were also to attack along the Pyrenees frontier; Charles, Duc de Bourbon, Constable of France, who had turned against his sovereign, was to lead a

[1] Hall, I, pp. 284–5.

[2] The collectors in North Wilts, for example, were Sir John Seymour, Sir Henry Long and Sir Edward Darrell of Littlecote. Darrell found eleven people worth £20 at Ogbourne St George, six at Mildenhall, eight at Preshute, seven at Avebury, one at Rockley and seventeen at Aldbourne. The tentacles of fiscal power already gripped the land. (See L. and P., III, II, 3584.)

[3] The Spanish envoy told Pope Adrian that, in view of the Turkish threat, Charles must so dispose that '*Gallos ad Italiam proficiscentes per caudam retrahat*—pull the French expedition into Italy back by the tail'.

force of Burgundians and German landsknechts against Lyons from Besançon, while Suffolk and the English army of over 18,000 men were to advance from Calais as far into France as they could get. The French king stood at bay in Lyons.

In July 1523, Wolsey had to report that the defences and supply of Calais were in a bad way, and the 'poore souldgiers far behinde un-payde of their wages'; Henry had resolved to limit his aims, and strike at a traditional English objective, and 'have the siege of Boulogne experimented'. He had at first been led on by disaffected Frenchmen, one of whom had 'hoped to see him crowned at Rheims', but Wolsey, he declared, had 'hit the nail on the head' in expecting that the Bur-gundians would 'stay' upon their own frontiers 'to the end that our money be spent among them'. He was not going to have his army sent into a 'distant land', dependent on people whose 'slackness and hard handling' he well knew;[1] and, on September 20th, he again ob-jected that the season was too late; that the new objective, Compiègne, was more difficult of access than 'interested' people pretended; that Boulogne would not be forced to surrender merely by being cut off, not besieged; that the Burgundians would have difficulty in 'providing carts', and that the French king might well do what he would himself, if he were in like case ('as our Lord keep him out of'), and take the offensive against Suffolk at once.[2] What with cold weather and lack of plunder, it would be hard, he thought, to keep the army from crying 'Home! Home!' Wolsey, still anxious, for the succession to the Papacy, to conciliate the Archduchess Margaret, brushed these sensible argu-ments aside: oddly enough, his master acquiesced, even saying he need not accept his advice simply because 'he had once given it'. But Henry's judgment was correct.

By the end of October, Suffolk, in full cry, had crossed the Somme and taken Montdidier. 'When they were all armed,' writes Hall, ecstatically, 'the trumpets blew; then towards the braie marched these valiant gentlemen with pikes and swords and cried Har! Har!' There was 'foining, lashing and striking . . .' But the Burgundians disbanded, as foreseen, and Suffolk had to withdraw to Valenciennes, 'after great journeys and little victory which caused the soldiers daily to die'. Henry reinforced him, saying,' We will in no wise that the army shall break'; but 'fervent' frost now set in, and 'in truth the soldiers would not abide'. Nor, now, did Wolsey, for good reasons, wish that they should. By December, Suffolk was back in England to face the royal

[1] L. and P., III, II, 3320.
[2] L. and P., III, II, 3346.

wrath, increased because Charles V, having secured his objectives in the south west, had failed to invade Guienne.

Wolsey had led his master into this fiasco in pursuit of his old ambition: since September, 1523, he had known that Adrian IV had been ill with renal disease. Sitting up in bed and speaking faintly 'like a man fatigated', the pope had told the cardinals that he was going to die. It was hard to say, reported the English agents, where the garland would light; if Wolsey were on the spot, he would be 'as sure of it as York'. And when the news of the pope's unlamented death arrived,[1] Wolsey told the king that, but for absence, he could count on the succession, though of course he would rather continue in the king's service. Before the eyes of king and cardinal rose the mirage of a papacy under their joint control; in fact, they were both little more than provincials compared to the cosmopolitan European realists with whom they had to deal, and to whom they were important mainly for their money. Charles V played them both with cool skill.

The usual intrigues now set in at Rome. The cardinals in the Sistine Chapel in their wooden cells, distinguished by letters and distributed by lot, were again walled in and guarded by the Swiss: while the voting was going on the roof cracked, but the architect said it was safe. The French cardinals turned up late, coming in booted and spurred, amid laughter, a gesture thought 'very dissolute'. By the eighth day rations were cut down, and by the twentieth the Roman populace were threatening the conclave with bread and water. Then a bishop, Cardinal de Grassis' son, dreamt he saw Cardinal Giulio dei Medici, an illegitimate member of that family, on the high altar, playing the pipe, the rest dancing. His dream proved correct; Medici had prevented anyone else being elected, and when his French-backed rival, Colonna, had asked him if he meant 'to stay in that prison for ever', he had sworn never to yield. The French had then abandoned Colonna, who had remarked '*Bien, je ferai un bon Pape pour le roy votre maistre*', and switched his decisive support. After a record conclave of over three weeks, Medici had been elected, on November 19th, as Clement VII.

It was a qualified victory for Charles V; he would have preferred a German, but had backed Medici as the candidate most likely to win; and the new pope, the Spanish envoy reported, was 'very reserved, irresolute . . . loves money, coquettes with the French'.[2] The emperor

---

[1] The Cardinals, parodying Tacitus, put on his tomb, *nihil in vita infelicitor contigit quam quod imperaret*: 'Nothing more unfortunate happened to him in his life than that he had to rule.'

[2] Fisher, op. cit., p. 252.

had never, of course, intended to have an English pope, and Wolsey had been subjected to the maddening, suave, diplomacy of which Charles was a master. He had naturally always, he told Wolsey from Pampluna, wanted him to be pope, but since Adrian's reported death, 'had dispatched no letter into Italy, as he had no assurance of the fact'. The cardinals were thus already in conclave, but though he thought it would be little use, he would write 'to show his good will'.[1] He had even told his ambassador to inform Henry that he had despatched a special courier, and enclosed copies of the letters of recommendation he had written. He did not say that the courier had been deliberately delayed.

Wolsey never forgave the emperor; but he put a good face on it; deliberately lied to Henry that he had nearly been elected, though well knowing he had stood even less chance than in 1522; and declared 'for my part I am more joyous than if it had fortuned upon my person'. 'How great a friend,' he exclaimed, 'your Grace and the emperor will both have in him!' They had to make the best of Clement VII, but, for both of them Cardinal Campeggio's deplorable remark that he 'hoped to find in Clement more clement skies' was to prove singularly inept.

V

Wolsey had now seen that Charles V meant him no good. He discouraged Suffolk's advance, with a view to switching to the French, but Henry continued to throw good money after bad. In 1524 he sent 100,000 English crowns to subsidize an offensive by Bourbon in Provence; in June the all too sensitive Pace was toiling over the Col di Tenda, 'so upright to ascend and stand that in many places it made us creep on all four, and so proclive in descent that, without great inforcement to go bolt upright', they would have fallen;[2] complaining also in July, from Lucca, of 'molestious passage of baggage': he had not 'dared to turn his horse travers for all worldly riches, nor even look down for proclivity and deepness of the valley'.

Henry now pledged himself, if Bourbon succeeded in attacking through Provence, to invade France in person; if he failed, it might be wiser to mediate, even veer, as Wolsey desired, again to the French. And Charles V was now not paying Wolsey his pension; it was as easy, the cardinal's agent complained, 'to get money from a stone as cash

---

[1] L. and P., III, II, 3559.
[2] Strype, *Ecclesiastical Memorials*, Vol. I, Appendix, pp. 20 ff. These experiences contributed to his breakdown the next year and to his recall.

from these people', and, by June 1524, Wolsey was already in touch with an agent of Louise of Savoy, the Queen Mother of France. The cardinal also approached the new pope to make an informal appeal for peace.

In the event the move proved premature. Bourbon had duly invaded Provence and laid seige to Marseilles, attempting to open a passage between Spain and Italy for Charles V, but the inhabitants had defied him; by the end of July, his troops had mutinied, and were retreating fast to Italy along the steep and twisting *via Aurelia* in the summer heat. Francis I, who had advanced from Lyons to Avignon with a large army, now thought he saw his chance: 'I am concluded,' he declared in October, 'and am resolved, to pass in person into Italy; and whoever shall advise me to the contrary shall not only be blamed, but incur my displeasure.' There was no more to be said: the king crossed the Mt Cenis pass, hot for the conquest of Milan. By the end of the month he took it, but plague broke out there, and in November, with the river Po swollen by the autumn rain, he failed to capture Pavia, losing three thousand infantry and four hundred gentlemen killed. The high-towered city was defended by Don Antonio de Leyva, so crippled by gout that he was chair-borne into battle, but one of the best soldiers of the day.

As the winter came on, the French position began to look precarious, and Wolsey's approaches to the French mistimed. The King of France, it was said, 'has made a very hasty invasion of Italy, and it will not be easy for him to return without risking his life and all that he has'. 'All the great lords,' it was reported, 'are obliged to go and warm themselves in the King's kitchen. The infantry lie in the trenches and dare not leave them lest they die of hunger and cold.' Henry roared with laughter at his rival's predicament, saying he thought it would be hard for him to get safe out of Italy.[1] Then early in March, 1525, the Archduchess Margaret told the English envoy, '*nous avons ce matin, ung peu avant notre diner, reçu les meilleurs nouvelles du monde d'Italie; le Roy de France est prisonnier, XIII M de ses gens tuez*'.[2]

At dawn on February 24th, the French had been caught between two fires: three thousand German and Spanish infantry, wearing white shirts, had assaulted the French camp, while the besieged imperialists in Pavia had broken out. The French chivalry, the king at their head, had charged the Spanish arquebusiers and pikemen: it had been

---

[1] E. F. Rogers, *Correspondence of Sir Thomas More*, pp. 313–14.

[2] 'We have this morning heard from Italy the best news in the world. The King of France is prisoner, 13,000 of his people killed.'

another Agincourt. Francis was hauled off his horse by his helmet: had not the imperial viceroy come to his relief, he would have been trampled down in the melée; it was even rumoured that he was wounded, but the abbot of Narjara told Charles V that in reality he 'had no wounds at all save a contusion of the leg, and a mere scratch between the fingers of his hand'.[1] When Henry heard the news, he was delighted: he had probably resented Wolsey's feelers for peace, and when the messenger from the archduchess found him in bed, he exclaimed 'you are as welcome as the angel Gabriel was to the Virgin Mary', and sprang up to tell the queen. 'Now is the time,' he told the imperial commissioners, his countenance beaming with joy, 'for the emperor and myself to devise full satisfaction from France. Not an hour is to be lost!' Before the imperial embassy in London, bonfires blazed in the spring evening; great casks of wine were broached.

Charles V, by contrast, received the news impassively in Madrid. 'A battle has been fought under the walls of Pavia,' they told him on March 10th, as he came from mass, 'the King of France is a prisoner and in your Majesty's power, and his whole army destroyed.' 'The King of France in my power, and the battle gained by us!' he exclaimed, and returned at once to the chapel to give thanks to the Virgin. 'Your majesty,' they said, 'is from this day in a position to prescribe laws to Christians and Turks, according to your pleasure': he merely remarked that he would now go into Italy, pacify Christendom and pursue his main object, a crusade against the Turks. He would take all advantage he could, but not actually depose Francis I. He had more constructive politics in mind.

Henry, on the other hand, either seriously or for political warfare, reverted to his old impossible ambition, to recover the realm of France by the sword. 'So long,' he now wrote to Wingfield, his permanent ambassador to the emperor, 'as the realm of France . . . situate in the heart and midst of all Christendom, shall remain in the hands of those who cannot, ne never will, cease to apply their wits, powers, thoughts and studies, to ampliate and extend their limits and dominions, never satiate ne contented with enough, there can never be rest, quiet and tranquillity in Christendom.'[2] It was 'notorious and manifest', he went on, 'that he ought to have the French crown': if not, that he had the right, by lineal succession, to Normandy, Gascony, Guienne, Anjou, Maine and Poitou. Since these territories could only be won by

---

[1] *Spanish Calendar*, III, I, p. 22. Russell wrote to Henry that Francis had blamed his Swiss, 'who had not done their part as they should have done'.

[2] Byrne, op. cit., p. 34.

'violence and puissance', never by consent, Henry instructed the ambassador to propose to Charles V an immediate, utterly impractical, joint invasion of France. They could enter Paris together; Henry would take the French crown, then proceed with Charles V to Rome to 'see the Crown imperial set on his head'. The Princess Mary could be 'transported' to Paris, where the emperor could marry her; in due course, he would inherit England and become the 'Peaceable Lord and Owner of Christendom'.

Such a project, if seriously meant, would not appeal to the realistic and dedicated mind of Charles V, who had no intention of making his uncle King of France. Although the Princess Mary answered his commissioners in such fluent Latin that, although she was nine, she seemed twelve, and sent an emerald ring to her fiance, which he put on his little finger, Wolsey must have well known that Charles would never install Henry VIII in Paris. The emperor had already deceived Wolsey over the papal election: now it was apparent that, wisely enough, he was going to let Henry's extravagant ambitions down as well. At the moment, however, though victorious, he was nearly bankrupt; since he owed vast sums to the English, both sides as yet were in two minds about breaking the alliance.

CHAPTER IX

QUICKSANDS OF DIPLOMACY

◙

IN spite of his ambitious designs, when, in 1525, Henry surveyed the scene at home and abroad, he may well have doubted if Wolsey was quite so successful as Wolsey wished him to think. Though the cardinal remained the magnificent ruler of England, with a European prestige, other able men were now coming up; one an insular conservative aristocrat; the other a new man of villein blood. Thomas Howard, already Lord Treasurer, had succeeded his famous father, victor of Flodden, as third Duke of Norfolk, at Whitsun, 1524; as Surrey, he had already campaigned in Ireland, Scotland and France. Thomas Cromwell, on the other hand, was the son of a drunken brewer and blacksmith at Putney, evicted from his copyhold for fraud, though he had in fact sired the greatest administrative genius of the age, and his daughter was to be ancestress of Oliver, Lord Protector of England.[1]

The Howards were East Anglian gentry who had married into the great mediaeval family of Mowbray, from whom their dukedom derived. Thomas, himself, now Norfolk, had married Elizabeth, daughter of the executed Buckingham; his heir, now Surrey, was to grow up a wild blade and a poet; his daughter to marry Henry Fitzroy, the king's natural son. Norfolk was a short dark soldier with a wary eye, a hatchet face and a cruel mouth: he was limited, hide-bound and deadly. Like his father, he served the crown out of prudence. 'Bear he never can prevail to lion,' he said, 'for lack of tail'; 'by God's body,' he was to tell More, '*indignatio principis mors est*.'[2] Arrogant in his degree, he could also remark 'Prince may make a nobleman but not a gentleman'; he thought England was 'merrier before the New Learning came up', and declared that he had never read the Scriptures, nor ever would. He was an untiring henchman of the king; when necessary, his butcher; and he came to regret helping Thomas Cromwell to power. Their

---

[1] She married a Welshman called Williams, whose son, Richard, was knighted, took his mother's name, and became great-grandfather to Oliver Cromwell. He was not, of course, as Hackett states, wildly (*Henry the Eighth*, p. 528), a 'descendant' of Thomas.
[2] 'The anger of the prince is death.'

rivalry reflected two worlds—ramified feudal family interest and landed power; and business, finance, centralized administration.

Cromwell was as great a thug as Norfolk, but plebeian, travelled, seasoned in the intrigues of Renaissance Italy. An able, thick-set youth, with a tight little mouth and porcine eyes, he had left home for the continent at eighteen, fought in Italian wars, worked for Frescobaldi bankers in Florence and English merchants in the Netherlands. He had even, it was said, clinched the favour of Julius II by presenting him with a dish of English 'jelly' when he came in from hunting; for the Holy Father had so enjoyed the dish, after a cardinal had tasted it for poison, that he had dispatched Cromwell's business at once.

By 1520 Thomas was well married and established in London; a rising lawyer, money-lender, accountant, and wool merchant, he could turn his hand to anything. He had probably, by then, entered Wolsey's service; by 1523 he was a Member of Parliament and drafted, and probably delivered, an able speech before the king.[1] It had been a striking speech, critical of the war, perhaps a *ballon d'essai* put up by the cardinal, by then trying to check the headstrong king. Right as it was to 'scourge' the French, who, if not, would 'scourge' others, Cromwell begged the king not to go over in person. He should 'restrain his high courage'; prosecute the war 'little by little', rather than 'send over all at once the power royal of the Kingdom'. If he did, the realm would be ruined, and forced to 'coin leather'; and if they advanced far into France, the enemy would cut their supply; as for the taking of towns, Henry well knew that the winning of Thérouanne had 'cost more than twenty such ungracious dogholes would be worth'. We had now no bases in France, save Calais, and the French were united as never before; rather the king should subdue Scotland and join that realm to his for ever.

Here was the voice of realism and business: it is unlikely that, directly or by report, it was lost upon the king; and, by 1525, Wolsey had assigned Cromwell a suitable task—the suppression of minor monasteries in the interests of his new foundations at Christ Church and Ipswich.

II

In 1525 Wolsey had more unpleasant matters in mind. As Cromwell

---

[1] L. and P., III, II, 2958. Cromwell discharged many lesser duties. That autumn, with other civic worthies, he 'presented' various householders before Alderman Warley, for 'defective pavements, a noisesome goose house', dangerous cellar doors, and a 'case very noisesome and odible', as well as denouncing a Spaniard for evil conversation and Spencer's, Harrison's and Badcoke's wives for scolding. (*Ibidem*, 3657.)

had warned the Commons, Suffolk's operations in France had been ruinously expensive, but Henry was still determined on the war. The king, Wolsey had to declare, was now going to France in person, thinking, after Pavia, to seize his chance, and, if he went, he must 'go like a prince'. By-passing Parliament, the cardinal demanded an 'amicable loan' assessed by commissioners and derived from the old feudal 'aid', payable when the king himself campaigned overseas. It was to be a sixth of lay property; a quarter from the clergy. When the City demurred, they were told 'it were better that some should suffer indigence than that the King should lack'; they should 'ruffle not in this case, for it might fortune to cost some their heads'.[1]

Wolsey also had to bully the clergy, who refused anything save the sum granted by Convocation. When, in fact, the matter 'was opened through England', writes Hall, 'how the great men took it was a marvel, the poor cursed, the rich repugned, the light wits railed, but in conclusion, all people cursed the Cardinal, and his co-adherents, as subversor of the laws and liberty of England. If men should give their goods by a commission, then it were worse than the taxes in France ...'; others said 'whatsoever was granted no good came of it'; and others ... 'that the cardinal sent all the money to Rome;' thus was the 'muttering throughout the realm'.

The resistance was not confined to London and the clergy: there was unrest in Kent, where men said they 'would have no rest of such payment as long as *someone* lived'; rumblings in Essex and Huntingdonshire; in Suffolk unemployed weavers began to 'rage', put themselves in harness and ring the alarm on the church bells. The Duke of Suffolk had to temporize: 'I will be your surety,' he promised, 'since ye be my countrymen.' When Norfolk, coming down from Thetford, with a 'power', asked their grievance, they all spoke at once. 'Who was their captain?' he demanded. 'My lord,' answered a 'well-aged man', John Green, 'forsooth, it is Poverty, for he and his cousin necessity hath brought us to this doing.'[2] After all, the year before, there had been news from Germany 'how uplandish men called the bowres [boors]' had risen en masse.

Henry, with his Tudor feeling for public opinion, now intervened. It was against his honour, he discovered, that the Council should attempt so doubtful a matter in his name; indeed, he had been misled. 'Well,' he

---

[1] Hall, II, p. 36.
[2] Hall, II, p. 43.

Brewer remarks that the story of Captain Poverty shows 'the melancholy and poetical temperament of the East Anglian as compared with the sturdier and more prosaic element of the South Saxons.' (Introduction, L. and P., IV, *LXXXIII*.)

complained, 'some have informed me that my realm was never so rich and that men would pay at the first request, but now I find all contrary'; then, in royal anger, he declared, 'I will no more of this trouble. Let letters be sent to all shires that the matter be no more spoken of. I will pardon all . . .' For the first time in his reign he had to yield.

Encouraged by the courtiers, Henry still wanted war, but he got all the credit for calling it off. Wolsey, already anxious to pull out, got none: he might pretend that his intercession had done the trick, but the people, wrong as usual, said 'God save the King, for the Cardinal is known well enough.'

So the invasion was abandoned—none too soon. After Pavia, Francis I had been conducted to the castle of Pizzigitone and committed to the custody of a Spanish captain; a reliable man, Pace reported, with two hundred men at arms and thirteen hundred Spanish infantry under his command. But Charles V knew it was impracticable to dethrone his captive; so with an air of studied moderation he was merely demanding the stiffest terms he could get. And he had long resolved to drop the English, having no desire to make his uncle too powerful and, all along been interested only in English money, of which he had great need, for even after Pavia, his troops were unpaid. He had long taken the measure of Wolsey; always avid, he said, for preferment, and so to be taken '*tamquam piscis hamo*—like a fish with a worm'. And the emperor had long resented, in his glacial pride, having to conciliate this upstart.

His new resident ambassador, Louis de Praet, a Burgundian noble, also despised Wolsey. After severe provocation, the cardinal had More intercept his dispatches, which made the attitude of the imperialists all too clear: 'If we obtain the battle,' de Praet had written, 'all will be well; our master will escape the danger of such friends and confederates as he hath hitherto had. I hope to live long enough to see our master properly avenged on this man (Wolsey), who is in great measure the cause of all the evil now befalling his Imperial Majesty.'

In March, after Pavia, Henry himself complained to Charles V of the 'indiscrete, disloyal and ungrateful proceedings of M. de Praet, your resident ambassador at this my court, whose conduct has been very different from my paternal affection towards you and the equally good intention of our most beloved Cardinal';[1] and, in this protest, '*T. Cardinalis Ebor*' concurred. But Charles told his ambassador that he had long trusted him entirely, and would be 'revenged on Wolsey in proper time'; already he was in touch with the Dowager Queen Louise of France, determined to rescue her son. The pope might say

[1] *Spanish Calendar*, III, I, 1525–6, p. 74.

that Francis I 'needed other help than women's tears', but Henry would never be crowned at Rheims.

Charles now decided to dispense with the English: he asked that the Princess Mary, aged nine, be sent out to Spain at once 'to learn the language' and with a huge dowry, knowing well the requests would be refused. 'I see no way,' he wrote that June, 'except for me to marry Isabella of Portugal, with whom the king offers a million ducats, but I shall not take any step without the consent of the King of England, as I have sent him my word. I wish for no war this year, but to attend to my marriage.'[1]

Princess Mary's grand match had now vanished. It was an appalling affront; Henry at once demanded that Charles pay his debts and cancelled the Treaty of Windsor. Wolsey, too, gave as good as he got: 'I know full well,' he told the Archduchess Margaret's commissioners, 'that we shall never get any assistance from you: but we shall do our best. Either by an alliance with the Turk—the Emperor's worst enemy —or by making peace with France, or by giving Princess Mary to the Dauphin.' By August 1525 Henry and the cardinal had sold their support to the French, cashing in, too, on the reaction in Italy, where, it was reported, many were glad to see the French overthrown, but sorry to be left a prey to the Spaniards, who for their cruelty were the most hated of all: already the pope, Venice, Florence, Siena, and Mantua were in league. It was therefore with satisfaction that in September Henry received the first instalment of a life annuity of 100,000 crowns a year from the French. Early in September, 1525, peace with France was officially proclaimed; and Henry offered his benevolent mediation in the predicament of Francis I. 'The Cardinal,' wrote de Praet, in October, 'has two ends in view, first to obtain great sums of money for the King of England under pretence of war; second, to keep the French King and the emperor in perpetual war and distrust.'[2] He was not far wrong; Wolsey had a financially exacting master, nor might England's position as a second-class power in a mere 'angle of the world', as Wolsey realized, be enviable should Habsburg and Valois agree.

III

When Charles V threw over the Princess Mary, he had thwarted the

[1] L. and P., IV, 1453. Charles was hardly popular with the Portuguese who, three years before, had petitioned him not to allow Spaniards to poach on their preserves in the East Indies. Charles—no romantic—had woundingly implied that they deserved no credit for their exploits; they had merely been driven overseas by poverty and mismanagement, and he would not hinder Spanish competition.

[2] L. and P., IV, 1702, quoted Fisher, op. cit., p. 257.

Charles Brandon, Duke of Suffolk. Portrait at Compton Wynyates
(Reproduced by permission of the Marquess of Northampton, D.S.O.)

Catherine Howard
From a miniature
(Reproduced by gracious permission
of H.M. The Queen)

8. Jane Seymour
   Portrait by Hans Holbein
   (Reproduced by gracious permission of
   H.M. The Queen)

Anne of Cleves
(Reproduced by permission of the
 President and Fellows of St John's
 College, Oxford)

dearest hopes of the queen. She had for years worked to obtain the splendid match, of which the offspring might be supreme in Europe and overseas, an emperor of the west. The slight from her own nephew, from whom Wolsey was now careful to cut her off, weakened an already difficult position. The problem of the succession had long haunted Henry's mind, for of Catherine's six children, Mary alone survived, and by 1525 it was clear that the queen was past bearing any more. Mary was the sole legitimate heir, and now her position was compromised. The English might have accepted the dazzling imperial marriage, but her projected betrothal to the Dauphin, a project her mother bitterly opposed, would be intensely unpopular: no French prince would come easily, even as consort, to share the English throne. And if she married a subject, there might be civil war at her accession.

In cold anger at the insult from Charles V, Henry now insulted Catherine by grooming his bastard for the succession. This fine boy by Elizabeth Blunt was six years old; he was now brought forward as a potential heir. In mid-June he was made Knight of the Garter, and Earl of Nottingham; then, led by Norfolk and Suffolk into the great chamber at Bridewell, created Duke of Richmond and Somerset. The child was given a great household, £4,000 a year, two cloths of estate, four state chairs of cloth of gold and velvet; four great carpets, vast quantities of linen. He was appointed to high nominal offices: Warden of the Cinque Ports; Lord of Ireland; Warden General of the Scottish Marches.

A well-known tutor was found for him, Richard Croke, a Greek scholar from Eton and King's, who had made a reputation in Germany and was a fellow of St John's College, Cambridge. The boy later went to live with this tutor in Cambridge at King's, where he was given the full discipline of Renaissance learning and where his aristocratic friends taught him, it was complained, to sing bawdy songs, hawk, and waste time on frivolous indoor amusements on wet days. He might, it was thought in 1525, marry his half-sister, or make a grand dynastic match. Meanwhile, Henry ordered Mary to Ludlow, away from her mother, to begin her duties as Princess of Wales. 'I am in that case,' wrote Queen Catherine from Woburn to her only child, 'that the long absence of the King and you troubleth me . . . it shall be a great comfort to me to see you keep your Latin and fair writing and all.'

Henry kept Christmas of 1525 at Eltham, where he had spent so much of his youth. It was called the 'still Christmas', he had so few attendants, being scared of the plague in London. He had also had a narrow escape that year when hawking. He had jumped a ditch with a pole such as now used in otter hunting; it had broken, and the king had fallen, head down, into the clay, to be pulled out, half suffocated, by an attendant.

In his *Remembrance* of 1519, it will be recalled, Henry the king had been pleased to put his household in profitable order without further delay. But abuses were still rampant; in the winter weather, king and cardinal went into them, drawing up the Ordinances of Eltham. There were too many yeomen of the guard, they discovered, very chargeable, and too many officers far stricken in age, waited on by their own servants, all living on the king. Pensioned off, they now left 'with lamentation'. The Ordinances now minutely described the hours and duties of the household; promotion by merit was made easier and menus fuel and candles cut down. The king's barber was enjoined to be scrupulously clean—the shaving water was scented with cloves—and the cooks had to see that scullions were properly clad and washed up properly; leavings and dregs were no longer to be flung into the court-yard, but collected for the poor. 'No dogs were to be kept within the palace,' save a 'few spaniels for ladies'; other dogs were to be kept in kennels.[1] Henry himself was to be treated with greater formality: yeomen-in-waiting were to keep the passage outside his Privy Chamber 'clear of rascals, boys and others' who had been accustomed to stand and stare, beg and, if given the chance, steal.[2] Two yeomen were now to sleep on palliasses outside the king's door under torches that burned through the night, and only those specifically invited were to hawk and hunt with the king. The pages were told to moderate their language, not make a noise or argue when playing cards or chess, and stop the game if the king came in. They were not to gossip about the king's movements either, whether by day or night. Only the select gentlemen of the bedchamber were to help the king to dress: the grooms of the chamber were merely to bring in and, if necessary, warm the clothes.

The king now also had a new property, though he did not at present attend to it; Wolsey, aware that his stock was falling, had presented him with the great brick palace of Hampton Court, later to be one of Henry's favourite residences. In return, Wolsey, who still used his old residence, now also had Richmond, to the rage of those who remembered the days of Henry VII.

---

[1] See again Neville Williams, *The Royal Residences of Great Britain*, p. 66, for an admirable summary.
[2] *Ibidem.*

IV

While in January 1526 these domestic reforms were being devised at
Eltham, the French king, who had been moved from Italy to Spain,
had failed to escape and, fallen ill, was forced to accept stiff terms. In
February, Charles V visited him himself, with high ceremony, and the
Treaty of Madrid was agreed. It marked a great but an illusory triumph
for the emperor: Francis first swore to keep the peace, a thing very
uncongenial to one of his temperament; he also surrendered the whole
rich Duchy of Burgundy, Charles V's most coveted objective, for he
was heir to Duke Charles the Bold; he gave up the County of Charolais
and his claims over Flanders and Artois and the rest of the Low Countries, as well as all his rights in Italy—in Naples and Sicily and Milan.
He further promised to discharge the emperor's debt to the King of
England, and provide 500 men at arms and 10,000 foot to accompany
Charles V to Rome, when he went there formally to receive the imperial crown. As hostages for this treaty, Francis handed over his two
eldest sons, the Dauphin and the Duke of Orléans and in return the
emperor conditionally offered him his sister, Eleanor, the Dowager of
Portugal, with a great dower.

Henry disguised his anger, ordered a *Te Deum* in St Paul's and bonfires to be lit in London, but the Londoners were sceptical: the French
king, they said, would never keep his promise. And they were not far
out; Francis was brought to the frontier near Bayonne, where boats
were moored in the Bidassoa; as the king stepped into the French one,
his two sons were received by the Spaniards, but the moment Francis
got near the French shore, he leapt from the boat, mounted a horse and
rode flat out for St Jean de Luz and Bayonne. More ceremoniously,
the emperor moved down to Seville, where he married the Princess
Isabella of Portugal, the fabulous riches of whose family, drawn from
the East and Brazil, are still commemorated in Belém and Batalha.

Henry, furious as he might be, had no wish, as the cardinal put it,
to leave one war to enter another. But he now edged nearer to the
French, congratulating Francis on his release, and expressing 'stupe-
faction' at the harshness of the emperor's terms. Bonds made in captivity, he suggested, preaching to the converted, had small effect in conscience and law; soon Francis I declared that the lawyers of his realm
had pronounced that anyone making a covenant to his own hurt was
not bound, and that he had not the power to give away crown property without the consent of the peers and estates of the French realm.
By May 1526 he had formed the Holy League of Cognac—a town still
distinguished by its *Place François I*; it came to include the pope,

Florence, Venice and the exiled Sforza Duke of Milan, expelled by the Spaniards. Henry thought it worth while to become 'Protector'.

But Charles V remained supreme in Italy. He was unable to take over Burgundy, and in May his allies, the Medici, were expelled from Florence, but in July Bourbon captured Milan, and his ally, Cardinal Colonna, in connivance with the Spanish envoy Moncada, took Rome, defeated the Swiss guards and chased the Medici Pope into the Castle of St Angelo.

This crisis, however, coincided with a European catastrophe: the Turks, under Suleiman the Magnificent, to whom the French had appealed after Pavia, had long been on the attack. Their crescent tipped battle-standards, draped with human hair, had already in 1522 been planted on the great battlements of Rhodes, after an epic defence by the Knights. Now, in June 1526, the uniformed janissaries, with a discipline and firepower unparalleled in the West and backed by hordes of Sipahi cavalry, had utterly defeated the Hungarians near the Danube at Mohacs. King Lewis, brother-in-law of the emperor, had fled and died, smothered in a morass by his own armour. The flower of the Hungarian aristocracy, recklessly brave and incompetent, had been butchered in battle, and over 1,500 prisoners had been massacred before the Turkish pasha's tent, the head of the Bishop of Colocz impaled before it on a spear.

In Rome the warring Christians paused: the pope convened the cardinals, the ambassadors; begged them to unite. All he got was fair words; in October Henry, not very helpful, wrote that he had wept over the loss of Hungary; it had been caused, he said by the dissensions of Christendom: when the other princes could agree, he would not be behindhand to join a crusade and he exhorted Clement VII to 'bear up'. But 'happy be we', wrote Henry's envoy in Paris, 'who through your Grace's policy have not been drawn into the Italian League, which now, through their negligence, is come to nothing . . . they reckon the pope is ruined and the French are slack and have little care for their own interests and none for those of Christendom.'

Now, Henry calculated, was the time to 'mediate'. Events in Germany had also got beyond the emperor's control; important cities were turning Lutheran, and that year the Protestant princes had formed the League of Torgau, synchronized with the League of Cognac. Charles must be anxious for a settlement and Francis for his son's return. Something might well come out of it, if Henry and the cardinal made themselves felt; they therefore decided to begin converting the peace concluded with the French into an open alliance.

V

All that summer of 1526, writes Hall, the king had taken his pastime in hunting: during August he had been merry in the great park at Petworth, where the court were lavishly entertained; then at Chichester and Arundel, where he had 'liked much' the castle, and the nobility and gentry had flocked to attend him. He had then proceeded to Winchester, Ramsbury and the Kennet valley, up to Bicester in the midlands. He disliked the French alliance, which was unpopular both in the City, with its interests in the Netherlands, and among the populace, with their traditional hatred of the French. Wolsey complained in September that he somewhat wondered that his highness demurred at lending his ship, the *Peter Pumgarnet*, to the French ambassador, who had offered to rig and trim her himself.

The king was also very particular about the design of the newly minted and depreciated crowns of the rose. And he found time to renew his attack on Luther, who, the year before, had alleged that the king's book was not his own, but that of a crafty sophist, in particular of 'that monstrous and public offense to God and man, the Cardinal of York, that pest of your realm'.[1] Henry again declared that he had written the book himself, and that England was well rid of the apostate priests who had left his realm to 'wallow in lust' in Germany: he inveighed against Frau Luther, formerly a nun, and exhorted the reformer to give her up.

The king's own way of life remained lavish: his wine bill that autumn for claret alone being over £700, with £14 17s 0d for 'suppers and banquets' on board the *Minion* and *Mary Guildford*, bringing it from Bordeaux. In December he allowed his sister, the Duchess of Suffolk, an easy settlement of her old debt as Queen of France, letting her pay £500 a year 'each December at Calais' on a liability of over £19,000, the payments to cease at her demise, when hangings and jewellery she had taken would revert to the crown.

But Wolsey was now gambling everything on his pro-French policy, the great galleon of his gigantic fortune set for hard weather; he still lived in the utmost splendour at York Place and Hampton Court, and his great new foundation, Cardinal College at Oxford, was going up. 'With what forwardness,' wrote Dr John London at the end of 1526, 'this magnificent work prospereth, going forward winter and summer!' Already the lodgings on the south side of the great quadrangle were finished, save only the battling of the stone work, and the tower was already as high. Towards the street, the king's arms and the cardinal's

---

[1] *illud monstrum et publicum odium Dei et hominum Cardinalis eboracensis, pestis ille regni tui.*

were already most curiously set over the gate, Wolsey's arms in gold and colour. And already the foundations of the great hall were six feet high and those of the cloister at ground level: the builders had finished the vast kitchen, with all its promise.

The dean and canons, indeed, inaugurated centuries of good living that Christmas, based on larders, pastry houses, slaughter and fish houses—'so goodly done that no two of the best colleges in Oxford had rooms to compare with them'. All could even·be cleaned with running water, at need; and an army of workmen were quartered where the old Peckwater Inn had stood. Would to God, exclaimed London, there were as many masons as stuff already carried—Cotswold stone from Burford and Barrington, limestone from Headington; more than £4,500 had been spent that year. As for the Fellows, they were already thought the 'flower of my lords' university'. 'If you were a continued dweller in Oxford,' London concluded, paying the greatest compliment in the local vocabulary, 'and did take a watchful regard unto the young college, but yesterday in a manner begun, you would not think but that it was a very old foundation.' The university authorities, too, grovelled to the cardinal. They understand, they said, that he intended not only to augment the salaries of all the college fellows, but establish new lectureships for the university itself.

On these great enterprises Wolsey, the former Bursar of Magdalen, had set his heart: he alone knew how precarious was their future, as he felt the sands of royal favour begin to shift, and sensed the implacable hostility of the magnates, the City, the people and the aristocratic, pro-Habsburg, circles round the queen. She at least, he knew, was vulnerable and he decided it was now her ruin or his.

VI

The opportunity to strike came in February 1527, when the Bishop of Tarbes arrived to negotiate the betrothal of the Princess Mary to one of the French princes. For the French raised a difficulty, concerted in collaboration with Wolsey, doubting the status of the princess, and 'whether the marriage between the king and her mother, being his brother's wife, was good or no: of which the first motion grew much business or it were ended'.[1]

Catherine had tried in vain to restore relations with Charles V; and in April she was horrified to learn from the imperial ambassador that for six weeks an appalling threat, in Wolsey's mind since the previous

[1] Hall, II, p. 80.

year, had been mounting against her daughter and herself. 'The Cardinal,' he wrote, 'to crown his iniquities' was 'working to separate the King and Queen ... and the plot was so far advanced that a number of bishops and lawyers had already gathered secretly to declare her marriage null'.

CHAPTER X

'THE KING'S GREAT MATTER'

✿

ONE evening in April 1527, as the touchy French envoys returned
from dining with the Tailors' Guild, two boys were pitching
down rubbish out of a gutter and they splashed a servant of the
Count of Touraine; the French took the matter up; sent for the Lord
Mayor, forced him to put the entire household in prison and send the
boys to the Tower, where one of them died and the other 'fell lame'.
The episode set the City again by the ears against the cardinal, the
architect of the French alliance.

And, indeed, he was on a risky course, a prince of the cosmopolitan
Church, accustomed to talk with royalties as an equal, his one discernible principle the interests of the papacy, he was playing fast and
loose with the city's economic ties with the Netherlands, to get his
own back on Charles V. Just as Francis I was determined on revenge, so
Wolsey's personal hatred of the emperor encouraged him to take risks
beyond the resources of an island power. Henry was now more wary
after the failure in France and the first climb down he had had to make
in his life before City and country over the 'amicable loan'; but the
cardinal, equally well aware of the risks, was committed to his attack
on the queen, the preliminary to Henry's marriage to a princess of France.

And here the king's personal wishes contradicted the policy of his
minister; for Henry contemplated remarriage in the interest of the succession, not within his own princely caste, but for love. 'It is a wonderful thing,' wrote Cavendish, 'to consider the strength of Princes' wills
when they are bent to have their pleasure fulfilled ... and among other
things there is nothing that makes them more wilful than carnal love.'
It was one thing to arrange a collusive divorce for high dynastic reasons;
another to 'wrong' Charles V 'in blood' by displacing his aunt for a
young woman of no dynastic consequence at all.

One of Henry's discarded mistresses, Mary Boleyn, now married to
Sir William Carey, had a sister on whom the king had long had an
eye. Anne Boleyn had been a maid of honour at the Court of France,
and when she had returned to England in 1522, on the eve of the second

French war, she was about sixteen. Already, in 1524, Wolsey had been instructed by the king to prevent her marriage to young Lord Henry Percy, heir to the Duke of Northumberland, telling him not to entangle himself with 'that foolish girl yonder in Court, Anne Bulleine'; it was said that the king designed to marry her to her cousin, Piers Butler, the son of the Earl of Ormonde, but, according to Cavendish, rumours of a different reason had got about, and when Anne realized the king's inclination, she began to 'look very haughty and stout'.[1] She also abandoned her intrigue with the poet Sir Thomas Wyatt, who complained in a sonnet:

> There is written her fair neck round about
> Noli me tangere,[2] for Caesar's I am,
> And wild for to hold, though I seem tame.[3]

This 'wildness' was combined with vivacity, a violent temper and a formidable tongue: Pollard's quaint remark that 'her place in English history is due solely to the circumstance that she appealed to the less refined part of Henry's nature'[3] hardly does her justice; and aspects of her high-strung personality, with its touch of Irish blood, were inherited by her daughter, Elizabeth I.

Anne was now about twenty-two, pale, vivacious, with black, slanting, eyes, a full mouth, smooth black hair. She came of a family founded by a silk and wool mercer of London, who had been Lord Mayor and had acquired Blickling Hall in Norfolk; her grandfather had married Margaret Butler, co-heiress to the Irish Earl of Ormonde;[4] her father, Sir Thomas, had married a niece of the Duke of Norfolk. He had been keeper of the Foreign Exchange, and ambassador to Francis I; by 1522 he was Treasurer to the Household, with estates at Hever in Kent and in East Anglia, including timber mills at Rochford, Essex. He was rich and pliable, and in 1525 he had been made Viscount Rochford, when Henry Fitzroy had been created Duke of Richmond.

[1] Op. cit., p. 58.

[2] '*Do not touch me*,' quoted by Pollard, op. cit., p. 152. Sir Thomas Wyatt, 1503-42, born at Allington Castle, Kent, son of Sir Henry Wyatt, who had been involved in the political struggles of Richard III's time, when he was racked in the presence of the King himself, and vinegar and mustard poured down his throat. But, according to tradition, a cat brought him a pigeon daily while he was in the Tower, so that he would ever after 'make much of cats as other men will of spaniels'. Thomas was esquire to the Body to Henry VIII, and accompanied Russell to Italy in 1527, after a chance encounter. 1529, High Marshal of Calais; 1533 Privy Councillor; Sheriff of Kent, and from then employed on Embassies to the Emperor. He was thus an important man of affairs, though his enduring fame was to be as a poet. (See pp. 461-2.)

[3] *Henry VIII*, p. 154.

[4] Pollard states that she was Anne's mother; but she was her grandmother.

This honour may have been earned by services rendered by Sir Thomas and his daughter Mary, but the earldom of Wiltshire and Ormonde, in November 1529, and the lordship of the Privy Seal in 1530, were to be due to the king's infatuation for his younger daughter.

This cunning and methodical character knew how to exploit her success: Anne, too—not a Howard for nothing—determined to make the most of it. For Henry could feel strangely romantic passion; odd in anyone so self-indulgent and experienced, with an option on most of the women of the court.[1] In the way of romantics, it seems, he always hoped the next one would be better.

Such was the contradiction between the aims of king and cardinal as they combined to oust the queen. In the spring of 1527, after the Bishop of Tarbes had questioned Mary's legitimacy, the Bishop of Lincoln and 'other great clerks', writes Hall, 'had told the king that the marriage between him and the Lady Katherine, late wife of his brother, Prince Arthur, was not good but damnable.' In May 1527, Wolsey, as legate *a latere*, collusively and secretly summoned Henry to appear before him in Warham's archiepiscopal court of Canterbury, charged with living in sin with his brother's widow. The object was nothing less than to annul the king's marriage.

But no decision was yet taken; in May, Rome had been sacked by a famished and unpaid Imperialist army and Clement VII besieged, in fear of his life, in the Castello of St Angelo. 'The Almayns', writes Hall, had 'got the wall', and killed 'IIIC Swyshes of the Pope's Guard'; their commander, the renegade Duke of Bourbon, Constable of France, had been shot in the thigh and died in the Sistine Chapel, but the Germans had overrun and sacked the city, while Clement and the cardinals again fled by a secret passage to the Castello. It had been a European scandal; 'never was Rome so pilled neither by the Goths nor Vandals'; the Spanish and German soldiers had spoiled virgins and ravished wives, 'punished citizens by the privy members to cause them to confess their treasure' and 'had one riding like the pope with a whore behind him'. The Germans had set about undermining the massive Castello, though the river and the foundations of Hadrian's tomb defeated them. But by July the pope had been forced to surrender and was entirely in the imperialist's power; he could hardly confirm a sentence of nullity on the marriage of the aunt of Charles V. 'Which, Sire,' wrote Wolsey to his master, 'is a matter that must needs stir the

---

[1] Mackie's opinion that the story of his promiscuous amours is a myth (op. cit., 325) is not borne out by much contemporary opinion, and it was widely held on the continent that his way of life accounted for his domestic disappointments.

hearts of all good Christian Princes and People to . . . the repressing of such Tyrannous demeanour. And surely, Sire, if the Pope's Holiness fortune either to be slain or taken, as God forbid, it shall not a little hinder your Grace's affairs which I have now in hand.'[1]

Exhorted by Wolsey to rescue the Holy Father, Henry replied, 'What should I doo? My person nor my people cannot him reskue, but if my treasure may help him, take that which to you seemeth most convenient.'

So Wolsey chose this occasion to consolidate the alliance with the French. In July 1529, he set off with full credentials and tremendous pomp and 'barrells of gold' and came to Calais. Already, in April, he had induced Henry to write to Francis I in his own hand, thanking his '*Frère et parfait Amy*', for '*tels oyseaulx que m'avez envoiez pour le vol du heron*', and signing '*bon Frère, Cousin, Compère et Allye*'.[2] The cardinal had never been in better mind, lecturing his mission on how to deal with the French, who would, he warned them, be as familiar as if they were intimates, and assume that the visitors could follow their language. They should answer, of course, with equal confidence, in English; 'Riche,' he had joked, 'speak to them in Welsh.'

When the English got to Boulogne, they found a pageant at the gate, depicting 'a nun called Holy Church whom the Spaniards and Almayn's had violated, but whom the cardinal had rescued and set up again, and another of the pope lying under the emperor sitting in majesty, whom the cardinal pulled down'.

Wolsey knew also, that he had the French king at a disadvantage, for, as the Hungarian envoy had informed him, he was 'destitute of good captains and money', and that 'the said French king considering the captivity of the pope, the detention of his children with the emperor, with the apparance of attaining Italy by the imperials, [was] marvellous perplexed, and for sorrow in manner given to melancholy, not knowing how to do'.[3] So the cardinal had met Francis I at Amiens, guarded by Greek and Albanian mercenaries, 'drawn up in a great piece of green oats'. By August, Wolsey had concluded a full French alliance; he had even proceeded to Compiègne, where he planned to hold a conclave of cardinals as vicar general for the captive pope, a design which failed.

But, already, Sir Thomas More reported to the cardinal, the king was

---

[1] State Papers of Henry VIII, I, p. 189.

[2] His Brother and perfect Friend . . . for some birds (hawks) you have sent me for the pursuit of the heron.

[3] S.P., p. 204.

restive, concerned about the threat to English trade with the Low
Countries which the pro-French policy would bring about, saying he
had considered within himself 'how loathe the Low Countries were to
have any war with him', and commanding Lord Sandys to 'hold back
his troops at Guisnes', lest the Low Countries 'reaped the goods of the
English merchants' and began 'some business upon the English Pale'.
And the king's misgivings were shared by the City; Hall writes that
when Wolsey defended the French alliance 'some knocked the other
on the elbow and said softly "he lieth".' But it was the king's mounting
passion for Anne Boleyn that brought about Wolsey's doom.

II

For Henry was desperately in love. Writing to Anne Boleyn, he reveals
himself more intimately than in his tremendous public utterances when
cornered or when pushing through some political move. Nine of the
letters are in French; eight in English, full of passionate anxiety and
desire to be loved. He wanted total intimacy, proof against the world;
Anne Boleyn played him as if he were a great salmon.

The letters, now in the Vatican, many of them in Henry's own even
hand, were written from the summer of 1528 to May 1529, when
Anne had withdrawn from Court to silence scandal. Henry laments
her absence; when he thinks how long it must be, he finds the prospect
intolerable, were it not for his hope of her unchangeable affection; he
sends her his miniature set in jewels. In his next letter, his instinct for
self-preservation returns; her withdrawal seems 'a very small return for
the great love I bear you, to be kept at a distance from . . . the woman
in the world I value most'. 'Consider well, my mistress, how greatly
your absence grieves me: I hope it is not your will that it should be so,
but if I heard for certain that you yourself desired it, I could do no other
than complain of my ill fortune, and by degrees abate my great folly,
and so, for a want of time, I make an end of my rude letter.'[1]

Then he is concerned about Anne's health; if she would 'retire to
the Sussex side' (of the Thames), she would escape the 'distemper', by
which, so far, no women have been taken ill at the Court. 'I beg you,
my entirely beloved, not to frighten yourself nor to be too uneasy in
our absence, for wherever I am, I am yours. My, H. Rex. lovely.
(Ma H.R. aimiable).'

[1] *Pensez bien ma mestresse que l'absence de vous faict me grief, esperant qu'il n'est pas votre
volonté, que ainsi le soit, mais si je entendoy pur vérite que volontierement vous le desiriez, je non
puis mais faire si non plaindre ma mauvaise fortune en rebattant peu a peu ma grande folie.*

Anne was playing him beautifully; doubt, anxiety, appeal for protection, successfully applied. He could not indeed divine her intentions; put himself 'in great agony' whether they were to his disadvantage or not. 'I beseech you now,' he begged, 'with the greatest earnestness, to let me know your whole intention as to the love between us two. I must of necessity obtain this answer from you, having been for a whole year struck with the dart of love (*ayant esté plus q'ung année atteinte du dard d'amour*).' He even promised to make her his sole mistress, 'casting off all others that are in competition with you'; soon he was promising to 'outdo her in loyalty of heart', signing '*H autre (A.B.) ne cherche R*, (H. no other (A.B.) seeks Rex).' The great fish was nearer the bank.

By September 1528 he had better news. 'And then I trust within a while after to enjoy that which I have so long longed for. . . . No more to you, at this present, myne awne darling, for lake of time, but that I would you were in myne arms, or I in yours, for I think it long since I kyst you . . . written after the killing an hart, at XI of the clock; minding with God's grace, mightily tymely to kill another, by the hand of him which I trust shortly shall be yours.' He sent her the venison; 'some fleshe representing my name, which is hart's fleshe for Henry, prognosticating that hereafter, God willing, you must enjoy some of mine, which, if he please, I wolde were now.' He sent another fresh buck killed with his own hand, 'hoping when you eat of it, you will think on the hunter'.

Still she kept him in anticipation, her absence 'wounding him more deeply than either words or writing' could 'express'. Then she was ill, and he would willingly bear half her sickness himself, in particular as it meant more of the 'tedious absence which had already given him so much uneasiness and were likely to give him more'. 'I pray God he would deliver me,' he exclaimed, 'from that troublesome tormenter.' His most trusted doctor was away, but he sent her 'the second, and the only one left'. The sweating sickness had struck his own household, but, thank God, they were all recovered. And when plans to meet were again thwarted—not, of course, through her fault—'I trust shortly,' he wrote, 'our meetings shall not depend upon other men's light handlings but upon your awne'.

They did meet, and the next letter came right from the heart: 'Myne awne sweetheart, this shall be to advertize you of the great ellingness [loneliness] that I have held since your departing . . . me thinketh the time longer . . . than I was wont to do a whole fortnight.' But he looked forward to their next encounter, and his book (another against Luther) was going well, 'in writing whereof I have spent about four hours this day', so that he had a headache. He signed, 'wishing myself (specially of an evening) in my sweetheart's arms, whose pretty duckys [breasts] I trust shortly to kiss.'

The salmon was practically gaffed.

Thus obsessed with Anne Boleyn, Henry had already cynically undermined Wolsey's whole policy. He had supplemented the official mission sent by Wolsey to Rome, in the charge of his new protégé Stephen Gardiner to expedite the divorce, by sending out his own confidential secretary, Knight, as well; he was to obtain a different dispensation for him to marry Anne, in spite of having made her sister his mistress and so contracted a prohibited relationship in canon law.

'I do now send you the copy,' he apparently wrote, 'of another [document] which no man doth know, but the which, I am sure, you will never disclose to no man living, for any craft that the cardinal or any other can find; willing you to keep it secret . . . desiring you to use all ways . . . to get access to the Pope's person . . . and in so doing I shall reckon it the highest service you ever did me.' And, of course, he must get absolved from the marriage to Catherine as well; '*pauca sapienti*', he concluded—'few words to the wise'. He thus double-crossed Wolsey's whole policy of a royal French marriage. The cardinal scotched the clumsy manoeuvre, but he knew, on his return from France in November, that Anne Boleyn had probably won, and that behind her were her Howard and Boleyn relations, avid for his ruin.

That December, the pope had been allowed to escape to Orvieto, thus rendering Wolsey's plan for a conclave superfluous. He was now pacifying the English envoys, hinting that, if Henry just took a new wife, the accomplished fact could be condoned. 'His Holiness,' Gardiner reported from Orvieto, 'is *Cunctator Maximus*', the greatest delayer. 'On the morrow we returned to the Pope's Holiness and spoke roundly unto him . . . and to that point that the King's Highness would do without him. His Holiness said he would it were done; and, to the other words, nothing but sighed and wiped his eyes and said he would he could help.' He had not been able to decide which cardinal to send to England, and 'wold that he might send noon'. Now he at last commissioned Wolsey and Cardinal Lorenzo Campeggio—long a protégé of Wolsey's, an expert cadger for English benefices and absentee Bishop of Salisbury who knew the English Court—to try the king's case in England. For in July a French army under Lautrec had mastered Northern Italy and was advancing south against the demoralized Imperial army, now withdrawn from Rome to defend Naples from the hired galleys of Andrea Doria. Although opposition from the City had forced Wolsey to call off the war, officially declared against the Low Countries in January 1528, the Anglo–French position was now stronger.

But Campeggio's power was limited: he was an expert in canon law, a *rusé* procrastinator, instructed to take no decision without reference to the pope, who would review it in the light of French or Imperialist success. He also suffered from gout and took over three months to get to Calais by October 1528.

III

Henry was now so entirely devoted to the lady that, soon after the put-up summons from Wolsey and the Archbishop in 1527, he had told Catherine they must separate, and, indeed, had long 'abstained from her bed'. The queen had replied with Iberian reproaches and tears; defied the Councillors; refused to leave the Court; declared firmly that she was Henry's lawful wife. She had also smuggled out a letter to Charles V at Valladolid, demanding that he intervene at once—which he had done.

Such was the impasse which Campeggio found as he moved painfully to London through the autumn countryside; he had now to calculate that the galleys of Andria Doria had been bought off from Naples, that the French army, rotten with plague and fever, had surrendered, and that Genoa, vital to their supply and of great importance to Charles V, had now, under pressure from Doria, changed sides. The two cardinals first suggested a compromise: could not Catherine retire, in the greatest comfort, to a nunnery, on Henry's guarantee that the Princess Mary would remain, after any male heirs, in the succession? The queen remained adamant, all her religious and dynastic feelings outraged; such hypocrisy, she said, would ensure Henry's damnation and her own. The legate had to report that a trial was inevitable, and that, in England, it would not be free. As arranged, he advised Clement in the last resort to revoke the case to Rome.

In November 1528, Henry summoned the nobility, Lord Mayor, Aldermen, principal merchants and lawyers to the great hall of his palace at Bridewell, where he harangued them. He had reigned, he said, for twenty years with victory, wealth and honour, but 'when we remember our mortality, that we must die, then we think that all our doings in our lifetime are clearly defaced . . . if we leave you in trouble. For if our true heir be not knowen at the time of our death, see what shall succeed to you and your children'; they had heard of the 'mischiefs and manslaughters' of old times. The 'great clerks' had told him that he had long lived in sin: 'Think, you my lords, that these words touch not my body and soul?' If the clergy could pronounce the queen his lawful wife, he would be thankful—she was of high lineage and of 'most gentleness and buxumnes'; if not, he could only lament his misfortune and lack of true heirs. 'These be the sores,' he concluded, 'that vex my mind; these be the pangs that trouble my conscience and for these griefs I seek a remedy.' The great assembly, packed to door and window, were impressed. But it was a gloomy Christmas at Greenwich in 1528; the queen very melancholy, amid feasting and jousts, masques and disguisings, though Campeggio's son was made a knight.

Through the spring of 1529 Stephen Gardiner and his colleagues were still pushing the king's interests with Clement VII; Anne Boleyn wrote to 'good Mr Stephyns', that she wanted no more false hopes, 'which do put me in more pain, *and they that are partaking with me*, as you well know'; she trusted that 'a hard beginning would make a better ending', and sent them all cramp rings. But, in May, her cousin, Francis Brian, was writing to Henry himself that 'neither fair means nor foul' would serve with the pope; 'if the cardinal feels aggrieved at the truth, let him'. But he dared not, he said, write the truth to his cousin Anne.

Campeggio had now been in England for months; there was nothing for it but a high drama at Blackfriars, with the cardinal legates in judgment and the king and queen in court. By June 15, 1529, Henry, without his queen, had come by water to Anne's father Lord Rochford's steps, waited for the tide, and gone down to Greenwich: 'I much fear,' wrote the French ambassador, 'for some time past the King has come very near Mademoiselle Anne, therefore you will not be surprised if they want to hasten (the trial), *car si le ventre croiste, tout sera gasté.*'[1]

The next day, Catherine saw Campeggio, who was in bed, and solemnly swore that in all her married life with him she had only slept with Arthur seven times and without effect.

On Friday, 18th, the two scarlet-robed princes of the Universal Church, hatted and gloved and ringed, moved majestically to their chairs of state behind a railed and carpeted table. Henry appeared by proxy; the queen, supported by four bishops and a great train of her ladies, made her grave Spanish obeisance to the court. 'A poor ignorant woman', unversed in the law, she appealed, on excellent advice, against any case pending in Rome being taken in London.[2]

---

[1] 'For if she gets in the family way, everything will be spoilt.' L. & P., IV, III, 5679.

[2] She had been allowed to consult the Spanish humanist Vives, to whom she had long been a generous patron; but, to her anger, he had refused to defend her in Court; he

Three days later, the king himself attended the court beneath a cloth of estate on the legate's right; the queen was on their left. 'Henry, King of England,' rang out the unprecedented summons, 'Come into the court!' whereat, says Cavendish, the king answered and said, 'Here.'[1] The queen made no answer to the summons, but rose and swept round the whole court to kneel before the king. 'Legates of the See Apostolic,' Henry began, 'I most heartily beseech you to ponder my mind and intent, which is to have a final end for the discharge of my conscience, for every good Christian man knoweth what pain and what unquietness he suffereth that hath a conscience grieved. . . .' No prince had a better queen, but he was deeply troubled in conscience: he could scarce study anything profitable to his realm and people.

In her metallic accent—Cavendish says 'broken English'—the queen contradicted him flatly: 'I take God to witness,' she said, 'that I have been a true, humble and obedient wife . . . and when you had me first, I take God to be my judge, I was a true maid, without touch of man.' Striking at his most sensitive spot, she concluded 'and whether this be true or not I put it to your conscience'.

Henry gazed straight before him, his conscience under control, while the queen, still on her knees, begged him to consider her honour, her daughter's and his own. He was not interested.

She rose, made her final reverence; then, an impassive Spanish dynast, unexpectedly took her way straight out of the court ignoring a further summons, her women applauding about her. Had the matter been decided by them, wrote du Bellay, the king would have lost the battle, for they 'did not fail to encourage the queen on her entrance and departure by their cries'. 'On, on,' she said, 'it maketh no matter. It is an indifferent court to me, therefore I will not tarry.'

At the next session Catherine was pronounced contumacious; and Warham cited signatures of the bishops who supported the king's case, including John Fisher of Rochester. 'No sir, not so, under your correction,' interrupted Fisher, 'for you have not mine, no.' 'But you were fully resolved,' countered Warham, 'that I should subscribe your name and put your seal myself.' 'All which,' replied Rochester, 'under your correction, my lord, is not true.' He then denounced the divorce entirely; no power could dissolve the marriage, human or divine and he would die for his opinion; he produced a booklet he had written. 'The affair of Rochester,' reported Campeggio to the pope, rather im-

---

retired, after six weeks in prison, to Bruges, where he wrote his famous Treatise on Education dedicated to a new patron, King John of Portugal.
[1] p. 128.

pressed, 'was quite unexpected and unforeseen and has left everyone in wonder. You already know what sort of man he is.'

The court turned to examine witnesses on the main point. Various elderly gentlemen were called; Thomas, Marquis of Dorset, thought Arthur had been about fifteen; a boy of good sanguine complexion, he had probably used the princess as his wife. Sir Anthony Willoughby gave directer evidence: 'Willoughby, bring me a cup of ale,' the boy had said in the morning, 'for I have tonight been in the midst of Spain.' 'My masters,' he had also boasted, 'it is good pastime to have a wife'; and when told at breakfast 'Sir, you look well after the matter', he had replied, 'Well enough, for one that has been in Spain.' At Ludlow, too, Sir William Thomas of Caernarven, had often conducted the prince in his nightgown to the princess's door: another witness, drawing a longer bow, thought that Arthur had never been the same boy after his marriage; it had caused his decline. Mountjoy, on the other hand, refused to commit himself, and the Bishop of Ely could say nothing of the words used because of the 'tumult'; he doubted if the marriage had been consummated; the queen, on her conscience, had repeatedly denied it.

The case dragged on; all concerned unaware that a new French army had been routed at Landriano, and that on June 29, 1529, pope and emperor had been reconciled and signed the Treaty of Barcelona. Worse still, for the cardinal, Margaret, Regent of the Netherlands, and Louise of Savoy, mother of Francis I, were in fact planning to meet at Cambrai to make a general peace, on the basis that Charles V give up his claims to Burgundy and the French their Italian demands, and that the French princes held as hostages should be restored. The English were to be left out: moreover, Clement VII had long decided, under pressure from Charles V, and on Campeggio's advice, to bring back the case to Rome, and, by mid-July he had revoked it.

Henry now sent the two dukes to require the legates to make an end; but Campeggio knew what to do: in eloquent Latin, he suavely announced that no cases could be tried during the summer vacation at Rome; naturally the Court in London came under the same rules, and the case must be adjourned till October. Nothing was said about revocation, but everyone knew what was implied.

Suffolk now 'gave a great clap on the table' and exclaimed 'with a hault countenance' that 'it was never merry in England while we had Cardinals amongst us'—a traditional remark, paralleled in Langland's fourteenth century *Piers Plowman*, '*The country is the curseder that Car-*

dinals comen in.' And Wolsey is reported to have answered, 'Sir, of all men within this realm, ye have least cause to dispraise Cardinalls; for if, I, poor Cardinall, had not bine, you should have at this present no head upon your shoulders, wherewith you might make any such bragge.' He referred, of course, to the time when he had saved Suffolk from Henry's wrath after he had hastily married the king's sister. 'You know best,' he concluded, 'what friendship I have showed you, which I have never revealed to any person alive before now. . . .' And therewith, writes Cavendish, the duke gave over the matter. But he had pronounced the epitaph of the mediaeval Church in England.

IV

Wolsey maintained all his state, only those knowledgeable at Court knew how precariously.[1] By July 22, 1529, he knew that the king's case had been revoked to Rome; and early in August, that the 'Ladies' Peace' had been ratified at Cambrai. His whole policy, domestic and foreign, was in ruins. Like Neville Chamberlain, Wolsey had gambled on a foreign policy that had not made sense, running contrary to the basic interests of the country.

Henry was forced to a re-appraisal of the facts: in September he was at Grafton, near Stony Stratford, and received both legates. He was gracious enough to Campeggio when he came to leave, but Wolsey was now told that the king was out hunting and would see him in London. Henry never set eyes on his great minister again. And Campeggio was seen off with insults; Henry had set the customs officers at Calais to search his luggage and the legate complained of their officiousness. How could he help it, wrote the king, 'if certain porters of ours had been rough'? Why take offence? 'As to your legateship, no wrong has been done to me or mine': Campeggio had only authority to conclude the case; failing that, he now had no standing. 'You may infer from this,' wrote the king, 'that my subjects are not well pleased that my case has come to no better conclusion.'

Then, early in October 1529, Henry struck Wolsey down. The

[1] In May and June 1529, all unknowing, his dependents in the West had sent up their tributes: four Avon salmon and nineteen lobsters from the prior of Christ Church; a great horse, a peacock, forty rabbits, six herons and two dozen quails from Sir Giles Strangeways; Thomas Trenchard had produced herons and cygnets and shoveller ducks; Master Arundel, beeves and a saddled nag; Sir John Rogers, four pheasants and six gulls. Master Philips, two kids, a peacock, a peahen, a moor hen—the last too much, one would think, even for Tudor taste. The Mayor of Salisbury had sent beeves and muttons; the Mayor of Poole a tun of white wine; the Controller, a barrel of salad oil and eight conger eels; the Customer, a hogshead of claret; the town of Wareham another, and the vicar of Canford two lambs, four capons and two geese. L. and P., IV, III, 5746.

antique writ of *praemunire*, revived in the case of Hunne, was issued against the cardinal, on the ridiculous charge that he had abused the powers of the legatine court, set up by authority of the pope, to the prejudice of the king. Soon the whole Church of England was to come under the charge, as the first step in its total subjugation, for Henry was now determined to 'possess himself of a sovereignty which none of his predecessors had ever supposed he had a right to, and which intruded itself into spheres of action and thought that had never been invaded'.[1]

Wolsey still affirmed that he would 'discharge him of all these light flea bitings and flies' stingings', and would yet 'so handle the matter that he should reign in more authority than ever he did and all quake and repent that had meddled against him'. But the charges mounted up, backed by clamour against his great *orgueil*—his odious pride; all the monstrous display and insatiable avarice. He was accused of impoverishing the nobility and the king's servants, 'yea, and the whole community, like for many years to be irrecoverable'. What mighty treasure the King's grace had at his entry! Why was it minished now?' He was blamed for the inflation—'the great decay and enorme ruin, scarceness and poverty'; for 'advancing his own high and prodigal palm'.[2]

[1] Sir D. Lindsay Keir, *Constitutional History of Modern Britain, 1485–1937*, p. 50.

[2] The hatred he provoked is vividly expressed in *Rede me and be not wrothe*, written by Protestant refugees in Strasbourg in 1528. A bogus coat of arms is thus described:

> 'Of the proude Cardinall this is the shelde
> Borne up betwene two angels off Sathan.
> The sixe bloody axes in a bare felde
> Sheweth the cruelte of the red man,
> Whiche hathe devoured the beautiful swan,
> Mortall enemy unto the whyte lion
> Carter of Yorcke, the vyle butchers sonne.
>
> The sixe bulles heddes in a felde blacke
> Betokeneth hys stordy seriousnes
> Wherefore the godly lyght to put abacke
> He bryngeth in hys dyvlisshe darcknes.
> The bandog in the middes doth expresse
> The mastif cure bred in Ypswich towne
> Gnawynge with his teth a kynges crowne.
>
> The cloube signifieth playne, hys tirranny
> Covered over with a Cardinals hatt
> Wherein shalbe fulfilled the prophecy
> Aryse up Iacke and put on thy salatt
> For the tyme is come of bage and walatt,
> The temporal chevalry thus throwen downe
> Whereby, priest, take hede and beware thy croune.'

See Edward Arber, *Reprints*, Vol. I, p. 19.

He still came at Michaelmas to hold his Court as Chancellor in full pomp; and when Norfolk and Suffolk demanded the surrender of the Great Seal, he insisted on seeing the king's own signature for their authority. But when he saw it, he broke down, and soon he had lost half his animation; the greatest example, wrote du Bellay, 'of fortune that one could see', pleading his case in bad rhetoric, for 'his heart and tongue failed him completely'. He wept and prayed to the ambassador to induce Francis I to intervene and 'withdraw his faithful servant from the gate of hell'. He expected, at least, perpetual imprisonment.

Henry took good care not to see him. 'Mademoiselle de Boulen,' the ambassador continued, 'has made her Friend promise that he will never give Wolsey a hearing, for she thinks he could not help having pity on him.' Even the dukes could not manage the king, although, as du Bellay shrewdly observed, 'these lords intend, after [the cardinal] is dead or ruined, to impeach the state of the Church, and take all their goods. . . . I expect they will do fine miracles.'

Already the ambassador was pointedly ignored, and complained himself that he cut a poor figure, made to ride a mule, ostensibly for fear of the plague, 'which had visited the animals', presumably the horses.

V

That autumn Henry summoned the famous Reformation parliament; it was to last, intermittently, for seven years, the instrument of sweeping administrative, social and religious change. There had not been a parliament since 1523; Wolsey had done without them, and they were still only 'an occasional if majestic expedient'.[1] Now from all over England came the knights and burgesses, representing, along with the nobility, the great interests that were to dominate the country for centuries. Many of their families were to be long established, some famous —a Sacheverell from Leicester; a Throckmorton from Warwick; a Sir Giles Alington; a Sir Roger Mynors; Thomas Wentworth; Sir Roger Townshend from Norfolk; Sir Edward Lyttleton; Sir Nicholas Wadham from Somerset; a Strangeways from Dorset; a Sir Richard Grenfelde (Grenville) from Cornwall.

The burgesses came up from the Cinque Ports, from Yarmouth, Colchester and Oxford; from the midland towns; from Guildford and Lewes. There were members from New Sarum and Old Sarum; for Ludgershall, Wootton Basset and Marlborough; they came up from Worcester and Ludlow and the Welsh border, and from far-away

[1] D. Lindsay Keir, op. cit., p. 38.

Newcastle and Carlisle; from Dorchester, Bridport and Chard; a
Treffry from Bodmin, a Tredenick from Lostwithiel.

Numbering less than 300 members from thirty-seven counties and
about a hundred boroughs, elected by forty-shilling freeholders in the
counties and by an oligarchy in the towns, they 'showed no desire
whatever to wrest the conduct of Government from (Henry's) hands'.[1]
They came, rather, intent on their local concerns; with the economy of
the realm; with the 'decay of husbandry; with weights and measures,
and 'cloth not to be exported unwrought'; with conveyance of coin
out of the realm and merchant adventurers who took 'too great
brokes'. They were concerned about heresy, but, outside London,
their grievances against the clergy were generally more practical than
doctrinal; against excessive fines for probates and mortuary dues, abbots keeping tanneries and trading in wool; non-resident pluralists;
'things', Hall alleges, 'which before might no wise be touched, nor yet
talked of by no-man, except he be made an heretic and lose all he had,
for the bishops were Chancellors, and had all rule about the King'.

But the new chancellor was a layman, Sir Thomas More; and with
Henry in his seat royal in the Parliament Chamber he made an elegant
oration. The king, like a good shepherd, he said, saw the need for
reform; and just as among a great flock some were rotten and faulty,
and the good shepherd sent them away, so he had now rid them of the
'great wether which is of late fallen, as you all know'. Wolsey had
craftily and untruly juggled with the king, but 'His Grace's sight was so
quick and penetrable that he . . . saw through him', and according to
his desert, the cardinal had been given 'gentle correction'.

The Commons then adjourned to their own place and elected
Thomas Audley, attorney to the Duchy of Lancaster, as Speaker in
place of More. By December 1529, they had produced an immense list
of Wolsey's alleged misdemeanours, but Henry allowed him, in return
for abject submission, to regain the archbishopric of York and substantial revenues. Soon the Commons were declaring their grievances
against the Church, so that Warham and the other bishops 'both
frowned and grunted',[3] and Fisher of Rochester exclaimed 'for God's
sake see what a realm the Kingdom of Boheme was, and when the
Church went down, then fell the glory of the Kingdom'. The Commons were furious, accusing him of calling them heretics and 'no
Christians, as ill as Turkes and Sarisans'.

After his disgrace, Wolsey had at once set about putting his immense

[1] Keir, op. cit., p. 39.
[1] Hall, II, 167.

possessions in order. Everything now belonged to the king; the 'goodly rich stuffs' were heaped on long tables in the gallery of York House; the cloth of gold and silver, the elaborate tapestries, the gorgeous copes, were hung along the walls. An incredible wealth of gold and silver plate was displayed, all carefully inventoried; chairs in black velvet, embroidered with cardinal's hats and double crosses in crimson satin and Venetian gold; curtains of 'changeable sarcenet'; fifteen great beds, fifty-nine counterpanes of satin and damask, quilts 'with my lord's arms', quantities of feather beds, mattresses, down pillows and blankets furred with white lamb. There were black silk pillowcases embroidered with fleur-de-lys, sixty carpets from Venice; even a close chair in comfortable black velvet, specially sent to the king.

As the cardinal left for Esher, a small house in Surrey belonging to the see of Winchester, his treasurer condoled that he would be sent to the Tower. 'Is that the good counsel and comfort,' asked Wolsey, 'that you can give your master in adversity? . . . I would you should know that it is untrue. . . . Though it hath pleased the King to take my house ready furnished at this time . . . I would all the world to know that I have nothing but it is his of right.' He also remarked, wrily, referring to the dun cow cognisance of the Tudors and the bull of the Boleyns,

> When Cowe doth ride the Bull,
> Then Priest beware thy skull.

But Henry was not yet decided to destroy this valuable servant and sent him a ring as token of good will: the cardinal, remarking that he had nothing but the clothes on his back, presented Henry, in return, with his 'poor Foole . . . I trust', he said, 'he will accept him—for he is for a nobleman's pleasure . . . worth a thousand pounds.' But the poor Foole 'took on like a tyrant' at being sent off; it needed six tall yeomen to convey him to Court, where Henry was delighted with him.

Two other more important characters now gravitated to the king's service. Thomas Cromwell, already well established, was deeply concerned for his career; standing in the window at Esher, the hard-bitten adventurer was seen to weep; he had a prayer book in hand and was saying mattins, 'which had bine a strange sight in him afore'.[1] 'Why, Mr Cromwell,' said Cavendish, 'what meaneth this dole. Is my lord in any danger?' But Cromwell was not concerned for the cardinal: 'I am like to lose all that I have ever laboured for,' he replied; he was 'disdained for his master's sake', and an 'evil name, once gotten', was 'not

[1] Cavendish, op. cit., p. 170.

lightly put away.' 'But this much,' he concluded, 'I will say to you, that I will this afternoon, when my master hath dined, ride to London and to the Court, where I will *either make or marre* or ever I come again.' And so one who was to be the greatest administrator of Tudor England passed from the cardinal's service on his way to the king's.

With Henry's approval, and at the last moment, Thomas Cromwell now became Member for Taunton in Somerset in the new Parliament, a seat in the gift of the see of Winchester where Wolsey's influence had long been decisive, and subject to the local influence of Sir William Paulet, whose family was to do well out of Cromwell's attack on the Church. Wolsey was now begging the king, 'humbly upon his knees with weeping eyes', to take care of his foundations at Oxford and Ipswich and imploring Cromwell's help; he had been so short of breath, he wrote, that he had nearly died; 'if you love your life come hither . . . forsake me not in my extreme need'. He must somehow, he kept saying, get the favour of Anne Boleyn.

Cromwell could hardly do that for him, but he defended his master so brilliantly in Parliament that he greatly increased his standing in the Commons.

Stephen Gardiner, who had also begun his career in Wolsey's service, had also passed to the king's.[1] He had been employed to further the divorce in Italy, and since 1528 had been one of the royal secretaries. By 1531 he would attain the great bishopric of Winchester. Strictly orthodox and cunning in the pursuit of power, he would represent the conservative aspect of the Henrician Reformation, suffer imprisonment under Edward VI, and, under Mary, enforce a Catholic reaction.

By Christmas the cardinal was so ill that Henry sent his own physician, Dr Buttes, to examine him: 'Have you seen yonder man?' he asked, 'how do you like him?' Dr Buttes thought the illness in part psychological; 'Sir,' he replied, 'if you would have him dead, I warrant he will be dead within these four days if he receive not comfort from you, and Mistress Anne.' 'Marry,' exclaimed Henry, remembering past services, 'God forbid that he should die! I pray you, Master Buttes,

[1] 1483–1555; the son of a cloth-weaver at Bury St Edmunds, he had studied law at Trinity Hall, Cambridge, where he became a Fellow. He became a tutor in Norfolk's household and private secretary to Wolsey. 1525, Master of Trinity Hall: 1529, Archdeacon of Norwich: 1531, Bishop of Winchester; Ambassador in France and Germany. He wrote *de Vera Obedientia* vindicating the King's authority against the Pope, but opposed Cromwell's Protestant policies. After the death of Henry VIII he was imprisoned, but became Chancellor under Mary. In 1554 he had the statute *de Heretico Comburendo* re-enacted. On his death-bed is said to have remarked *'negavi cum Petro, exivi cum Petro, sed nondum flevi cum Petro'*. (I have denied with Peter, and gone out with Peter, but I have not yet wept with Peter.) He was buried at Winchester, where his chantry remains.

go again unto him; for I would not lose him for twenty thousand pounds!' He told Buttes to accept no fee, and sent Wolsey another ring; even persuaded Anne, his 'good sweetheart', to send him a gold tablet. Wolsey cheered up, though his own Venetian doctor, Augustini, applied leeches and 'vomitive electuaries'.

VI

In the spring of 1530 the cardinal went reluctantly north to his diocese of York, restored to a see 'long destitute', as Henry wrote, 'of an archbishop there resident'. He still had a hundred and sixty persons in his train and twelve carts for his own stuff, and he distributed ample bounty at Peterborough for Maundy Thursday, when he washed the feet of fifty-nine poor men, the number signifying his own age. The king even wrote specially to Lord Dacre to show him a benevolent mind, according to his dignity: Henry, it seemed, might allow him an honourable retirement, in particular as he had seized York Place and most of Wolsey's colossal wealth.

But the king was besotted with Anne Boleyn: Sir John Russell told that shrewd Savoyard lawyer, Eustace Chapuys, the new ambassador from the emperor, that the lady had been so furious with him for defending Wolsey that she had cut him for three days; he still thought the cardinal might make a come-back, 'considering his courage and ambition', but for Anne's being so accomplished a mistress of intrigue.

But Wolsey played into her hand; though surrounded by spies, he found the habit of power politics ineradicable. Soon he was approaching the French king and Charles V; writing to Rome; up to no good. Then the king fell in a rage with the Council—slow, tortuous, Norfolk; hearty, crooked, Suffolk; subservant secretary Gardiner and the rest: 'The Cardinal,' he shouted, was 'a better man than any of them for transacting business', and repeating this twice, he left the room.

So the Norfolk–Boleyn interest went into action; Anne, herself, weeping and 'regretting her lost honour', even threatening to leave the king. Henry prayed her, with tears, not to speak of the affair, but nothing would calm her but the cardinal's arrest.

Up at Cawood, in early November, in the archiepiscopal palace near York, Wolsey was preparing for his installation: able and irrepressible, he had again been living in great splendour and had become vastly popular in the north, that stronghold of the old religion. So grand and cosmopolitan a figure must have greatly impressed the diocese; he insisted, however, that his enthronement was not to be at all pompous

—no processional carpet; he would go, in all humility, on foot, 'in the raumpes of his hosen'.

It was too late; the spies, the intrigues and the importunities had done their work; and the pope, it was said under Wolsey's influence, had now officially forbidden Henry to marry the lady, or anyone else, while his case was pending. Informed of this late in October 1530, the infuriated king ordered Wolsey's arrest for high treason.

It is recorded that, on All Souls' Eve, Wolsey was at dinner when a strange accident occurred: as his company rose from table, Dr Augustini's great gown of 'boisterous' Venetian velvet overset the cardinal's heavy cross which struck the chaplain, Dr Bonner, on the head. 'Hath it drawn any blood?' asked Wolsey, as they all stood aghast: it had, and he shook his head, saying '*malum omen*'—ill luck.[1]

On Friday, November 4th, again at the end of dinner, when Wolsey was 'at his fruites' in his private room, the young Earl of Northumberland, whose marriage, as Lord Henry Percy, to Anne Boleyn Wolsey had scotched, and Sir Walter Walche, of the King's Privy Chamber with a concourse of gentry, entered the great hall at Cawood, having seen to it that the gates were secured behind them. Told of their arrival, Wolsey appeared imperturbably urbane: he was sorry he had dined, that there was not enough fish. He then bade the earl hearty welcome; led him to the big fire, remarked how well he had followed his advice and kept his father's servants about him, for he recognized some of them.

Horribly embarrassed, the earl managed to whisper, his hand on the cardinal's arm, 'My lord, I arrest you for high treason.' Wolsey stood stock still, speechless. Then demanded to see written authority: but Walche had just secured Dr Augustini by brisker methods, saying: 'Go in traitor, or I shall make thee.' And when Walche appeared, Wolsey, recognizing a Gentleman of the Privy Chamber, gave in: 'Spare me not,' he said, 'I will obey the King's will.' He then surrendered his keys, while the treacherous Venetian doctor, tied to a horse, was bundled off to London, to give evidence on the correspondence with the pope.

Next day, the cardinal rode to Pontefract amid the lamentations of his household and the townsfolk: he feared to go to the castle, where

[1] Cavendish, op. cit., pp. 234 ff. His eyewitness account, a masterpiece of Tudor English, on which this description is based, was not printed until 1641, when certain interpolations were added as indirect propaganda against Archbishop Laud, and it is argued that this incident was taken from a similar episode in Laud's life; but Holmes's edition, here quoted, based upon a manuscript owned by the antiquary Stowe and collated with two others of Tudor date by Dr Christopher Wordsworth, includes the story.

Richard II had met his fate, 'and lie there and die like a beast'. He was conducted to the abbey. From there he was brought to Doncaster, and so to the Earl of Shrewsbury's lodge at Sheffield Park, where he was civilly entertained for nearly three weeks, while the evidence was further sifted in London. Would he 'care to kill a hart'? they asked, but he no longer cared for hunting; elderly and ill, he was now 'taken with a thing about his stomach as cold as a whetstone'; then with dysentery. And now they brought him worse news, disguised as good. Sir William Kingston, Constable of the Tower, had arrived himself with twenty-four of the royal guards. . . . 'Gentle Mr Kingston', they said, would conduct him to the king: he had always said he wanted to come before the king's majesty. But Wolsey knew what that meant: 'Mr Kingston, Mr Kingston,' he reiterated, and gave a great sigh, having, it seems, also some superstition that he would die at Kingston-on-Thames. So when the constable knelt in greeting, he bade him leave the kneeling to him —'a wretche replete with misery'. A polite message from Henry produced the reflex—'I trust he is in health and merry', but the cardinal was now too ill to move. Kingston, he said, was bringing him to a 'fool's paradise': 'I know what is provided for me.' That night the dysentery grew appallingly worse, and when, at last, he was brought to Leicester Abbey, he could hardly sit his mule. They were received by torchlight in the November dusk; as Kingston helped him up the stairs, he had 'not felt so heavy a burden in his life': 'Father Abbot,' said the cardinal, 'I am come to leave my bones among you.'

It took Wolsey nearly two days more to die; harried by demands from the king to reveal £1,500 he had salted away. Clear-headed to the last, he knew he could not live; if the flux and fever did not clear, he said, either excoriation of the entrails, frenzy, or death must ensue, and the best of these was death.[1] 'If I had served God,' he said, 'as diligently as I have done the King, he would not have given me over in my grey hairs'; as for Henry, he was a prince of royal courage and princely heart, and rather than miss any part of his will and pleasure, he would endanger the loss of half the realm: 'therefore, Mr Kingston,' he concluded, 'be advised what you put in his head for you shall never put it out again.'

And so died Thomas Wolsey, Cardinal Archbishop of York, at eight of the clock, as he said he would, and was buried, the day after, by torchlight, at four in the morning. Such was the catastrophe of a most

---

[1] It is unlikely that he took, or was given, poison; though Dr Augustini was rather rapidly restored to favour, having given a bond to the King for £100, to be forfeited if he revealed certain secrets he had given Norfolk in writing. L. and P. IV, III, 6738.

formidable and brilliant man, the last great mediaeval prelate to hold sway in England; a man of wide horizons and European ambitions, not interested in trade or the rising middle classes or the gentry, the masters of the future, but the last splendid, corrupt, symbol of an order becoming obsolete.

The king who heard of his death was fiercer, shrewder, and harder than the splendid boy Wolsey had fascinated in 1512. Huge, thick, and hearty, the monarch was shooting at a target at Hampton Court, and Cavendish, summoned to an audience—to be grilled, handsomely rewarded, and taken into the royal service—leant against a tree to await his pleasure, lost in thought. Henry came suddenly behind him and clapped him on the shoulder: 'I will make an end of my game,' he said, 'then I will talk with you.'

Soon, handing his bow to a yeoman, the king bade Cavendish follow; then, in a russet velvet gown furred with sables against the November cold, he examined him closely for a whole hour. Cavendish would not go unrewarded, he said, if he revealed the whereabouts of Wolsey's £1,500. A certain priest had it, he answered, but 'no one could charge him with it but only I'. 'Keep this gear secret,' said Henry, 'between you and me, for if I hear any more of it, I shall know by whom it came out. Howbeit, three may keep council, if two be away; and if my cap were privy to my council, I would cast it in the fire and burn it.' What wonder that the monarch 'could not abide to have any man stare in his face; or to fix his eye too steadily upon him when he talked with them'?[1]

[1] Ellis. Series III, vol. III, p. 102.

CHAPTER XI

'COWE DOTH RIDE THE BULL'

❖

THE king who had broken Wolsey and kept his own counsel so close was at the height of his powers; capable, when roused, of masterful decisions. He was now to throw an instinctive, tactical, political genius into action, and become the figure Holbein would depict: 'a terrifying tyrant balancing a massive bull's torso on legs like pillars, the head thrown back and up in the bull's posture of challenge and defiance, the heavy bearded jowl, the self indulgent mouth, the small predatory nose, the flat hawk's eyes gleaming with malice and attention'.[1]

Henry had always been hard and cunning: Pollard thought him a political innocent till he was in his late thirties. 'Suppose,' he wrote in 1902, 'there ascended the throne today a young prince, the finest oar, the best bat, the crack marksman of his day. . . .' Like some successful Oppidan of Dr Warre's Eton, this paragon had long been slow to develop, negligent in business, duped by elderly continental politicians. Yet no one brought up at Henry VII's court and endowed with Henry's cold intelligence could have had many political illusions, and his elaborate Renaissance education and theological interests had made him much more subtle and perceptive, whatever adolescent posturings romances of chivalry had encouraged. And the arrogant, self-righteous complacency, which was growing with decades of adulation and success, came from an early conviction of the separateness of royalty. Sixteenth century dynasts were a caste apart who thought their subjects not fully human; beings to be patronized, exploited and discarded. Few of them were constantly concerned with business and high policy, so important to serious historians; and Henry, like Francis I, spent most of his time, as he was expected to do, living, representatively, like a king; in a round of jousting, hunting, shooting and gambling for immense wagers; playing royal tennis and bowls, moving from one palace to another, avoiding the plague.

His accounts reveal the casual routine of the household. Ball, the

[1] Mattingly, op. cit., p. 97.

king's dog, gets lost in Waltham Forest; Cutte his spaniel, is apt to stray—in 1530 someone has 10s for retrieving him; in 1531, a poor woman gets 4s 6d for the same service. When the monarch bawled 'Cutte', did the courtiers reflect on the meaning of the name? Patche and Saxton, the king's fools, are always on hand; Peter Tremazin rides two horses at once; an 'Almayn' turns up 'bringing a lion'; a 'fellow with a dancing dog' is rewarded, and 'the frantyke man' at Woodstock gets £4 13s 3d. In June 1532, a great fish is 'hunted' at Greenwich and the watermen are heavily tipped.

Hunting was an obsession and only a few sedentary officials thought it a martyrdom; when Henry shot a tame buck by mistake, he amply compensated the owner, while 10s was paid for a cow that the Lady Anne's greyhounds had managed to kill. People would bring in casual offerings; the water bailiff of London, a live seal; a man from the Abbot of Gloucester, baked lampreys: when the Provost of Eton sent cakes, the messenger had 5s. Offerings of game and fish and cheese came in; filberts and cherries, lettuce and cucumbers, grapes and pears in season. There were constant masses and saints' days, receptions to ambassadors and state banquets; water parties and disguisings—elaborate dressings up. Musicians flocked to the court; the royal choristers were cherished and trained and someone even got 10s for 'bringing nightingales for the King'. Henry also bought a remarkable quantity of books.

In such a rich tumultuous life of pleasure and occupation, Henry naturally held the chores of government in some distaste: as a matter of policy, he seldom attended the formal meetings of the Council, though he would discuss business informally with a group in a gallery or a garden. His pleasures came first; though terrified of plague, and preternaturally wary of dynastic danger, he took appalling risks when jousting, 'having no respect or fear of anyone in the world'. In 1524 he had nearly been killed by Suffolk; 'Having a new harness made of his own device,' writes Hall, 'such as no armourer before that time had seen,' he had 'thought to essay the same at the tilt,' but forgotten to put down the viser. Horrified spectators cried 'Hold! Hold!', but Suffolk, his helmet closed, neither saw nor heard. So the two had met head on and Suffolk's spear had struck the king on the forehead, thrust the whole helmet back, full of splinters. Terrified, he had sworn never again to run against the king; but Henry had magnanimously declared 'none was to blame but himself', and run several more courses to show himself intact. He went on taking these risks, well into his forties; in 1536, he was concussed and unconscious for two hours.

None of these things impaired his ability and he always set high standards in his immediate entourage. In 1527, for example, he had insisted on getting rid of an incompetent chaplain by making him coadjutor to the master of Southwark Hospital, since he ought to be provided for, 'being a gentleman born': once rid of him, he said, 'he might, as he shortly wold, have a better learned man in his place'. But Henry was developing an increasing callousness, a coarsening fibre, a habit of regarding his closest companions as expendable.

Not that his sexual adventures—of which he was already boasting to his wife in 1514—had led to radical disease. It is widely believed, and still asserted, that Henry was syphilitic—hence, it is argued, the disabilities of his descendents and the failure of his line. But the case is quite unproven.

The theory was started, obscurely, by a Dr Currie in 1888[1] and popularized, by implication, in a short, sensational, anonymous and disreputable article on *Some Royal Deathbeds* in the *British Medical Journal* of 1910.[2] This gave an appalling picture, based on no contemporary evidence, of the dying monarch as 'a mass of loathsome infirmities' and 'festering sores', giving off an intolerable 'stench'. The next, and most influential, popularization came from MacLauran's *De Mortuis* in 1930, but this relied heavily on Pollard's erroneous statement that Catherine gave birth nine times instead of six. The whole case has since been virtually destroyed by J. F. D. Shrewsbury's *Henry VIII, a medical study*.[3]

For there is no conclusive evidence, he insists, from Catherine's misfortunes, from Henry's medical history, or from the fate of his descendants, that he suffered from syphilis. Out of six births to Catherine, one son survived for fifty-two days, and Mary lived well into middle age: such mortality was 'more probably a feature of the time, not of the line'.[4] Moreover Henry had married Catherine when he was eighteen; he was a golden boy, a Renaissance paragon; had he contracted syphilis, he would have already been disfigured. For the 'Great Pox' or 'French Pockes' was an appalling disease which had erupted in Europe in 1493, probably from the New World, and its repellent symptoms could not

[1] *Notes on the Obstetric histories of Catherine of Aragon and Anne Boleyn.* Edinburgh Medical Journal.

[2] Vol. I of that year, p. 1303.

[3] *Journal of the History of Medicine and Allied Sciences,* Vol. VIII, Winter, 1952, pp. 141–85. q.v. for a masterly analysis. See also F. Chamberlin, *The Private Character of Henry VIII,* 1932, and R. S. Ellery, 'Must Syphilis Still Serve?' *Medical Journal of Australia.*

[4] Shrewsbury, p. 147. Pollard invented a premature boy born in 1514 by confusing an entry in a fire-damaged manuscript which referred to the consecration of the battleship of the *Henri Grace a Dieu* with the christening of an infant. Apparently, in all, he invented three miscarriages.

have been concealed. Henry's political enemies would have made savage propaganda out of his condition, while, had Catherine shown symptoms of the disease, she would certainly have been put away. But she died of coronary thrombosis, probably aggravated by anxieties and humiliations; the doctors at the autopsy found her healthy, save for her heart, which was 'black and hideous'. 'When,' Shrewsbury insists, 'historians, whether lay or medical, arraign an individual before the bar of history, and accuse him of voluntarily acquiring and knowingly transmitting a dangerous disease, that has most serious social implications, I consider it incumbent upon them to present much stronger evidence in support of this accusation than is furnished by Catherine of Aragon's obstetric history.'[1]

None of Henry's children, either, showed symptoms of syphilitic disease. Mary was short-sighted, but not deaf; she had a rough, mannish voice, a glum expression and a frightening stare, nor could she have children; but none of these handicaps would have derived from inherited syphilis. Edward VI's right shoulder was higher than his left, so that the organs on his left side were compressed, and he died at sixteen of a tumour of the lung, aggravated by poisonous medicines. Queen Elizabeth I lived to a ripe age; though sexually perhaps abnormal, she was a brilliant personality of immense vigour;[2] and Henry Fitzroy, Duke of Richmond, was considered very handsome, though he died of consumption at seventeen.

Henry's offspring were hardly a biological success, but there is no conclusive evidence either of syphilis, or of sudden 'degeneration', setting in after 1530. Henry was then, in fact, at the height of his powers; and he was still to be capable of going on campaign in 1544, riding from Calais to Boulogne, and, in the year after, of 'hawking for pheasants'. He was never incapacitated in mind, either; all too clearheaded, he was to examine and underline, on his deathbed, the evidence for the treason of Norfolk and Surrey.

It was rather the effects of hereditary gout, aggravated by gross feeding—for he was a 'Tudor Gargantua'—that killed him, not syphilis. The first severe symptom is not recorded until 1537, when he developed 'a sore leg that no poor man would be glad of'.[3] This was an ulcer or occluded sinus, due to 'crystals of sodium biorite in the body tissue which may have worked into swellings near the joint and discharged,

---

[1] Op. cit., p. 158.

[2] 'Five of the greatest medical authorities . . . in the English speaking world all rejected the idea that Elizabeth ever suffered from syphilis. In face of this weight of medical opinion further discussion about Elizabeth is superfluous.' Shrewsbury, op. cit., p. 169.

[3] Pollard's statement that he had it not long after 1530 cannot be sustained.

Prince Edward by Hans Holbein
(Reproduced by permission of the Director, Kunstmuseum, Basel)

10. Thomas Howard, Third Duke of Norfolk, by Hans Holbein
(Reproduced by gracious permission of H.M. The Queen)

causing agony'.[1] Along with rising blood pressure—he complained of headaches—and derangement of the kidneys, this gouty affliction would account for the change, in late middle age, and not before, 'of the young Prince into a jealous, suspicious, lonely old despot, without inventing a terrible mental and moral degeneration for which there is no shred of evidence, and invoking a late nervous manifestion of syphilis to explain it'. 'No one,' Shrewsbury concludes, 'can say with certainty that Henry VIII never acquired syphilis; but no one has the right to accuse him of the voluntary acquisition of the disease, in my judgement, without presenting much more convincing evidence than has yet been supplied.'[2] It is time that historians stopped repeating the accusation as a fact.[3]

The personality which had emerged by 1530 to take full charge of affairs was in fact consistent; for long well able, if put to it, to take control; endowed with a cold political instinct which grasped situations in human terms, if liable, when thwarted, or maddened by women, to blind rage. Henry was instinctively much more subtle and empirical, more *en rapport* with the feeling of the country, than the ruthless careerist, Wolsey, a great prince of the cosmopolitan Church, or the self-made administrative genius Thomas Cromwell, ultimately his master's slave. In his very casualness, he carried the bulk of the people with him. 'Henry,' writes Dr Rowse, 'had the gentry, the townsmen and the people generally with the monarchy, even if they did not always see eye to eye with his doings. . . . That was the strength of his position; it was really unassailable.'[4]

On the continent, on the other hand, where he could hardly play from strength, save for his nuisance value and his money, he had to adapt his policies to the shifts of greater dynasts.

II

It was this discrepancy between the king's internal and external powers which led to the break with Rome. Henry had already remarked in 1515, on an occasion of religious controversy, that 'the Kings of England had never had superiors on earth. Patently he had neither doubts nor surprise in the matter: it had never occurred to him that any power outside England could possibly thwart him. It is not too much to say

[1] Shrewsbury. op. cit., pp. 182–3.
[2] Op. cit., p. 184.
[3] Among recent writers, Lucy Baldwin Smith, in *A Tudor Tragedy*, p. 133; and Sir Charles Petrie, in *Philip II of Spain*, p. 198.
[4] *Tudor Cornwall*, p. 239.

that the Reformation got under way when he found out that in this he was wrong.'[1] Continental politics, in fact, had determined that the Pope could not accommodate him in ways which had respectable precedents, and in the face of the revocation of the divorce case to Rome, Henry appears to have been nonplussed. For some time he stalled, casting about for a way round.

One way, convincing to public opinion at home, if not on the continent, was to canvass the opinions of the universities of Christendom, an expedient suggested by an obscure Cambridge scholar who now entered great affairs. Early in August 1529, when Henry was on progress at Waltham in Essex, it chanced that a fellow of Jesus College, a Cambridge acquaintance of secretary Gardiner, was tutoring the sons of a gentleman of the neighbourhood. Thomas Cranmer came of small Nottinghamshire gentry and had been brought up to country life and to 'ride rough horses, so that, being archbishop, he feared not to ride the roughest horse that came to his stable, and when time served . . . he would both hawk and hunt, and would sometimes shoot with the long bow, but many times kill his deer with the cross bow, and yet his sight was not perfect '.[2] But he had begun his education the hard way. A 'mervelous severe and cruell scholemaster', according to his victim's account, had 'so appalled and daunted' him that he had never recovered his 'audacity'. He had then taken his fill of scholastic learning at Cambridge—of 'the dark riddles and quiddities of Duns'—and had become, as he remained, immensely learned, a theologian and bibliophile, a literary genius who bequethed a superb liturgy to the Anglican Church.

Cranmer now took his first step to greatness and the stake, by suggesting that the 'King's great matter' should be submitted to the universities. Henry was delighted: 'Marry,' he swore, 'that man hath the right sow by the ear' (or 'the sow by the right ear'). He sent for Cranmer, a pliable, if tenacious, cleric, who had taken Holy Orders late in life, and placed him, a tame apologist, in the house of Anne Boleyn's father, now promoted from Viscount Rochford to Earl of Wiltshire, to 'pen his mind and opinion'.[3]

Cranmer soon widened his horizons, for he went with Wiltshire to Bologna, where he witnessed the spectacular meeting of Clement VII

---

[1] G. R. Elton, *The Reformation in England*, Cambridge Modern History, Vol. II, p. 229 1958.

[2] See *Narratives of the Days of the Reformation*, ed. J. S. Nichols, Camden Society, 1855.

[3] As a Fellow of Jesus Cranmer had 'chanced' to marry Black—or Brown—Joan, employed, or resident, at the Dolphin Inn, Cambridge, but he had been re-elected to his fellowship after her early demise. Hence the allegations that he once had been an 'ostler' or 'kept an ale house'.

and Charles V, when it is said that Wiltshire refused to kiss the Pope's foot, though his spaniel had licked it. And Cranmer visited Venice and Rome, when he was well received.

Meanwhile, by February 1530, Henry had sent Commissioners to put the question of his divorce to Cambridge, long a hotbed of Lutheran ideas; but they only got a favourable verdict by the time-honoured device of referring it to a committee under the influence of heads of houses. Oxford concurred, by similar means and a similar majority, and during the summer, the main French universities, under political pressure, also replied favourably, as did the ancient and famous foundations of Bologna, Ferrara and Padua. The Spanish and Neapolitan universities naturally favoured the queen, while the Lutheran Germans, to Henry's disgust, having laxer views on marriage, saw no occasion for a divorce at all. But Henry could now cite, for home consumption, the favourable opinions of more 'great clerks', foreign as well as English.

He also had another weapon to hand. When, on the first crisis of 1529 he had summoned the Reformation Parliament, they had run hot on the scent of clerical abuses. They had attacked the church courts, cut down probate and mortuary fees, tried to limit non-residence, before he had prorogued them, that December. Now, when Parliament and Convocations met again in a second session, in January 1531, Henry decided further to soften up the clergy. He alleged that the whole Church, like Wolsey, had incurred the penalties of *praemunire* for recognizing the cardinal as legate, to the detriment of the Crown.

This cynical charge at once brought abject submission: the convocations surrendered to the indictment and paid the immense sum of £118,000 for pardon. They also gave a conditional recognition that the king was 'their singular lord and protector, only and Supreme Lord, and, as far as the Law of Christ allows, even Supreme Head'. The king's hand was now strengthened not only by the support of the universities, but, more importantly, by Parliament, though it was still assumed that the pope would decide his 'great matter'. The impasse remained, the discrepancy between the king's power at home and abroad.

III

Henry, in his practical manner, now felt his way towards a revolutionary line of attack: if he could blackmail the pope by bringing pressure in England, so much the better; if not, come what might, he would be judge of his own case. As the ruler of the sovereign 'empire' of England, he would go his own way.

The Reformation Parliament remained the obvious instrument to hand; first to bring pressure on Rome; then, if necessary, to cut a way out by Statute Law made by king in Parliament. In the spring, 1532, came the first move. An attack, probably drafted by Cromwell, now a Councillor, and, by April, master of the king's jewels, was opened on the rights of the clergy to their own jurisdiction. By May Henry was demanding their total submission; they must now make no new canon law without his own licence, and submit to a drastic revision of existing laws by thirty-two persons, half of them laymen appointed by the Crown. On the following day, the king told the speaker that the clergy were only 'half, indeed, scarcely, his subjects', and that prelates, on consecration, took an oath to the Pope clean contrary to their oath to him. Five days after, he received the Submission of the Clergy; the first position in his strategic campaign to win control of the Church had been won, and his success was marked by the resignation of Sir Thomas More from the Lord Chancellorship of England.

Henry next engineered an Act of Restraint of Annates which the pope would well understand; so many bishops, it seemed, were so old that too much money would have to be paid to Rome in premiums by their successors. The act was, of course, conditional on the king's assent, he was careful to inform the pope; not to be given until Easter of the following year: 'You should instil into their ears,' he wrote to his envoy in Rome, 'how incessant have been our efforts to resist the importunity of our people for passing the statute.'[1] With an eye on the popular support essential to his strategy, he also explained to the speaker of the Commons, that it was 'grudge of conscience' that made him abstain from the queen's company, not foolish or wanton appetite: after all, he was forty-one, he said, 'at which age the lust of a man is not so quick as in lusty youth'. It was a terrible thing to have lived in sin with his brother's wife.

Meanwhile he was losing £45 at 'shovel board' to Anne Boleyn's brother, Rochford, and in May, paying £12 to 'the sergeant of the cellar' who had won it off the lady at bowls.[2] In June, at Eltham, he paid for a black satin nightgown for the Lady Anne—doubtless it matched her eyes—and accepted a present of 'marmalado' from Thomas Cromwell. In August he was fishing at Hampton Court with an 'angle

[1] Fisher, p. 315, quoting L. and P., V, 886.
[2] Henry's poorer subjects were not allowed to follow his example. In 1531 'no one having less than £20 was to play any game for money or other thing, unless it be shooting with a long bow or playing for meat or drink, to be had at the same time as the said playing'.

rod'; then he moved to Woodstock, and an Italian got 5s for presenting him with a melon at Abingdon.[1]

Having fixed the clergy at home through their submission, and, he hoped, the pope abroad by the threat of withdrawing Annates, Henry now set about repairing his interrupted alliance with the French. He even braved the channel crossing and 'men were sorry to hear,' writes Hall, 'that the King's should pass the sea in winter'. He had also determined that there should be no doubt of the status of the lady; on September 1, 1532, at Windsor, Anne Boleyn was created Marchioness (technically Marquis) of Pembroke in her own right, with the large endowment of £1,000 a year; in October the king was meeting large bills for silks and furs, and betting high with Norfolk, her uncle, and with Rochford, losing £93 and £116 at dice. And when, that month, he proceeded from Greenwich, by Sheppey, to Canterbury and Dover, he took the marchioness with him.

In August Archbishop Warham, that battered and tenacious character, had died aged eighty-two; he had been served with a writ of *praemunire* for consecrating a bishop before confirmation by the king, and had known what that meant. But, at last, he had turned and defied Henry; asserted that archbishops had the right to consecrate freely 'time out of mind', that 'this article was one of the causes for the death of St Thomas ... I think it better,' the old man had written, 'to suffer the same than against my conscience, to conform to the article for which St Thomas died.' But the strain had killed him, and his secretary had suffered a nervous breakdown, even lost his faith; 'nearly hanged himself with his own tippet', said he would 'proclaim the King a traitor' and, again, attempted suicide with a penknife.[2]

The obscure Cranmer, not Gardiner, was to be his successor, for politic Gardiner had been in two minds about the submission. Summoned back from another mission to Germany and Italy in October 1532, the ingenious scholar, his mind in liturgical niceties, was to be Primate of England, ready to do as he was told and find reasons for doing so. He had now remarried—this time to the niece of the German theologian Osiander—and the king and Cromwell had another hold over him, should their consciences take an orthodox turn.[3]

Cranmer did not arrive until January 1533. 'There was never a man came more reluctant to a bishopric,' he was to say, 'than I did to that.'

---

[1] Privy Purse accounts, L. and P., III, pp. 747 ff.

[2] L. and P., X, 113.

[3] Cranmer had already sent her on ahead to England, and by her was to have a son and two daughters. After his death, she married a Protestant printer, Richard Whitchurch and after him, Bartholomew Scott, a Surrey J.P.

When Henry and the marchioness with a brilliant entourage landed at Calais in October 1532, Francis I had to receive them with appropriate splendour. The two kings met between Abbeville and Boulogne, Henry in russet velvet and gold braid loose over it; Francis in slashed crimson with cloth of gold 'plucked out through the cuts'. The combined cavalcade set forward over the chalk downs to Boulogne, hawking as they went. There the huge English king bent to embrace the three boy princes of France, now restored to their father, but Henry could bring only Henry Richmond, 'full of favour and beauty, the King's bastard son of England'.

Anne, Marchioness of Pembroke, glittered in the queen's jewels: and when, in masking disguise—cloth of gold and crimson tinsel—she danced with Francis I, Henry, with bluff humour, twitched aside the lady's mask and the French king had to talk to her direct. After the kings had taken leave of one another with 'princely countenance and hearty words', personal diplomacy, it seemed, had again consolidated a precarious alliance.

It was now November: great storms and tides struck the coast—three feet above the wharf at Antwerp, inundating Zeeland and maritime Flanders; the king was held up at Calais, and only got back by a hurried crossing at midnight. Safely in Kent, he lost £9 to the lady at 'Pope July game'. Installed again at Greenwich, he set little store by Clement VII's warning to return, on pain of excommunication, to his wife; he told him that as a fisherman, the successor of Peter, he should 'pull his nets softly, or he might break them'.

IV

By January 25, 1533, Henry had married Anne Boleyn, for she was pregnant. The fact was kept close, so that the pope should not refuse the bulls for Cranmer's consecration: once installed, the new archbishop could by-pass the papal jurisdiction, and, while the case was still pending at Rome, pronounce the king's marriage a nullity. There was not much time to lose.

The Reformation Parliament now reassembled for its next session, with speaker Sir Thomas Audley promoted Lord Chancellor in place of More, at present honourably retired. They rapidly passed a momentous act in Restraint of Appeals which declared England an 'Empire' under a monarch supreme over Church and State; 'a body politic compact'. No one could now appeal out of the realm to the Court of Rome, and the king's causes could be tried only in the upper house of a subservient convocation. The act was revolutionary, cutting off a sovereign state from the spiritual jurisdiction of the cosmopolitan church.

The marchioness was by now rather hysterical: 'Will you send me some apples?' she asked Wyatt, who knew her well, and may have warned Henry against her. 'I have such a longing for apples! Do you know what the King says? He says it means I am with child! But I tell him—No! No! It couldn't be. No!' And she laughed and ran from the room.[1] In March she was entertaining the king in her richly tapestried dining room, with its superb new golden 'sideboard'. She sat on his right, and Henry was so excited it was hard to follow what he said: 'What a great dowry the Marchioness had got! . . . What a rich marriage! . . . all we see and the rest of the plate belongs to her!' Talking for two hours in the garden, the king bored Chapuys, running on and on against the pope, reiterating how Charles V had owed his election to himself. Like a picador with a bull, Chapuys planted some darts in the royal hide: Queen Catherine—now Princess Dowager by act of parliament—might withdraw to Spain, the people were very loyal there; or she might make a good governor of the Low Countries. 'These remarks,' reported the ambassador, 'set him thinking.'

Henry returned to blackguarding the Pope, who would never, he said, convoke a General Council, 'seeing the ugly bastinadoeing he would get. . . . Consider,' he said, 'the vanity of his foot being kissed.' He had just seen a book from the pope's own library claiming all monarchs as his feudatories, and 'for his part, he meant to repair the errors made by Henry II and King John'. With insular arrogance, he praised his French allies—they had so much improved it seemed they were Englishmen!

At this time, too, with nice irony, Henry informed the pope that, though he had once written a book in his favour, he had now studied theology more deeply and found the contrary to be correct; but if the Holy Father gave him cause to study deeper, he might reconsider his views.

Oddly enough, in February 1533, after the usual stiff fees had gone to the cardinals concerned, but mainly through pressure from the French, Clement VII had granted the bulls for Cranmer's consecration: probably he was thought harmless. By April, Henry's new archbishop could preside over a Convocation of sixty-six divines. The pope, they soon decided, had never had power of dispensation, if a brother's widow had been carnally known; and, by forty-four to 'five or six', determined that known she had been. John Fisher, 'the most holy

[1] Mattingly, op. cit., p. 256, quoting S. P., I, 390.

learned prelate in Christendom', alone among the bishops, contested their opinion. Not long after, he was in the Tower.

Cranmer, already perjured by taking the customary oath of obedience to the pope, after penning a secret document repudiating it as a 'form', was now beseeching the king, 'very humbly', for licence to determine the 'great cause of his matrimony'; rumours, he said, were rife, among the common people. 'The letter,' writes Mattingly, 'in its first draft was already a masterpiece of official absurdity . . . but the crawling phrases were not abject enough for Henry.' He sent it back with annotations in the royal hand and changing the words 'beseeching your Highness most humbly upon my knees' to 'prostrate at the feet of your Majesty beseeching'.[1]

Henry now declared that his conscience put him in such fear of God that he could not refuse the archbishop, though recognizing no spiritual superior on earth, and the farce culminated in a small ecclesiastical court at Dunstable Priory, where the last spur of the Chilterns overlooks the East Midland plain, four miles from Ampthill, Queen Catherine's place of banishment. Summoned to appear, Catherine refused to attend: she had for years been appealing to the only court she recognized, at Rome. She was now again pronounced 'contumaceous', and on April 23rd sentence was given by Archbishop Cranmer for the king's divorce.

Henry explained once more to Chapuys how he must have male heirs. Could he be sure, said the ambassador, of having them? 'Am I not a man,' said the monarch, touched to the quick, 'like other men?' And he said it three times. Further, he declared, if he had ever admitted that Catherine had come to him a virgin, it had only been his fun—'as a man jesting and feasting says many things not true'. And when he said that, he began to crow, 'Tell me, how have I paid you off? What more could you have?' Then, wrinkling his forehead and turning fierce, he declared that all resistance would be useless: Charles V had no right to interfere, or try to make him go on living in sin.

But Catherine, the 'old widow Princess', still blamed Henry's state of mind on the concubine. He was not, she always maintained, ill-natured in himself; it was 'this Anne that had put him in such a perverse and wicked temper'.

V

Easter saw the triumph of Anne Boleyn and Whitsun her coronation: already she was boasting that she would have Princess Mary as her

[1] Op. cit., p. 258.

maid, or 'marry her to some varlet'. On Easter Eve she went to mass in royal state, openly as queen, loaded with jewels and wearing gold frieze; Norfolk's daughter, the affianced of Richmond, carried her train, and sixty maids of honour followed her: 'All the world,' wrote one observer, 'was astonished, not knowing whether to laugh or cry.' When London preachers told their congregations to pray for 'Queen Anne' people walked out with 'ill looks'; the Lord Mayor instructed the city merchants not to 'murmur' and to stop their apprentices gossiping and, 'what was more difficult', their wives.

London was consoled with fabulous pageantry, in which the lord mayor and aldermen were particularly honoured; Henry ordered celebrations to be organized to the last detail, on a tremendous scale. His reign was a paradise for external, as well as interior, decorators.

Cranmer having now declared officially that Anne Boleyn had been married to the king, her coronation took place. The lord mayor, the city companies—haberdashers, mercers, grocers, were rowed down to Greenwich, preceded by a float with a great dragon 'casting wildfire' and 'wild men' making 'hideous noises', and by another with the new queen's device of a white falcon, crowned, on a mount surrounded by girls and roses. Off Greenwich, the whole procession turned upstream and cast anchor, 'making great melody'. Then, at three o'clock, Queen Anne, in cloth of gold, entered her barque, and the whole flotilla, joined now by the barges of the bishops and high nobility, rowed back to the Tower; a Venetian spectacle, covering the Thames from bank to bank, with banners glistening in the summer sunshine, bells 'clinquant' and fluttering streamers—'a triumphant sight to see as they passed upon the water' with 'the marvellous swet armone of the sayd ynstermentes', sounds which 'be a thyng of another worlde'. At the water steps of the Tower, to the sudden thunder of guns, Queen Anne came ashore through a lane of spectators, to be received by Sir William Kingston, by Gardiner of Winchester and Norfolk; within, stood the huge, splendid, king, who clapped his hands to both her sides, publicly emphasizing her condition. That evening they supped privately in the Tower.

The next day Queen Anne proceeded to Westminster, with the Lord Chief Justice and the judges in scarlet: costly and cunning pageants were laid on; there was a tame poet at Cornhill, and Nicholas Udall, the fashionable pioneer of Tudor drama, destined, from 1534 to 1541, to be Headmaster of Eton, and though hardly a success, afterwards Head-master of Westminster, had composed suitable verses in the vernacular.[1]

[1] R.Ms. 18. A LXIV, B.M.

The reigning Headmaster of Eton, Robert Cox, had also turned out some brisk Latin:

Iam diadema gerit nobilis Anna sacrum,[1] etc.

So the fountains ran with wine, but hostile witnesses allege that the cheering was thin; that the lord mayor, told to command people to shout, had said he could not command their hearts; that Anne's fool had to yell at the crowd 'Ye have all scurvy heads and dare not uncover'. But the Londoners, anxious about the Flanders trade, certainly bawled '*Orson queneve, and France dogue*' at the ambassador of the Most Christian king.[2]

They saw an elegant lady in white cloth of gold in a litter of white damask, her black hair hanging down under a coif with a circlet of gems; and, that night, Anne, lodged at Whitehall, paid another secret visit to the king. Then on Whit Sunday, June 1st, in purple velvet furred with ermine, she was crowned in the Abbey with the heavy crown of St Edward, then with a lighter one. At the banquet in Westminster Hall there were four tables running its whole length; Suffolk, gorgeously arrayed, rode up and down on a courser caparisoned in crimson, while Henry looked on from a latticed closet, where he sat with the ambassadors of Venice and of France—the last glad, doubtless, of the privacy. There was the usual crying of largesse, and presentations of plate, the new queen acting her part with a great sense of occasion.

But the king had caught a Tartar in Anne Boleyn; high-strung, neurotic, she always knew her own mind even in trifles; 'touching your monkey, the queen loveth no such beasts, nor can scant abide the sight of them',[3] but she 'set much store by a pretty dog'. Moreover she was all too articulate, 'incessantly crying after the King'; he was soon even a little afraid of her and her tantrums soon made him look ridiculous.

Already, by August, she was furiously jealous, for Henry, sated, had turned to other women. She ought to 'shut her eyes and endure' it, he told her, as her betters had'; he could, after all, 'humble her in a moment more than he had exalted her'. They did not speak, it seems, for two days. Dynastically these tiffs counted for little, as the king was convinced Anne would bear a son, and 'holding it for certain', as the physicians and astrologers all said so, he presented her with 'one of the richest and most triumphant beds'.

Then, on Sunday, September 7th, in the afternoon, at Greenwich,

---

[1] 'Now the noble Anne bears the sacred diadem.'
[2] Whoreson knave.
[3] L. and P., VIII, 1084.

Queen Anne gave birth to a girl. The event was 'the edge of the cloud that ultimately blotted her out',[1] though the child was to be Elizabeth I, the greatest of the queens of England. The astrologers and sorcerers were much reproached, but the king put a good face on disappointment; bells pealed and bonfires flared; a *Te Deum* was sung in St Paul's and on the following Wednesday the lord mayor, Sir Stephen Pecocke, 'in a gown of crimson velvet with his collar of S. S. and all the Aldermen in scarlet', came again by barge to Greenwich, where the high nobility and courtiers were assembled. Between autumnal garden walls hung with arras and along paths strewn with green rushes, they proceeded to the Church of the Observant Friars; and here the child was carried to the silver font, overhung by a crimson canopy and railed with red. The Dowager Duchess of Norfolk held her, wearing a mantle of purple velvet, her long train furred with ermine; Cranmer was godfather; the dowagers of Norfolk and Dorset, godmothers; and 'this done,' writes Hall, 'Garter Chief King of Arms cried aloud "God of his infinite goodness, send prosperous life and long to the high and mighty Princess of England, Elizabeth", and then the trumpets blew . . .'[2] There was an immense torchlight procession—five hundred torches borne by the royal guards and servants and more by the gentlemen—back to the Queen's chamber. The mayor and aldermen were suitably thanked, then 'had to the cellar to drink, and so went to their barges', while the early autumn dusk settled over the brick and plaster palace and the Thames ran steady and full to the sea.

VI

So long as their uncomfortable alliance lasted, Henry and the French king were extremely formidable, as the pope well understood. Three English merchants from Antwerp might report in December that the Captain of Gravelines had warned them 'if your King take not back his Queen again within thirty days, I would advise you, nor none of your nation, not to pass this way, but to keep you at home; for if you do I will take you as good prize', and Chapuys might advise the emperor to keep the Straits of Gibraltar against English ships, and forbid the cloth trade with Flanders; but Charles V had more urgent cares in mind.

The English merchants had not, and the French were as unpopular at Court as in the City. Du Bellay, their ambassador, had a way of showing off, 'carping' rapid French at the Council, alleging English

[1] J. E. Neale, *Elizabeth*, p. 15.
[2] II, 243.

political greed, and reflecting on the handicaps of those ignorant of his language. When the old Earl of Shrewsbury, 'palsied from the wars,' gave 'neither care nor countenance to this jolie man', not understanding a word, the ambassador even remarked that his ignorance was a 'lack in his nobility'. The remark was translated, and Shrewsbury got to his feet, knit his brows, laid hand to dagger, and so 'set his countenance that the French hardie ambassador changed colour wonderfully'. 'Saith the French whoreson so?' he shouted. 'Marie, tell the French dogge again, by sweet saint Cuthbert, if I know one pestilent Frenche woorde in all my bodie, I would take my dagger and dig it out before I rose from table.' And they could tell the 'tawny whoreson' again that the English had 'to eat up their beasts fast, otherwise they would be so many they would devour their masters'. Du Bellay was quite put off his dinner, 'but drank wondrous oft'.[1]

Henry knew that the war was detested, and did his best to promote morale, alliances, and defence. A memorandum to the king's Council made in September 1533 recommended that all bishops—'especially those nearest the Court'—should be asked whether they could prove that the 'so-called Pope of Rome' was above a General Council, or the General Council above him? All the nobility, bishops, and civic authorities were also to 'disparage' the Bishop of Rome informally, as well as officially, and so spread the idea among the people. Spies were to be sent into Scotland, to see if the Scots were intriguing with 'any outward prince', and ambassadors sent to conclude an ambitious league with the kings of Poland and Hungary, the dukes of Saxony and Bavaria, and the Landgraf of Hesse, as well as with Lubeck, Dantzig and 'other steddes (harbours) of the Haunse Tutonyk'.[2] Forts along the Scots border were also to be strengthened; the king's navy, guns and munitions of war, 'bows, etc' to be repaired and provided for.

And in theological warfare Cranmer was not backward; he declared that Christ had named no head among the apostles; that it was uncertain if St Peter had ever been in Rome, and that 'to judge from their lives, the faith of many Popes was not good': the present one, in particular, was 'corrupt both in person and government'. A General Council was, of course, superior to the pope, though not to princes, and if any of them had acknowledged him 'by mistake', they might 'pull their necks out of the yoke as men may escape from a robber'.[3] More coarsely, one of Cromwell's agents remarked that, if the pope and emperor would

[1] Cavendish, op. cit., pp. 81–2.
[2] L. and P., VI, 1487.
[3] L. and P., VI, 1488.

consider what harm Henry might do them, 'the Pope might rather wish to wipe his arse by license with his briefs than to send them into these parts or elsewhere'.

Henry was now even swearing revenge on His Holiness, 'if it cost him his life, wife and children'; and told his envoy, Sir John Wallop,[1] to warn the French king he would 'give the Pope such a buffet as he had never had before'. On this note of vigorous controversy and defiance, Henry, Queen Anne, and the Court celebrated Christmas: Cromwell, too, tireless, omnicompetent, coming to the height of his powers, had got a great many presents that December of 1533, including 'an ambling gelding' and 'a porpoise'.

[1] Soldier and diplomat, of Farleigh Wallop, Hampshire, of the family afterwards Earls of Portsmouth. He served in the Low Countries, and as Commandant at sea; fought against the Moors for the Portuguese and with Surrey in Ireland and France. Envoy to Margaret of the Netherlands, to Prague and Vienna; ambassador to France and Lieutenant Governor of Calais, 1530; through the 'thirties again in France and resident ambassador in Paris, 1539. Knight of the Garter, 1543. Lieutenant of Guisnes, d, 1551.

CHAPTER XII

'A BODY POLITIC COMPACT'

❖

BY 1534 Henry was well set on his new, insular, course. Over the next six years he sanctioned radical administrative changes which form the turning point of his reign. In April, Thomas Cromwell, long a power behind the throne, managed to oust Gardiner from the office of principal secretary, and began to make it something new. Indeed he 'made the secretary supreme in the internal administration. . . . In all the advanced states of Europe—in Spain and France as well as in England—the Secretary of State comes to the fore as the executive agent of a new type of government . . . [Wolsey] the last mediaeval Chancellor, was followed by the first modern Secretary of State'.[1]

As the crisis developed, the king also came to employ a specifically Privy Council. It sat more often and, if the Council attendant was with the king, other members continued to sit to deal, on their own, with routine business in London. This trend increased as the crisis mounted, and in other ways also a new bureaucracy, independent of the House-hold, began to grow up; the administrative sequel to the assertion of empire and to the supremacy of statute law made by King-in-Parliament.

Historians have called the change a 'revolution' marking the rise of the modern sovereign state, though perhaps the 'claims of the modern unitary state had in fact been conceded in the course of the preceding centuries',[2] and the 'revolution' was simply 'a resumption of normal development after a period of emergency'. If so, it has been argued, the term is 'misleading, demanding a heightening of contrasts and an exaltation of personality' which seems 'harmful and essentially false'.

But whether or not Cromwell and his master were reviving inherited powers, Cromwell certainly 'overhauled the machinery of govern-ment as it had never been overhauled since the reign of Henry II; and he overhauled it so drastically that much of it was not radically altered till the reign of Victoria'.[3] Yet they did not regard themselves as revolu-

---

[1] G. R. Elton, *The Tudor Revolution in Government*, pp. 300–2.
[2] See S. C. Harriss, *Medieval Government and Statecraft. Past and Present.* July 1963.
[3] H. R. Trevor-Roper, op. cit., p. 74.

tionaries—never a popular term among the English; and if, in fact, they made a 'revolution', it was limited, as usual, by what the public would stand, and called something else.

Along with these rapid and concentrated administrative charges, went the nationalization of the Church. It brought the '*Ecclesia Anglicana*', a new term, out of the main community of Catholic Christendom, and confirmed the revolt of another northern people against the Italianate papacy which had begun, to Tunstall's distress, among the Germans. But Henry remained strictly orthodox, unlike the monarchs and princes who had turned Lutheran; his objects were always political. He wanted his entire 'empire' of the British Isles, and to have it both ways. Yet the political alliance made, the new 'Church of England' went its own way.

Henry's assertion of 'empire'—a mediaeval term—was not original. Even in France and Spain the monarchs, though doctrinally orthodox, were coming to control their clergy at the expense of Rome; and by the 'thirties, Lutheranism and other forms of Protestantism had officially come to stay in Germany, in much of Switzerland, in the great Baltic cities, in Denmark, and in Sweden. Here, indeed, is the closest parallel; Gustav Ericksson Vasa, a violent and enormous man, with whom Henry had much in common, had seized the Swedish throne in 1523, broken the Danish hold over Sweden and turned on the Church. As Henry was to use Parliament, so Gustav had already used the *Riksdag* to bring the weight of nobles, burgesses and people against the clergy, hand over much wealth to himself and the monastic estates to the nobility. Henry was to plunder the monasteries; Gustav had already seized a bell in every church, and provoked a 'bell revolt' of the peasantry, not unlike the Pilgrimage of Grace of 1536; they had thought that the bells had cleared the air of demons. He was to authorize a translation of the Bible into Swedish and to transform the electoral kingship of Sweden into a monarchy backed by an economic expansion he personally encouraged. Henry's new state and Reformation was not, as some English historians seem to imply, unique. And like Gustav Vasa, in the last resort, though all was done in due constitutional form, he was responsible for this revolution himself. His attack on the Church was to consolidate the power of the new aristocracy, gentry and merchant capitalists who bought the Church lands and whose interest coincided with those of the new monarchy, though afterwards they overcame it, so that, in England, the king never became absolute.

During the spring of 1534 the Reformation Parliament confirmed the Submission of the Clergy, ratified and reinforced the Acts of Appeals and Restraint of Annates, and gave the Crown control over the election of bishops. In March, an Act of Succession confirmed the rights of Henry's offspring by the new queen: in the autumn session, too, parliament passed an Act of Supremacy, uniting the 'Imperial Crown of England' with the headship of the Church, claiming that the king had supreme spiritual jurisdiction. They also gave him, annually, one tenth of the Church revenues to be based on a new assessment, and extended the definition of high treason. Casual talk could now cost a man his life, and anyone refusing the oath of succession became liable to 'Misprision of Treason'.

These measures provoked widespread, if ineffectual, opposition. Queen Catherine, the 'old princess dowager', had now been relegated to a grim, moated manor house at Kimbolton, near Huntingdon: she remained quietly irreconcilable, in touch with Charles V. Preoccupied as he might be with immense responsibilities, and cautious of direct attack, he could always threaten the vital trade with the Low Countries. The peasants muttered that 'since Queen Anne came in' the crops had been terrible; unemployment and inflation were getting worse. The arrogance of the new queen and the arbitrary cruelties of the king made many of the great nobles uneasy, and when an epileptic 'new-found Saint', known as the Maid of Kent, began to prophesy in Catherine's favour, she had been exploited, in very high quarters, for political ends. She would testify with her tongue protruding and with staring eyes, and 'a voice came out of her belly speaking sweetly of heaven and terribly of hell'. She would even dictate letters purporting to come from heaven to earthly creatures.

Henry and Cromwell soon scotched her: by April 1534, the 'Mad Maid' and her followers had been executed, but not before Catherine's two most distinguished supporters had also been laid by the heels. John Fisher, Bishop of Rochester, was already in the Tower, and Sir Thomas More, who had 'stood out against all the realm in opinion', was now charged with 'misprision', and sent to join him. They were in greater danger when, in March, the pope at last decided the long-drawn divorce case in favour of the queen. It was small consolation to Henry that Clement VII died that September, for he was succeeded by the hard-bitten Alessandro Farnese, Paul III; less irresolute than his predecessor, as his portraits witness.

On January 15, 1535, a memorandum was made in the Privy Chamber at the king's personal command. In the presence of Sir Thomas Audley, Lord Chancellor; the Duke of Norfolk; the Earl of Wiltshire; Thos. Cromwell, Chief Secretary, and others, Henry ordained that his style henceforth should be: 'Henricus Octavus, Dei Gratia Angliae et

Henry Howard, Earl of Surrey, by Guillim Stretes
(Reproduced by permission of His Grace the Duke of Norfolk)

12. Henry VIII presenting the Charter to the Barber Surgeons

Franciae Rex, Fidei Defensor et Dominus Hiberniae, et in Terra Supremum Caput Anglicanae Ecclesiae.'[1] The title confirmed the Act of Supremacy, asserted that Henry justly and rightfully ought to be supreme head of the Church of England, and in effect gave him the temporal rights and prerogatives of the pope. This final definition brought the doom of some good men, the dissolution of the monasteries, the transformation of the Church, and an immense shift of social and economic power among the ruling classes, decisive for England.

The detested queen, Anne Boleyn, still had a strong, if now inter-mittent, hold over the king. Her extravagance was resented; people said 'since the new Queen was made, there had never been such a pilling and polling of the realm', or even 'the king is an heretic and liveth in adultery'. As usual, there had been sporadic discontent in the West Country, though the main resistance was in the North. At Ilchester, Somerset, in the spring of 1532, the idea had been canvassed that a re-deeming hero, perhaps King Arthur, would come out of the West. 'The White Hare shall drive the White Greyhound into the root of an oak,' said one Richards, 'and the King be driven out of England and killed at Paris Gate.' And one Horlock said they would have no more kings in England, and 'such a gap in the West that all the thorns in the realm should not stop it', and 'there should come out of the West one that should bring snow upon his helmet that should set all England at peace'.[2]

The authorities now clamped down on the most ordinary expressions of discontent: when Sir Walter Stonor, for example, thanking Crom-well for 'the recovery of his poor house at Stonor and all the manors the King had given him', reported Margery Cowpland—'a marvellous drunken woman, somewhat straight of her wits, and her husband out of his mind'—for abusing the king and queen, he put her at once in Wallingford Gaol and awaited instructions.[3]

But Anne could still feast the king, and 'get up fine mummeries'; and, that month, Henry bought, among more massive purchases, 'a gilt flagon with the King's and Queen's arms with H and A on the cover', the stopper, significantly, with a 'crown imperial'; two bowls similarly engraved, and 'pots' with H and A, as well as a new strainer for oranges and a pair of gilt snuffers.[4]

---

[1] Henry the Eighth, by God's Grace King of England and France, Defender of the Faith and Lord of Ireland, and on Earth Supreme Head of the Anglican Church.

[2] Report from Ilchester Gaol. L. and P. Addenda, I, I, 768. See Christopher Hill, *Puritanism and Revolution*, p. 55, for the persistence of such legends among the people.

[3] L. and P., VIII, 844.

[4] L. and P., VIII, 44.

II

At the end of April 1535, John Houghton, the beloved and learned prior of the London Charterhouse and head of all the Carthusians in England, the priors of the Charterhouses at Axholme, Lincolnshire, and Beauvale, Nottingham, along with Dr Reynolds of Sion Abbey and a young priest, Robert Feron, were all indicted for treason and exciting sedition, having refused the oath of supremacy. 'Since the realm of England was first a realm,' Feron had declared, 'was never a greater robber against the commonwealth . . . than is our King. He boasteth himself above all other Christian kings . . . being puffed up with vain glory.' He had prayed that Henry would die, like 'the most wicked King John, or the manqueller Richard, sometime usurper'. His life was 'more stinking than a sow . . .'; look how many 'matrons of the court' he had violated, and now he had taken for 'his wife in fornication this matron Anne'. Reynolds, too, had remarked succinctly 'until the King and the rulers of the realm be plucked by the pates, and brought, as we say to pot, shall we never live merrily in England'. 'I have all the rest of Christendom in my favour,' he had said; 'I dare even say all this kingdom . . . for I am sure the larger part is at heart of our opinion.' Asked by Cromwell, 'Who are they?' he replied, 'All good men of the Kingdom'; when ordered to hold his tongue, he answered contemptuously, 'judge me according to your law'. Some of their objections were hard to answer: when Houghton asked how the king, a layman, could be head of the Church, Cromwell told him to be quiet, and countered: 'You would make the King a priest.'[1] Cranmer mildly suggested that it would be best for them all to recant; if they were sent to him, 'he supposed he might do much'.

He had misjudged his men. All but Feron, who had turned king's evidence, were hauled to Tyburn and hanged 'with great ropes', in turn, the others watching; then cut down, ripped up, their arms torn off, their hearts cut out and rubbed in their faces, their quarters stuck on long spears.[2] They remained, it is said, resolute to the end.

It was something new, wrote Chapuys, that young Richmond, Norfolk, Wiltshire, and other magnates had stood 'quite near the sufferers'; the king himself, it was said, would have liked to see the butchery, 'which was very probable seeing that nearly all the Court were there': indeed, among some courtiers, disguised and masked as Scottish borderers, had been one to whom extraordinary deference had been paid.[3]

[1] L. and P., VIII, 661.
[2] L. and P., VIII, 662.
[3] L. and P., VIII, 666.

Other Carthusians were sent to the Tower by the cartload; some had been chained upright for days; some 'died in prison with stink'.

During the summer two more important victims perished. When the new pope, Paul III, against strong advice, had made John Fisher of Rochester a cardinal, Henry had sworn to give him another hat and send his head to Rome for the other. Early in June Fisher was confronted with a bewildering number of accusations, going back over years, mainly connected with his support of Queen Catherine. He was now seventy-four—reported by the English at Calais to be 'ninety' and 'like not to live a month'. 'I know not who they were,' he would reply; or 'I am not certain, but I think I have written seven or eight'; or, 'I am quite ignorant of the author, but suspect, from the style, it was Cornelius Agrippa.' On the essential point he remained as clear and adamant as the Carthusians: the king was not, and could not, be the supreme head.

Henry gave him short shrift. On June 15th, Fisher was roused in the early dawn: he would suffer, they said, between nine and ten. As the immensely distinguished, emaciated, cardinal mounted the scaffold on Tower Hill, he was dazzled by the morning sun: '*Accedite ad eum et illuminamini,*' he said, '*et facies vestra non confundentur.*'[1] But the 'headless carcass of the Chancellor (of Cambridge) was left naked on the scaffold for the rest of the hot June day, saving that one, for pity and humanity, cast a little straw upon it'.

Henry remarked that his death had been the least cruel that could be devised: he had not been poisoned nor boiled in lead, nor hanged, nor burned nor tortured, but 'sworded'. Fisher's intimate possessions were confiscated for the king—a little flat book with a gilt cover and the French king's arms on the inside; a mitre set with counterfeit stone and pearl; knitted gloves with gold set on the backs; some silver gilt plate.

III

Henry, meanwhile, was merry at Windsor. Queen Anne was again pregnant, and in June Sir William Kingston was writing 'she hath as fair a belly as I have seen'. The king, it seemed, now enjoyed persecuting priests; showing himself his own power. His reputation abroad was appalling: 'The affairs of England,' wrote one Italian, 'are commonly managed more than barbarously'; even Henry's ally, Francis I,

---

[1] Psalm 34, v. 5. 'Come into his presence and be enlightened, and your countenances shall not be confounded'; quoted by H. C. Porter, *Reformation and Reaction in Tudor Cambridge*, q.v. p. 18.

confessed that it was 'almost impossible to bear with him'. 'Sometimes,
said the King of France, 'he almost treats me like a subject . . . but I
must put up with it. This is no time to lose friends.'

The court had never been gayer, for the king liked more and more
company; the new mode of Italianate sonnets was coming in; the
women's dresses were fantastically elaborate, the fashion of vivid make-
up showing off the Queen's black, slanting eyes, framed in her three-
cornered, jewelled hoods over fine linen. The splendid horses sped over
the park, and music floated out on the June air. The young Henry,
Earl of Surrey, Norfolk's son, incongruously a poet, was to recall good
times at Windsor, remembering his friendship with the boy Richmond,
his junior by sixteen months.

> '*The sweet accord, such sleeps as yet delight,*
> *The pleasant dreams; the quiet bed of rest,*
> *The secret thoughts, imparted with such trust . . .*
> *The friendship sworn, each promise kept so just.*'[1]

The tastes of the court in general were less romantic. Someone had
written a parody of the Apocalypse, and Henry 'walked ten miles at
two o'clock one night and got into a house where he could see everything'. He was delighted to see himself cutting off the heads of the
clergy; and, wanting to laugh at his ease, he even 'discovered himself'
to the spectators, who, hearing an enormous man bellowing with
laughter, may already have had their suspicions. Henry told Queen
Anne that she really ought to see the show.

At the end of June he was reiterating his commands to the clergy
and schoolmasters to denounce the pope and erase his name from the
service books, 'the same to be declared to the people at the assizes'. The
Bishop of Chichester published throughout his diocese 'the King's
most dreadful commandment as to the Union of the Supreme Head of
the Church of England to the Imperial Crown'; and the Bishop of
Lincoln told Cromwell that, not having enough clerks to copy the
declaration, he had ordered 2,000 copies to be printed.[2] But the Archbishop of York was less efficient; 'I cannot,' he wrote, 'be in all places
. . . nor can I put learning and cunning into the heads of those who
have it not.' Not only ignorance made his clergy difficult: it was hard,
wrote one of Cromwell's officials, to 'beat the King's authority into
the heads of the rude people of the north', and the Bishop of Bangor

---

[1] See John Gough Nichols, *Memoir of Henry Fitzroy*, Camden Miscell, Vol. III, p. lxv.
[2] L. and P., VIII, 922.

confessed that he did not know Welsh: would it be enough to have the declaration set out by others?

IV

Henry now killed an even more famous victim. Sir Thomas More, after his long imprisonment, well knew his fate; he had once said, 'if his head would win the king a castle in France, it should not fail to do so', and he had early decided that he could not take the oath of supremacy without risking perpetual damnation. Deprived of ink in the Tower, he had to use charcoal. 'Other pens,' he wrote to his daughter, Margaret Roper, 'have I none here; and therefore can I write you no long process, nor dare adventure . . . to write often. But take no thought for me, whatsoever you shall hap to hear, but be merry with God.'[1] He had taken his final position on the supremacy and was becoming less interested in the world. 'I have in good faith,' he told Cromwell, 'discharged my mind of all such matters, and neither will dispute King's titles nor Pope's; but the King's faithful subject I am.' He would not 'meddle in the world again . . . his whole study would be upon the passion of Christ and upon his own passage out of the world'.

In discussion with Richard Riche, the king's Solicitor General, he had said the last word; 'suppose it should be enacted by Parliament that God should not be God, and that opposing the Act should be treason; and if it were asked of you, Ric: Riche, whether you would say that God was not God according to the Statute, and if you were to say so, would you not offend?' It was impossible, Riche replied, for God not to be God; as for the king, he had been 'constituted supreme head on earth of the Church of England'. Whereat More—no mean persecutor of heretics in his day—asserted mediaeval doctrine: a king, he said, can be 'made by Parliament and deprived by Parliament, to which every subject being at the Parliament can give his assent: but for the Primacy (of the Church) a subject cannot be bound, for he cannot give his consent to that in Parliament'. The king might be accepted in England, yet many foreign countries did not accept him: no national Parliament could make its own spiritual jurisdiction.

Judgment was given ('as usual'), for high treason, but More was still offered pardon. 'I pray God preserve me,' he answered, 'in my just opinion even to death.' 'Since I am condemned,' he concluded, 'and God knows how, I wish to speak freely of your Statute. . . . For seven years that I have studied the matter, I have not read of any approved

[1] Chambers, op. cit., p. 317, quoted from Works, 1557, pp. 1446-8.

doctor of the Church that a temporal lord could, or ought to be, head of the Spirituality.' He had affirmed another mediaeval argument.

'What, More,' exclaimed Chancellor Audley, bringing out the old cliché, 'You wish to be considered wiser . . . than all the bishops and nobles of the realm?' 'My Lord, for one bishop of your opinion,' More answered, 'I have a hundred saints of mine; and for one Parliament of yours, and God knows what kind, I have all the general councils for a thousand years.'

'Your malice,' interjected Norfolk drily, 'is now clear.' 'What I say,' More replied, 'is necessary for the discharge of my conscience and the satisfaction of my soul.' Then, with the disgust of a great lawyer, he continued, 'I say further, that your Statute is ill made'; they had no authority, 'without the common consent of all Christians, to make a law . . . against the union of Christendom'.[1] The conflict between the nation state, claiming 'empire' or sovereignty, and the old Catholic European Christendom had been concisely defined.

There was no point in further discussion. Guarded by archers, More was brought back from Westminster to the Tower. Margaret pushed through the guard and embraced him, unable to speak. 'Asking leave of the archers,' her father told her it was God's will; that she had long, anyway, 'known the secret of his heart'. She tore herself away but ran back again to embrace him; he only bade her pray to God—and this 'without tears or change of face or colour'. 'Our Lord bless you,' More wrote in a last letter to Margaret, 'good daughter, and your good husband, your little boy and all yours and all my children, and all my Godchildren and all my friends.'

The king had kindly commuted the appalling sentence for treason at Tyburn to beheading in the Tower, and on July 6, 1535, Henry and the Council sent a message betimes that More was to die that morning; Henry particularly charged him 'not to use too many words', but graciously allowed his family and friends to attend.

More came to execution in a coarse frieze coat, carrying a red cross. He was physically broken, but steadfast; reproached for a legal judgment, he said he would make it again; and he made some wry jokes. As the Sheriff's officers helped him up the scaffold, he said, 'when I come down again, let me shift for myself'; he then tipped the headsman a gold angel, told him he had a short neck, and concluded 'let me lay my beard over the block lest you cut it'. After the heavy chunk of the axe, people remembered his short speech: he had died, he had said, the king's faithful servant, but God's first.

[1] L. and P., VIII, 996.

V

With an enormous entourage Henry had left Windsor on summer progress to Bristol the day before. He moved by Reading to Abingdon and Woodstock; at the end of July, he was at Tewkesbury and Gloucester, and arrived at Bristol in mid-August. He came back, in September, through Winchester and Alton; had to avoid Farnham because of the plague, and returned, by Basing, to Windsor by the beginning of October. He enjoyed showing himself to the people, sensing the trend of opinion, putting things to rights.

Hated as he now might be, his prestige was enormous. The English then liked their king to be a terror; Henry's accomplices, and even his victims, grovelled to him with masochistic abjection; as if this immense, unpredictable, temperamental figure symbolized the life and luck of the people, a monstrous mascot or father-figure, whose wrath guaranteed their security. As he cut his way into a secularized future, into a world increasingly run by laymen for laymen, he remained the semi-divine Prince, embodying the king-worship of his time; caught up, like the rest of them, in a political convention as entirely taken for granted as the lethal conventions of national sovereignty between modern great powers.

So great was this prestige, so submissive even his enemies when caught and killed—as the victims of the great carnivores are said to fall into a detached stupor—that he could literally, for reason of state, get away with murder. Backed now with new statutory powers, master in his own house, Henry and Thomas Cromwell looked about for fresh revenues for their near-bankrupt empire.

VI

It was this threat of bankruptcy and the fear of foreign invasion that drove Henry to follow up Cromwell's new administrative drive and the legal subjugation of the clergy by the attack on the richest and most vulnerable aspects of the church, which was to have such permanent social effects in England. The dissolution of the monasteries was designed to bring in vast revenues to the crown, and in the short prospect, it did so; it also bound the new and old great magnates and the rising gentry and their dependents to the monarchy, and to the alterations it had made.

In their immediate predicament Henry and Cromwell had little choice; they were faced with an economic crisis due to forces outside their control, or probably their understanding. Early Tudor England had been relatively prosperous; the rich, at their main meal at ten or eleven, consuming vast quantities of meat, game and fish, ale and wine; the middle-class a rude plenty of roasts and pies and stews, pickled herrings and cold meats. In spite of Henry's injunctions, beer had now supplemented ale, for the hops better preserved it. The poor used salt bacon, thick soups and 'whitemeats'—cheese and dairy produce—and a coarse bread, all despised by the upper classes:[1]

> '*Owe Englische nature cannot lyve by Rooats,*
> *By water, herbys, or such beggarie baggage;*
> *Geeue Englishemen meate after their old usage,*
> *Beiff, mutton, veale, to cheare their courage.*'[2]

Probably all but the poorest had been tolerably fed, if chronically scorbutic and through excess of calcium liable to the stone.

But, after 1525, serious inflation and hardship had begun: it was to continue through the rest of the reign and beyond. By 1540 the price of food had risen 30 per cent; by 1547 even more. New men made their fortunes, but the lower classes and skilled artisans were hit, and the poor became much worse off. Unemployment, though recognized as a responsibility by the state, was countered by inept legislation and savage penalties. Henry was angered and nonplussed.

Wolsey had had little understanding of finance, and the resistance he had met in 1523 and the subsequent climb down by the king himself had shown up his miscalculations: the City had declared firmly that the money was not there. As early as 1526, Henry had begun the debasement of the coinage which was to reach its climax after 1542: indeed, 'in his borrowing and in his sale of lands and debasement of the currency Henry (was to) leave an evil legacy behind him'.[3]

The European inflation, which left the English government nonplussed, had begun when the Fuggers of Augsburg and their like had

---

[1] Henry VIII, says Drummond, made an unsuccessful attempt to proscribe the use of hops, and his own brewer was forbidden to use them. Beer had first come in from Flanders in the previous century, and was still regarded with suspicion, as 'the natural drynke of a Dutcheman'. But by the end of Henry's reign it had become part of the national mystique. 'For your wine, we have good ale bere, metheghlen, sydre and pirey, being more holesome . . . for us than your wines, which maketh your people dronken, as prone and apt to all fylthy pleasures and lustes.' 'And a deep distrust of water,' says Drummond, 'is not surprising, for the character of the water supply was, with few exceptions, appalling.' J. G. Drummond and A. Wilbraham, *The Englishman's Food*, Cape, 1939, p. 87, q.v. for the best account.

[2] Quoted, op. cit., p. 54.

[3] Mackie, op. cit., p. 413. Having raised the value of gold, Henry, in his last years, coined his own plate and bullion at a profit, at the price of his credit abroad.

exploited the silver mines of Saxony and Tyrol, putting more coin into circulation; after 1530 there followed a very gradual influx of gold and silver from the Americas, though its effect was not felt so swiftly as formerly believed. In England the price rise was encouraged when Henry spent the Treasure bequeathed by his father on ruinous wars, repeated on a greater scale in the closing years of his reign.

But there were those who gained by the economic change; new capitalists were rich in cash and avid for land, while landowners with little capital and fixed rents were in difficulties; land came into the market, and was bought up and exploited by men determined to make it pay. Since 'sheep were the most profitable cattle', land was put down to pasture and tenants evicted, in spite of the government's legislation. Already, in 1515, an Act had been passed against enclosures, and, two years later, Wolsey had appointed a commission to examine the problem. But the economic revolution had continued: neither the king nor his ministers could control its social results. The West Country was particularly hit; in 1530, Bristol, long the most important city in the West, petitioned against the unemployment caused by the rise of capitalist factories outside the town, working on a greater scale than the old local economy, and employing villagers on piecework. About 900 houses, the king was told, had 'fallen down'; grass grew in the streets; the tolls on shipping had to be increased and petitioners demanded to be relieved of the upkeep of the castle, now in ruins.[1] Lyme Regis in Dorset complained that it was a great pity 'such a proper town' should 'be so lost, and but new-builded within sixty years by Edward IV'. Henry himself had been there, said the burgesses; he would know what substantial customs would be lost on wine, salt fish and linen, if the town and quay decayed. Ilchester, the antiquary Leland recorded, had been a 'very large thing, and one of the ancientist towns in that quarter', but it was now in 'wonderful decay, as a thing in a manner razed by men of war'.[2] Sherborne, on the other hand, which depended only in part on the cloth industry, 'but most by all manner of crafts', was the most flourishing town in Dorset, next to Poole, now in sudden expansion through the decay of Wareham, reduced to growing garlic in the area 'now within the walls fallen down'. Indeed, Poole, once a 'poor fishear village', much of it in living memory 'covered with sedge and rushes', was now the most flourishing port in the county.[3] Such shifts of the economy were paralleled in East Anglia and the West

[1] L. and P. Addenda, I, I, 238.
[2] *Itinerary of England*, ed. L. Toulmin Smith, Vol. I, p. 156.
[3] p. 254.

Riding of Yorkshire, as the cloth trade 'became a wholesale business operated by men who understood competition better than custom':[1] the prosperity of the ports varied accordingly.

Henry's attempts to relieve distress and promote employment were vigorous but not always wise. In 1529 he had tried to divert the Merchant Adventurers from exporting undressed cloth to the Low Countries to exporting it already dressed, thus giving more skilled work at home. At once the clothiers protested that the government—not for the first or last time—did not know what it was doing. The 'common people of those parts', they pointed out, 'wore garments of sundry colours not worn in England, which colours cannot be made save with undressed cloths', long an expanding export (it rose from 80,000 to 120,000 during the reign). But they could never export it dressed: the buyers refused to pay an economic price.

On the agricultural front there was little understanding of the facts, either; when, in 1531, the Reformation Parliament enacted that no subject should retain more farms than he could occupy for the maintenance of his own household, they were trying to stop the ocean with a broom. Nor did Henry's government deal wisely with unemployed and migrant labour; they tried to force it back into the old framework of locality and 'degree' and the dawn to dusk toil of mediaeval agriculture. They tolerated the 'impotent' but not the 'valiant' or 'lusty' poor and tried to have them set in the stocks and returned to their parishes with a flogging. Such measures, intelligible in view of the menace of roving 'sturdy beggars', were ineffective and 'the cruelty of the act (of 1536) is as appalling as its inefficacy'.[2] They marked, however, Henry's personal concern for the condition of the deserving —never the idle—poor, already apparent in the Privy Remembrance of 1519; a recognition that the destitute were a charge on the lay authorities, central and local, foreshadowing a system of poor relief original at that time.

Most advice available to the king on this count was too conservative. In a paper of 1538 on '*How the common people may be set aworke*', current economic changes were firmly ignored; the labour force was to be put back on the land, and cloth made only in the old centres. Men should be 'set to work the earth with ploughs' and 'in good towns to make cloth'; the 'ancient men of every village' should declare what ground had gone out of cultivation, for if it were reclaimed, '30,000 men servants (some say 100,000) who now live in miserable ease',

[1] Mackie, p. 463.
[2] Mackie, p. 454.

could be 'set to husbandry'. Unemployment could also be cut down if pirated editions of English books, printed abroad, were forbidden: printing (already an important industry) would then become 'a science by which men will wax rich who are now but beggars', and the uncharitable fashion of printers and booksellers to print anything which proves vendible, in despite of the first printing of it, would cease.

After all, the wealth of the realm arose from the work of the common people; there must be comprehensive protection from foreign competition; the king could not gather yearly more than was brought in, and in England 'where no gold and silver grows', God had ordained that gold and silver be brought in by the export of cloth. 'Only a rich realm' and a traditional economy could 'make a rich king'.[1]

So the price rise was countered by piecemeal orders: in 1541 the Lord Mayor of London was told to proclaim that no English merchant or king's subject should be so hardy as to sell the very best and finest sugar above £8 a pound, and the 'coarser sort' at lower rate, on pain of imprisonment.[2] Arbitrary laws restricted the extravagance of the rich: at one 'messe' an archbishop, duke, marquis or earl could have seven main dishes; viscounts, barons or bishops, six; substantial knights and squires, five; others, four, though soup, salad, eggs, tripe, calves feet and entrails, puddings and fruits, did not count.[3]

But the inflation went on; by the late 'forties, Hales would write, 'within these VIII years you could buy the best pig or goose that I could lay my hands on for 4d, which now costs me 8d'.[4] The rising capitalists added farm to farm; colonizing the waste, evicting tenants, if often putting them to more productive labour. And soon the new men were to find new openings, as when Tucker of Burford got the abbey at Abingdon, and William Stumpe of Malmesbury—though he helped the townsmen buy the splendid abbey church for their parish from the king—turned the rest of the abbey buildings into a factory, so that 'its vast houses of office' were 'full of looms to weave cloth in', and turning out 3,000 cloths a year.[5]

Henry was always in favour of stability and distinction of degree, and against the 'idle' poor. He could amend the phrase that 'Almighty God indifferently (impartially) regarded rich and poor', by adding 'touching the soul', against Cranmer's protest that God regarded them impartially in body as well 'rich or poor, free or bond'. And in a text

[1] L. and P., Addenda, I, II.
[2] Acts of Privy Council, Vol. VII, p. 113.
[3] L. and P., Addenda, I, II, 1880.
[4] *Tract on the Causes of Dearth.*
[5] Leland, I, p. 132. Stumpe did not, as often stated, exploit the abbey church itself.

stating that the rich should be diligent dispensers and stewards of their wealth, he could insert that the idle poor did not deserve it: 'There be many folk which had liever [rather] live by craft and begging sloth-fully. . . . We think it right necessary that such should be compelled by one means or another to serve the world with their bodily labours, thinking it small charity to bestow alms on them.'[1] Even in his will, Henry was to provide that the 1,000 marks distributed at his funeral should go to the deserving poor—'not to common beggars, as much as may be avoided'.[2]

[1] See the King's comments on this. *Institution of a Christian Man* in *Miscellaneous Writings and Letters of Thomas Cranmer*, ed. J. E. Cox. Parker Society, II, p. 82.

[2] L. and P., XXI, II, 634.

CHAPTER XIII

THE MONASTERIES
DISSOLVED

W HEN Henry seized upon the wealth of the monasteries he acted
in part as an Erasmian reformer, if immediately 'for the augmentation of his treasure and maintenance of his estates and wars'. And
he was exploiting mediaeval precedents, if the rise of the gentry, which
the sale of monastic lands confirmed, was already far advanced. The
dissolution, also, hardly worsened the plight of the poor, increasingly
victims of inflation. Yet the change marked the passing of a traditional
society:

> *'Level, level with the ground,*
> *The Towres doe lye,*
> *Which, with their golden glittering tops,*
> *Pierced once the skye.'*[1]

And Shakespeare was to write of *'bare ruin'd choirs, where late the
sweet birds sang'*.

Contemporary conservatives felt hatred, not sentiment: in 1536 the
rebels in Lincolnshire fastened up one of Cromwell's servants in a bull's
hide and baited him to death with dogs. But many of the populace still
thought Henry 'a redolent rose, and ever of gentle nature'; it was the
upstart Cromwell, out to enrich king and State by any means, who
was detested:

> *'Thy coffin with gold fillest thou apace*
> *Both plate and chalice come to thy fist.'*

In 1511 Bishop Fisher of Rochester had endowed St John's College,
Cambridge, with the revenue of the nunnery at Higham in his diocese;
but Wolsey, as cardinal-legate, had really set the precedent and pace
when he had suppressed twenty-one minor monasteries to endow his
foundations at Oxford and Ipswich.[2]

[1] Elizabethan *Ballad of Walsingham Abbey.*
[2] See Geoffrey Baskerville, *English Monks and the Suppression of the Monasteries*, Cape,
1937, on which much of this account is based.

'The first entrance was a precedent given by Cardinal Wolsey,' Grafton writes, 'who under pretence . . . to build his sumptuous colleges, dissolved certain small houses. I doubt not with good warrant from Rome, he did make to loose in others the conscience towards [them].' Wolsey had also developed techniques of systematic slander, leading to dissolution: 'He was more successful in suppressing monasteries than in reforming them; but since he was unable to reform himself, this is perhaps natural.'[1] He had taken timber for the roof of Cardinal College, and sold off bells and lead: 'The Cardinal's dissolution made all the forest of religious foundations to shake; justly proving the King would finish and cut the oaks, seeing the Cardinal had begun to cut the underwood.'

Thomas Cromwell, with his experience in the cardinal's service, was the recognized expert on precisely these affairs. As supreme head of the Church, the king was determined on what he held to be reform; and Cromwell, already in control of the whole administration and now appointed Vicar General with overriding powers not from parliament, but from the king, had no qualms either. He was determined to make the realm solvent. There were already big expenses on the Scottish border and in Ireland, on coastal fortifications, and on Calais—where workmen were difficult to come by, formed a rudimentary trade union, went on strike and got better wages for gathering the harvest. There was also the king's lavish programme of building. The obvious answer was to plunder the Church, for then, as now, privilege and powerlessness made the owners of inherited wealth vulnerable.

II

In January 1535 the *Valor Ecclesiasticus*, an unprecedented assessment of Church revenues, was set in train and completed by September; a remarkable achievement. No valuation had been made for centuries, and it was found that the income amounted to £300,000 a year, an immense sum, not surprising since the clergy owned well over a quarter —perhaps a third—of the lands of England.

The monasteries had always been an essential part of the mediaeval establishment. Apart from their primary function of prayer and praise, the important ones were centres of popular pilgrimage, of local charity, of education for well-born boys—Eton and Winchester were still mainly for poor scholars. Many houses had libraries stocked with illuminated books and maintained clever young monks at the uni-

[1] Op. cit., p. 103.

versities. Though not so rich or numerous as those on the continent, the monasteries were part of the traditional ways of life—particularly in the north. Rooted in their localities, they harboured many unsuitable people, for they would take in novices with family connections but no vocation for religion, and parents would say: 'If thou shalt be a monk or a canon, then shalt thou have plenty of delicate meats.' Founders had given heavy endowments, an after-life insurance, and their kin retained rights of residence: local gentry and retired soldiers or civil servants would buy '*corrodies*', life pensions in a monastery, with their own quarters. Loans and leases were given on favourable terms to the abbot's relatives; a whole tribe of stewards, bailiffs, auditors and overseers lived off the revenues, and often wasted or diverted them; there were innumerable ploughmen, shepherds, huntsmen, carpenters and domestic servants. Headships were coveted for relations of those powerful at Court. Lady Carey, sister of Anne Boleyn, tried to nominate the prioress of the ancient nunnery at Wilton. When Wolsey had refused her, and imprisoned the nuns who objected to his own candidate, Anne Boleyn had been enraged.[1]

Local magnates also influenced monastic elections: young Henry Fitzroy, Duke of Richmond, anxious to exclude a stranger, wrote to Cromwell in 1534 about the abbey of Bindon in Dorset, with its delectable fish ponds. 'It adjoins land of mine in Purbeck,' he said, 'and the convent will look after my deer. Please give the monks licence to elect their own abbot.' After the dissolution, the burgesses of Dorchester got most of that property; as the Dorset rhyme has it:

> '*Fordington Cuckolds*
> *Have a-stole Bindon bells.*'

The grandest houses had long been used as hotels by the royalties and magnates. At Butley Priory 'the King's gay sister, Mary, dowager Queen of France and Duchess of Suffolk, spent three summer vacations with her train of ladies and gentlemen. Here she hunted the fox . . . supped with the flattered canons in their little private garden, and once, driven indoors by a storm, hastened to finish her supper in the monastic church. On another occasion her husband, Suffolk, planted the members of his private chapel upon the house, which proceeded to keep them for nine months. And Butley was not the only East Anglian priory used as a cheap hotel by this handsome and popular couple.'[2]

[1] Op. cit., p. 68.
[2] A. G. Dickens, *Thomas Cromwell and the English Reformation*, pp. 28–9.

The major houses were thus part of the great world; rich, enmeshed in a network of local interests with the gentry, many of whose younger sons they employed. Some of the wealthiest were augustly old, coming down from Anglo-Saxon times, endowed by legendary kings, containing fabulous relics set in splendid shrines; famous centres of pilgrimage, blazing with gems and gold. But minor houses were often decayed, the prey of incompetent heads and their kin; in debt, understaffed, broken down. Between these extremes were houses whose life went pleasantly on—Lacock nunnery was admirably conducted—and many harmless monks were like idle Fellows of eighteenth-century colleges, very few in relation to the hordes of servants and hangers-on; concerned mainly with good living, often keeping mistresses round the corner. It had all gone on since time immemorial, mainly through the belief in purgatory and the efficacy of prayer: 'I pray for all' was the motto of the clergy, the justification of the religious. But now, when

> '*The masters of Arts*
> *And Doctors of Divinity*
> *[Had] brought this realm*
> *Out of good unity*',

the very existence of purgatory was being questioned.

III

There were 563 religious houses of all kinds containing 7,000 professed male religious, 2,000 nuns, and about 35,000 laymen. To discredit the monks with Parliament, always anxious to shift taxation on to the clergy, it would be best to prove how immoral they were and so rouse that blend of cant and cupidity already characteristic of the English middle class.

It is fashionable to ignore this gambit, but it was very important at the time and played with gusto, on good evidence. The records prove that this aspect of the Reformation was pushed through with hypocrisy, sadism and malice, by men who enjoyed bullying the weak and who grovelled to their masters while feathering their own nests. If most heads of houses and senior monks were transformed into secular clergy or well pensioned off, and few tears need be shed over their fate, the spirit of the main attack was poisonous. To Cromwell and his agents the mysteries of the mediaeval Church were a bag of old tricks: they were out to find damning evidence and they did so.

In July–December 1535 a rapid and comprehensive general visitation of religious houses was launched under the authority of Cromwell, vicar-general to the supreme head. His principal agents were Dr Legh, a clerical lawyer of 'satrapic countenance' and 'young and intolerable elation', a terror to the provincials he harried; Dr Layton, afterwards Dean of York, who had a nose for the obscene and a brutal, Rabelaisian humour; and Dr London, Warden of New College, who had so enthusiastically described Wolsey's Oxford foundation, and who was less radical, as became his office, but who ended his life in prison, having over-reached himself in attacking Cranmer. Dr John ap Rice was mobile and eager, more humane than Legh, whom he denounced to Cromwell as 'too insolent and pompous' and apt to 'handle the fathers very roughly'.[1]

The visitors insisted on the full mediaeval protocol and procedure, and questions took the traditional form. Was divine service properly conducted at the correct hours? How many attended it? Who were exempt? Did women resort to the monastery 'by back ways or otherwise'? Did the monks all sleep in dorter (dormitory) and feed together? Was discipline fair, impartial and enforced? Were accounts kept, and did the head of the house render the accounts annually? Was the monastery in debt? What leases had been granted, and did the abbot or prior favour his relations? What fees were taken from novices, and were they properly instructed? Were meals over-sumptuous? Did the brethren dress extravagantly? In general, were there any complaints?

These routine questions, pressed home, soon revealed 'evil lives, murders, sodomies, whoredoms in destroying of children, for forging of deeds and other infinite horrors of life'.[2]

And subordinates were encouraged to denounce their superiors: old scores were paid off. It is astonishing what an amount of ground Doctors Legh and Layton, London and ap Rice were able to cover.

The visitors at once found what they wanted in London, where the Prior of the 'Crossed Friars' was caught, very conveniently, 'in bedde with his hoare and both nakyd' at eleven in the morning. He went on his knees and bribed his visitors with £30 not to let on, but he was arrested on the spot. The Abbot of Rievaulx in Yorkshire, on the other hand, in his obstinacy and 'parvarse' mind, refused to acknowledge Cromwell's authority and 'departed', arrogant and intransigent. The Prior of Bridlington, in the same county, merely pleaded ill-health,

---

[1] L. and P., IX, 622.

[2] The fullest accessible account is given in *Three Chapters of Letters relating to the Suppression of the Monasteries*, ed. Thomas Wright, Camden Society, No. 26. q.v.

but at the Abbey of St Mary's at York the monks were 'wurse and wurse', and the visitors investigated the primitive methods of contraception in vogue.[1]

Soon, in the West Country also, Dr Layton found the required depravity: at Maiden Bradley, near Bath, was 'a holy father prior, and hath but six children, and but one daughter married yet of the goods of the monastery, trusting shortly to have the rest'. His sons 'be tall men waiting upon him', and he thanked God he never meddled with married women but always with maidens, the fairest that could be gotten, and always married them right well; indeed the pope, considering his fragility, had even given him 'licens to kepe a hore'.[2] At Bruton, Layton collected 'God's coat, Our Lady's smock, part of God's supper, and Mary Magdalene's girdle', presented by the Empress Mathilda and used to relieve women in labour. At Glastonbury he secured the famous 'thorn' sprung from the staff of Joseph of Arimathaea—'two flowers wrapped in white and black sarcenet, which, on Christmas even, will spring and bud and bear blossoms'.

But even he failed to find 'ill living' at either monastery; merely reporting that the 'brothers be so straight kept they cannot offend, but fain would if they might'. At Bath Priory, however—although the prior had sent Cromwell a leash of Irish hounds—monks were 'more corrupt than any others in vices with both sexes' and £400 in debt. At Farley, Somerset, a cell of Lewes, the prior had 'only eight whores'; the rest of the monks fewer; the place was 'a very stews, and unnatural vices are both here and at Lewes, especially the sub-prior, as appears by the confession of a fair young monk'. At Edington in Wiltshire—the superb church remains—the youngest brother had had to leave under a deserved cloud. At Abbotsbury, in Dorset, where the ruins of the great abbey still overlook Chesil beach and the ancient swannery, the abbot was accused of wrongfully selling timber, plate and jewels, and keeping women, 'not one, two or three, but many'. At Cerne Abbas, in the interior, where the giant cut in the hillside bore witness, then as now, to a pagan past, the abbot was accused of 'keeping concubines in the cellars', letting the church go to ruin, and supporting his bastards out of the church funds. He 'finds sumptuously a son of his by Joan Gardeners', and another 'called Harry, whom he begot on Alice Roberttes, to the great scandal of our religion in the town of Cerne'. He would openly solicit, it was said, honest women in the town.[3] But

[1] Wright, p. 97.
[2] Op.cit., p. 58.
[3] L. and P., VIII, 148.

confined for the visitation during the September harvest, the monks begged that he might 'ride abroad about the affairs of the monastery', as had the Abbot of Sherborne: their livelihood depended on the farms.[1] This request was echoed from Forde Abbey, from Abingdon and many other houses.

Away in Kent at Langdon, a small Premonstratensian house near Folkestone, Dr Layton found the place 'sore in decay and the abbot unthrifty', and in a note 'scribbled this Saturday', described how he had 'gone to the abbot's lodging, joining upon the fields and woods, even like a coney clapper [rabbit warren] full of starting holes', and knocked on the door. Hearing only the barking of the abbot's little dog, he stove in the door with a poleaxe, 'whereat th' abbot's whore, alias his gentlewoman, bestirred her stumps towards the starting hole': an assistant took the 'tender damsel' away to Dover, there to be set in a 'cage' for eight days. In Dover and Folkestone, on the other hand, the monasteries were in good order.

At Whitby Abbey, up on the north-east coast, 'a picturesque but disorderly institution', Abbot Hexham 'took his cut at the proceeds of piracy, while his servants waged ruffianly battles with the fishermen in the town below'.[2] In one Sussex house the abbot was so incompetent that the visitor thought it 'expedient for me to tell the poor fool how he shall do with his monks'. Other fathers had 'used bawdy words to ladies' at the confessional.

Back in Wiltshire, at Marlborough, friars had been caught 'sticking fast in windows, naked, going to drabs, so that a pillar was fain to be sawed to have them out'; others were 'plucked from under drabs' beds', some fighting 'so that the knife had stuck in the bone'. But the mayor had put in a word for one of the accused, charged with using a girl 'naughtily'; he knew the wench himself, he said, and thought the friar should be let off.

At Lichfield 'an old beldame' said that two of the nuns were with child, but at Leicester the abbot was 'doing very well', though some 'factious' canons were accused of the usual vices. At Ramsey Abbey in the Cambridgeshire fenland, all was well, but the visitors plundered a charter of King Edgar in an 'antique Roman' hand. At Walsingham in Norfolk, Sir Thomas l'Estrange found alchemical instruments in secret places, and pots and bellows. Here the prior was 'charged with an amazing range of offences: he had his faction among the deep drinking canons and committed management to the lay Seneschel's wife, a

[1] L. and P., IX, 256.
[2] A. G. Dickens, op. cit., p. 28.

crony of the heartier canons and reputedly the prior's mistress'.[1] At Pershore, amid the Worcestershire orchards, a Benedictine monk, Richard Beerly, blackguarded his colleagues to Cromwell himself. 'Now I will instruct you somewhat of religious men,' he wrote, 'monks drink a bowl after collation till ten or twelve of the clock, and come to mattins dronke as myss (mice), and some at cards and some at dice, and at tables.' He implored the vicar-general to find him secular employment and 'save his soul'. At Eynsham, on the Thames above Oxford, the brethren appeared but 'a raw sort of religious persons', but, in general, wrote Legh, it was 'the black sort of devilish monks' that were 'past amendment'.

If the report was unrepresentative of many well conducted and harmless houses, and the picture was what the visitors required, it is unlikely there was so much smoke without fire.

IV

While the visitation went on in September 1535, Henry proceeded to Portsmouth to inspect repairs to the *Henri Grace à Dieu*; then, by Southampton, to Salisbury, where wheat, that harvest, was as much as 12s a quarter in the market; indeed, that year, people were complaining, 'As for salt fish you will not believe how dear it is, both ling and haberden [Aberdeen herrings].' Henry moved on to Winchester and took 'certain rich unicorns' horns' from the treasure. He was still immensely popular, so obviously what a king ought to be, that his ministers were only the 'sharp thorns under the goodly rose'. People, of course, feared an interdict; they would 'get no more burial than dogs'; a few conservatives said 'all realms christen had forsaken us, save only the Lutherans', and some even hoped to see the king 'glad to take a boat and flee his Kingdom' and 'that mischievous whore, his queen, brent [burnt]'.

Meanwhile, as Chapuys reported, Queen Anne Boleyn still ruled the king; he would become 'worse until utterly ruined'. And he was grumbling, in a sinister way, about the Dowager Queen Catherine and the Princess Mary, for he could not, he said, stand the trouble and 'suspense'. Parliament, he hinted, should release him: '*Cette diablesse de concubine*,' wrote Chapuys, would 'never rest until he is freed from these poor ladies'. When Henry's threats made the courtiers gloomy, he shouted that wry faces were of no avail; he would free himself, if it cost him his crown, and when Mary had complained of solitude, he

[1] A. G. Dickens, op. cit., p. 27.

even declared 'soon would he provide that she should need no company'. 'The ill will of the King of England to the Princess,' commented Charles V, 'is cruel and horrible.' Henry even swore to fulfil an old prophecy that at the beginning of his reign he would be gentle as a lamb and at the end worse than a lion. As, indeed, he did.

These private exasperations did not, of course, distract the king from government: he was concerned, that autumn, with the blocking of rivers by weirs, and ordered abbots and landowners up and down the country to have them 'plucked up'. Among other remembrances on more pressing business, is a note on 'how to restrain young men from marriage until they be of more potent age', and to stop 'tall and puissant persons' marrying 'old widows'. Merchants, too, ought to be restrained from speculating in land, and keep their capital fluid for commerce.

But Cromwell took the main burden; tireless, immensely able, he went his way to make Henry 'the richest King that ever was in England'. His own huge bribes and perquisites rolled in, garnished with lesser but significant benefits; the abbess of Godstow sent him a 'dish of old apples' and 'two Banbury cheeses', while 'her brother Sir Richard Bulkeley would scrape together a paltry 25 marks; but for Cromwell the only value in this lay in the fact that the Bulkeleys were prepared to pretend that they thought him a gentleman'.[1]

One country squire promised 'as many pheasants as his hawks would take'; another sent partridges that his goshawk had taken.

It was a cold winter in 1535–6, and when some Londoners made snowmen of the pope and the cardinals, 4,000 people came to see the fun. Henry declared, 'If the Emperor and the Bishop of Rome and all his adherents were to combine against England, he was so prepared that he did not fear their malice.' It was the sort of remark that made him popular.

V

At Kimbolton, the gloomy moated house near Huntingdon, where the Dowager Queen Catherine had now been shut away separated from the Princess, she lived on; ill, impoverished, in fear of poison, often in prayer on her knees. In spite of his menaces, Henry did not dare to kill her, formally or informally; now she relieved him of his anxieties, not before she had written a magnanimous letter to the man she still loved. 'My most dear lord, King and husband,' she began, 'The hour of my

[1] David Mathew, *The Celtic Peoples and Renaissance Europe*, London, 1933, p. 43.

death now drawing on, the tender love I owe you forceth me to . . . put you in remembrance of the health and safeguard of your soul, which you ought to prefer before all worldly matters, and before the care and pampering of your body, for the which you have cast me into many calamities and yourself into many troubles. For my part, I will pardon you everything, and wish to devoutly pray God that He will pardon you also. For the rest, I commend unto you our daughter, Mary. . . . Lastly, I make this vow that mine eyes desire you above all things.' Unlike his later wives, Catherine had loved Henry for himself: they had been young together.

Henry was delighted at her death. 'God be praised,' he exclaimed, 'we are now free from all suspicion of war!' In yellow silk 'for mourning', he danced in the candlelight in the winter dusk and displayed the infant Princess Elizabeth in his arms. But Queen Anne had little to give her joy; her hold had long been weakening over her husband, who had taken up with a new girl the year before; the courtiers were now watching 'like vultures'.[1] While Catherine lived, a divorce from Anne would have only revived old troubles; now all would depend only on whether the child the queen was carrying was a healthy prince.

VI

The visitation of the monasteries had now done most of its work. Dr Layton's and Dr Legh's findings in the province of York, compiled in February, had provided even more scabrous evidence, just what was wanted. They must have grilled the monks and nuns with the zeal of Viennese psychologists; at Garadon were five homosexuals, 'one with ten boys'; at Holy Trinity, York, 'one with six'; at Warter, the prior, Will Holme, was incontinent; Jack Jackson guilty of 'incest with a nun'; at Calder, one Matthew Ponsonby showed peculiar depravity.

The monks, also, it seems, regularly got the local girls and wives with child: a nun, Margery Benbury, too, *peperit semel ex presbytero*, 'gave birth once by a presbyter', as did Margaret Shakelady of St Mary's, Chester: while at Monks' Arden Margaret Lepton 'gave birth by a regular canon'. At Selby one of the monks was incontinent 'with five or six married women'; at Conyshed, one had taken on six, another ten.[2] Here the principal relic was again a girdle good for those lying in. At Monks Lampley, Mariana Wryte, *ter peperit*, had given birth three times, and Johanna Snaden, *sexties*, six. In Norfolk, wrote

[1] J. E. Neale, *Queen Elizabeth*, p. 17.
[2] L. and P., X, 364. (Cleo M.S. E IV, 147, B. M.)

Dr ap Rice, the situation was no better: vice was endemic; Robert Codde, Prior of Pentney, was incontinent, 'as appeared from the confession of the Abbess of Marham'; at Westacre and Binham, inmates admitted unnatural vice, though those at Beeston Priory, near Cromer, were relatively chaste.

All this went on against a background of childish superstition. Women would make offerings to the images of St Bride 'for cows lost or sick'; among treasured relics was the wymple of St Etheldrede, good for sore throats; also her comb, good for headaches, and the rod of Aaron, good for children with worms. But most relics were obstetrical: at Kirkstall the girdle of St Bernard—of all people—was prized for those in labour, as, oddly, the tunic of St Francis and part of St Thomas's shirt, as well as the girdle of Mary Magdalene; at Pontefract 'Thomas of Lancaster his belt' and hat were held efficacious.

Vile as may have been the motives of the visitation, the cumulative, tabulated evidence illustrates the effect of celibacy on an uncouth but vigorous people. Indeed, in view of the vices 'prevalent among priests, as well secular as regular, as well as the youths who are not yet married', the two fathers with the cure of souls at Dereham, Norfolk, advised that 'the remedy of marriage be granted to such'. Many inmates, realizing that they had mistaken their vocation, asked the visitors that they should be 'released from religion'.

But Henry always remained set against clerical marriage. If the clergy raised families, he said, they would become much too powerful. It was monastic property that interested him; by the spring he had all the evidence he wanted, and, in March 1536, he came down in person 'among the burgesses of Parliament, delivered them a bill, and bade them look upon it and weigh it in conscience'. They must not, he told them, astutely, pass it merely as his own will, but 'try to see if it be for a common weal to his subjects to have an eye thitherward'.

The resulting act shows how shrewdly the moral aspect had been stressed. It began 'Foreasmuch as manifest sin, vicious, carnal and abominable living is daily used among the little and small abbeys', and went on to suppress them. Many large houses had also been discredited, but it was thought they had thrown the lesser ones to the wolves. 'In this time,' Grafton writes succinctly, 'was given to the King, by consent of the great and fatt abbots, all religious houses that were of the value of 300 marks and under, in that the great monasteries should be continued still. But one said in Parliament that these were as thorns [bushes], but the great abbots were putrified old oaks.'

In fact of course the Dissolution went on; over the next four years all the greater houses were to be dissolved. The king appointed a Court of Augmentation of the Revenues of the King's Crown to receive the spoils and dispose of jewels and plate. Lead from roofs was melted and sold.

VII

Down in Wiltshire in September, Henry had visited Wolf Hall on the southern fringe of Savernake forest. His host, Sir John Seymour, was then the hereditary Ranger, his office symbolized by the already ancient carved, silver-bound hunting horn, still an heirloom of his descendants. The Seymours were unimportant, but long established, and Lady Seymour was descended from Edward III. Their eldest daughter, Jane, was just twenty-five; small, fair, self-contained, she contrasted with the hectic, domineering Anne Boleyn—that 'night crow'. Henry found her very attractive and he made her lady-in-waiting to the queen; like an enormous, insatiable pigeon, he paid her romantic, if dishonourable, court at Greenwich—offering jewels, even a bag of gold pieces.

'There is nothing,' she replied, 'I value so much as my honour; if the King's Grace wisheth to send me a present of money, I humbly ask him to reserve it for such time as God will be pleased to send me an *advantageous marriage*.' Henry was only allowed to see her if her brother, Sir Edward Seymour, was there: she remained 'unassuming' but 'inviolably chaste'.[1] Perhaps to distract his mind, Henry went jousting and, in mid-January, as already observed, crashed in the lists, concussed and unconscious for two hours. Jane now brought herself to accept a locket with the royal miniature, and let her sovereign 'take her on his knee' in the queen's ante-chamber. Here Anne found them, and made an appalling scene. 'Be at peace, sweetheart,' protested the king, not for the first time and doubtless thinking of her child; but, in hysterics, she tore the locket from Jane's neck, cutting her own hand. Then, on January 29, 1536, prematurely, she bore a dead boy and thus 'miscarried of her saviour'.[2]

Henry came lowering to her room; told her the disaster was her own fault; she retorted that it was his for carrying on with 'that wench, Jane Seymour'. He replied roundly, 'You shall get no more boys by me. . . . I will speak with you,' he concluded, with ambiguous menace, 'when you are well.' That day he declared privately that he had been seduced by witchcraft and was free to take a new wife; and that day,

[1] See Hester Chapman, *The Last Tudor King*, pp. 19 ff. for a good account.
[2] J. E. Neale, *Queen Elizabeth*, p. 17.

also, saw the not very elaborate funeral of Catherine of Aragon in Peterborough Abbey.

Jane Seymour now retired to Wolf Hall. Soon Henry was writing, in a more restrained tone than he had written to Anne Boleyn: 'My Dear Friend and Mistress, The bearer of these few lines from thy entirely devoted servant will deliver into thy fair hand a token of true affection'; she should disregard a 'ballad of great derision' about them both, and he hoped shortly 'to receive [her] in these arms . . . I end, for the present,' he wrote, 'Your own loving servant and sovereign, H.R.'

Cromwell had long been at odds with his Boleyn patrons, who were hindering an understanding with Charles V; Chapuys reports how Henry and his Councillors were standing in loud discussion, when Cromwell broke away, exhausted with vexation, sat down on a coffer and called for a drink, until the king came striding after him, 'confusedly and in anger'. Henry then told the ambassador that he was 'no longer a child', they must not give him 'the stick and the caress', and he 'played with his fingers on his knees as calling a child'. As to helping Charles against the Turks, Chapuys might remind his master that one should renew old friendships before putting people to expense. The king then returned to his old line that it was through him that Charles had acquired the empire, and that after Pavia his nephew had let him down by refusing to make war on Francis 'because he was his prisoner'. During this tirade, Cromwell had been silent, afterwards saying that he had never known the king so contrary, and that he who trusted the words of princes was not wise.

The ambassador let Henry boast himself to a standstill, but Cromwell had been so angry that he had taken to his bed: if it were lawful, Chapuys concluded, to speak what one thinks of princes, he could say something of this King and so could Cromwell. It was under the pro-French influence of Anne Boleyn that Henry had taken the bit between his teeth; Cromwell decided that she must go.

He had long spied upon her, and, by April, a secret commission was examining the evidence. 'On May Day,' writes Hall, 'was a solemn joust kept at Greenwich, and suddenly from the jousts the King departed, having not above six persons with him, and came to the palace at Westminster. Of the sudden departing many men mused, but most chiefly the Queen.' Next day, she was sent to the Tower, accused of treason, adultery and incest; soon Cromwell was writing that the fame of the queen's incontinent living was 'rank and common' and discovering a conspiracy so dangerous that he 'quaked' at it. The indictment—or frame up—alleged, with dates, that, over three years, Anne had procured five men to 'violate' her, one of them George Rochford, her own brother, alluring him 'with her tongue in the said George's mouth and the said George's tongue in hers'.[1] The others were Henry Norris, Squire to the King's Body, Master of the Hart Hounds and Hawks, and steward, among many other things, of Oxford University, Minster Lovell and Burford in the Cotswolds; William Brereton, who had lands in Cheshire and offices in North Wales; Sir Francis Weston, both of the king's Privy Chamber, and Mark Smeaton, a musician, 'one of the prettiest monochord players and deftest dancers in the land'. 'Does not the lad play well?' Anne had remarked; then, it was alleged, he had been smuggled into a closet for candied fruits, and Anne had told her old servant, Margaret, to 'bring her a little marmalade'. 'Here is the marmalade, my lady,' the old reprobate had replied, whereat the queen had grasped the youth ('who was all trembling') and made him come to bed. There he had 'soon lost his bashfulness and remained that night and many others'. He had then attracted suspicion by getting too 'smart and lavish in his clothes'.[2]

All the accused denied the charges, save only the 'organist', who admitted, under threatened or actual torture by a knotted rope twisted round his head with a cudgel, that he had 'violated' her three times.

It was further alleged that the queen had promised to marry one of them 'when the King was dead'; had said that Henry was impotent, and even *laughed at him*, his clothes and his verses. She had also, it was said, tried to poison Richmond and the Lady Mary. Indeed, when the former, now far gone in consumption, came to say goodnight to his father, Henry wept, telling him to thank God he and his sister had 'escaped from the hands of the accursed whore'. The king also had the poet, Sir Thomas Wyatt, sent to the Tower, on suspicion of being the queen's lover, and Wyatt remarked: 'The King well knows what I told him before he was married.'[3]

During this painful crisis, prolonged by the obstinacy of the accused —had not Henry, riding from the joust, offered Norris pardon if he would confess?—the king kept to his garden, only going out by boat at night, 'banquetting with ladies' and returning after midnight, the music sounding over the water, to the scandal, or amusement, of

[1] L. and P., X, 876.

[2] See *The Chronicle of Henry VIII, King of England*, being a contemporary record . . . written in Spanish by an unknown hand, ed. M. A. S. Hume, Bell, 1889, pp. 56–7.

[3] According to the *Spanish Chronicle*, Henry, after Anne's execution, said to Wyatt: 'I am sorry I did not listen to thee when I was angry; but I was blinded by that bad woman.' P. 69. Her 'badness' was perhaps a desperate attempt to get a son.

London. 'You never saw Prince or man,' reported Chapuys, 'make greater show of his horns. . . .'

Jane Seymour, meanwhile, remained quite firm, even when Henry arranged for her brother to take over one of Cromwell's apartments, accessible by a covered way. But in the Tower Queen Anne disconcerted her gaoler, Sir William Kingston, who had received her so differently before her coronation. 'Shall I go into a dungeon?' she had asked, 'sank down' and wept; then 'fallen into a great laughter'. 'I am clear,' she had cried, 'from the company of man as from sin, as I am clear from you, and I am the King's true wedded wife.' Next day she was even 'merry' and 'made a great dinner'. The king, she said, did it to prove her; and, again, she laughed and laughed; 'I would to God I had my bishops,' she ran on, 'they would all go to the King for me.' The talk reverted to the musician, Mark—always the worst-dressed man in the house; he wore 'yerns' (jeans?) because he was 'no gentleman', and he had never been in her chamber, save at Winchester, when she had made him 'play the virginals above the King's room'.

On May 15th, the queen and Rochford appeared at the bar of the Tower before a tribunal of peers, over which their uncle Norfolk presided, and on which their father, Wiltshire, sat dumb. Queen Anne, with her sense of occasion, appeared as 'unmoved as a stock', with 'the bearing of one coming to great honour'; graciously she returned the formal salutations; strenuously and ably, point by point, she contested the charges.[1] The king himself is said to have remarked, 'She hath a stout heart, but she shall pay for it.' Rochford, too, defended himself so well that odds were ten to one on an acquittal: Sir Thomas More himself, it was said, had not replied better.

At that level, there was now no law in England save the monarch's will, and the monarch was very angry: 'when,' indeed, 'he had read the confessions, his meat did not at all agree with him.'[2] Norris, Brereton, Weston, Mark the musician, had already been condemned, and Cromwell hastened to tell Gardiner that he would get him £200 of the £300 'out among these men'; that zealous Protestant, the elo-

---

[1] She did not, however, write the superb letter to the King for which she was long famous. 'Never had Prince a more dutiful wife than Anne Boleyn . . . you chose me from a low estate and I beg you not to let an unworthy stain of disloyalty blot me and the infant Princess, your daughter,' and concluding, 'my last request is that I alone bear the burden of your displeasure. If ever I have found favour in your sight, if ever the name of Anne Boleyn has been pleasing in your ears, let me obtain this last request.' The letter was a forgery, a fine stroke of Elizabethan political warfare. That it was 'not really either written or composed by Anne Boleyn,' says James Gairdner, 'the handwriting, the style indicates beyond reasonable doubt.' L. and P., X, 341 n.

[2] *Spanish Chronicle*, p. 62.

quent Dr Barnes, applied for Rochford's Mastership of Bedlam (Beth-
lehem) Hospital; he would rather have it, he said, than a bishopric.

Anne was sentenced to be burnt (as a witch), or beheaded, at the
king's pleasure; her brother to die by the axe. He and the others
suffered first; all died 'charitably', praising their merciful prince, in the
hope, presumably, of protecting their dependants. Sir William Kingston had already written to know the king's 'pleasure touching the
Queen and also for the preparation of the scaffold'. The day after, on a
May morning—it was the 19th—black-eyed Anne Boleyn, the most
fiery and dangerous of Henry's wives, 'looking frequently behind her',
mounted the scaffold on Tower Green. It was built high so that all
could see her. She had hoped, almost to the last, to go to a nunnery,
then complained when her execution was put off. As she reached the
platform, four young ladies following, she appeared exhausted and
bewildered; 'Good Christian people,' she said, and her voice strengthened, 'I am come hither to die, according to the law, and I will
speak nothing against it.' She then cried mercy to God and the king—
'for a gentler nor a more merciful prince was there never'—and then 'I
take my leave of you and the world, and I heartily desire you all to
pray for me'.

She was stripped of her short mantle furred with ermine and took
off her white hood ('which was English made') herself. One of her
ladies handed her a linen cap, and she put up her hair. Another girl
bandaged her eyes.

A last mercy had been accorded. The headsman of St Omer—
Kingston calls him *Executur of Cales* (Calais)—the deftest, most fashionable expert of the day, had been specially brought over at short notice,
with his great beautifully balanced sword. Anne had made macabre
jokes about her slender neck: one hiss and flash of steel and the tragedy
was done.[1]

At home and abroad there was a great sensation. There is news from
England, they were saying on the continent, that the so-called queen
was 'found in bed with her organist'; that the king's mistress 'had *six*
lovers, one being her brother', and the like. 'As none but the organist
confessed,' said critics, 'the King invented the device to get rid of her.'
But the execution was popular in England.

More soberly, the power politicians re-assessed the position. The
pope began to excuse himself for having made Fisher a cardinal, and

[1] According to one version, the sword was hidden under a heap of straw. The headsman,
pretending to turn to the steps, said, 'Bring me the sword,' and as Anne turned to look,
struck before she knew what was happening. (*Spanish Chronicle*.)

Charles V offered his uncle the hand of the Infanta of Portugal.

Henry had other ideas. Archbishop Cranmer, supremely and expressly advised, had now discovered that the king's second marriage had been null: Anne had a pre-contract with Northumberland, and, after all, her sister, Mary, had been the king's mistress. On the day of Anne's execution, Cranmer was thus able to give Henry and Jane Seymour special marriage licences, dispensing with banns. On the 21st they were betrothed, and on the 30th privately married in the queen's closet at York Place. By the end of June, Jane was proclaimed queen.

Parliament now passed yet another Act of Succession: the Lady Mary remained barred; the infant Princess Elizabeth—the 'little bastard', as her enemies called her—was also declared illegitimate, and the succession was settled irrevocably on the king's offspring by the new marriage. Henry took overriding powers to determine the future, and made elaborate plans in case of a minority. In July Richmond died, aged only seventeen: all was now set for a new deal, the ill-fated union with Queen Catherine over, the scandal and obsessions over Anne Boleyn obliterated.

The new queen seemed shy and sequestered, but Henry doted on her. Her badge supplanted the falcon crest of her predecessor; a new royal barge, copied at the king's command from the Bucentaur of the Doge of Venice, conveyed the royalties to Westminster, and a survey was made of the queen's new lands in Hampshire, Wiltshire, Devon and Somerset. 'We have found all the Queen's farmers and tenants as glad of her grace as heart can think'; the crops looked promising, 'so that people do note the year to be the year of peace here in England, which men were wont to seek in Rome'. At Court the summer went by in a round of masques, jousts and festivities, centring on a benigner prince.

CHAPTER XIV

CRISIS SURMOUNTED:
A TUDOR PRINCE

HENRY seemed now at a new peak of power. The execution of the Carthusians, of Fisher and More, and the attack on the monasteries, had horrified Catholic Europe; but Pope Paul III could not achieve the coalition of France and a united empire which alone could have brought the heretic king to book. Charles V had his hands full on the Danube, in Germany, Italy, North Africa and the Spanish Colonies in America; that cold realist knew the facts of power, and he told the Lady Mary to make the best terms she could. At home, resistance seemed crushed; if Queen Jane could give Henry an heir, the dynasty might at last be secure.

Henry had never appeared more magnificent. He had long been building lavishly; York Place, Wolsey's huge residence, with its courts and gardens, had superseded the old palace at Westminster, and was becoming Whitehall, the centre of government. In 1536 Cromwell noted, in his own hand, how much building the king had done 'since I came to his service'; how he had 'built the place at Westminster with the tennis plays and the cockfights, and walled the park with a sumptuous wall, and built St James's in the Fields, a magnificent goodly house'. St James's still stands, in its Tudor dignity of dark brick, and from its balcony the sovereigns of England are still proclaimed.

Soon Henry was to begin Nonesuch, the fantastic palace near Ewell, Surrey, with its pinnacles and pavilions, designed to compete with the great châteaux of Francis I, and, under Elizabeth, to attain European fame. Hampton Court, his main residence in later years, had now been taken over from Wolsey and transformed into the great palace, with its vine and maze, that stands today. New lodges and gateways had been put up at the Tower and at Windsor; Greenwich further embellished, the gardens enlarged. The king had long been buying lands and houses up and down the country, and he set particular store by the woods behind Portsmouth for his ships: Henry was already the greatest builder of the English kings.

But behind this apparent power and magnificence, there was danger: 1536 saw the biggest crisis of the reign, met by the king with cool political judgment and calculated bluff. The dissolution of the monasteries and the attack on traditional religion were now provoking widespread resistance, particularly in the north, where the Reformation was 'an alien and southern thing'.[1] When, in the summer, 'New Articles of Religion devised by the King's Highness to establish Christian quietness and unity' and known as the Ten Articles, were promulgated, they were subscribed by both Houses of Parliament. But they were violently unpopular, though Henry himself had been constrained, he said, to put his own pen to the book; for 'they treated of no more than three sacraments, where always the people had been taught seven'. Further, with new-fangled efficiency, many of the old holidays were abolished, particularly 'such as fell at harvest time, the keeping of which was much to the hindrance of the gathering of corn, hay, fruit'.[2] Taxation, too, was heavily increased.

Discontent was less formidable in the south, but it was there. In mid-June, on the feast of Corpus Christi, a preacher at Sturminster Newton, Dorset, had told the people to keep their old holidays, offer candles and 'beware of heretics and of reading *this New Testament in English*': if the king and the emperor didn't go to Hell, the devil didn't live there. At Eynsham, Oxford, one John Hill had said that Norris and Weston had been 'put to death only for pleasure', and that he 'trusted to see the King of Scots King of England'.[3] The bailiff of Bampton, too, hoped to see the Scot 'wear the flower of England'; the vicar of Hornchurch, Hampshire, had said 'the King and his Council had made a way by will and craft to put down all manner of religious . . . but they would hold hard, for their part, which [was] their right; [and] the King could not pull down none, nor all his Council'. For one articulate clerk or yeoman, dozens felt the same.

In spite of the formal understanding and politeness, latent French hostility was also obvious; the Mayor of Dover, for example, reported that a Dutch hoy out of Middleburgh bound for London with hops and linen, had been boarded by a Frenchman three bowshots off shore, and men and boxes cast into the sea: the owner's son, a lad of fifteen, had been rescued by a 'mackerel man'. There were many complaints of systematic poaching of fisheries and casual piracy: they mounted up.

Since her mother's death, the Lady Mary had appealed to Cromwell

[1] David Mathew, *Celtic Peoples and Renaissance Europe*, p. 5.
[2] Hall, II, p. 269.
[3] L. and P., X, 1205.

to be allowed at least to write to her father; so Henry told Norfolk and the Earl of Sussex to 'go bird-catching' and persuade her to admit that he was supreme head. But Mary proved so obstinate that they told her 'if she were their daughter, they would beat and knock her head against the wall and render it soft as baked apples'. The king was furious with her: even Cromwell was terrified of what he might do, and, when Queen Jane intervened, Henry told her not to be a fool. By the end of June, Mary had been so far broken, and so cautiously advised by Charles V, that she had made abject submission—signing the document, her partisans explained, 'without reading it'. Her guilt and remorse were to have their sequel in the reign of 'Bloody' Mary. At present she was cowed.

II

Henry was not to have it all his own way in theological warfare, either. In July 1536, the month in which the Ten Articles in which he had a hand were authorized, he received a letter written in Venice from his cousin, Reginald Pole. Since the king, cited to appear before a General Council for the following year, had asked, hopefully, his views on papal supremacy, Pole had given them: he enclosed a work called *De Unitate Ecclesiae*, on the unity of the Church. It was an extremely unpleasant book, blistering and disrespectful, as from one royal kinsman to another, for Pole thought Henry's incursions into theology puerile. It had been written, said the author, with all the wit and learning he had, to save Henry from frightful dishonour and danger, in this world and the next. He hoped his cousin would yet return to the fold.

Since Henry had opposed the calling of a General Council without the express consent of all Christian princes, 'especially such as have within their own realms and seigneuries *imperium merum*, that is to say the whole, entire, and supreme government of all their subjects', and the English clergy had acquiesced, Pole now felt it his duty to intervene, as the only one of the nobility, educated by Henry from a boy, capable of doing so. He bitterly reproached him for executing the Carthusians and Fisher and More—could hardly write for tears at the thought. He even compared the king to Nero and Domitian, and appealed to Charles V to protect Christians against an enemy worse than the Turk. While Charles was crusading in Africa, the so-called Defender of the Faith had attacked Christendom more cruelly than did the heathen, and for twenty-seven years, too, Henry had 'plundered' his subjects; 'made a sport of the nobility'; made himself detested by the people, and 'torn like a wild beast the men who were the greatest honour to the Kingdom'. The pope, Pole warned him, would expel him from the Church as a 'rotten member', and he recalled the fate of Richard III. As a final insult to one who prided himself on his theology, Pole's covering letter told Henry to appoint a real expert to read the book and give his unbiased opinion: Tunstall would do. Not surprisingly, the summary was endorsed 'abbreviations of a certain evil-willed man who writ against the King's doings'. But Henry dissembled his hatred: sent a mild answer; invited Pole to England to talk things over. Pole was too intelligent a fly to enter that parlour: under Mary, he was to get his revenge.

<h2 style="text-align:center">III</h2>

Far worse was to come. By the autumn of 1536 Lincolnshire and the north was seething with discontent; the plundering of the small monasteries and the obvious threat to the great ones had confirmed popular fury. The old feudal detestation of a centralizing monarchy and of 'villein blood' in the Council combined with perennial poverty, aggravated by the inflation to rouse serious, deep-rooted opposition.

The north, indeed, had never been brought under proper control: Richmond's nominal lieutenancy had been a farce, and Tunstall, appointed to the great palatine Bishopric of Durham in 1530, had never been effectual: the Earl of Northumberland, who had managed to arrest Wolsey, was ill and notoriously bankrupt; resentful, pensioned by the king.

But the first flare-up came in Lincolnshire, a popular movement encouraged by priests and led by 'one who named himself Captain Cobbler'. The people said that the monasteries had been 'great maintainers of sea walls and dikes', and marched under a rustic banner of the Five Wounds of Christ, a plough and a horn. Spontaneously, or coerced, many gentry joined them, though many were uncouth enough—'such a sight of asses, so unlike gents for the most part'.[1] On October 6th, Lincoln, under its towering cathedral, was taken. The insurgents, in the English way, did not regard themselves as rebels; they were protesting against evil Councillors, not attacking the king; they demanded that taxes be diminished, heresy be put down; that the dissolutions should stop. 'Friends,' they said, 'now is taken from us four of the sacraments and shortly we shall lose the other three, and then the faith of Holy Church shall utterly be suppressed and abolished.' Soon

---

[1] Baskerville, p. 160, op. cit.

no man would be able 'to marry . . . or at length eat a piece of roast meat, but he should . . . first pay the King'.[1]

Henry reacted with royal rage, flung their demands in their teeth, reinforced Suffolk at Stamford with artillery, the decisive arm. Already the insurgents were at cross purposes, and he denounced them, himself, in the high Tudor style, afterwards used by his daughter Elizabeth. 'How presumptuous then are ye,' he wrote, 'the rude commons of one shire, and that the most brute and beastly of the whole realm, and of least experience, to find fault with your Prince.' Parliament, not Cromwell, had decreed the dissolution of the monasteries: 'We wolle that ye . . . should well know that this is granted to us by all the nobles, spiritual and temporal, of this our Realm, and by all the Commons in the same Act of Parliament, and not set forth by any Councillor or Councillors upon their mere will and fantasy.' As for the monks, they were an 'unthrifty sort of vicious persons' who wasted their substance, while the people's 'own natural Prince, sovereign Lord and King' had 'spent more in their defence of his own than six times they [the monks] be worth'.

The insurgents' demands were of course 'mad and unreasonable; unmete and dishonourable', and he would never admit them. And if they had not the 'grace and naturalness to consider their allegiance', the rest of the realm, he doubted not, had. They must surrender their leaders, return to their homes, and face such 'condign punishment' as he and his nobles should think fit. If not, he concluded, 'then by your obstinacy and wilfulness [you] put yourselves, your wives, your children's lands, goods and cattle, beside the indignation of God, in utter adventure of total destruction and utter ruin by force and violence of the sword'.

Before this leonine and politically able roaring, now backed by the reinforcements hastily assembled and—as Henry himself arranged— paid in advance 'to give them better courage',[2] the rising caved in. Suffolk, under instructions, if necessary, to 'destroy, burn and kill man, woman and child', reoccupied a sullen Lincoln.

But the crisis was not over; on October 13th a more massive revolt broke out in Yorkshire and spread over the north. It began at a meet held ostensibly for cub-hunting, and was led by a capable lawyer and local squire, Robert Aske. He called the movement 'The Pilgrimage of Grace for the Commonwealth', and his followers marched under a banner with Christ on the Cross on one side and a Chalice and Wafer (Hall calls it a 'cake') on the other. Northumberland was now incapa-

[1] Hall, II, p. 270.
[2] L. and P., Addenda, I, 1106.

citated; Tunstall lost his nerve and fled to Norham Castle; soon the insurgents were in York. Lord Darcy of Templehurst, the veteran Warden of the forests north of Trent, shut himself up in Pontefract castle, along with the Archbishop; but they also had to surrender and join the rebels. Aske established himself there, keeping great state; negotiating with the king's enemies in the Low Countries, while over thirty thousand insurgents, including four peers and many of the gentry, gathered at Doncaster under the banner of St Cuthbert, who, before Flodden, had so well defended the north: they were 'warlike men, and well-appointed'.

Against them Norfolk and his supporting peers had only eight thousand men, many of them disloyal; but the late October rain had so flooded the ford and meadows that one army 'could not come at the other'. To gain time, he civilly met the leaders on Doncaster bridge, and rode down with two of them to Windsor to present their demands to the king.

Henry privately declared the truce a 'blot on his honour', but he dissembled; further annoyed, probably, when a Windsor butcher, inflamed by a priest's sermon and offered too little for a sheep, exclaimed, 'By God's soul, I would rather the good fellows of the north had it among them, and a score more of the best I had.' The culprit had been hanged at once on a new gallows before the castle gate, and the priest on a tree at Windsor bridge.

Henry now replied, with cunning and in his own hand, 'with no creature privy thereto until it was finished'. He attacked the vague doctrines of the insurgents: for his part, he would live and die in the faith of Christ; and exactly what did they mean by the liberties of the church? As for villein blood in the Council, there had been more lawyers and priests in it when he was crowned: 'How come you to think that there were more noble men in our Privy Council then?' He concluded, with a bland assumption of power, 'To show our pity, we are content, if we find you penitent, to grant you all letters of pardon, on your delivery to us of ten such leaders of this rebellion as we shall assign to you. Now note the benignity of your Prince, and how easily bloodshed may be eschewed. Thus I, as your Head, pray for you, my members, that God may enlighten you for your benefit.' Seldom has a weakish hand been more coolly played.

Norfolk returned to Doncaster, authorized to offer a free Parliament and a free pardon; Darcy was conciliated; Henry even brought himself to summon Aske to London, entangling that political innocent in friendly discussions, playing for time. By January 1537, Aske was going up to Yorkshire to persuade his followers to disband and the main crisis was over.

There remained some flickers of revolt, convenient for the king's still implacable purpose. 'I fear me', said a Yorkshire yeoman shrewdly, 'the gentlemen will deceive us the commons, and the King's Grace intends to perform nothing of our petitions. Wherefore I think best to take Hull and Scarborough ourselves betimes.'[1] They failed to take them; Darcy and Aske, now compromised, were brought back, bound, on horseback, to the Tower. On a market day in July, at York, where, said the king, 'he had been in his most frantic glory', Aske was dragged on a hurdle through the streets and hung in chains high above the city to die.

Norfolk, meanwhile, had put down a peasant rising in the Lake District and established himself at Carlisle. Through the spring and summer of 1537 Henry's revenge went on: in Yorkshire important abbots and local gentry were executed; in Lincolnshire thirty-six of the commons hung; seventy-four at Carlisle. 'You shall in any wise,' he wrote, 'cause such dreadful execution to be done upon a good number of the inhabitants of every town, village, and hamlet that have been offenders in the rebellion, as well by hanging them up in trees as by quartering of them and the setting of their heads and quarters in every town, great and small, as they may be a fearful spectacle to all other hereafter that would practice a like matter.'

The victory was the king's own; but Cromwell, with his 'villein blood', had also triumphed; all he stood for—the secularized state—had been the target of the revolt. But even Cromwell may have afterwards remembered the words of Darcy before his execution in the Tower. 'Cromwell, it is thou that art the very original and chief danger of this rebellion and mischief, and art likewise causer of the apprehension of us that be noble men . . . and I trust that, ere thou die, though thou wouldst procure all the noblemen's heads within the realm to be stricken off, yet shall there one head remain that shall strike off thy head.'[2]

That Christmas of 1536, the Thames had frozen so thick that the heavy king and his pale, delicate queen, wrapped in furs, could proceed on the ice to Greenwich amid the plaudits of the Londoners. The political ice had been thinner.

In January a proper Council of the North was devised with a reluctant Tunstall as president: 'The said bishop,' it was urged, on his behalf,

---

[1] Quoted by Fisher, op. cit., p. 414.
[2] Fisher, op. cit., p. 412.

'is in hate with the people of the north . . . which might be occasion to make them grudge against the King.' He was even 'unfurnished of cart and horse, wheat, malt, wine and of other things, saving only some beefs and muttons'; how could he entertain? Yet, if he did not, he might 'bring the King's authority amongst wild people into contempt, which God forbid'. He begged to retire to a cure of souls and 'meddle no further with worldly business'.

Henry increased his stipend to £800 a year and commanded him to serve: the Council of the North now had a secretary and a board of three lawyers and civil servants, as well as a few local magnates and gentry: it was a compact, relatively efficient body, though it was to have little success.

But the crisis had its most important effect on the central administration. The king by now had a regular Privy Council—as he called it himself, writing from Windsor—of which the fluctuating Council Attendant was only a part. Cromwell had noted, in 1534, that he must remind the king 'for the establishment of the Counsayle'. 'Now everything,' writes Dr Elton, 'points to its having been organized before the second half of 1536, when attendance on the King grew regular, meetings became more frequent, and membership settled down to fixity and permanence.'[1] And doubtless the demands of that autumn—the need, perhaps, to shield Cromwell—had confirmed the change. But it was not until August 10, 1540, after Cromwell's fall, that nineteen men described as his *Highness Pryvy Counsaill whose names hereinafter ensue*, met to appoint a clerk and provide for the keeping of a register, that this vital development was formalized.[2]

IV

By the spring of 1537 the new queen was pregnant. Anxious to shield her from all distress, Henry told Norfolk in March that he could not preside over the newly formed Council of the North at York, lest 'upon sudden and displeasant rumours' in his absence, the queen might 'take . . . such impressions as might ensue no little danger or displeasure to the infant'.[3]

---

[1] G. R. Elton, *The Tudor Revolution in Government*, p. 342. q.v. He lists the following Councillors: Cromwell (Vicegerent and Lord Privy Seal), Cranmer, Audley (Lord Chancellor), Norfolk, Suffolk, Exeter, Oxford, Sussex; the bishops of Durham, Hereford and Chichester; Lord Sandes, Chamberlain to the Household; Fitzwilliam, Lord Admiral, Paulet, Kingston, Sir John Russell, and Sir Edward Seymour, now Viscount Beauchamp. (p. 339.)

[2] P. 317.

[3] Chapman, op. cit., p. 23.

It was easier now to countenance the Lady Mary as she had made submission. Queen Jane told her husband that she now had no 'equal' with whom 'to be merry . . . unless it would please you that we might enjoy the company of the Lady Mary's grace at Court; I would make merry with her'. 'We will have her here, darling,' Henry replied easily, 'if she will make thee merry.'[1] When she appeared, now aged twenty, short, bustling, deep-voiced, in full state, her ladies about her, the king characteristically put the blame for their estrangement where it did not belong: 'Some of you,' he remarked, 'were desirous that I should put this jewel to death.' In the resulting silence, Jane remarked suavely that 'it had been great pity to have lost your chief jewel of England'. 'Nay, nay,' said the king, bluff and hearty, 'Edward . . . Edward . . . clapping the Queen on the belly.'

But his other daughter, the four-year-old Elizabeth—'as toward a child', her governess had written, 'and as gentle of conditions as ever I knew in my life'—seemed firmly and finally put aside. 'Why, Governor,' said this very sharp child, 'how hath it, yesterday Lady Princess, and today but Lady Elizabeth?'[2]

Through the summer domestic tension grew, but the king had one satisfaction. Reginald Pole had now been made a cardinal, and in February sent north as legate *a latere* to foment the now extinguished northern rebellion from the Low Countries. He had been hopelessly late: the French king had ordered him out of France; the Archduchess Margaret of the Netherlands had refused to harbour him; he had got no further than Cambrai, whence he had been conducted to Liège, and by September, he was back in Italy, his mission a failure.

On October 9th, St Edward's Eve, 1537, the queen fell in labour; three days later, she bore a son. The rejoicing was tremendous; dancing and bonfires all over the country; thanksgivings, feasting, the salutes of guns. London went wild, with fountains spouting wine and heavy civic pageantry. The court ceremonies reached their brilliant, crowded climax as 'the right excellent and noble Prince' was christened Edward, after Edward IV and the sainted Confessor. The Lady Mary was godmother; the Lady Elizabeth, carried by two lords, held the baptismal robe. Henry was ecstatic, as the spectres of disputed succession and foreign intervention diminished: he held the child and wept for joy. The curse, it seemed, had at last been lifted; Jane might well have more sons and the Tudor dynasty be secure.

Their luck did not hold; three days after the christening, Queen Jane

[1] Chapman, op. cit., p. 24.
[2] *Ibidem*, p. 25.

was delirious with puerperal fever. The crowds, the notabilities, the deputations—though cut down by Henry's command—had been too much for her; she had sat through one pompous reception lasting six hours. Queen Jane fought her illness for five days, and on October 25th, she died.

Henry left at once for Windsor and 'kept himself close for a long time'. 'Divine Providence,' he wrote to Francis I, 'hath mingled my joy with the bitterness of the death of her who brought me this happiness', for Jane Seymour was the wife he loved best, and he directed that he should be buried with her in the great royal vault beneath the chancel of the nearly completed St George's Chapel, Windsor.

He turned to a detailed plan for the Prince's household: elaborate precautions were to be taken against infection; baths and lavatories installed; casual visitors fended off, dogs and beggars kept out; passages and cooking utensils were to be spotless. All this Henry himself supervised with his wonted and formidable grasp.

But the infant prince faced other, political, dangers. Henry had now entirely repudiated the authority of Rome. 'All his learned men,' he had written to Paul III that year, had declared 'that the Roman bishop has no more jurisdiction over his subjects than the Bishop of Mayence or Trèves or any other foreign bishop.' He had refused to attend a general council in Mantua, where, he said, 'the bishop and such as he reign[ed] in noisy pomp'.[1] Led by the pope, the hostile continental powers at once refused to recognize Edward: Princess Mary, they still insisted, was the legitimate heiress, through her mother a European royalty in her own right. Henry knew that he must now so organize and defend his kingdom that his son, even if still a child, could hold it. This objective was to dominate the rest of his reign.

V

During 1537 the dissolution of the monasteries had gone on. Henry was out for their property to pay for administration and war, but, brought up in the Erasmian new learning, he had his humaner purpose on a magnificent scale. Had he not written, in his own hand (and his own spelling and, probably pronunciation) that he proposed 'Gode's worde myht the better be sett forthe, chyldren brought up in lernyng, Clercs nuryshud in the universities, olde servants decayed to have lyfinges, allmes housys for pour folke to be sustaynd and reders of Grece Ebrew and Latyne to have god stypende, dayly almes to be

[1] L. and P. Addenda, I, 1221.

mynystrate?' He intended an entire reorganization of the Church.

Cromwell's visitors were already attacking some scholastic pedantry at Oxford and Cambridge. In September 1535, Dr Layton had established a new lectureship in Greek at Oxford; one in Greek and Latin at New College and another at 'Allsowllen', as well as others at Merton and Queen's. Every scholar had to attend one lecture a day, on pain of loss of his dining rights, for the visitors had known how to hit where it hurt. The old scholastic learning was being put down: 'We have set Duns (Scotus) in Bocardo (the stocks),' Layton had written, 'and banished him Oxford for ever.'[1] He was too optimistic—turn nature out, in new guise she will return. Duns' writings, meanwhile, had 'been made a common servant to everyman, fast nailed up on posts in all common houses of easement';[2] and New College quadrangle had been 'full of leaves of Duns': Mr Greenfield, a Buckinghamshire gentleman, had been seen gathering them up as 'blownsheaves' to make a circle round his deer to keep them in a wood and make 'a better cry for his hounds'. Layton had also tried to reform morals; forbidden laundresses to come to the men's chambers: 'No doubt,' he had chaffed Cromwell, 'the honest matrons will sue you for redress.'

These changes had been welcomed by twenty progressive Fellows of Magdalen. Indeed, they had written, they could not sufficiently thank Cromwell; the young men had hitherto been so 'blindly instructed' in logic that they 'could not know whereabouts they went'; now beneficent government had prescribed a proper way and order. And they had warned Cromwell to ignore the 'sinistral informations' of the reactionary party in the College.

At Cambridge, too, the new learning—so unpopular in Erasmus' times there—had been officially encouraged. Cromwell had now succeeded Fisher as Chancellor,[3] and had at once made himself felt. He had confirmed that daily lectures should be given in Greek as well as Latin; that all scholars should read the scriptures for themselves; that civil, not canon, law should be studied and scholastic philosophy forbidden: even

[1] Duns Scotus, c. 1274–1308, an Oxford Franciscan who had taught the primacy of will over intellect. 'No man,' writes Osborn Taylor, 'ever drove either constructive logic or the subtleties of critical distinction closer to the limits of human comprehension or human patience. . . . If you enter *his* lists you are lost. The right way to attack him is to stand without and laugh. That is what was done afterwards, when whoever cared for such reasonings was called a Dunce after the name of the most subtle of mediaeval metaphysicians.' (*The Mediaeval Mind*, II, pp. 543 ff.)

[2] L. and P., IX, 350.

[3] Thus, in due course, contributing, all unknowing, to a record: five Chancellors to be executed in a century. The others, besides Fisher, were Protector Somerset, Northumberland, and the Elizabethan Earl of Essex.

antique ceremonies, so dear to academic minds, were to be abolished; they hindered 'polite learning'. Scholars had still to read Aristotle; but the reformers 'Rodulphus, Agricola, Melancthon, Trapezuntius, etc. as well', and not 'the frivolous quibbles and obscure glosses of Scotus, Burleus, Anthony Trombet, Bricot, and Bruliferus'.

These injunctions had been enforced under pain of the indignation of the Erasmian king himself. At the universities there was now official enthusiasm for the new learning, and, at the end of his life, Henry founded the two largest colleges in both.

VI

Through 1538 the attack on the lesser religious houses continued; in 1539 it began against the 'great and solemn' ones as well. If Henry meant to divert massive endowments to other forms of learning and piety, Cromwell had to fill the coffers of the state, depleted by growing administrative costs and by defence. Again invasion threatened; Cardinal Pole— 'enemy to God's word and his native country'—continued his plotting, and the king decided to destroy all potential claimants to the throne—centres of 'malice domestic' and foreign intrigue.

Henry's first cousin, Henry Courtenay, Marquis of Exeter, was descended from a sister of Edward IV. He had vast estates in the West, where he was regarded as a potential successor, even supplanter, of the king: 'Our master,' one of his servants had said in 1531, when the divorce had outraged opinion, 'shall wear the garland at the last.'[1] Exeter had long conciliated the king, but his wife had been intimate with the Queen Dowager Catherine and involved with the crazy Maid of Kent; Henry had already warned him and his friends that they 'must not trip or vary for fear of losing their heads'.

The other royal collaterals, descendants of Edward IV's brother Clarence, were the aged Countess of Salisbury, mother of the detested Cardinal Pole, and her sons, Henry Pole, Lord Montague, and Sir Geoffrey Pole. All, like Exeter, had been in touch with the cardinal; and all were now in dire peril, for they had lost their last opportunity. 'The Pilgrimage of Grace,' writes Dr Rowse, had been 'the only chance for the small aristocratic circle of seizing fortune by the forelock. They did nothing; or rather their class feeling made them rally to the king against the northern men, and, after that, they were isolated and lost.'[2]

---

[1] A. L. Rowse, *Tudor Cornwall*, p. 235, q.v. for an account of him and of the consequence of his ruin in the West: 'The ruin of a noble house such as this was like the foundering of a great ship.'

[2] Op. cit., p. 237.

By 1538 there was evidence to convict them all. Sir Geoffrey Pole turned king's evidence, and both Exeter and Montague were executed for treason that December, while the old countess was imprisoned in the Tower. 'In your conferences with the Emperor,' wrote Henry to Sir Thomas Wyatt, now an Ambassador, in February, 'you shall ever inculcate the ingratitude of the Poles ... who by counsel of the Cardinal, his brothers Montague and the Marquis of Exeter, with their adherents, have ... imagined the way to destroy us and our dearest son, the Prince, with the Lady Mary and the Lady Elizabeth, our daughters, for to take upon them the whole rule, whereunto the said Marquis [had] fixed his mind and sought his opportune occasion for ten years. . . . All these things have been disclosed by Sir Geoffrey Pole, Montague's brother.'

Soon Cromwell was noting, among urgent memoranda, 'a (retrospective) bill of attainder to be drawn up for the Marquis of Exeter, and his complices. A like to be drawn up for the Lady Marques and the Lady of Salisbury.'[1] All their great properties came to the crown, many of them to form part of the royal Duchy of Cornwall; others of the vast Russell estates in the West. Henry had finished off the Yorkist house of the White Rose.

VII

As part of this vendetta, which the king pursued implacably, two more of the great abbots perished, following the execution of the abbots of Woburn and Colchester the year before. 'The Abbot of Reading,' noted Cromwell, notoriously, in September 1539, 'to be sent down to be tried and executed at Reading, with his complices, similarly the Abbot of Glaston, at Glaston.' They had been intimates of the Poles and Courtneys and the pre-arranged decision was political.

Their abbeys were also very rich, Glastonbury the grandest in Somerset. 'The house,' wrote Cromwell's agents, 'is great, goodly, and so princely we have never seen the like.' There were two parks, four outlying manors, 'a great mere ... five miles in compass, well replenished with great pikes, breams, perch and roach'. 'We would,' they wrote, 'that your lordship did know it as we do: then we doubt not but that [you would] judge it a house meet for the King's Majesty and for no one else.' 'We trust,' they concluded, 'that there shall never come any double-hood [religious] within that house again.' They nosed around for treasure 'hid or mured up'; found £300 and a fair golden chalice, hidden, they said, by Abbot Whiting himself—who had 'ymbecelyd'

[1] L. and P., XIV, 655.

[embezzled], they alleged, enough to 'begin a new abbey'. They had put him in the monastery tower, 'being a very weak man and sickly'. His study had yielded a book against the king's divorce, but no letter that was material. But by November 15th, the abbot had been 'arraigned and put in execution' for robbing his own church; dragged through the town on a hurdle to 'the hill called Torr'. Here, on that autumn day, high above the Somerset meadows, he was strung up: he took his death 'very patiently'. Sir John—now Lord Russell,[1] newly appointed steward of the Duchy of Cornwall and Lord President of the Council of the West, endowed with huge estates—told Cromwell that the body had been divided into four parts and the head stricken off; one quarter sent to Wells, the others to Bath, Ilchester and Bridgewater, and the head stuck over the abbey gate. 'I commit your lordship,' Russell concluded, 'to the keeping of the Blessed Trinity.' A century later, Somerset folk were still saying, 'Remember how poor Abbot Whiting was used.'

Cromwell's men now busied themselves with auditing and selling up the enormous, ancient property. They pensioned most of the remaining monks, paid off the servants with half a year's wages, sold the cattle for cash. The local gentry closed in, a Paulett begging the surveyship for his brother: 'I assure your Lordship he has been very diligent to serve the King.' It is the tone of the Roundhead sequestrators after the Civil Wars, if the form of the cant differs.

The destruction of famous shrines also continued, emphasizing the final break with Rome in a way the people would understand. In the great Norman cathedral at Durham, the shrine of St Cuthbert was smashed with sledgehammers, and the saint's body relegated to the vestry; even the tomb of the Venerable Bede was desecrated. The great rich shrine at Bury St Edmund's in Suffolk proved 'very cumbersome to deface'; here were 'the coals that St Lawrence was roasted withal', the parings of St Edmund's nails, St Thomas of Canterbury's penknife and boots; relics, also, that brought rain and prevented weeds growing in corn.

Sir William Bassett at Buxton Wells removed the healing image of

---

[1] John Russell, afterwards first Earl of Bedford (1486–1555), who had come to Court when Philip and Juana of Castile had been driven to take shelter in Weymouth in 1504, came of a Dorset family with connections through the wine trade with France and Spain. He became the most successful of Henry's soldier diplomatists; fought in Flanders, lost an eye at Morlaix in 1522, served as a diplomat in France and Italy. He acquired Chenies in Buckinghamshire by marriage, and now acquired vast properties in the West Country. Comptroller of the Household, 1537; Privy Councillor; Baron Russell of Chenies, Lord High Admiral, 1540–2; Lord Privy Seal, 1542; Executor of Henry VIII's will and owner of Woburn, Bedfordshire, 1547.

St Anne, defaced the 'tabernacles', took away the votive crutches shirts and sheets, and sealed up the baths and wells. The image of our Lady at Lewisham was 'put in a chest, locked and nailed, with her coat, cap and hair, with divers relics, and the blessed knife that killed King Edward' (stabbed at Corfe Gate, in 978): 'I missed nothing,' wrote Dr London, 'but only a piece of the holy halter Judas was hanged withal.' The image of the Welsh giant Darvell Gadern, the 'gatherer' which could pull souls from hell, was burnt beneath an Observant friar, once confessor to Catherine of Aragon, who lost his nerve and clung to the ladder.

The visitors, like the agents at Glastonbury, would point out smugly what pains they were taking for the commonwealth; one, who had put down the Blackfriars near Fisherton bridge at Salisbury, cadged for their 'stuff', and thanked Cromwell for a warrant 'to take a stag in Purbeck'.

There was a brisk trade in the general debris: the iron and stained glass in the windows of Bordesley Abbey, Worcestershire, brought 17s 8d— 'sold to Raffe Sheldon and a Mr Markham', who also got 'the old broken tile house'. 'Candlstix, brass potts, a great basin, a cope of tawny damask', timber work in the high choir, 'an alabaster altar'—all went; two 'portatif organs' fetched 2s and 'old books in the vestry, VIIId'. At Evesham Abbey 'no little spoil was made by unauthorized people', but the authorized agent reserved the best bed for his local patron, and 'as for the table at Worcester, I am right well contented that your wife shall have the same . . . God send us merry meeting'.

These representative minor sales, paralleled all over the country, were eclipsed in 1538 by the greatest plunder of all. The shrine of St Thomas of Canterbury, famous all over Europe, yielded two great chests of jewels that each took six or eight men to carry, as well as, apparently, twenty-four wagon loads of other treasure. Henry declared the saint 'a rebel'.[1] In March 1540, Christ Church Canterbury and Rochester were dissolved and Waltham Abbey in Essex surrendered.

In spite of these spectacular political crimes and calculated iconoclasms, Henry was aiming at a salutary reconstruction of the Church, and he was too shrewd a realist not to give most of the religious a generous deal. As already remarked, many abbots and monks became bishops, deans and canons in transformed foundations, as at Peterborough, and Osney, near Oxford, whose abbot became the first bishop of that see. The heads of houses were very well pensioned indeed; Abbot Reeve, for example, of Bury St Edmunds where the shrine had been so hard to deface, was a 'merry old man, fond of the ladies, fond of his

[1] J. D. Mackie, op. cit., p. 396.

glass, fond of the gardens of his country houses';[1] he got 500 marks a year—a huge income—and it was no one's fault that within six months he died of old age. Abbot Segar of Hayles, Gloucestershire, also got a handsome annuity: he was glad to escape the restrictions of his calling —'Glad,' he said, 'to live in the light.'[2] The abbot of the splendid monastery at Beaulieu, Hampshire, obtained ample compensation: 'Thank God,' he said, 'I am rid of my lewd monks';[3] and the Abbot of Pershore obtained a country house with a garden and orchards and a pool. The abbesses of Wilton and Shaftesbury were handsomely pensioned. The monks not given alternative positions were given 'capacities' to take ordinary livings and substantial sums to tide them along.

'The religious of all ranks,' concludes Baskerville, 'got a great deal more out of the dissolution . . . than is generally recognized.' Nor is it likely that they had been less rapacious landlords than anyone else: 'Does anyone seriously maintain,' he writes, 'that the colleges of Oxford and Cambridge are easier landlords than private individuals? Their bursars see that they are not.'

The evictions, in fact, were timely, recognizing the tide of opinion and economic interests and they occurred before the full tide of anti-clericalism could mount up, as on the continent, where in the end the religious orders often met a much worse fate.

Henry, it seemed, also, as well as profoundly changing the universities and the church, had laid the foundations of an absolute monarchy. But it was the nobles and the rising gentry who mainly profited by the up-heaval. Henry himself had no illusions; as when he told his Seymour brother-in-law, who had accused the new bishops of lack of hospitality: 'I know your purposes well enough; you have had among you all the commodities of the abbeys, which you have consumed, some with superfluous apparel, some at dice and cards, and other ungracious rule, and now you would have the bishops' lands and revenues to abuse like-wise.'[4]

But the Government was insolvent; it started selling off the lands at once, and by the end of the reign two thirds had gone. The remaining properties were mostly on leases, now often altered to twenty-one years instead of sixty, so that fines for renewal were more frequent and higher. It is often forgotten that the most massive grants, worth £20,000 a year, went to the clergy, all but three, out of fifty-five, by way of ex-

[1] Baskerville, op. cit., p. 189.

[2] Op. cit., p. 190.

[3] P. 252.

[4] J. G. Nichols, *Narratives of the Days of the Reformation*, Camden Society, 1859, pp. 262–3.

change for the endowment of new and better foundations. But great magnates came next, with lands worth £16,000 a year: they included Cromwell, Norfolk, Suffolk, Wriothesley, grandfather of Shakespeare's patron, Southampton, and Russell. The city merchants, between them, got lands worth £6,000; Sir Richard Gresham bought immense areas of Yorkshire and London aldermen speculated in a big way. Crown officials and king's servants both got £3,500 worth; the lawyers, surprisingly, only bought property worth £1,500 a year; but eleven enterprising doctors obtained twenty grants worth together £500, a similar amount to that of the clerks and yeomen. Lands worth £23,000 went to persons at present unknown.

There were many transfers and sub-sales: 'very few humble people,' writes Fisher, 'were among the original grantees. On the other hand, there was an extremely brisk speculation in land during the last decade of the reign, many people buying licences to alienate a few days after they had secured a grant.'[1] The monastic lands were thus very widely distributed and a great 'interest' in the Reformation emerged which even the Marian reaction could not upset: it 'confirmed a decisive shift in power within the landed ruling class from the great feudal families, with their centrifugal traditions, to the aspiring gentry and new men who were coming up into their places through royal favour'.[2]

> 'Bitter it was, oh, to view
> The sacred vyne,
> While the gardiners played all close,
> Rooted up by the swine,'

an Elizabethan would write, and John Aubrey, that seventeenth-century romantic, would think 'the tingle tangle of their convent bells made very pretty music, like the college bells in Oxon'; yet the change had to come, and the blackmail, cant, violence, and destruction masked a much more sensible settlement than partisan historians have been inclined to admit. But Henry himself, and his successors, got no more than a transient benefit, for he had raised up an interest stronger than the crown, and 'the long term outcome of the Reformation was the opposite of that intended by the Machiavellians who had created it'.[3]

[1] *History of England*, Vol. V, Appendix II, p. 500.
[2] Christopher Hill, op. cit., pp. 34-5.
[3] Op. cit., pp. 38-9.

CHAPTER XV

'ILL-CONDITIONED WIVES'

H ENRY was now much concerned at the turn of continental power politics. In June 1538, the pope, the emperor and the King of France made the Truce of Nice, and at Aigues Mortes, in August, Charles and Francis planned a joint crusade against heresy, at home and abroad. At Rome the destruction of the famous shrine of St Thomas of Canterbury was the final outrage; in December, Paul III launched the Bull of Excommunication and deposition drawn up in 1535, and was planning a coalition of the emperor, the French and the Scots against the heretic English—as Wyatt put it, reporting from Nice, 'the emperor and the French King and Bishop of Rome assembled, pretending a union of the world'.

'We cannot a little marvel,' Henry wrote to his ambassador in Paris, 'at the very frosty coldness and slack remissness [the French] show now'; an invasion fleet was gathering at Antwerp and the Privy Council had been ruefully debating 'points to be considered if the intercourse with Flanders were broke'. It had 'so long been so profitable' and the king and the merchant adventurers had invested thousands; Calais would be the best alternative outlet.

The defences of the coast were also inspected and heavily reinforced. Cromwell noted, among other urgent business, the 'places where fortification is to be made'; Berwick, Carlisle, Holy Island, Tynemouth, Hull, Lynn, Yarmouth, Lowestoft, Aldborough, Orwell, Tilbury, Gravesend, the Downs, Calshot point, Portsmouth, Hampton water, Lyme, Plymouth, Falmouth, Fowey and Milford Haven, as well as Calais and Guisnes.[1]

Already in 1537 the Lord Admiral had reported that they had viewed Calshot point and devised a tower to be set at the Western entrance to Southampton water; 'it would there so strengthe all that quarter . . . that none should lie there neither come to any road or channel thereabouts, unless he come in and go out at the Needles'. At the entrance to the Solent an ancient fort had also been transformed, and a new one

[1] L. and P., XIV, I, 655.

devised opposite, on a 'hard sand' called Hurst. Like Calshot ('a strong castle late builded,' writes Leland), Hurst Castle still stands, and Charles I was to be confined there on his way to London and death. 'The people of the Isle of Wight,' the commission also reported, 'are all, both gentlemen and others, well minded to defend their country . . . saying they will stake their coasts and cast their ditches anew towards the low water mark, then, when their enemies land, it shall be dangerous to them.' They would, they promised, make their bulwarks stronger and 'keep their beacons . . . on every hill right well'. The commission also sent Cromwell 'some more cockles of Shelsay which are not quite so good as they would be at the full of the moon'.[1]

Henry had already put a castle, still extant, where Chesil Beach in Dorset joins Portland Bill; and, in 1539, as president of the Council of the West, Russell surveyed the entire west coast down to Cornwall. Next year, the forts at Pendennis and St Mawes guarding Falmouth were already begun, designed by a German expert; the interior of St Mawes 'built of the white free stone on the shore between Pentewen and Blackhead'.[2] 'Both castles remain,' writes Dr Rowse, 'two of the most beautiful examples of the military architecture of that time.'[3]

Such were the defences made in the West. Along the South-East coast were forts at Rye, Sandgate and Dover 'under the Castle'; the 'great castle of the Downs', and the 'bulwark at Gravesend'. Eastward in East Anglia, Henry commanded the inspection of Harwich: here the people were ready and diligent; had made trenches and bulwarks and demanded guns; they had even offered to pay for the powder. A substantial blockhouse was built opposite; the local justices alerted, beacons tended, and craft ordered to sea 'to set wisps on fire' if they saw the enemy. In the far north, Newcastle-on-Tyne was repaired, and in 1540 Henry was ordering the Bishop of Carlisle back to his diocese with the wages for the king's workmen upon the new fortress there; the bishop had stayed in the south 'rather to have lingered the time at Eton than for any just cause'.[4]

By the Spring of 1539 the fleet was concentrated at Portsmouth and urgent missives were sent out commanding the magnates to provide archers and gunners for the ships. 'That most pestilent idol,' wrote the king, 'the bishop of Rome' was 'minded to rob and spoil the realm' and

---

[1] L. and P., XIV, I, 573.
[2] Leland, op. cit., I, p. 202.
[3] *Tudor Cornwall*, p. 247.
[4] Act of Privy Council, VII, p. 88.

'invert good religion', so they were each told to provide forty able men for the sea: 237 letter missives also went out to the gentry, asking them how many men they could raise for the king's service.[1] In May Henry reviewed 15,000 embattled Londoners at Westminster.

Meanwhile, in Flanders, all English ships were put under arrest and English diplomats forced to pay excise on their beer. 'They were the first,' they complained, 'that ever paid it'—18d a barrell—'but they must pay or lack drink.'

Henry now wrote to the emperor in Spain warning him that Cardinal Pole, on his way there, again up to no good, would 'pour forth the venom of his serpent nature'; Charles should ponder how odious and detestable traitors ought to be to princes. That realist remarked, with characteristic ambiguity, that he 'felt cumbered between his friend and his conscience'; by December 1539, Henry was offering the hand of the now illegitimate Lady Mary, formerly affianced to the emperor, to the Protestant Philip, Count Palatine of the Rhine.

II

Henry himself was also once more looking for a wife. The Dowager Duchess Christina of Milan, a niece of Charles V by his sister, the Queen of Denmark, and widow of elderly Francesco Sforza, last Duke of Milan, who had died in 1535, was considered. But she declined the honour, reputedly observing that she would marry the King of England if she had two heads. Enquiries were also made at the French Court, ribaldly received, and the French ambassador pointed out that the ladies of his country were not to be inspected like ponies.[2]

But Cromwell, deeply committed to a forward Protestant policy at home, was pushing his master into a German alliance which could put pressure on Charles V in the Netherlands. The Lady Anne of Cleves was pock-marked and thirty-four; she could only speak German, and her main accomplishments were needlework and the favourite German game of *Skat*; but her brother, Duke Wilhelm of Cleves, had a nuisance value against the emperor, the more so when he inherited Gelderland. Between Rhine and Meuse, thirty miles west of Nijmegen, Cleves had strategic importance; the duke also controlled Berg, and Julich which lies between Maastricht and Cologne, increasing the threat to the

[1] L. and P., XIV, I, 12. In South Wiltshire, Alington could raise five men; Fittleton, thirteen; Brigmerston and Milston, five; Great and Little Durnford, fifteen; Bulford, nineteen, and the town of Great Amesbury and West Amesbury, forty-eight. (Musters, Hundred of Amesbury.)

[2] Mackie, p. 403.

emperor's communications between the Rhineland, Germany and the Low Countries. The Cleves family were still Catholics, but Anne's sister was married to the Lutheran Johann Friedrich of Saxony. Henry's relations with the Schmalkaldic League would be improved; and Cromwell may have wanted much closer commitments with the great Lutheran Baltic ports.

Henry was now restless; wary that he was being pushed too far. But Cromwell, led on, like Wolsey, by a dangerous foreign policy, took a grave risk; he told his master that everyone praised the beauty of the princess of Cleves—'as to her face as to her whole body'. She might not be musical or well educated, but such skills were considered in Germany bad form; 'and your Grace's servant, Hans Holbein' (retained by Henry for a large annual fee) 'hath taken the effigies of the Lady Anne'. In fact the picture was too flattering: 'while the famous Holbein portrait now in the Louvre is no aphrodisiac, it does at least omit the traces of smallpox which less respectful eyes were quick to observe'.[1]

Her arrival confirmed Henry's worst suspicions. 'The King's Majesty,' reported Fitzwilliam, now Earl of Southampton, from Rochester, 'upon the sight of her person was not contented.' 'How like you this woman?' the king asked Lord Russell, obviously expecting the answer 'no'. 'Do you think her so fair as she hath been made out to me?'[2] Russell, the perfect courtier, replied, with maddening tact 'that he took her not for fair, but for brown complexion'. 'Alas,' muttered the exasperated monarch, turning away with 'a sore troubled countenance', 'whom shall a man trust?'

It was the depth of winter; Henry had brought sables down to Rochester for his bride, but could not now bear to present them. When he kissed her, he showed 'misliking'; indeed, appeared 'nothing pleasantly disposed'. Reluctant as a huge sulky bull, he told Cromwell that 'he had a great yoke to enter into'; and when, at length, he 'marched forward' said that he 'must needs'. On January 6, 1540, amid great splendour, the marriage took place: 'Surely, my lord,' Henry remarked, 'I liked her before not well, but now I like her much worse.'

Eight days after, Cromwell was saying ruefully that 'the Queen was still a maid for the King's Highness . . . the King's Highness liked not her body'. He had not yet 'carnally known' her and could not, 'for the disposition of her body, be provoked there unto'. As for Henry, he soon declared 'that he mistrusted her to be no maid, by reason of the looseness of her breasts and other tokens': he could 'have none appetite',

---

[1] A. G. Dickens, *Thomas Cromwell and the English Reformation*, E.U.P., 1959, p. 164.
[2] Strype, *Ecclesiastical Memorials*, I, Appendix, p. 309.

he complained, for 'displeasant ayres'. He lamented the state of princes: poor men could choose.

Dr Chambers, the king's physician, was consulted: he advised his master 'not to force himself', while the king complained that he felt unwontedly 'indisposed' and 'could not overcome the loathesomeness ne in her company be provoked or stirred to that Act'. Yet, the elderly tyrant told Dr Buttes that during his enforced continence he had twice given proof of virility (*duas pollutiones in somno*) and thought himself 'able to do the Act with other than with her'. This sad state of affairs was confirmed by the new queen. 'Why,' she told her ladies, indiscreetly, 'when he comes to bed he kisseth me, and taketh me by the hand and biddeth me "good night, sweetheart", and in the morning kisseth me and biddeth "farewell, darling".' Among his intimates, Henry called her 'The Flanders Mare'—a phrase which redeems much. Cromwell had made the same fatal mistake as Wolsey: he had made his master look a fool.

III

The personal affront put the king in dangerous mood. The fiercely deterrent and conservative Six Articles had been acclaimed by most of the London populace, who detested new fangled ideas; and, abroad, the pro-Lutheran policy no longer made sense, as the accord between the emperor and the French had already worn thin. In February 1540, Henry told the Lutheran envoys that he had no need of German soldiers for his ships; they were anyway always seasick. In March Gardiner boldly denounced the Protestants in St Paul's; the redoubtable Dr Barnes denounced Gardiner; and Henry himself, always fascinated by theological warfare, condescended to intervene. In the end Barnes refused to recant, even for the king, and was clapped into the Tower, along with two 'hot gospellers', Jerome and Garrett.

Cromwell now asked Gardiner to dine, in an attempt to settle their differences as between men of the world, and his guest astutely let him believe that they were agreed: in fact his hatred was implacable, and he thought Cromwell was on his way out.

Yet on April 18th, Henry seemed to veer round. Cromwell was suddenly made Earl of Essex and, next day, Lord Chamberlain of England, with appropriate revenues. Thus fortified, he so managed the new Parliament and the convocations that he got the equivalent of three million for his master; and, for good measure, he plundered the property of the Knights of St John, whose aged prior died of shock.

Yet Gardiner's calculation was correct: since April Cromwell had
been menaced by a new, insidious attack. Norfolk and Gardiner,
between them, were luring the king into a new marriage, this time in
the Catholic interest. Catherine Howard ('Haward' they spelt it, phonetically) was about twenty-one, Norfolk's niece, the empty-headed
daughter of Lord Edmund Howard and Jocasta Culpeper. She was
short, plump, vivacious, with auburn hair and hazel eyes, physically the
most attractive of Henry's wives, and first cousin of Anne Boleyn.
When Anne of Cleves' German entourage had been sent packing, the
girl had become one of her ladies, and 'the King did cast a fantasy on
Catherine Howard the first time that ever his Grace saw her'. Henry
was frequently rowed across to Lambeth, where she lived with the
dowager Duchess of Norfolk; soon the Howards were advising her
'in what sort to entertain the King and how often'. They particularly
praised her 'pure and honest condition'.

By May 6th the new Earl of Essex had long scented danger. 'The
King liketh not the Queen,' he told Secretary Wriothesley as they stood,
pensive, at a window.[1] 'For God's sake,' replied Wriothesley, 'devise
how his Grace may be relieved.' 'Yea,' said Cromwell, 'how?' 'I cannot suddenly tell,' answered the Secretary—no friend, though Cromwell had got him the appointment—'For God's sake devise relief for
the King or we shall both smart for it.'

Cromwell now stepped up the theological warfare; Bishop Sampson
of Chichester and Dr Wilson, a royal chaplain, were arrested as papalists
who had denied the king's supremacy; in desperation, Cromwell even
introduced a new treason bill; and it was rumoured that he would
arrest five other conservative bishops. The king watched the contest
glumly.

On the afternoon of June 10, 1540, Henry struck. The Privy Council
was in session, the windows open to the June air, as business proceeded
round the carpet-covered table. Suddenly, to the brisk tramp of armed
men, there entered the captain of the king's guard and arrested the
'villein' minister for high treason. Lantern-jawed, malignant, the Duke
of Norfolk darted at Thomas Cromwell and ripped the collar of St

[1] Sir Thomas Wriothesley (1505–1550), first baron Wriothesley of Titchfield and Earl
of Southampton; e.s. of William Wriothesley, York Herald; educated St John's College,
Cambridge, in Law; 1530 Clerk of the Signet; employed on diplomacy and administration. With the king at Windsor in crisis of 1536; obtained monastic lands at Beaulieu and
Titchfield, Hants; 1538, Ambassador to the Netherlands; 1540, Joint Principal Secretary;
1544, Lord Chancellor and baron Titchfield; 1545, K.G.; Earl of Southampton 1547. His
grandson, the third earl, was probably the youth to whom Shakespeare's sonnets are
addressed.

George from the upstart's neck; Southampton ripped the garter from
his knee. Even the hard-bitten victim lost his poise and threw his bonnet
on the floor, shouting, in rage and frustration, that he was no traitor.
Was this his reward? he demanded, his small eyes gleaming with a
hatred equal to Norfolk's colder malice. It was odd that he should have
expected one.

The greatest administrative genius of the reign was done for. He had
so shifted and modernized the structure of Government, so much increased the Privy Council's efficiency that a grand vizier was no longer
so necessary. Nor had he any party behind him; in the Council all were
enemies: 'The service of a suspicious monarch had created in the
governing groups an atmosphere devoid of generosity, fair play, friendship or any loyalty except to sovereign or to self.'[1]

The fallen minister was conveyed down river to the Tower; and,
that night, his enemies 'banquetted and triumphed together', though
some, fearing he might yet escape,' dared not yet be merry'. They were
reassured when the king's servants came to Cromwell's house, listing
and packing up the furniture and silver. This sign was always thought
conclusive.

On June 29th an Act of Attainder passed the Commons, condemn-
ing Thomas Cromwell as heretic and traitor. He was charged with em-
bezzlement and with licensing heretics to preach, but the gravest
charge was his villein blood and presumption: had he not once declared
that 'if the lords would handle him so, he would give them such a
breakfast as was never made in England'? Had he not overridden the
great prelates, since, the Protestants admitted, he could not abide their
'snuffing pride'?

One more service was demanded: to provide evidence, eagerly
rendered, to release his master from Anne of Cleves. At midsummer the
queen had been quietly relegated to Richmond, a healthier place, the
king considered, than London; and on July 9th both Convocations
declared the marriage void. There had been a pre-contract, it was discovered, with the Marquis of Lorraine; Henry explained that the matter
was urgent, 'for so might the succession of this realm be called in doubt
ever after, whether it were lawful or no, whensoever the son of Lorraine would make his claim by his pre-contract, it should break the
King's marriage'. The Bishop of Rome would take advantage, 'being
mortal enemy to the King', to slander the succession of this realm.[2]
Nor had the union been consummated, and 'matrimonie non consum-

---

[1] A. G. Dickens, op. cit., p. 170.
[2] State Papers, I, CXXXIX, p. 636.

mate' was under the disposition of the church, so that 'the church thereof may dispose, and a second matrimonie consummate could take
away the first non consummate'. The king's virtuosity in argument had
never been more acute.

Parliament soon passed a bill of dissolution and Anne was pensioned
off with the great manors of Richmond and Bletchingley and the
enormous income of £4,000 a year. She was advised to write, with just
the right blend of humbug:

'Pleasith your most excellent Majesty to know that though this case
must needs be most hard and sorrowful to me, for that great love
which I bear unto your most Noble Person, yet having more regard for
God and his Truth than to any worldly affection, I acknowledge myself
hereby to accept [the judgement of the Clergy], entirely putting myself
to Your Highness's goodness and pleasure, most humbly beseeching
Your Majesty that though . . . the pretended matrimony is royal . . .
yet it will please you to take me for one of your most humble servants,
and so to determine of me, as I may sometimes have the sight of Your
Most Noble Presence, which I esteme a great benefit, and that Your
Highness will take me for your sister . . . Anne, Dochter of Cleyffs.'

She took the parting cheerfully and bought a great many new
clothes. Already, it was rumoured, falsely, that Catherine Howard was
pregnant, but the Council begged Henry 'to turn his most noble heart
to love'.

From his room in the Tower Cromwell wrote long, frantic letters
to the king. The script conveys, as nothing else, how rattled he was; his
normally efficient late mediaeval handwriting, crowding down the un-
headed page, folded and refolded (they had no envelopes) into a small
oblong packet, becomes blotched when the pen runs too fast, or the
writer omits, in his haste, to sand it.[1] The letters are those of a modern,
commonsense, man of business, rather vulgarly asserting ties with a
heartless royal dynast, aloof in his caste. A subtler man than Cromwell
would have known that prince and subject were at cross purposes.
'What labours, pains and travail,' he wrote, 'have I taken according to
my bounden duty, God alone knoweth, for if it were in my power, as
it is in God's, to make your Majesty to live ever young and prosperous,
God knoweth I would. . . . Your Majesty hath been the most bountiful
prince to me that ever was King to his subject; yea, the more like a dear
father (Your Majesty not offended) than master.' 'Prostrate at your
feet,' he wrote in his final appeal, 'the frail flesh inciteth me continually

[1] B. M. Cott, Tit, B.I.

to call to your Grace for Mercye and Pardon. . . . I call for mercye, mercye, mercye.' This *cri de coeur* was not cowardice: in the convention of the time, it probably tries to avoid the mutilation to which a commoner was liable or the flames to which a heretic would be consigned.

If that was his object, Thomas Cromwell succeeded: on July 28, 1540, he was beheaded at Tyburn. He apparently died affirming the 'Catholic faith of Holy Church'; 'and then,' writes Hall, 'he made his prayer, which was long, but not too long . . . and so patiently suffered the stroke of the axe by a ragged Boocherly miser [wretch] which very ungoodly performed his office.' The poet Surrey, Norfolk's heir, expressed the feelings of the nobility: 'Now is the foul churl dead,' he remarked, 'so ambitious of other's blood. . . . These newly erected men would by their wills leave no nobleman on life.'[1]

On the same day, privately, at Oatlands, with characteristic timing, 'the King took to wife Catherine, thinking now in his old age [he was just forty-nine] to have obtained a jewel of womanhood'. But the jewel, like Cromwell's thick neck, was flawed.

Two days after, the three Protestant ideologists in the Tower perished. Robert Barnes, William Jerome and Thomas Garrett were drawn to the stake and burned as 'detestable and abominable heretics': 'Junker Heinrich,' commented Luther, 'means to be God.' That year, too, Richard Mekins, a boy of fifteen, was also burnt for heresy by zealous Bishop Bonner of London, who had hitherto supported Cromwell and was now anxious to conciliate Gardiner. The boy had been made to declare that he learnt his heresy from Barnes and doubtless the bishop felt an example should be made; but there were those who felt he should have spared the child, 'seeing he was such an ignorant soul'.

IV

Henry was re-invigorated by his marriage. The full splendour of Tudor pageantry was deployed; the queen's state barge, manned by twenty-six bargemen and twenty attendants, swept down river with flashing oars, the deck strewn with fresh rushes and rosemary. The city magnates were rowed to meet her, banners displayed, while the guns thundered from the Tower; jewels and brocades, pearls and sables were heaped on her; lavish grants of land sustained her dignity.

Indeed, the king's régime became rather hectic. He rose at dawn, heard mass, rode out early to hunt; returned to a gargantuan meal at

[1] L. and P., XXI, II, p. xli.

ten—'marvellous excessive', it was observed, 'in eating and drinking'. Despite his gross bulk, his bloated jowl, his now ulcerated leg, his mounting blood pressure, he was at the apex of his personal rule— vigilant, incalculable. He now struck right and left against potential danger, real and imaginary; deliberately, he spread terror.

He also insisted on greater privacy. 'The King's pleasure is,' minuted the Privy Council, in October 1540, 'that they should no longer molest his person with any manner of suit'; such suits should now be written and delivered to the Council Attendant; and only the grooms of the Privy Chamber were to serve the King, and 'not to suffer the pages or other persons to intermeddle . . .'

Strict precautions were again ordered against infection, and infected families turned out of Windsor, with compensation promised, though tardily paid; the perennial battle for order in the itinerant court went on, as Henry moved on progress, that August, to Reading, Ewelme, Rycott, Ampthill and Dunstable and back to Windsor and Hampton Court. Tapsters who vagrantly followed the Court from place to place and caused the price of victuals to go up were set in the pillory; local poachers were forbidden to take partridges and pheasants with 'any nets trammells or other gins'.

But amid his many preoccupations that year Henry had refounded Westminster School. There had long been 'boys of the Almonry' and 'grammar boys' attached to the abbey; on the dissolution of the monastery, Henry had himself taken charge and made the school an integral part of the new foundation, for in the 'Booke of the erreccion of the King's College', the names of the forty King's Scholars 'follow immediately after those of the Dean and Prebendaries. The king seems to have taken the school under his special protection, and the appointment in 1543 of Alexander Nowell as headmaster was to open a new era in the history of the school . . . he has a claim on the gratitude of posterity both as the writer of the shorter catechism and as the inventor of bottled beer.' He also introduced the annual Latin play, and appointed a *Praepostor Immundorum* 'whose duty it was to keep an eye on yill kept hedys, unwashed faces, fowle clothis and sich other'.[1]

Next year, the king was to find the affairs of Eton, another royal foundation, less happy. The playwright, Nicholas Udall, appointed, as already observed, headmaster in 1534, in the flush of enthusiasm after the queen's coronation, had been a great success with the boys. A Wykehamist and a notable flogger—he would beat fifty-three strokes at a time—he wrote plays for the scholars to act, in particular *Ralph*

[1] L. E. Tanner, *Westminster School*, pp. 4–5, q.v.

Royster Doister. But in March 1541, strange goings on came to light, for a London goldsmith was accused of buying certain images of silver and other plate stolen from the chapel, and 'Nycholas Uvedale, Scoolmaster of Eton, beyng sent for as a suspect to be counsail of a robbery lately committed at Eton by Thomas Cheney (and) John Horde, scolars of the said scole, did confess that he did comitt buggery with the sayd Cheney sundry times heretofore . . . where upon he was committed to the M'shalsey' (prison).[1] The headmaster solicited temporary reinstatement so as to pay his debts (he had done much entertaining): 'For the love of Christ,' he wrote to Wriothesley, 'consider in what extremitys and distress I am constitute. . . . Bee good maister to me this oons [once].' Scipio Africanus, he pointed out, had been riotous and dissolute in youth, and the young Q. Fabius Cunctator had a shocking reputation. 'Forget,' he begged, 'that is past'; he hoped 'to be hable to shake it of within two or three yeres at the uttirmust'.[2]

And, indeed, it was impossible to keep Udall down; the fashionable playwright was made much of at the court of Edward VI and Mary, and ended up, as successor to Nowell, headmaster of refounded Westminster.[3]

Christmas of 1540 was kept with great magnificence; Anne of Cleves, to show there was no ill feeling, cheerfully visited Hampton Court, where 'the two queens danced and drank together', but the political atmosphere remained tense. 'This prince,' wrote Marillac, 'having offended many people, has occasion to distrust others, and shedding blood upon any suspicion only makes distrust to increase.' Describing Lord William Howard, the new ambassador to France, he wrote that 'like several other lords, he would rather live in France than here, where they are under continual suspicion'.[4] Henry even turned on two of his most trusted servants, on rumours of their behaviour on embassies abroad. Bound and fettered, Sir Thomas Wyatt was marched off by archers to the Tower: 'No one dared say a word for him, and by their fine laws he must be judged without knowing why'; there could, indeed, be 'no worse war' than the English carried on against each other, and as long as they did so, they would not attack France.[5] Sir John Wallop, that reliable war horse and diplomat, was also arrested.

Not to be put down, Wyatt pointed out that he had to ingratiate himself with Charles V at Nice; described how he had 'trotted up and

[1] *Acts of the Privy Council*, Vol. VII, p. 157.
[2] *Letters of Eminent Literary Men*, Camden Society, XXIII, pp. 1–7.
[3] See C. Hollis, *Eton*, p. 36. 'Headmasters,' he writes, 'are infrequently hanged.'
[4] L. and P., XVI, 466 and 467.
[5] Marillac, *ibidem*, 467.

down in that hell through heat and stink': he was released at the request of Queen Catherine, 'on hard conditions that he take back his
wife, from whom he had been separated for fifteen years', but only to
die at Sherborne the following year, returning from Falmouth, where
he had met envoys from the emperor. Wallop, accused of praising the
pope, was let off 'for slipperiness of memory, being a man unlearned',
and restored to the captainship of Guisnes. But both arrests showed
Henry's extreme suspicion of well-tried men.

His vigilance now also extended to smaller matters; that year, he
was furious with the Council for sending some thieves, who had
organized an elaborate robbery at Windsor, to common prisons, not
the Tower, 'as though you made no difference between the enterprise
of robbing His Majesty and the attempting of the same towards any
mean subject'. They were to be sent to the Tower at once, and 'the
maker of their instruments strictly examined to get to the bottom of
the affair'.[1]

Church as well as state was entirely subject to the king's imperious
will: following Henry's Erasmian policy, the great and ancient foundations, Winchester, Norwich, Durham, Ely and Worcester were
transformed, as deans and canons (often the same persons) replaced the
monks; lesser but venerable sees, Carlisle, Coventry, Rochester, were
also adapted. Henry created six new bishoprics, Peterborough, Chester,
Oxford, Gloucester, Bristol and Westminster: save for the last, they
endure still. In a grandiose transformation, he had envisaged many
more. But orthodoxy was preserved and the clergy remained celibate.
Yet out of this revolution, came the Church of Andrewes and Laud; in
the long run, that of Trollope and Dr Grantly. The king would also
endow Regius professorships of Divinity, Hebrew, Greek, Medicine
and Civil Law at Oxford and Cambridge, with all their interesting
consequences, and give a charter to the Royal College of Surgeons and
have his portrait painted presenting it to those skilled in the 'noble
science and cunning of surgery': it is hard to say which looks the more
dangerous, the giver or the recipients of this document.

V

In spite of the new Council of the North at York, which was not unpopular, rebellion still smouldered in the district. The 'faithful people
of this boreal region' had never understood what was going on in the
south, and had not, apparently, quite learnt the lesson of the Pilgrimage

[1] *Acts of Privy Council*, VII, p. 684.

of Grace. 'Anno Domini 1539,' wrote a northern chronicler, 'all was suppressid furiously under foote (even as th'olly temple at Hierusalem was handlyde when the Chaldees had dominion thereof) . . . and all this ungratiousness cam thrughe cowncell of one wreatche and heretike Crumwell . . . which Crumwell was headyde for highe treason in the yeare after.'[1] The great minister's fate had given a wrong impression that the old ways were to return; and all the north country, as the French ambassador reported, was still 'very unstable because of rigorous rule and excessive taxation'.

In April 1541, there was a new rebellion in Yorkshire, when a plot was laid to kidnap or kill the Bishop of Llandaff, Lord President of the Council of the North, at Pontefract Fair. Henry had the ringleaders executed at Tyburn, and a local magnate, Sir John Neville, beheaded in York for not betraying what he knew. He also took the occasion to kill off the aged Countess of Salisbury who had been in the Tower since 1538. In March, Scut, the queen's tailor, had made her a furred night-gown and a worsted kirtle[2]; now, without even being told the reason, she was sent the way of her son, Lord Montague, to the block, a spectre of mediaeval royalty, 'the last of the right line of the house of Plantagenet'.[3]

Henry also gave another brutal warning to the nobility in general. Lord Dacre of the south, a popular young blade with estates in Sussex, had chanced, in a moment of choler, to kill a 'simple' poacher, after his deer; far from condoning this casual offence, Henry condemned Dacre to die. The horrified Council sued for his pardon, but the young nobleman was actually led on foot through the city to Tyburn and, on June 29th, strangled like a common murderer. His three associates, all proper young gentlemen, were also hanged. People were shocked; the king did not even respect degree, and 'great moan was made for them all'.

Having, at one swoop, cleared the Tower, Henry set out on an elaborate progress to the north. He was in no good mind; had declared he 'had an unhappy people to govern whom he would shortly make so poor that they would not have the boldness or the power to oppose him'. The king had, indeed, suffered a seizure in the spring, when his ulcer had 'clogged' and he had gone black in the face; he had refused

---

[1] Robert Parkyn's 'Narrative of the Reformation.' *English Historical Review*, January 1947.

[2] Acts of Privy Council, VII, p. 147.

[3] The year after, Wriothesley got the stewardship of her immense properties, mainly in the West Country, and the mastership of 'the hunt of deer in all these'. L. and P., XVII, 1154 (6).

even to hear music, and had barred his bedroom door for a week against his young wife, who had selected for her device 'No other Will than His'.

But never had a Tudor progress been more impressive as the great cavalcade moved north in the late summer weather to cow the areas of rebellion. Hunting as he went—two hundred stags were killed at Hatfield alone—Henry moved through Lincolnshire to York, there to receive submission, apologies and fines. To martial music his files of archers entered Lincoln with drawn bows; the royal guards followed, pikes and axes at the ready; a galaxy of brilliant chattering courtiers and women contrasted with the ponderous dignity of the great magnates of the Council.

The civic authorities hastened to bring tribute; Stamford with twenty pounds, Lincoln with forty, Boston with fifty. As the king entered Yorkshire, he was met by two hundred of the gentry, with four thousand tall yeomen, well horsed. They all made submission and presented £900 through Sir Robert Bowes; then, on September 16th, the Archbishop of York with three hundred clergy came out to meet him, bearing £600: the mayors of York, Newcastle and Hull gave £100 apiece. Henry turned east and devised fortifications at Hull, then, crossing the Humber, returned through Lincolnshire to Hampton Court. Here, on All Souls' Day, in fine fettle, he gave thanks to God for the 'good life he led and trusted to lead' with the new queen.

But enemies of the Howards were closing in; Catherine was quarrelling about precedence with the Lady Mary; she had no child, and she had not been crowned. She was never to be so: on November 2nd, discreet Archbishop Cranmer, always hostile to the Howards and Gardiner, but not having the heart to tell Henry the facts to his face, slipped a letter into his master's hand. It contained circumstantial evidence of the queen's habitual misconduct before her marriage, based on the testimony of members of the household of the dowager duchess of Norfolk where Catherine had been brought up.

For John Lassells, Cranmer's zealous Protestant informer, had a sister, Mary Hall, 'nurse'—in the sense of Juliet's 'nurse'—in that rather scandalous Howard establishment. At first the king affected to take little notice, though he ordered further investigation; he was preoccupied with the illness of Prince Edward, now aged four, who had a 'quartern ague' (malaria); at first refused to believe the boy was ill; then sent for a whole concourse of physicians.

But soon all the queen's past came out. The household of the dowager duchess, near Horsham, had been no school of virtue and

refinement; *Fais ce que vous voudrez* had been its motto—do what you
like, though the duchess would occasionally clout the girls on the head.[1]
Catherine, it was alleged, had carried on with Henry Manox or
Mannock, like Mark Smeaton a musician, a player of the virginals,
ever since she was thirteen. Mannock confessed that the duchess had
'caught them and beat them' for making love, and charged them 'never
to be alone together again'; he had also 'felt more than was convenient'
(suitable), and knew certain secret marks on her body, though he
'swore upon his damnation' he had done nothing more. Her next
affair had been more regular: Francis Dereham, one of the Duke of
Norfolk's gentleman pensioners, used to visit her in the dormitory of
the duchess's household, both at Horsham and Lambeth. The maidens
used to steal the old lady's keys and admit their lovers to clandestine
feasts of strawberries, apples and wine—'very bad', it was said, 'for
their complections'. Here Dereham and Catherine used to 'kiss and
hang by their bellies together as they were two sparrows'. 'Hark to
Dereham broken-winded,' the girls would giggle; and, indeed, he
confessed that 'he had known her carnally many times both in his
doublet and hose, between the sheets, and in naked bed'. An understanding, he said, had been reached between them.

In face of these confessions (afterwards confirmed by Catherine), the
king ordered her to keep to her rooms. She made a last frantic attempt
to see him; ran screaming down what is now the 'haunted' gallery at
Hampton Court to intercept him at Mass. She was held back by force:
that afternoon, November 6th, the king went for a hunting picnic,
and, in the autumn dusk, he was rowed to London for an emergency
session of the Council. He never saw Catherine again.

Henry sat speechless, 'pierced with pensiveness'; the last romantic
illusion of youth gone. Then, perhaps to the embarrassment of the
hard-faced Councillors, he began to cry. As Marillac reported, with
relish, to his master, 'The King has changed his love for the Queen into
hatred, and taken such grief at being deceived that of late it was thought
he had gone mad, for he called for a sword to slay her he had loved so
much. Sitting in Council, he suddenly called for horses without saying
where he would go.' He was, indeed, quite *hors de propoz*, 'out of
order'. He had sworn that the wicked woman had 'never such delight
in her incontinence as she [should] have torture in her death', and,
finally, he 'took to tears, regretting his ill luck in meeting such ill-
conditioned wives and blaming the Council for the last mischief'.
Chapuys, the imperial ambassador, also reported, 'It is like the case of

[1] L. and P., XVI, 1320.

the woman who cried more bitterly at the loss of her tenth husband than at the death of all the others together; though he had been a good man, it was because she had never buried one of them before without being sure of the next.'

On November 7th, the queen herself was interrogated. Her enemies had ample evidence of her past before marriage: now, to obtain a kill, they had to convict her of adultery. 'If there be none offense sithence [since] the marriage,' declared the old Duchess of Norfolk, 'she cannot die for that was done before.' But Cranmer was already saying, 'You may see what was done before marriage; God knoweth what has been done since'; and Henry had instructed the Council 'not to desist until you have found out the bottom of the pott'.

There was, indeed, new evidence to hand; with incredible folly, the queen had made Dereham her private secretary and also started an affair with Thomas Culpeper, her kinsman, a well-to-do young gentleman of the king's Privy Chamber, with nothing against him, save that he had once 'violated the wife of a park keeper in a thicket'. During the progress to the north, Culpeper had frequently met the queen on the backstairs, though she 'had been in fear that somebody should come in'.

It was Lady Rochford, widow of Anne Boleyn's brother, who was thought the 'principal occasion of her folly'. She, too, was sent to the Tower, where, under interrogation, she went mad. The queen, it appeared, had called Culpeper 'her little sweet fool,' and a Mistress Morton deposed, vaguely, that 'Catherine had looked out of the window at Culpeper after such sort that she thought there was love between them'; and since she had been 'closetted with him for five or six hours', it was 'thought for certain they had *passé oultre*'. More conclusively, perhaps, the queen had written to him, laboriously, in her own hand: 'I never longed so much for a thing as I do to see you and speak with you . . . it makes my heart die to think what fortune I have that I cannot be always in your company. . . . I would you were with me now that you might see what pain I take in writing to you. Yours as life endures. Katheryne.' On November 11th, the queen, now hysterical, was removed to Sion House, and there lodged without any cloth of estate. Henry told Cranmer to examine her, 'if her wits were such' that he 'could do so without danger', and he found her, he told the king, 'in such lamentation and heaviness as I never saw no creature, so that it would have pitied any man's heart to have looked upon her'. He had begun by declaring the king's mercy, instead of the law, lest she might be 'driven into some dangerous exstacy' or else into 'a very fransy'. He sent, enclosed, all he could get out of her; sufficient, he thought, to prove a contract with Dereham, although she maintained it was no contract, for she declared that 'all Dereham did to her was by force and, in a manner, violence rather than of her free consent and will'.[1] Her state jewels were confiscated. Next day, she denied the more deadly charge of adultery with Culpeper, but, on the 13th, he confessed that he had 'meant to do ill with the Queen and that likewise the Queen so minded to do with him'. Meanwhile, Protestants were saying, sanctimoniously, 'What if God worketh to make the Lady Anne of Cleves Queen again?', and 'What a man is the King! How many wives must he have?' Tartly, Gardiner told a German diplomat 'that the King would never take back the said lady'; what had been done was founded upon good reason, whatever the world might allege.

It was now proclaimed that the 'Queen had forfeited her honour' and she petitioned Henry for mercy 'most humbly on hands and knees', admitting Mannock's familiarities, and that Dereham had 'used her in such sort as a man doth his wife'. Yet, as apparent from Cranmer's report, in her high Howard pride, she never admitted the *de facto* marriage with Dereham which might have proved she had never been queen, and even saved her life. She denied intercourse with Culpeper; confessed herself 'blinded with love of worldly glory', and appealed to her 'benign and merciful prince'.

Early in December, Dereham and Culpeper were arraigned at Guildhall; Dereham, like Mannock, was hanged, cut down alive, his guts and members burnt before his face, and the remains quartered. Culpeper, as a gentleman of the Privy Chamber, was allowed to die by the sword. Their heads were set on spikes on London Bridge.

The Norfolk clan now paid the penalty of their miscalculation. Defiant, a former intimate of Catherine of Aragon, irrepressibly loquacious, scornful doubtless of the Tudors, the old duchess was clapped in the Tower, with her daughter, Lady Bridgewater, and her son, Lord Howard. She proved 'testy'; Lord William, too, 'stood as stiff as his mother . . .' and 'Bridgewater [showed] herself her mother's daughter and [would] confess nothing'. The Duchess's jewels were thought 'very base', and though it was hoped to make her 'cough up' more, she had 'much trash in her baggage'; and there was not room for all the Howards and their servants in the Tower. Would Henry, asked the Lieutenant, allow some of the royal apartments to be used? Could he 'lend them his double key'? The king does not remember, he was told,

---

[1] *State Papers*, I, CLXII, pp. 689–90.

'that he has any double key, but permits the locks to be altered'. The dowager took to her bed.

Norfolk left for his estates in East Anglia, disavowing his relations. In mid-December, he wrote to the king: 'I learnt yesterday that mine ungratious mother-in-law (stepmother), most unhappy brother and his wife, with my lewd sister of Bridgewater, were committed to the Tower.' What with this, and 'the abominable deeds' done by his two nieces (Boleyn and Howard), and the reputed treason of his kin, he feared that the king would 'abhor him and never speak to him again'. Prostrate at the king's feet—like Cromwell—he reminded him that he had turned informer, and begged 'some assurance of the King's favour, without which he would never desire to live'.

The duchess, complaining loudly of the mid-winter discomforts of the Tower—she could not, she said, 'live in it'—pleaded for greater liberty in her confinement. Henry, personally, turned her request down, and she now 'coughed up' £800, 5,000 marks and £1,000 in plate.

The king continued to be furious; the more so for the condolences of Francis I, who had told his good brother to consider that 'the lightness of women cannot bend the honour of men'. The Council, reported Marillac, were doing all they could; but the king had gone 'twenty-five miles from here with no company but musicians and ministers of pastime and spent most of his time hunting, seeking to forget his grief'.

On December 16th a special commission indicted the young queen for 'presumptive treason', in that she had before her marriage 'led an unlawful, carnal, voluptuous and licentious life'; though she had a secret contact with Dereham, she had 'arrogantly contracted and coupled herself in marriage to the King'. More succinctly, it was said 'she had been found an harlot before he married her and an adulteress after'. The trap had closed. 'It looks,' wrote Marillac, 'as if the end of these tragedies will be no less scandalous than pitiful.'

VI

In the midst of domestic disaster, Henry kept Christmas 1541 at Greenwich, his experienced political acumen unimpaired. At the end of December, he gave Chapuys a masterly and defiant survey of the whole field of foreign policy. If the Danes were in league with the French, 'they could do him little harm—neither Swede nor Dane, especially as the Dane [Frederick I] was so old'. Naturally Charles V had failed to clean up the pirate base at Algiers; he had not employed pilots who

HENRICVS DEI GRA REX ANGLIE ·

13. Henry VIII from a
line engraving by
Cornelius Matsys

Henry VIII with his
jester. Mallards
Psalter
(Reproduced by
permission of the
British Museum)

14. Catherine Parr, attributed to Holbein
(Reproduced by permission of the administrators of the estate of the late Mr J. F. Minke

knew the North African coast.[1] If the emperor wanted war with England, he hoped that 'his fleet would return in disorder to Sicily . . . or be wrecked on the coast of England and take shelter under the bulwarks he had himself erected on the coast'. He had no use for king or emperor, and recalled past occasions 'when he had looked for help and found none'; and that Francis I was again soliciting the Turk who, as Henry's ambassador to France had put it, had 'that year raised the siege of Buda and advanced further and besieged a place called Pest', to invade Europe.[2]

On January 21, 1542, a bill of attainder was brought in against Catherine. But she never answered it; in February she was conveyed in a closed barge from Sion to the Tower, passing under the heads of her lovers, impaled on London Bridge. Silly, flighty, inconsequent and attractive, she knew how to die. On the night before her execution, she sent for the block and rehearsed the correct way to place her head, begged that her sins should not be vented on her family, and asked that her servants be provided for.

On the 12th, a little group assembled in the winter morning at the place of execution, where Anne Boleyn had died. Catherine had to be helped up the scaffold, almost too exhausted to speak: it is unlikely that she said, 'I die a Queen but would rather die the wife of Culpeper.' The axe made short work of her delicate neck.

Lady Rochford, now apparently again in her senses, was also butchered, but the Howards managed to outface their setback; the duke regained power; the dowager duchess and her relatives were released.

Much sympathy was felt for the monarch. On January 16th, in Parliament, everyone had spontaneously bowed to the name of 'such an exceptional Prince'.

[1] Charles V's landing at Algiers, that October, had been ill conducted and a gale had so wrecked his fleet that many of the documents of the Imperial Chancellery had been lost; Cortes, the conqueror of Mexico, had told him he could yet take the city, but he would not take the further risk.

[3] L. and P., XVI, p. 690.

CHAPTER XVI

ENTIRE EMPIRE

❈

WHILE Henry and Cromwell had been transforming Church and State and successfully defying formidable coalitions abroad, they had also consolidated their rule in Wales, dealt carefully and not unsuccessfully with Scotland, and attempted to solve the problem of Ireland. Now, in spite of Cromwell's fall, the king's domestic troubles, and fluctuating threats from the continent, Henry's position was better within the island 'empire' that it had been in Wolsey's day. How had this change come about?

As Pollard well remarks, Henry was a 'great unionist, though separatist as regards his wives and the Pope';[1] Wales, Scotland, Ireland, had all long felt the pressure of his will; if Cromwell had done the main work, his master had been behind it. North Wales, the principality from which the Tudors had emerged, was already shired; Pembroke, Glamorgan and Monmouth had been part of the Lancastrian inheritance, and under Sir Rhys ap Thomas all the country had been tolerably ruled. His grandson, Sir Rhys ap Gruffydd, had been less tractable and, in December 1531, he had been executed in the Tower.

In 1534 Cromwell had taken over; a council of the Marches of Wales had been established under one of his protégés, Rowland Lee, Bishop of Coventry, a forthright character, 'not affable to any of the Welshry'. He had claimed to have strung up Welshmen by the thousand; 'Thieves I found them, and thieves I shall leave them,' he had written, and, indeed, 'cattle thieving was endemic in these mountainous pastoral areas, as on the borders. To this, the Welsh added another vice, the forceable carrying off of widows. Extreme poverty was at the root of it all.'[2] Then, in 1536, Henry had shired the whole country, largely confirming the old divisions in the north, but creating new shires and boroughs, all now represented in the English Parliament. English law had superseded tribal custom and blood price paid in cattle; the old jurisdictions had been replaced by Justices of the Peace;

[1] Henry VIII, p. 291.
[2] A. L. Rowse, *The Expansion of Elizabethan England*, p. 289.

authority had been diffused, and Wales incorporated into Henry's empire by statute, the first Act of Union in the history of the British Isles. Thus the 'manifest robberies, murders, thefts and other malefacts' had been put down, and those unable to speak English excluded from office. Most of the people had been reconciled to these measures since they were intensely loyal to the dynasty and felt that Henry had their interests at heart; he instructed the Council to respect their feelings. By 1543 the Council of Wales and the Marches was to be further reinforced, the union completed.

II

Naturally Ireland had long proved far more intractable. The negative policy of the early 'twenties, rejecting both conquest and plantation, already described, and pursued in spite of Surrey's advice, had got nowhere, though, considering Henry's continental commitments, it had served its turn. By 1526 the Geraldine Earl of Kildare, *Garret Oge*, had been summoned to London and held hostage for two years, and with the rise of the Boleyn influence, his position had been further undermined. Anne Boleyn's grandmother had been a Butler, her cousin was Earl of Ossory; they were all sworn enemies of the Geraldines. And, as relations had worsened with Charles V, Ireland had again become a potential base for foreign attack.

In 1529 Henry had appointed young Richmond as nominal lord lieutenant, and, next year, superseded Kildare by Sir William Skeffington, known as the 'Gunner', for he was expert in artillery. In 1532 Kildare had been restored, but, by February 1534, again recalled and lodged in the Tower, leaving his son Thomas, Lord Offaly, as his vice-deputy. Offaly, known as 'Silken Thomas', *Tomás an tSioda*, from his elegant clothes, had been a charmer of twenty-one. But soon the Butlers had got to work, and put out a rumour that his father had been done to death in the Tower; frantic at this news, and worked upon by the Gaelic chanting of a harper, *Tomás* had raised rebellion and declared himself the 'Pope's man'; Dublin had been besieged and the English primate of all Ireland slain on the beach.

The Gunner had now been sent out again; the pope had been persuaded to put *Tomás an tSioda* under a curse so frightful that Kildare had died in the Tower when shown it, and Maynooth castle had been smashed by the English guns. The survivors, given the 'pardon of Maynooth', had then been massacred—an ominous precedent for Irish history. In August 1535, *Tomás an tSioda* had surrendered and, in the following year, his five Geraldine uncles had been trapped: by February 1537, Henry and Cromwell had hanged the lot.

The fall of the Kildares had confirmed a radical change of policy. Lord Leonard Grey, made deputy in 1536, had convened an Irish 'Reformation' Parliament which had imposed a religious revolution on the English model; the authority of Rome had been repudiated, and Henry accepted as supreme head of the Irish Church; abbey lands had been confiscated and the wearing of Irish dress within the Pale forbidden; Irish minstrels and bards had been banned. Ireland, it had been proclaimed, was the 'King's proper dominion of England, and united knit and belonging to the Imperial Crown of the same realm': an English archbishop named Browne had been appointed. Then the final Irish resistance had been crushed. A Geraldine League, including Desmonds, Macarthys of the south-west, and Conn O'Neill in the north, had tried to restore the surviving Geraldine, a half brother of 'Silken Thomas', aged eleven. They had been defeated at Bellahoe, but the boy had survived, smuggled out of Ireland to Florence in 1541, a more promising environment.[1]

Though Grey had been recalled, accused of intrigue with the Irish, and executed in 1541, when Henry had cleared the Tower, the king now had a free hand. Cromwell, too, was dead, but Henry determined to treat Ireland as they both had Wales. In January of that year a surprisingly optimistic paper headed '*For the Reformation of Ireland*' had put the case for this decision. Wales, it was pointed out, was loyal because never under a deputy, but subject to 'Seneschels' and justices in each shire; so might Ireland be pacified, and the *Kerne* and *Gallóglach* take to tillage and fishing. If the great chieftains were won over, the rest would follow, for they had 'pregnant and subtle wits'; told they would not be banished but hold their land from the king—'as O'Donnel hath done and O'Neill is trying to do'—they would become tame.[2]

Henry sent out a new lord deputy, Sir Anthony St Leger; and in June 1541 had himself proclaimed by the Irish Parliament as king, not merely lord, of Ireland—a title originally conferred by the Pope—and confirmed as head of the Irish Church. The great chieftains were flattered and conciliated, encouraged to surrender their lands, regranted on terms better for them than for their people. But in March 1542, Henry had to raise another 'amicable loan' to reduce Ireland to 'the knowledg of God and good civility', as well, of course, as to

---

[1] He was allowed to return under Mary, but 'never went back to Irish ways'. Curtis, op. cit., p. 175.
[2] L. and P., XVII, 68.

crusade against the Turk and his (French) adherents. It was to be repaid, said Chapuys, at the 'Greek Kalends'; no one expected repayment, but 'put a good face on it'. For Ireland there was never enough.

St Leger and the Council for Ireland explained, that spring, how difficult it was to raise cash. The Irish would rather keep *Gallóglach* costing £40 or £50 a year than pay £5 in rent. Many castles needed repair, and it was hard to find horses; Kildare had kept two or three hundred stud mares, but all were now dispersed. The king, they advised, should organize new studs, a popular move that Henry could well make, since he had revolutionized the standard of horse breeding in England, having himself two stables of a hundred horses each and drawing a hundred and fifty yearly from his studs in Nottinghamshire and Wales. The Irish magnates were confidently expected to follow suit.

The great Irish chieftains were also now made peers; if Ormonde came in, Desmond would follow, and the English, as St Leger put it, would have 'a Roland for an Oliver'.[1] But, in May, he told Henry that the MacWilliam, who had petitioned to be made 'grand captain of his county, as the earls of Ormonde and Desmond were in theirs, and to have some honour',[2] had excused himself—plausibly enough—for being in arms in league with other septs: his county, he had said, lay far from the Pale, and 'he had to adhere to some Irish for defence against others', for no captain of his, he explained, had died in his bed, but all slain by Irishmen. It would be wise, thought St Leger, to pardon him, for his county adjoined the Ban, 'where all the salmon fishing is, and his obedience would improve the fishing'. As for the O'Neill, he had promised submission, 'if an Irishman was to be trusted'; and St Leger had 'drawn his strength' by promising his *Gallóglach* the waste mountainous county of Mourne, so that at least for the moment 'no man ever saw O'Neill so tractable'.[3] Soon, indeed, O'Neill was declaring that, if 'only he had the money', he longed to go and see Henry himself; as this hint was 'beyond all expectation', the English tried to 'furnish' him, 'although sterling money was scant to be had'.[4] By July, Marillac was reporting the Count 'Apmont' (Desmond), 'an Irishman of the quarter of the savages', had come to do homage to Henry as King of Ireland. As Henry returned from mass, Desmond and three others were observed to take leave of the king very humbly—'all the

---

[1] L. and P., XVII, 314 (referring to the famous companions in *The Chanson de Roland*).
[2] *Ibidem*, 146.
[3] *Ibidem*, 340.
[4] *Ibidem*, 664.

while the King or their interpreter spoke, they were on their knees'.[1] The English, he said, hoped much from the example.

Encouraged by this submission and having long 'exhausted infinite treasure in the Reformation of Ireland', Henry decided in August 1542, 'now that most of the inhabitants had been brought to obedience', to set up two Councils, one in the West, including Ormonde and Desmond; the other in the North with O'Neill and O'Donnell. Since, moreover, as among the Welsh, compounding of felonies for fines had made 'the King's laws sound strange', the Irish laws were to be abolished. The Redshanks, seasoned mercenaries from south-western Scotland, were also to be expelled, for they bought peel towns and castles, and 'greatly coveted to populate [the country], the same being the most vile in their living of any nation next Irishmen'.[2]

Henry also attacked the Irish Church, told the English bishops of Dublin and Meath to instruct their Irish colleagues to renounce popish doctrines, though, in this context, the English Act enforcing the continent living of priests was not to be implemented.

If Henry hoped much from the apparent submission of the aristocracy, it is odd that he should have still tried to force the Reformation on Ireland. The plunder of abbey lands infuriated the people, nor was there, as in England, a native capitalist class to buy them up and prove a bulwark of the new order. In the long term, the Anglican Church of Ireland was to settle in, but already, by July 1542, James V of Scotland had given safe conduct to two Spanish pioneer Jesuits, Salmeron and Casata, sent to Ireland, through his kingdom, from Rome, an action, he said, showing how solicitous his Holiness was for Ireland as its people. And it was rumoured, to the horror of the Irish, that English Primate Browne would burn the *Baculum Jesu*, the crozier with which St Patrick had banished the snakes; as, indeed, the new archbishop did.

III

Such was Henry's 'empire' in Ireland by 1542—still a problem shelved rather than solved. The other potential part of the 'empire' had long been equally intractable. In 1542, agents of James V, arrested in Ireland, had admitted that if Henry 'made any business in France', the Scots would 'straight molest him'.

It will be recalled that Henry had for years tried to conciliate the Scots in vain, but since the 'thirties his hold over his nephew had

[1] Chapuys, L. and P., XVII, 468.
[2] Certain devices for the reformation of Ireland, L. and P., XVII, 690.

diminished. Margaret, dowager of Scotland, was now dead, and the boy, James V, was dominated by the pro-French faction, led by the warlike David Beaton, cardinal-bishop of St Andrews. When in 1541 James had refused to meet his uncle at York, it had been only the last of many frustrations. As far back as 1534, the king had been trying to fix an interview, thanking his nephew in effusive terms for a present of falcons, and making James V—who had all the Stewart charm and incompetence and already a train of bastards—a Knight of the Garter. He was now, Henry had pointed out, in the august company of the emperor and Francis I. Two years later, Henry had again sent the bishop-elect of St Asaph 'dulcely to inculce James' to meet him and stress the great honour and comfort that would come of the interview, to be held well within England. All had come to nothing: in 1537 James had gone to France and married the delicate Princess Madeleine, daughter of Francis I, the worst defiance he could have made. 'If Scotland keeps him [Henry] in apprehension,' the papal nuncio in Paris had remarked, with a fine flair for essentials, 'it will make him keep his money to himself—not give it to the emperor.'[1] Further, in his hatred of his step-father, the exiled, pro-English, Angus, James V had actually burnt Lady Glamis, Angus' sister, and beheaded his brother-in-law, the Master of Forbes, on charges of conspiracy. Nor had the death of the young Queen Madeleine in 1538 deflected the French alliance: he had married the more forceful Mary of Lorraine, daughter of the Duc de Guise, widow of the Duc de Longueville.[2]

More or less blandly, Henry had ignored even these moves, contenting himself with avuncular advice; telling his nephew not to plunder his subjects and 'gather into his hands numbers of sheep, and such other vile and mean things ... being the livings of poor men, therewith to advance his revenue'. He should follow his own example, he wrote, and seize the lands of the monks who occupied so much of Scotland to the 'maintenance of their voluptie', seeing their 'untruth and beastly living';[3] James could then 'live like a King and yet meddle not with sheep'. He reminded him also, from over thirty years' experience as a ruler, that honesty was the best policy.

Now, against this exasperating background, Henry decided on a stronger line. In February, 1542, he instructed his ambassador to Scotland to tax his nephew with refusing to come to York, and, when James declared he had needed the consent of the French king, Henry

---

[1] Byrne, op. cit., p. 284.
[2] See their picture at Hardwick, Devonshire collection.
[3] Byrne, pp. 288-9.

called off further contact. 'We would be loathe to put him' (again), he wrote, 'to so great pains, seeing he cannot without leave of others do it.' It was incredible that James had asked advice of another prince 'to have met with such an Uncle as, since his tender age, [had] showed himself so careful over him'.

In March Henry seriously considered a scheme put up by Sir Thomas Wharton, Governor of Carlisle, to kidnap the Scots king. But even the Privy Council were shocked at the 'taking of a king in his own realm by subjects of his Uncle'; they would not, they said, have dared to discuss such a thing without express command. And the castle concerned, they said, was miles inside Scotland, the country around Dumfries thickly inhabited; if the plot were discovered, what slander and deadly feud! And what if King James were slain? They could not possibly advise it; Wharton, though he had meant it well, should 'surcease' and 'make no living creature privy to such matters, save upon some future command of the King'.

IV

To such expedients had Henry's attempt to bring Scotland into the orbit of his island empire been reduced, yet his main policy had achieved much success. He had nationalized the Church, broken opposition at home; defied the pope and two great continental monarchs; and now it looked as if continental power politics were again giving him another chance.

The truce of Nice in 1538 between Charles V and Francis I had long worn thin, and by December 1541 the Marquis of Guasto, Spanish Governor of Milan, had committed a notable international outrage; he had executed two French envoys, Fregoso and Ricon, on their way to negotiate with the Grand Turk—a violation Francis I had said, self righteously, of the *ius gentium*—the Law of Nations. Another major European conflict was clearly brewing up, and Henry again determined to exploit it—this time, in tune with popular feeling, against the French.

The memory of Catherine Howard was soon blotted out. On January 29, 1542, even before her execution, the king gave a round of banquets—twenty-six court ladies at table at once, the king 'making them great and hearty cheer'. He was now, the French ambassador reported, in better spirits, but 'very stout, much resembling his maternal grandfather Edward IV being about his age . . .' though he seemed very 'old and grey since the *malheur* of the last queen'.[1]

[1] L. and P., XVII, 178.

By new laws, any queen would now have to confess the slightest previous misconduct on pain of death, and all who knew of any had to reveal it within twenty days, on pain of forfeiture of goods and imprisonment for life. The competition for the monarch's hand can hardly have been very hot.

But Henry might well be in better mood, for now France and the empire were again on the verge of war. In January 1542, Paget[1] had reported from Paris a significant scene: French agents had seized Marano, a strategic port on Friuli on the Adriatic, which belonged to the emperor's brother, Ferdinand of Austria, and set up the French king's arms. When he had received the news, Francis I had sent for the ambassadors of the Empire, Venice and the pope; should he, he had demanded, accept the town? If not, the captors would hand over the port to the Turks. The imperial ambassador had replied that the king ought first to hang the bearers of the dispatch and then do his best to hang those that still held the city. '*Tout bien, monsieur l'ambassadeur*,' the king had answered, referring to the outrage at Milan, 'I may not kill ambassadors, as your master does'; and as for hanging those who had meant to do him a service, he would reward them. Again, what ought he to do? accept Marano or give it to the Grand Signor? It was blackmail, and the representatives of the empire, Venice, Mantua and Ferrara in Paris, were all, Paget reported, 'ready to weep and think Italy lost, seeing the preparations the Turk makes and the friendship he found in France'.[1]

Yet the French were still supposed to be bidding for the hand of that politically hardy perennial, the Lady Mary (she had again been seriously ill), though Francis I was asking if Henry really expected him to marry his son, the Duc d'Orléans, to a bastard? Norfolk now told the French envoys in London, 'Sirs, to be plain with you, I think that my master, being so wise a man as ye know he is, and doth so well know his affairs, shall think this matter not so earnestly meant or spoken.' But the negotiations had their use; they brought pressure on Charles V, as had the failure of the Diet at Ratisbon in 1541, when the Protestant princes, with English encouragement, had again remained irreconcilable.

[1] Sir William Paget, 1505–63, son of the Sergeant of the Mace to the City of London, he was educated at St Paul's school and at Trinity Hall, Cambridge. Employed by the Boleyns and by Gardiner; Clerk of the Signet, 1532; Knighted, 1537; Secretary to Anne of Cleves, since he could speak German; Clerk to Privy Council, 1540; Secretary of State, 1543; Knight of the Garter, 1547; Chancellor of Duchy of Lancaster, 1st Baron Paget, 1549; on Somerset's Fall, deprived, but reinstated under Mary. Lord Privy Seal, 1556.
[1] L. and P., XVII, 55. (Record Office. Copy in Caius College, Ms. 597, p. 25.)

V

The emperor, indeed, might well be forced into an English alliance, and a concerted attack on France. But the allies would have to move fast; already the French were moving into Luxembourg and threatening Antwerp. And first Henry had to deal with Scotland, for the Scots were now in a defensive league with France, Denmark, Sweden and the duchies of Prussia, Gelderland and Cleves.

And in August 1542, a final insult occurred: the Warden of the Middle Marches, Sir Robert Bowes, along with Angus, descended from the Cheviots on Teviotdale, 'burnt certain towns and recoiled homeward'; but 2,000 'shouting' Scots 'prickers'—light horse—ambushed them at Haddon Rigg. Bowes and his brother had been taken, along with other gentry, and four or five hundred men; Angus just got away 'after great debate with himself'; others only escaped 'by speed of horse'.[1]

Henry deeply resented this fiasco: he had personally instructed the authorities to stock up with supplies and ammunition at Berwick and Carlisle, Norham and Wark; he had ordered the Council of the North to have their country ready at an hour's warning and swift posts to be laid on; guerrillas, the king had said, should be sent into Scotland to burn and ravage if the Scots attacked. Only two days before Haddon Rigg, the Privy Council at Hampton Court had ordered much gunpowder, 1,500 bows, 1,000 sheaves of arrows, and 3,000 bills to be shipped to Berwick.

So now, following up his kingship of Ireland, Henry claimed the sovereignty of Scotland as well. He declared open war, and wrote a long, retrospective manifesto. 'It hath been very rarely and seldom seen before,' he wrote, 'that a King of Scots hath had in marriage a daughter of England: we cannot, ne will not, reprehend the King our father's act therein, but lament and be sorry it took no better effect'.[2] 'We trusted,' he went on, 'the tree would bring forth good fruit that was of the one part of so good a stock.' He recalled, in detail, all the Scots raids, treacheries and diplomatic deceit: while they had spoken fair, their deeds had been as 'extreme as might be, and his subjects spoiled'. And now, having captured Bowes and his company, the Scots even refused to put them to ransom in the accustomed way; Henry could only forget fair words and consider the king of Scots deeds.

By October 1542, Norfolk, Southampton, and Hertford were in York, vowing to 'purge the dishonour of Haddon Rigg'. But there

[1] L. and P., XVII, 662–3.
[2] Byrne, pp. 296 ff.

was no Wolsey or Cromwell to organize supplies; the hasty march from York to Berwick was gruelling; biscuits and beer were held up at sea and 'the carriages of the county so feeble' that they could take only one pipe each; the men had to drink water for four days on end, and when they got beer, had only enough for six days, rating every man a quart a day.[1] The bridge into Berwick broke down, and five men were drowned.

It was now late October, and the main army could do little; they only raided west over the Border along the north bank of the Tweed to burn Kelso and returned to base. Nineteen men died from drinking 'puddle water', and it was 'never thought Englishmen would endure with so little and yet go forward'.

With exasperated, tireless grasp of detail, the king bombarded Norfolk with suggestions and advice: but Norfolk was ill, 'his old disease of the lax marvellous sore on him'. Shooting the great ordnance at 'bushments' in the hills and hanging spies had been all they had done. Henry replied, with unexpected mildness, that he was sorry 'with all their good will to serve and the great charge incurred, the damage to the enemies [was] like to be so little'; they must 'better foresee hereafter'.

Southampton, long desperately ill, his hand so trembling that he could not sign reports, had now succumbed, ending, in this horrible campaign, the successful career begun, as Sir William Fitzwilliam, in France. Norfolk still declared that his men, 'like true men, laying aside their sorrow, were bent to do what they came for', but begged the king to send up Russell to be Warden of the Marches; failing him, Hertford must take over;[2] for himself, he could not take the office— another Scots winter with its vehement cold would kill him. So Henry appointed Hertford Lord Warden; but he, too, complained that he was unsuitably provided; found 'but a bare tent, more unfurnished than the meanest gent in the field'; and, being a stranger, he said, he could barely rule the company.

The raid, however, had provoked the Scots to attack. In late October, James V was outside Edinburgh castle, with his bishops and nobles, the

---

[1] L. and P., XVII, 975. (Norfolk and others to the Council.)

[2] Sir Edward Seymour, Earl of Hertford and 1st Duke of Somerset, 1506–52, son of Sir John Seymour of Wolf Hall, Wiltshire and brother to Queen Jane. 1524 Esquire to the King and in 1529 Esquire to the Body; 1536, Viscount Beauchamp of Hatch, Somerset; 1537, Earl of Hertford; 1541, Knight of the Garter; 1543, Lord Great Chamberlain; 1544, Lieutenant General in the North; 1544, and Lieutenant of the Kingdom. In conjunction with Paget he defeated the Norfolk interest and after the death of Henry VIII seized power as Lord Protector. He was ousted by Russell, Herbert and Warwick, and executed in 1552.

oxen for his gun carriages lowing in the morning mist; all the flower of Scotland, including Highlanders—'wild northland men'—were eager for battle, the more so as they were to have £4 Scottish (£1 sterling) a month, and 'all they could win'. The English were destroying 'man, wife and bairn'; in mid-November James sent 18,000 men south-west by Melrose to strike at Carlisle.

'An espial reports,' wrote Sir Thomas Wharton, 'that two powers of Scotland will invade this Friday morning . . . with wallets': there was a full moon, so Wharton lit the beacons and concentrated all the forces of the county at Carlisle: he had only 3,000 spears, but the Musgraves and Grahams of the Border were thought likely to turn on the enemy.

On November 24th the Scots army attacked. Emerging from the Esk valley, east of Dumfries, their infantry came on over the debateable ground. But as the English foot advanced to meet them, Wharton observed that their cavalry had been slow in getting forward; there had, in fact, been a dispute over the command, for James had given it to his young favourite, Sir Oliver Sinclair, and the Scots had dismounted to argue. So Wharton launched his whitecoat cavalry at them before the foot joined battle, and caught the Scots nobles between Solway Moss and the Esk.

It was a rout: the Scots panicked, leaving their 'wallets' behind; many were killed, others drowned—three days after, ten bodies were drawn with fishing nets out of the Esk. Glencairn, Maxwell, Lord Flemyng; the King's minion Sir Oliver; earls, barons, two hundred lairds, thirty standards and twenty guns were captured. 'There are now in your hands,' wrote Hertford to the king, 'men who, with good order, may make the peace, or the conquest, of Scotland.' It seemed another Flodden, the handstroke of God, thought Hall, for the cardinal of Scotland—empowered to lay England under an interdict had the invasion succeeded—had 'promised them heaven for the destruction of England'.

James V was ill and had merely watched the battle; he now turned and rode hard for Stirling to get round the Firth where English ships threatened the capital, 'speaking displeasant things against his borderers.' He made first for Tentallon Castle, where his current mistress lived; then, at Falkland Castle, his hunting palace which still stands, he took to his bed. Here his rage and despair were aggravated when some soldiers 'surlily demanded their pay with threats', and by news of another outrage. The English Somerset Herald, after negotiating the exchange of the prisoners of Haddon Rigg, had been stabbed in the December dusk, two miles south of Dunbar, by two destitute English refugees, anxious to win favour with the Scots. They had cut down his horse boy and stabbed him, yelling for help, in ten places, but the herald's colleague Berwick Pursuivant, had made off: 'Fie,' the assassins had exclaimed, 'the heretic has escaped!'[1] This violation of the laws of chivalry further disgusted King James, who at once wrote to his uncle that he would apprehend the killers.

But even worse was to come: on January 6th, prematurely, the queen, whose two infant sons had already died, bore not a longed-for prince, but a girl. 'The de'il go with it,' exclaimed the Scots king of his Crown, 'it will end as it begun; it came wi' a lass and it will pass wi' a lass.' He was wrong; but so, in the black northern winter, remembering the daughter of Robert the Bruce through whom the crown had come to the Stewart line, and repeating in his fever 'Oh fled Oliver! Is Oliver there? Oh fled Oliver!'—died James V; and so began the life of Mary Queen of Scots.

Down in London, Henry played a cool, experienced, hand. Twenty-four of the principal Scots prisoners were brought south to the Tower, paraded through London to Westminster and lectured by Gardiner; then, at Christmas, lavishly entertained. The king, he said, more regarding his honour than his princely power, was content to show them 'kindness for unkindness, right for wrong'.[2] All were released and taken care of by the English nobles; indeed, 'they never had greater cheer'. Glencairn got £200—at least £5,000 in modern money; Lord Flemyng, the same; Sir Oliver Sinclair, £66 13s 4d. And Henry called off the war. As that rising man, John Dudley, son of the hated minister executed in 1510 and now Lord Lisle, afterwards Earl of Warwick and Duke of Northumberland before he, too, perished on the block, told his master, it did not 'beseem the king's honour to make war upon a dead body or a widow or a suckling'; and, besides, the rain had bogged down the army and now the snow had fallen. The king turned to diplomacy and planned to marry Prince Edward to Mary Queen of Scots. As Henry feasted that Christmas of 1542, the year ended in apparent peace, the entire empire of the island now at last in the king's hands; Wales incorporated, Ireland quiescent, Scotland, it seemed, subdued. All was ready for the attack on France.

VI

For on the continent the war was now open; in July, Francis I had

[1] For an elaborate account of this episode see L. and P., XVIII, I, 26. Surprisingly, the boy survived.
[2] Hall, II, p. 340.

defied the emperor and the Habsburgs were also engaged on two other fronts; on the Danube against the Turk for Buda-Pest; in North Africa, in a disastrous combined operation against Algiers. In April Henry had himself ridden down to Dover to inspect the forts; since he would strike across country, he had told Marillac, where there would be no suitable lodging, he need not accompany him. Marillac suspected that he would cross to Calais. In May, too, Chapuys had been in Flanders, concerting arrangements. With an apparently consolidated empire behind him, and the two great powers of Europe at war, Henry meant to take his long-planned revenge on his cousin of France, and tighten his grip on the Straits of Dover. He had even, that year, thought of ordering some kettledrums, 'to be played on horseback after the Hungarian manner'.

CHAPTER XVII

MATRIMONIAL PEACE:
ANGLICAN SCHISM

✿

ON January 1543, unaware that James V was dead, Paul III, still intent on his revenge against the arch heretic, had granted six-tenths of the Church revenue of Scotland over two years for the war against 'Henry, son of perdition and Satan, who bears himself as King of England'. The king now sent Suffolk as his lieutenant to the border with authority over Hertford, and told the Scots Council he was determined on the union, 'either by conformity, as he desired, or otherwise'. He offered Arran, the protector, and the principal nobles of the Council of Scotland, bigger pensions 'than anyone else in Christendom would pay' if they 'went on a straight foot with him'. His grandniece, the infant Mary Stewart, the 'daughter of Scotland', was to marry Prince Edward; if she died, Henry would himself take control. Meanwhile, he had time to thank the Duke of Prussia for some falcons, saying how he took pleasure in hawking when wearied of public affairs; he was also stocking the new park at Waltham with deer; fallow deer from Waltham Chase, twelve stags from Bedwell Park.

Francis I, in Poitou, also took his pleasure that winter. Paget reported that he never stayed two nights in one place, disposing himself according to reports of 'great harts', and 'wearying everyone with his intention to keep carnavel at Fontainebleau'. But his war strategy was shrewd; he was concentrating on Flanders in collaboration with the Danes, now blocking the Flemish trade with the Baltic, while French ships were, unofficially, harrying the English trade with Bordeaux.[1]

---

[1] The French were then more aware of oceanic strategy than the English. Early in his reign Francis I had founded Le Havre, and in 1541 they were 'seeking the Trade of spicery by a shorter way than the Portingales use', i.e. by the '*mare glaseanum*', 'the sea of ice'. Jacques Cartier, who had first sailed from St Malo in 1534, and, the following year, explored the St Lawrence up to the site of Montreal, was now sent there again, with 500 or 600 'footmen', under Captain Marotte who had been in exile for Lutheranism. His men, Wallop reported, were 'malefactors and vagabonds who can well be spared, so that if they never return it will be no great loss'. L. and P., XVI, 488.

Francis also sent money to Marano, this time with Venetian con-
currence, to help keep the emperor occupied with the Turks as well as
in Italy, and prevent him reinforcing the Netherlands; Charles V, now
middle-aged and intermittently crippled with gout, was all the more
anxious for English subsidies in view of his crushing responsibilities
and the situation on the Danube and North Africa.

Henry, on the other hand, after his stroke of luck against the Scots,
was once more 'feasting ladies'; he might, it was rumoured, even marry
the Dowager (Guise) Queen of Scotland, and, by February 1543, he
was at last telling the French that their demands for the Lady Mary's
long-discussed dowry were unreasonable; unless they had better pro-
posals, it was not worth his seeing them again. He could not 'con-
descend' to such terms with honour, and Francis should be more
moderate 'as becomyth oone frend to doo with another'.[1]

He now finalized the elaborate secret treaty with Charles V. They
would both require the French king to cease making war on the
emperor and holding 'intelligence' with the Turk; restore Marano to
Ferdinand and pay the arrears of Henry's pension. The contracting
parties also agreed to make a joint invasion of France within two years,
with 20,000 foot and 5,000 horse, the invasion to last four
months.[2]

Henry was now the more anxious to bring the Scots to heel: though
Lisle was telling Suffolk, there was 'like to be great ruffling in Scotland',
for the powerful lords Argyle and Huntley were 'drawing one way',
threatening to set Cardinal Beaton at liberty again or 'make a worse
reckoning.' But Henry renewed the 'abstinence from war' for another
four months: after all, he could not, he said, otherwise 'sit still with
honour'. Sir Robert Bowes and the other prisoners had now, at last,
been released, and the Scots laird, Murray, even remarked that the two
realms, united, would be 'strong enough to pluck the great Turk out
of his den'.[3]

This laudable project was far from the minds of most of his countrymen; more blood cried aloud for vengeance, and religious fanaticism
now further divided the Scots. The pro-English party had encouraged
protestant ideas, which took on among the people. In 1541 Calvin's
Institutes had appeared in French, in the year that their author had
finally settled in Geneva, and he was to find a champion in John Knox.
The Scots were further enraged when the English Parliament asserted

[1] S.P., I, 728, 731.
[2] L. and P., XVIII, 144.
[3] L. and P., XVIII, 155.

Russell L.d Privy Seale.

with one Eye.

15. Pencil drawing by Holbein of the First Earl Russell. Windsor Castle
(Reproduced by gracious permission of H.M. The Queen)

16. William, First Earl of Pembroke. School of Eworth
(Reproduced by permission of the Earl of Pembroke)

that the 'late pretensed King of Scots was but an usurper', and that the time 'was ripe and propice' for the recovery of Henry's right and title for the Scots crown.[1] When, therefore, on July 1, 1543, the Scots representatives were induced to sign the Treaties of Greenwich, the first of which was a treaty of peace, and the second a treaty of marriage between the infant Mary, Queen of Scots, and Prince Edward, aged five, the agreement meant nothing. This aspect of Henry's policy for an island empire had already failed.

The Irish, on the other hand, were superficially more tractable: on the same day as the Scots treaties were signed, an elaborate ceremony was laid on for them. Enthroned under his Cloth of Estate at Greenwich, with all his Council and the Scots representatives about him, Henry created the O'Brien Earl of Thomond; taking a sword of state from Lord Lisle, he 'girt it bawdrick wise' about the kneeling Irish chieftain, while his patent was read out. McWilliam attained his coveted honour as the Earl of Clanrickard and Dunkellyn; and Donough O'Brien became Lord Ibracken. Henry then put chains of gold about their necks and knighted them; gave them robes of estate and paid all debts. Led by the trumpets and officers of arms, and accompanied by their sponsoring English peers, they all went to dine in memorable, convivial splendour.

II

When she observed that the king was paying court to her, the widowed Lady Latimer, born Catherine Parr, is said to have remarked that it were better to be his mistress than his wife; but by April 1543 Scutt the tailor had made her a whole trousseau—a 'slope hood' and tippet; French, Dutch and Venetian gowns; Venetian sleeves and pleats; French hoods and linen. And by June, when the king was at Harwich inspecting the haven, and the emperor was in Germany, in his horrid little travelling chair, on his way to Flanders, it was observed that my Lady Latimer was at Court, along with her sister, Anne Herbert, in company with Lady Mary and Lady Elizabeth. A new, intelligent influence was to come into their disrupted and precarious lives, for, unlike Catherine Howard, Lady Latimer was well educated and of amicable disposition. She was thirty-one and rich, and had already been married twice; Sir Winston Churchill calls her 'a serious little widow from the Lake District',[2] and she was a daughter of Sir Thomas Parr of Kendal,

---

[1] Wriothesley, *Chron: I*, 140, quoted by Pollard, 327
[2] *A History of the English Speaking Peoples*, II, p. 64.

Westmorland, Comptroller of the King's Household to Henry VII, who had died when she was a child. Since she had to make her way, her mother had her educated in Latin, Greek, Italian and French.[1]

On July 12th, in the queen's closet at Hampton Court, under a special licence from Cranmer which dispensed with banns and with 'none opposing and all applauding', Henry married his sixth and last queen. Asked by Winchester if he took her as his wedded wife, the king, always hopeful, answered with 'joyful countenance (_hilari vultu_), Yea.' Both the princesses were there, along with Russell, William Herbert,[2] the new queen's brother-in-law, and other intimates. Not the Howards.

Unlike the Norfolk nieces, Anne Boleyn or Catherine Howard, the new queen was not in the least arrogant at her elevation. 'It having pleased God,' she wrote to her brother, Lord Parr, 'to incline the King to take her as his wife, which was the greatest comfort that could happen to her, she asked him to let her know of his health as friendly as if she had not been called to this honour.'[3]

The Court was thankful that the king should be settled and in better temper—though, to the Catholic faction, Catherine was tarred with the Protestant brush. Only one person was furious—Anne of Cleves. She had been glad enough for young Catherine Howard, but this was too much; she declared that she would 'like to be in her shirt (without her £4,000 a year) with her mother', in 'despair' at 'the espousal of this third (new) wife'. Catherine Parr was 'not nearly so beautiful' as she was, and, besides, there was no hope of issue, seeing that she had none with her two former husbands. 'A fine burden,' she said, 'Madame has taken on herself,' alluding coarsely to the king's gross bulk.

[1] Her first husband had been Lord Borough of Gainsborough, who had died 'very old and distracted of memory' in 1529; her second, John Neville, Lord Latimer, of Snape Hall, Yorkshire, whose family had been involved in the Pilgrimage of Grace; he had died in 1542. Sir Thomas Seymour, the Lord Admiral and brother of Hertford—who was later, as the Dowager Queen's fourth husband, to make a pass at the young Princess Elizabeth—had wanted to marry her, but, by the spring of 1543, had been 'overruled by a higher power'.

[2] He was the younger son of Sir Richard Herbert, gentleman usher to Henry VII and Constable of Abergavenny Castle. A mad fighting young fellow, says Aubrey, 'Black Will Herbert' had killed the Sheriff of Bristol, fled and taken service with Francis I, who had recommended him to Henry VIII. By 1544 he was to get the rich nunnery of Wilton, and Church lands at Ramsbury in North Wilts, and in 1551 to be created Earl of Pembroke, the founder of a famous family. He died in 1570. Aubrey describes him as illiterate; 'strong sett but bony, reddish favoured, of a sharp eye, stern look'. Under Mary, he was to be turned out of Wilton, but, after her death, to come back 'like a Tygre' to expel the nuns, crying 'Out, ye Whores, to worke, to worke, ye Whores, goe spinne.' _Brief Lives_, ed. O. Lawson Dick, p. 142.

[3] L. and P., XVIII, I, 918.

In fact, 'Kateryn the Quene K.P.', as she signed herself, proved a benign influence; well able, next year, to act as Regent, like the first Queen Catherine, when Henry was at the wars in France. She encouraged Mary to translate Erasmus' paraphrase of the Gospels, and employed the repentent Nicholas Udall to edit the book; Elizabeth, now eleven, submitted scripts to her; Prince Edward was to thank her for accepting 'so gentylly my simple and rude letters', call her *Regina nobilissima* and *mater charissima*, and compliment her on '*vostre belle escriture*'.[1] And she could manage the king himself; now no less dangerous and still immensely able, but entering, in his early 'fifties, on what he himself described as his 'old age'.

III

The new queen shared her husband's passion for theology. Here Henry had loosed forces he could not control, and he now tried to stabilize doctrine. As Pollard remarks, 'to devout but fundamentally irreligious minds, men like Henry VIII and Louis XIV, rites and ceremonies are a great consolation and Henry seldom neglected to creep to the cross on Good Friday', though he would 'row up and down the Thames in his barge for an hour after Evensong on [the] Holy Thursday [before]', with his pipes and drums playing'.[2] He always thought himself strictly orthodox and had promised the emperor that he would 'well foresee that no new naughty traditions' would be made in his realm; like his successors, he retained the title, long cancelled, of Defender of the Faith.

One of Richard Hunne's crimes in 1514 had been to possess 'divers books prohibit and damnyd by the law, as the Bible in English'. Now, since 1538, the 'Great Bible' or 'Cranmer's Bible' had been in all the Churches and the clergy commanded to 'exhort every person to read the same'.[3] And along with it, the government had imposed a service book in English, with the Creed, the Lord's Prayer, and the Ten Commandments. The drive of the new capitalists for monastic lands had been paralleled by the habit of reading and hearing Bible and Liturgy in the native tongue, the old numinous run of Church Latin superseded by familiar words.

By 1543 the king felt that this doctrinal trend had gone too far. He had already attacked the 'lurking Anabaptists', and the marriage of the

---

[1] 'On your beautiful handwriting.' Ellis, II, Series I, pp. 131–2.

[2] op. cit., p. 311 and n.

[3] It was a modified conflation of Tyndale's 'heretical' translation from the Hebrew and Greek, and of Coverdale's version from the Vulgate and Luther. It was nominally by Thomas Mathew, in fact by John Rodgers, afterwards burnt.

clergy 'contrary to the wholesome admonitions of St Paul'. Even the archbishop had to conceal the existence of Mrs Cranmer, who, according to popular rumour, was carried in her husband's baggage train in a specially constructed trunk. Now, in 1543, Henry launched a double attack. That spring Parliament passed an Act for the Advancement of True Religion; it condemned unorthodox translations and restricted the reading even of the Great Bible; women and the lower orders were not allowed to read it at all. Savage penalties were also threatened against clergy who preached against the official line. In May, too, the service books were adapted to the use of Sarum.

The other attack was made by the king himself. The 'Bishops' book' or *Institution of a Christian Man* of 1537, never officially sanctioned, was now superseded by a *Necessary Doctrine and Erudition of any Christian Man*. Henry wrote the preface himself; cited the approval of the lords spiritual and temporal and of the nether house. The new book was to be a 'true and perfect doctrine for all his people'; Winchester as well as Cranmer had a hand in it, and it affirmed transubstantiation, the celibacy of the clergy, and all seven sacraments.

Henry had taken immense trouble in its production, and his own copy of the original 'Bishops' book', used for the revision and inscribed 'the King's commandment is that I should not be had out of the Privy Chamber', intimately reveals his mind. It shows how acute and practical he was, and how much he let Cranmer stand up to him. To the definition of God's omnipotence 'all subject to it and cannot resiste . . . the same', Henry added, 'but by his grace'. He thus left a loophole for anyone, like himself, *en rapport* with the Almighty. Cranmer, however, thought 'the words better out'; for God gave 'not his grace to let [frustrate] his own power'.[1] Then the king's commonsense was outraged by a phrase in the Lord's Prayer. 'And lead us not into temptation', he argued, should read, 'Suffer us not to be led'; but Cranmer retorted briefly, 'Christ taught us thus to pray'. Anxious to strengthen government, Henry also wished to supplement 'we must heartily forgive those that trespass against us' by 'and commit the punishment of the offender (being contrary to God and the Prince's laws) to the order of Justice'. He pointed out, too, that people knew quite well that they did not forgive their neighbours, and so omitted the prayer, thinking (as Latimer had put it) 'to do their neighbour a foul turn with a

---

[1] *Corrections of the Institution of a Christian Man by Henry VIII, with Archbishop Cranmer's annotations. Miscellaneous writings and letters of Thomas Cranmer*, ed. J. Cox, Parker Society, 1846, Vol. II, pp. 83 ff. Cox considers that the corrections were made in 1538, not, as Strype considers, in 1542.

better conscience'. The king also asked Tunstall if he really imagined that a felon would confess, if told that he must do so before being acquitted? He then discussed Origen on Psalm 37, Ciprian *de Lapsis*; Isaiah 43, and Solomon on Proverbs 18.

In spite of this shift back to orthodoxy, Cranmer remained in high favour. He always answered the king's enquiries at once, sending him succinct, tabulated answers, 'which,' Henry said, 'he could never get with no such readiness of none, no, not of all his chaplains and clergy about him in so short a time'. And Henry understood Cranmer's literary genius.

This was well for the archbishop, for that spring the king had to defend him against a dangerous attack. Gardiner, 'wily Winchester', had not forgiven Cranmer for getting Canterbury: the ablest of the conservatives, he was destined, under Mary, to send Cranmer to the stake.[1]

The archbishop had sentenced two prebendaries of Canterbury for denouncing the English Bible, and one of them, in connivance with Gardiner, set on Dr London, Warden of New College, whose services in liquidating monasteries are already familiar, to denounce the archbishop for heresy. Winchester now presented the accusation to the Council: he demanded a commission of enquiry, 'if the King was so content'.

Fortunately for Cranmer, Henry was not content. One evening, early that summer, as he came in his barge by Lambeth Palace and the archbishop emerged to pay his respects, he hailed Cranmer to join him. 'Ah, my chaplain,' he remarked genially, 'I have news for you. I know now who is the greatest heretic in Kent', and taking the articles of accusation from his sleeve, he presented them to the archbishop. But when Cranmer suggested an enquiry, Henry replied, 'I will commit the examination hereof wholly to you, and such as you will appoint.' They would hardly then, Cranmer naïvely objected, be impartial: 'Well,' answered Henry, conclusively, 'it shall be none otherwise. For

---

[1] He judged everything politically; including Erasmian learning, when it caused trouble. In 1542, as Chancellor of Cambridge, he reproved the humanist, Sir John Cheke, for introducing a new pronunciation of Greek. Erasmus, he admitted, had backed the change, and doubtless modern pronunciation differed from the original; but he thought Cheke's innovation 'arrogant'; moreover, it would weaken the prestige of the seniors. Cheke replied that the new pronunciation was popular abroad, but Winchester still forbade it. Cheke then asked him, as a personal favour, to remit the edict; but Gardiner gave the well-worn bureaucratic reply that he could not cancel it for one person; the old pronunciation should be continued, not because it was right, but because it was used; best to leave well alone. He hinted that Cheke, much as he liked him, had better be careful. L. and P., XVII, pp. 327, 479, 803.

surely I reckon that you will tell the truth; yea, of yourself, if you have offended. And therefore make no more ado but let a commission be made out to you and such others as you shall name, that I may understand how this confederacy came to pass.' The tables had been completely turned.

Henry at once ordered the houses of the main signatories to be searched. 'What will they do to you,' he exclaimed, with prophetic foresight, 'when I am gone?' The sequel was disastrous for Dr London: he was convicted of perjury, deprived of his offices, and died in prison.

Though Cranmer was cleared, Henry had cause for alarm, for heresy was rampant. One Kentish curate had, reasonably enough, remarked, 'If singing and playing were to God's honour . . . think you that our Prince would have pulled down those abbeys as he hath done?' 'Our Lady,' it had been said, 'was no better than other women, but a sack to put Christ in'; a 'priest's crown was but a balaam's mark', and the conservative clergy were 'pope-holy knaves'. Parson Cooper of Tenterden had declared that God was 'neither pleased with fasting nor discontent with eating', and Margaret Tofts had said her daughter could piss as good holy water as the priest could make any: one heretic 'would have neither ringing nor singing and cared not if he were buried in a ditch'. 'Hast thou authority to absolve me or give me penance?' another had asked a priest, 'Nay, thou mayst keep sheep.' Worst of all, another had said of the king's own injunctions, 'A fart for them!'

Arguments had led to violence: 'Dost thou call it [the sacrament] thy maker?' Henry Bird had demanded in 1542, 'Call it no more so, for if thou dost, I will kill thee!' Authority was undermined; 'No knave priest', said another, 'should know their minds, only God.' Even Wykeham's College beside Winchester—in Gardiner's own see—was infected; one of the ushers—William Forde, himself a Wykehamist— had become a Protestant. There were many golden images by the church door, and his study adjoined it, so he tied a long cord to them, linking them together; then, 'being in his chamber after midnight, he plucked the coorde's end and, at one pull, all the golden Gods came down with *Heyho Rumbelo*'. 'It wakened all men with a rush, amazed at the terrible noise and grievous sight,' but the usher was innocently in bed, the cord cut. Yet he was, of course, vehemently suspected; his scholars 'cried and railed' against him and he 'led a dogge's life, among them', being later badly beaten up.[1] Such were the goings on provoked by religious strife.

[1] *Narratives of the Reformation*, Camden, op. cit., p. 30.

With his political sense sharpened by experience, and in spite of trimming doctrinal sails to the shifts of power politics abroad, Henry tried for the rest of his life, and as far as he could, beyond, to reconcile the opposing attitudes of Cranmer and Gardiner and their political allies and exploiters, while finding both sides useful as the shifts of power politics abroad happened to demand.

IV

On June 18th, Chapuys asked the English authorities to let him see a ciphered letter 'found within the Frenchman's shoe'; if it was Marillac's cypher, he said, he could read it. And on June 22, 1543, still thinking the Scots situation favourable, Henry had sent a defiance to the French. By July he was officially at war, and, that autumn, sent a token force, under Sir John Wallop, strictly ordered to husband his artillery and ammunition, to help the emperor besiege Landrécies. But already, by July, the martial Cardinal Beaton, who had re-organized his power at St Andrew's, was marching on Linlithgow with 6,000 men, and by September the Protector, Arran, made off to Stirling, and went over to the cardinal. Now, Henry wrote, he saw 'the [dowager] Queen [of Scots] at the order of the cardinal, one man his enemy directing all things, and all their conjecture deceived'. In December 1543, after the English had seized some Scots ships, there was a riot in Edinburgh, and the infant Queen of Scots, crowned at Stirling, was removed from Henry's reach.

But the continental expedition paid off. Early in November, Wallop reported to the king that Charles V himself had arrived, 'armed, upon a little Turkey horse'; '*Dieu mercy*,' he had remarked, '*je suis tout gueri pour cambattre mes ennemyes*.'[1] Surrey and Wallop had attended a big council of war, which had decided to threaten the French flank. But Francis I had decamped with his army during the night, commanding all muleteers to take away the mules' bells, and carters 'not make any yerks with their whips'; 'trumpet there blew none, nor yet stroke of drum'. The French had also left much wine, many tents, some gun powder. And Charles V had agreed to let Henry have the master gunner 'that made the bullets artificials'.

Foul weather had now set in and they had broken camp; but many Spaniards offered to serve the king; if he wanted Spanish arquebusiers, he could have them; they were much the best. Wallop had conserved the artillery and was bringing it to Calais, if he could get cart-horses.

---

[1] 'God be thanked, I am quite cured [from the gout] to fight my enemies.'

In mid-November, having taken leave of the emperor who was at Cambrai, Wallop summed up the campaign. There was never such a war, he told the king, where there was so much to learn, both before Landrécies and at the emperor's coming. Many Spaniards, Germans, and Italians, he again emphasized, were anxious to serve Henry next year. Besides the arquebusiers, Count von Mansfield of Saxony had offered 5,000 foot, and out of Italy the Duke of Mantua's bastard, 'Alex: Gonzage', offered 4,000 and 300 mounted arquebusiers as well. Wallop had made a book of these names, but he warned his master 'it was evil meddling' with the Italians, having had 'good experience thereof this year to be either too wise or too false'.[1]

All was now set for the next year's campaign. Henry kept Christmas, 1543, at Hampton Court in full state. On Christmas Eve he came out from high mass, moved heavily to his presence chamber, and there, beneath his Cloth of Estate, created his two brothers-in-law, Lord Parr and Sir William Parr, respectively Earl of Essex and Baron Parr of Horton. Both were already Knights of the Garter, but at the Chapter that day Sir John Wallop, after his successful campaign at Landrécies, was also made a member of the Order, 'to the joy of all present', and supplied from the Great Wardrobe with eighteen yards of crimson velvet for a gown, hood, and tippet, and ten yards of white sarcenet for lining.[2]

The gargantuan court feasts, that Christmas, were provided by a master cook and by no less than thirty assistants in the kitchens, eleven in the pastry house and twenty-five in the pantry; though the launderers were, oddly enough, only five. The musicians and jesters and hangers-on who had survived the Eltham reforms flocked round their newly-married master.[3]

Along with the lurking violence, smooth deceit and false politeness at the summit of affairs, Henry's court was, also, still, a highly sophisticated centre of music, literature and learning. As already recorded, Sir Thomas Wyatt, far the best court poet, had died the year before. But he had left a fine legacy to the few who had read his manuscripts; indeed, as an Elizabethan was to put it, 'in the latter end of [Henry's] reign sprang up a new company of courtly makers, of whom Sir Thomas Wyatt the elder and the Earl of Surrey were the two chief-

[1] L. and P., XVIII, II, 385.
[2] L. and P., XVIII, II, 517.
[3] That year orders were still being made against idle persons haunting the court; no one was to keep any page or boy contrary to the king's ordinance, or keep greyhounds without his leave, and 'furthermore the King commandeth that no person keep any firretts' (ferrets). L. and P., XVIII, II, 542.

tains; who having travelled in Italy and there tasted the sweet and stately measures of Italian poesie, as novices newly crept out of the schools of Dante, Arioste and Petrach, they [had] greatly polished our rude and homely manner of vulgar poesie from that it had been before'.[1]

There had been nothing 'rude' in Wyatt's masterpieces;

> *'They flee from me that sometime did me seek*
> *With naked foot stalking within my chamber:*
> *Once I have seen them gentle, tame, and meek*
> *That now are wild, and do not once remember*
> *That sometime they have put themselves in danger*
> *To take bread at my hand; and now they range,*
> *Busily seeking in continual change.*
> *Thanked be fortune, it hath been otherwise*
> *Twenty times better; but once especial —*
> *In thin array, after a pleasant guise,*
> *When her loose gown did from her shoulders fall*
> *And she me caught in her arms long and small,*
> *And therewithal so sweetely did me kiss,*
> *And softly said, "Dear heart, how like you this?" . . . '*

Or in his

> *'My lute awake! perform the last*
> *Labour that you and I shall waste . . .*
> *My lute, be still, for I have done.'*

But the other highly accomplished poet still at court, Henry Howard, Earl of Surrey, was back from the wars. He was also a master of new Italianate meters 'and first of all Englishmen in translating the fourth book of Virgil'; but he was too much involved in the highest politics to last long. Henry's Court was, as ever, brilliant, and, in it still lurked death.

---

[1] Quoted *Arbor*, Elizabethan Sonnets, I.

CHAPTER XVIII

LAST ADVENTURE AND
NEAR BANKRUPTCY

✸

BEFORE invading France, Henry had to settle Scotland: after Arran's desertion and the abduction of the infant Mary Queen of Scots, finally taken for refuge to Inchmahone Priory on Lake Monteith, he had at once reinforced the border garrisons, and ordered them to raid regularly into Scotland and burn the crops; he had also prohibited the export of corn, iron plough-shares and horse-shoes. The best course, he decided, short of conquering Scotland, was to knock out Edinburgh and Leith and paralyse the Scots before he invaded France. In March 1544, Chapuys told his master that 'the King was on the point of reducing Scotland to such extremities that she would be no help to the French', and Henry had himself written: 'We, from this moment, repute, consider and hold the Scots our enemies.' He urged Charles V to declare war on them, and his instructions to Hertford were specific and brutal; 'to sack Leith and burn and subvert it, putting man, woman and child to fire and sword without exception when any resistance shall be made against you'.[1]

The king now had a great reputation in the Celtic Highlands and Islands, where news travelled fast. One John Elder, for example, 'map-maker', a 'Redshank' or Pict, educated, he emphasized, at St Andrew's, sent him a map drawn from his own travels in the north and west. He had heard, he wrote, how the king had 'pardoned the rebel Lords of Ireland, creating them earls and lords, bestowing riches upon them and sending them home in gorgeous apparel'—the sort of gesture the Highland world understood. Scotland, of course, had been part of the empire of England before the coming of Albanectus, Brutus' second son; and he denounced Beaton, 'the pestiferous Cardinal, his blind bishops and other false crafty bores' who 'had drunk the French King's wines'. He hoped Henry would 'smoke the papistical foxes out of their caves'.[2]

---

[1] Byrne, p. 346.
[2] L. and P., XVIII, II, 539. The Highlanders, he pointed out, were not, as alleged, intrinsically 'rough footed', but looked so because they wore leather boots with holes to let the water run away, with the hair outwards.

Since the English were short of maps, the gift may have come in useful.

On Sunday, May 4, 1544, Hertford's fleet entered the Firth of Forth. The army landed within a mile of Leith, and he ordered his cavalry forward; the whole force, in three 'wards', advanced to secure the harbour and land the guns. They found 6,000 Scots, horse and foot, with light artillery and some local peasants and 'rascals', drawn up along a brook. The 'stout' Cardinal Beaton himself was there, along with Arran, Seton and other lairds, 'dressed', as Lisle told Paget, 'in a frock of yellow velvet, cut and pulled out with tinsel sarcenet; but when he perceived that the English had a great devotion to wet their shoes to come to his holiness, like a valiant champion, he gave his horse the spurs'.[1] Half-an-hour's fighting 'right sharply handled on both parts' was enough; then the English, Hertford informed the king, attacked Leith so boldly that town and ordnance, 'such as it was', were taken before nightfall, 'and the enemies fled out'.[2] They found it richer than they expected any Scottish town to have been, with plunder worth £10,000—much of it grain—and 'two fair ships of the late Scottish king in the harbour, the *Salamon and the Unycorn*'. These would return with the navy.

Having secured their base, the English now advanced on Edinburgh. Provost and burgesses tried to gain time: if Hertford guaranteed them against the 'power of Scotland', they said, they would change sides. True to instructions, Hertford rated them for resisting his master's Godly intent, 'to revenge which', he told them, 'he was now sent'. He would have their town and castle to use as he thought fit; and when the Provost said he must consult his colleagues, Hertford told him that he 'came not to condition or treat with them'.

During this haggle, the Earl of Bothwell and Lord Hume had entered Edinburgh, as intended, with 2,000 men; but now, under covering fire from the archers and hackbuttiers, the English stormed the city. A big canon blew in the main gate and 300 of 400 Scots were slain in the assault, though Bothwell and Hume retreated to the castle which remained impregnable. The invaders wasted no time on it, but proceeded 'utterly to ruinate the said town with fire'; Edinburgh burnt for three days; and 'we burnt the Abbey called Holy Rood House and the palace adjoining the same'. Then 4,000 English light horse from the border arrived and wasted the country, rounded up cattle that had been driven out for safety.

All these atrocities were briskly completed; by mid-May, Hertford had evacuated Edinburgh and Leith, having burnt every house to the

[1] L. and P., XIX, 481.
[2] *Ibidem*, 472.

ground. He also burnt Seton Castle and the best gardens and orchards
in the country, for Seton had helped to get the cardinal out of prison:
he also advanced on Dunbar, caught the people unawares by a trick 'so
that their first sleeps closed in with fire' and they were 'suffocated and
brent'. A final blow was struck, down at Jedburgh, in June, where 'all
was burnt, and the Abbey likewise'. The Irish, Hertford told the king,
'have done good service and are dreaded by the Scots as they take no
prisoners'. On the border, too, there now remained no fort where the
Scots could assemble: the victory, wrote one pious informant, 'was
rather a miracle than otherwise; God be praised for all! In these victories,' he asked, 'who is to be most highest lauded but God, by whose
goodness the Englishmen have had a great season of notable victories?
. . . And for the continuance of God's favour let us pray for the prosperous estate of our noble and valiant Lord Governour and King, for
whose sake doubtless God shall spread his blessings over us!'

But, back in London, certain high persons reported the victory 'in-
accurately', to the slander of the king's captains, and were commanded
by the lord mayor to bring their 'books' to be burnt within twenty-
four hours. The rumour also ran in Venice that 16,000 Englishmen had
been slain—the king's host broken. In time the facts spoke for themselves;
Henry's orders had been carried out to the letter; and the Scots, if
united by a new hatred, had been knocked out for the year. When, late
in June, Henry married off his neice, Lady Margaret Douglas, daughter
of his late sister Margaret by Angus, to Mathew Stuart, fourth Earl of
Lennox,[1] the rise of another pro-English party in Scotland was still
handicapped, as Lennox put it to Queen Catherine, 'by the coloured
falsehood of the Lords of Scotland'.

II

The enormous expense of the invasion being mounted against France,
on top of the expense of the Scottish expedition, had already brought
the king near bankruptcy. Cromwell had tried to make him the richest
king that was ever in England, but Henry had already run through
much of the wealth which Cromwell had piled up; huge sales of Church
lands went on apace, and when the 'common voice reported' that the
king himself would go overseas to the war this year, the City knew
what that meant. On May 16, 1544, while Hertford was making his
bloodstained withdrawal from Scotland, the Government, as it oddly

[1] Henry, Lord Darnley, the son of this marriage, married Mary Queen of Scots and
became the ancestor of the Stuart Kings of England and Scotland.

put it, 'enhanced' the value of the coinage by raising the price of gold.

The debasement of the coinage now coincided with the inflation hitherto creeping, now acute, and the king's credit steadily diminished; in June he had to pay 12 per cent; 14 per cent in August; 16 per cent by September: he was selling lead from the plundered monasteries. Yet, as a whole, the economy was expanding; financially inept as the Government might be, as were all sixteenth-century governments, they were not able to interfere as much as they wished in a prosperity which sustained relatively heavy taxation.

The year before, a subsidy of £183,000 had been voted: Parliament now had to relieve the king from repaying the large 'loans' already incurred—an action 'justified on the grounds that it gave parliamentary sanction to a situation which was already irremediable'.[1] This complicity with the king's demands increased royal favour: the Commons in particular, now felt more important. In 1542 they had demanded, through their Speaker, Sir Thomas Moyle, 'liberty of honest speech' and free access, through delegations, to the king. In 1543 they had also established their freedom from arrest. For George Ferrers, an official of the King's Chamber and Member for Plymouth, had been imprisoned by the City authorities on a suit for debt, incurred by a guarantee. The House had arrogantly sent the Sergeant with the mace to get him out, and in the fracas the mace had been broken. But Henry had strongly backed the privilege of the Commons; Ferrers was vindicated. 'We are informed,' said the king, 'by our judges, that we at no time stand so highly in our estate royal as in the time of Parliament'. As the royal necessities increased, so the power of the Commons' purse began to tell.

Early in May, secretary Wriothesley succeeded Audley as Lord Chancellor and became a peer: but no one stepped into Cromwell's shoes. Cromwell had left a far better instrument of government, but Henry kept it under his own hand. There was now quite a well-established bureaucracy; the Councils for Wales and the North and Ireland; courts for collecting the various royal revenues; a court to survey the crown lands; the Stannary courts in Cornwall; and, independently, the justices of the peace, well under control, administered local affairs. All centred on the Privy Council; the prerogative law courts through the chancellor, the Church courts through the archbishop, and through the court of Star Chamber, in reserve. The Privy Council itself, now, since 1540, contained twenty members, with a permanent clerk; the major routine officials tended to stay in London, though sometimes with the king.

[1] Mackie, op. cit., 439.

The records still give an impression of abject dependence on the monarch: the more so as the Council was rent by factions worsened by religious strife, both sides jockeying for position on the king's demise.

III

But that now hardly seemed imminent. Grey and bald and gross, Henry was better; and domestically more content than since the death of Queen Jane. He was eager to launch in person his long-planned attack on France; liked the visiting Duke of Albuquerque, a 'ceremonious' visiting grandee from Spain; 'much desired his company for the enterprise of France'; even sent a courier to Charles V to arrange it. He had the Don feasted and shown his principal royal houses; his rich possessions; his plate. The Spaniard told his friends that 'but for the emperor's service he would not abide there an hour', but 'out of duty' he remained. Charles V had now declared war on the Scots and relations improved.

The object of Henry's war was strictly limited. Calais was now the only English foothold on the continent, and Boulogne, round the corner of Cap Griz Nez, was a potential threat. The king was determined to secure it, and so consolidate his command of the straits. The strategic danger was still a union of the French and Scottish crowns, which could have made Scotland not a bridle, but a stranglehold for England; in temporary alliance with Charles V, Henry's objective makes sense—granted that it was worth keeping the foothold in France. The war was also a last fling; an expression of royal vanity and rage; after all, kings then went to war because that was what kings did. 'Whether such conquests would be worth the blood and treasure they would cost was an irrelevant absurdity. Nobody expected that they would.'[1]

Much thought had been given to the expedition: that spring Norfolk had summarized the Council's views on the best route for the king to take. 'Item,' he wrote, 'it is thought the best way is to go by the frontiers of Flanders unto that passage where the Duc of Suffolk came over the ryver of Som [Somme] at his retourne out of France [in 1523], which is two miles on this side of the town of Veele [Abbeville] in Vermandoyse.' The king, too, always concerned for his horses, was buying up Flemish mares (he preferred real ones); but their principal industry, the Flemish authorities complained, was the breeding of

---

[1] Mattingly, *Renaissance Diplomacy*, p. 163. Sir Thomas More, in *Utopia*, had thought the same thing.

horses: were all the 200 Dunkirk mares, they asked, in fact for the royal stables?[1] But they had to let them go.

On July 14, 1544, Henry sailed for France, with his two trusty, ageing Dukes, Norfolk and Suffolk, the flag of St George at the masthead and 'such a porte of the nobilitie and yeomanry of England as neither been lyke known by experience nor yet read of in history'. The English were supposed, as planned, to strike across the Somme, and Charles V to advance on Paris from St Dizier on the Marne. In fact, neither king nor emperor intended to take much of the campaign and Henry, as indicated, cared only about Boulogne, 'that fortress', he told the queen, 'which was to the realm most displeasant and noisesome'. The other objective was Montreuil—Monstrell, Montrulle or Mutterell the English called it. Situated on the river Canche, inland from Etaples and the modern Le Touquet, the town was a potential base from which to defend Boulogne or to attack Abbeville.

Always a man of moods, Henry was in high spirits, stertorous, unwieldy, but still a soldier, reliving the old campaigns in Flanders, when he had written back, boasting, to his first queen. He now wrote to Catherine Parr, also a competent Regent, giving highly technical details of the campaign. On her side, she wrote, 'I cannot quietly pleasure anything until I hear from your Majesty', her words, indeed, 'not only written with ynke but moost truely impressed on the hart . . . lest I should be tedious to your Majesty I finish this my scribbled letter'.[2] 'The king's prosperous health and that of his family are not a little to my comfort,' wrote Russell to Paget, in August: 'the King has better health and works better and more than I would have thought', wrote Chapuys.

As in 1513, the July rain set in; Henry rode over the open country behind Cap Gris Nez to Marquise, north of Boulogne, in a thunderstorm. There were similar difficulties of supplies, and Norfolk decided not to assault Montreuil but starve it out. Criticized, he wrote to Suffolk, 'I am sorry in my old days to be thus spoken of, but some men's doings are better spoken of than others'; he would rather have someone 'whom the King trusted to report truly' than £500. Suffolk sent him Cavendish, long, since Wolsey's fall, in the king's service. Russell also sent fifty Cornish miners, 'the best that Godolphin could choose', for the mining and investment of the town; already, by mid-August, the besieged were eating horse flesh, and the governor saying that the English would 'take him by the "bec" [beak] not the hands'.

---

[1] *Spanish Calendar*, VII, p. 229.
[2] Strype II. Repository of Originals, p. 33.

The main objective remained Boulogne, where the king was impatient for results. A wagon containing his personal weapons and enormous armour broke an axle tree for lack of grease, and two men who spoke the language were told off to supervise the French carters; Hunt, the king's blacksmith, was killed by a chance shot. On August 21st Henry himself mustered the expensive High Almayn horsemen now come in, but vile weather continued: on September 4th, in another thunderstorm, the English threw 'wild fire' into Boulogne, and by the 11th the king, with Surrey and Lord William Howard, 'took his stand to see the fall of the Castle'. 'I never in my life,' wrote one eye witness, 'saw the King so joyfull and in such good spirits . . . so elated.'[1] French offers of peace had been brushed aside: Henry was determined on his kill, and felt he was conducting the entire campaign. There was so much to do, he wrote to the queen, 'in foreseeing and caring for everything ourself as we have almost no rest or leisure to do anythynge'.

On the 13th the French duly surrendered; the inhabitants had been promised safety but many refugees left the town; men, women and children, wagons and horses, they trudged past the bulky splendid king as he sat to take the surrender, the Germans drawn on one said, the English on the other, the Master of the Horse holding a naked sword before him. After the first miserable cortege, came the 2,000 men of the garrison in ranks of five. But soon another storm wrecked the royal pavilions, damaged shipping in the habour and blew down the tents.

On the 18th, Henry and the stately Albuquerque made their formal entry into conquered Boulogne: back in England, the queen ordered processions of the clergy and 'thanks for the benefits God had heaped upon us'. Like Catherine of Aragon, she was working well with the Counsellors at home: it was best, she had written, to keep the Scots warring on all sides; she had encouraged Lennox on his expedition from Bristol up the west coast to Dumbarton. It failed, but not before she had piously attributed an unachieved success to his now serving a master 'whom God aids'.

The sequel at Boulogne was less exhilarating than the surrender: indiscipline broke out and one of the Germans 'stuck an Englishman with a boar spear in the throat without any occasion given'; indeed, the Almayns 'set nothing by no man and ate twice what they should'. Some drunken German horsemen got into Etaples, 'strangely' sent there by Charles V, and refused to leave until paid. Norfolk sent his cousin, Sir Edmund Wyndham, to 'hang up' some of the English for looting, and 'do his best to cause the Almayns to come hither', which,

[1] *Spanish Calendar*, VII, p. 264.

he feared, 'would not come to pass'. Montreuil remained untaken, though the king mustered his battle before the main gate, and knighted those distinguished in the taking of Boulogne.

IV

There was now good cause for the English to pull out, for Boulogne had been captured against a background of frenetic diplomatic intrigue; the attempt to take Montreuil was abandoned. Both Charles V and Henry were out to double-cross each other, and the French had long been negotiating with the English to break up the alliance. Unfortunately Charles V, to whom the affairs of England were not of the first importance, had got in first; on September 19th, the day after Henry had made his formal entry into Boulogne, the emperor had signed a treaty at Créspi with momentous consequences to Europe. It declared perpetual peace and a reversion to the *status quo* as at the truce of Nice; it detached Francis I from the Turks and recognized a Spanish domination of Italy that was to last for two centuries. To mark the close of that long conflict, the princess of Spain, daughter of Charles V, was to marry the Duc d'Orléans. Leopold of Austria, King of the Romans, the pope, Venice, the monarchs of Poland, Portugal and Denmark, were all included, and Henry, though formally 'comprised' subject to his consent, was left to face the infuriated French.

Already many of the emperor's German mercenaries were changing sides, strictly against instructions as the emperor assured Henry, but since Charles V could not control or pay them (left in garrison at Vitry-les-Français, the Germans had burnt the place down) he was glad to see them go. There was no need, anyway, wrote his shrewd minister Nicholas Granvelle, to fear the enmity of England: Henry had shirked out of the campaign and 'not for the first time made himself the emperor's enemy without being able to hurt him'. 'It is a maxim,' Granvelle concluded, 'to regard the reality of treaties in conjunction with what is possible . . . ' 'We have done nothing,' wrote Charles V, keeping a poker face, 'of which the King of England can possibly complain.'[1]

Told of the *fait accompli*, Henry, too, remained impassive, though he 'doubted if the Spaniards would put up with being ruled by a descendant of Francis I, the greatest enemy the Emperor ever had'. After all, he had obtained his objective. Already, in mid-September, he had told the Cardinal of Arras, the emperor's envoy, that 'the season being so far advanced, he had decided that the army should not move further

[1] *Spanish Calendar*, VII, p. 377.

into France, and had issued orders to that effect'.[1] Indeed, his Privy Council had told him that the period in which, by treaty, the allied armies were to keep the field would expire in a fortnight; as an old connoisseur of diplomatic irony he had even hinted that Charles V, by advancing so dangerously far into France, might have forced the English to go beyond their obligations.

Much as he doubtless relished this gambit, Henry had given Charles V the excuse he wanted; and when Chapuys told him to his face that he had 'consented' to the Peace of Créspi, the king 'changed colour several times'; 'he would like to know,' he shouted, 'how anybody dared assert it!'

The tactical situation now looked rather dangerous. The Dauphin, with an 'enormous' force, including Gascon and Italian mercenaries, was said to be advancing on Boulogne, and the French fleet from Le Havre might attack the vulnerable shipping off Etaples. In August there had been a scare at Portsmouth, when forty-four sail were seen going up Channel 'under the Wight', though they turned out to be Spaniards and 'Portingales'. Many English ships were also guarding the east coast and the autumn fogs made the task difficult. 'After my umbell comendassens,' one sea captain was writing, phonetically, to the Council, 'may it please your lordships to advertize that Monday last there fell suche a mist whare we lay in Orwellwaies [near Harwich] that on of us colde nott see a nother lying at a nanker'.[2] Even in the Straits of Dover, the English, their main force covering the Channel at Portsmouth, had to rely in part on the emperor's ships.

It was a humiliating position. Wriothesley appealed to God and blackguarded the French: 'God is able to strength his own against the Dyvel, and therefore let not the Queen's majesty in anyways trouble herself, for God shall turn all for the best. And sure we be that the King's Majesty's person is out of all danger, and so be the rest, too, I doubt not, for it shall not yet enter into my creed that the Frenchmen will cope with us, whatsoever brag soever they set upon it.'[2]

It was time, nonetheless, for Henry to return: 'I would wish the Majesty of England,' wrote Norfolk, on whom the responsibility lay heaviest, 'at least back in Calais.' Soon it was put about that the king, after his honourable conquest of the town of Boulogne, was 'now minded to repair to England'; beer and wine were laid on in such places in England where he would lodge, and on September 29th Paget wrote

[1] *Spanish Calendar*, VII, p. 336.
[2] S.P., I, p. 772.
[3] *Ibidem*, I, p. 767.

from Boulogne, 'tomorrow, God willing, the King's Majesty will take the Seas'.

Next day Henry embarked, after dinner, 'quite buoyant and joyful, and determined not to lose the town'. Only when Chapuys, who accompanied him to ship, assured him of his master's good faith, did he reply shortly 'I have always heard fine words—I wish to see them put into effect'. With this parting shot, and escorted by the imperial warships, the monarch returned, for the last time, to his island.[1]

V

The two dukes, along with Gardiner and Paget, were left to do the best they could. There was sickness in Calais ('I have my nagu a gayne a moos as yll as never I had hym'); the small craft off Etaples and Boulogne were rotten with the great rains; there were daily 'frays with the Almayns' in which the Irish took part; there was 'no carriage for the mills and brewhouses, the horses being dead'. And how to get the guns from Montreuil over the ford at Etaples? The dukes retired on Calais, along with the Councillors still in France.

Back at Hampton Court, Henry was furious. 'The King thinks his honour touched,' they were told, 'if his army should retire at the enemies' coming into the field.' As for the Councillors, he commanded them to return to Boulogne at once: 'We think you should satisfy his Majesty,' wrote their colleagues at home, 'touching your proceedings with all diligence.'

They obeyed, and Henry was pacified. But not quiescent; on November 11th he sent them the 'form of the plat' (map) of the fortifications beside the Old Man (a tactically important tower), to which he had made some additions. 'To make the corner of the bulwark cover the flanks,' the king thought, 'with stakes and rods wound together and other timber you may keep them up as well as if they had been made of turf'; the galleries should be 12 feet wide, 'with boards two inches thick, and so full of holes that a great number may shoot out of them at a time'. His grasp of detail was unimpaired.

Meanwhile, Charles V had written begging Henry to promote 'such good and holy work as Peace between two Christian princes is'; and

---

[1] An occasion for Young Roger Ascham to present him with his *Toxophilus*, a treatise on archery. 'I being at my book at Cambridge,' he wrote, 'did offer something on his victorious return.' It dealt with an English matter, he emphasized, in the English Tongue, 'a pastime honest for the mind, holsom for the body, fit for everyman, vile for no man'. His 'zeal to set forward shooting' pleased the King, who accepted his book in his gallery at Greenwich, and accorded Ascham a pension of £10 a year.

Gardiner and Hertford, sent to Brussels, reported that the emperor was entertaining the French queen, the Duc d'Orléans, and the Cardinal of Lorraine. But the Spanish estates (confirming Henry's opinion) would not agree to the marriage of their princess with Orléans, 'who could evil see, and one of his eyes is eaten with small pox'; Francis I, too, was said to be longing for the return of his ladies, one of whom was his present mistress. By December, Charles V, sick of the gout, had retired to his native town of Ghent, intending, it was said, to go into Germany.

The danger of a coalition against England, fomented by the pope, was thus no longer acute, though Cardinal Beaton was begging more help from Rome, 'seeing the tender age of the infant [Scots] queen, the lamentable death of the late King and the rage and cruelty of the enemies'. But the pope was concerned with far more momentous plans: he had just issued a Bull for a free grand Council of Christendom at Trent, under the Dolomites north of Verona, timed for the spring of 1545.

Keeping Christmas 1544 at Greenwich, Henry licensed his subjects to equip privateers against the French, and told Cranmer to see that the clergy paid up their subsidy by January 15th. He also 'forgot', Chapuys reported, to enquire for the health of Charles V; but coming out of his pew after Mass, told him he was 'ten times better', and 'added, very loudly', that since his return, 'those people [the French] had been much whipped both by land and sea'. They had 'paid their scot lately by reason of the great quantity of French wine seized by his ships of war'; and indeed twenty-five Frenchmen, laden with red claret and white, had been brought into the Thames, 'taken round Wight and Rye'. When Chapuys thanked the queen for her kindness to the Lady Mary, she replied that she did not deserve his gratitude; what she had done for the princess was far less than she would have liked to do, and she hoped that God would avert the slightest dissension with the emperor; both sovereigns were so 'good'.[1] All was now peace in the royal family; on New Year's eve, the Lady Elizabeth sent her stepmother a godly little book *A Mirror or Glass of the Sinful Soul*, a French rhyme translated into English prose, private for the Queen; she wished her 'prosperous issue and a year of health and joy'.

[1] *Spanish Calendar*, VIII, p. 2.

CHAPTER XIX

INVASION FOILED: ROYAL THEOLOGY

❖

Henry, at fifty-four, now had to face the most serious invasion threat of his whole reign, the entire resources of France concentrated on England. In February 1545, he wrote a letter of his own penning to Sir Henry Wootten, ambassador to Charles V, instructing him to reproach the emperor for 'making peace with the common enemy, leaving us in the war. . . .' 'Having aided him in every tempest from his youth until now,' he wrote, 'we are discouraged by the discourtesy he now shows us.' Doubtless the cause was his Council's 'sinister and wrong informations'; the ambassador was to press him to 'annul this peace, so disagreeable to most people'. The king's fixed idea that Charles V, his junior and sometime nephew, ought to take his advice was ineradicable: beyond overwhelming the English envoys with courtesies, Charles V remained unmoved.

The Scots were now again in the field, led by Angus—for he had finally turned against the king—and, like Arran, they defeated the English at Ancrum Moor. Sir Ralf Eyre, Warden of the Middle Marches, advancing on Jedburgh, was set on, made to fight on foot and killed; 1,400 men were slain or taken: 'lack of good order', it was reported, had caused the reverse.

Lennox, too, from Carlisle, having failed to take Dumbarton, was still 'not so fortunate as he might have been': he desired revenge, above all, on Angus; wanted to raise men from the west coast and the Islands to march on Stirling—an impracticable plan. Two French ships were already in Leith with artillery, gunpowder and money; and on March 18th, Arran, Cardinal Beaton and Angus proclaimed, rather wildly, in Edinburgh that all men from sixteen to sixty were to make ready to come to the border with fifteen days' victuals on twenty-four hours warning: 'they say', ran the rumour, 'ten thousand well-geared men will be ready by the full moon'.

These gestures were in part political warfare, made in conjunction with the French; but the threat kept considerable and expensive forces

in the north at a critical time and morale there was patchy. Of the
ten gunners in the important castle at Berwick-on-Tweed, old Shrewsbury was informed, 'but four could shoot'; when the captain was away
his son ruled—'a very wilfull young man', and the constable regularly
opened the 'postern gate leading to the white wall, night and morning,
to let Lord Eures' sheep in and out'. In the event, the French were to
land in Scotland that summer, and Hertford again to devastate the
valley of the Tweed.

But the main threat remained against the south coast. A fleet of over
a hundred and fifty ships was already mustered at Le Havre; its objective, in conjunction with an attack on Boulogne, Portsmouth, the Isle of
Wight and the invasion of England.

II

If the English were ready for them, the credit was due mainly to the
king. The navy had now become a 'permanent service with ships,
men and administration renewed in unbroken succession until our own
day. Henry VIII was the author of that'.[1] Though still built of unseasoned timber and normally laid up in winter, the new ships were
equipped with powerful guns. The old tactics of grapple and board,
used in the ineffective battles of the king's youth off Brittany, had been
long abandoned; the new *Great Harry*, launched in 1541, was a ship
of over 1,000 tons, and there were great expectations of the latest,
heavily-gunned, *Mary Rose*. And the new galleasses, of lower super-
structure but fully rigged, with auxiliary oars, were highly adaptable.

Ever since, as a splendid youth, Henry had gone aboard in a sailor's
'coat and trousers with frieze cloth of gold and a large whistle', he had
loved the sea; he had fostered the new dockyards at Portsmouth, Deptford, Woolwich, and lately commanded a detailed pictorial survey of
the whole south coast. The forts guarding the island, from the north
east to Cornwall, were now in being; the king, Cromwell and the
Council had seen to that.

Oceanic enterprise, too, had been developing: in 1540 a Brazilian
Cacique, in whose lower lip was set a precious stone about the bigness
of a pea, had made a sensation at court, and by 1542 Southampton merchants had set up a fort at Bahia. To the north, the oldest trade of all
with Newfoundland for fish, had been further expanded when factories
had been set up to split and cure the catch on the spot. All this Atlantic
enterprise meant more skilled navigators; more boys bred to the sea.

[1] J. A. Williamson, op. cit., p. 166.

Tudor administration and resources could not, of course, keep fleet or forts permanently ready. They had to guard the Channel, the straits of Dover, the east coast, and keep the army defending Calais and Boulogne supplied; already they were overextended, but the potential was there.

Henry reinforced the main fleet at Portsmouth with ten extra ships and with French prizes, while the Privy Council ordered search to be made among the French prisoners for pilots. In May 1545, the king himself, seeing a certain 'flitte of Portugals was due', commanded Lord William Howard to try 'with all gentleness and good and doulce [sweet] words to retain two or three notable ships which his grace was informed were with them, well trimmed with ordnance'. He had been advised that the King of Portugal would not object.[1] Flemish hoys and 'pinks' carrying food and munitions to France were to be arrested and 'unladen'—their cargoes bought up.

The forts which the king and Cromwell had placed at strategic places about the coast were now operational, but there were never enough guns. If a French army equipped with artillery and 'hackbutts' (muskets) had landed, the English bowmen would have been outclassed; moreover the bowyers complained that one Peter van Helden had cornered the whole import of bowstaves and was driving up the price: Henry himself at once ordered that the price be fixed. And so short was the king of professional soldiers that the authorities at Calais were told to enrol Albanian deserters from the French king 'if they could be trusted'.

The French, still heavily attacking Boulogne, now planned to take Portsmouth, win control of the Channel and cut the English supply; Francis I, 'like to die', but game to the last, had ordered up twenty-five galleys and some carracks from the Mediterranean to Le Havre, while Charles V, annoyed at the English blockade, was already arresting English merchants in the Low Countries. Lisle took the fleet across the channel, for a spoiling attack on Le Havre, but the French were too strong for him to go in. And by July 1545, they launched the most dangerous invasion that had come against the island since 1066. On the 18th, a big fleet, with pikemen and hackbutiers crowded aboard, were sighted from Portland.

At Portsmouth July 23rd was hot; hardly a puff of wind stirred the smooth waters of the harbour. Henry was at dinner in the flagship when the French were reported in the offing, and within two hours a

---

[1] *Acts of Privy Council*, VII, p. 186.

'fleet of great force' was threatening the most important naval base in England.

The king hurriedly went ashore, and the fleet made what sail it could to come at the enemy; but the wind would not serve; only the galleasses, 'the rowing pieces', got out and set on the French. Then, in the late afternoon, a sudden breeze stirred the sultry air, and the great ships began to move. D'Annebault, the French admiral, did not like the look of them, or of the channels of the harbour, or of the chances of a south-westerly gale, and he had begun to draw off, when a spectacular catastrophe struck the English. Suddenly the great *Mary Rose*, turning to catch the wind, heeled over and sank.

Henry cried out in anguish at the sight; the vice-admiral, Sir George Carew, and over 400 men perished; only twenty or thirty of the crew were saved. 'I made enquiries of one of the survivors,' wrote a Flemish merchant, 'and he told me that the disaster was caused by their not having closed the lowest row of the gun ports on the side of the ship.... The ship was turning . . . when the wind caught her sails so strongly as to heel her over and plunge her open gun ports beneath the water, which flooded and sank her.'[1] 'The ship,' Grafton corroborates, 'by too much folly was drowned in the midst of the haven; for she was laden with too much ordnance and the ports left open.'

The French fleet pulled out and lay off Chichester bar; then, with a west wind rising, moved up Channel to be free of shoals and get searoom; they threatened Seaford and raided and burnt Brighton. Sir Edward Gage warned the justices of Kent that twelve score sail of French ships had landed 20,000 men—all Kent must repair hither, he wrote, for their repulse; 'Haste, haste, post haste', he marked the letter, 'for thy life, haste!' But in mid-August a second action off Shoreham proved decisive. There was again little wind and again the galleasses went in; after a sharp exchange, both fleets anchored for the night, but by the morning, the French were gone. They had sickness aboard, food and water were short in the overcrowded ships and there was nothing for it but to retire to Le Havre.

This deliverance caused bewilderment, even some disappointment, among the levies of the English countryside. 'If they come,' the Norfolk levy had asked their duke, 'for God's sake bring us between the sea and them.' On the Isle of Wight, indeed, the French had made landings at Bembridge and Shanklin; 'the man who killed one of them', it was reported, 'had great praise from the gents and sogyars, that say with what spyryt and stomak a [he] did yt': he was sent up to the king

[1] *Spanish Calendar*, Vol. VIII, p. 190.

with the spoils. But the Worcestershire equivalent of the home guard drew a complete blank. In mid-July they had set forward from Worcester towards Portsmouth, and, after three days' marching, had got mid-way between Wantage and Newbury. Here they were met by orders from the Council to go home, which they obeyed. Then Mr Sergeant Knottisford arrived from Malvern and told them to set forward for Portsmouth again; since he could show no warrant, they were deeply puzzled: 'Wee surely arre,' wrote their captain, 'so perplexed and put in doubt that wee know not what is to be chosen for the best.' They decided to call it a day.

So the invasion threat was past, but the French were increasing their attack on Boulogne and the war there was to continue through the winter; in the north the French, as already described, were still a nuisance, and the cost of the war was rocketing.

III

'In an age,' wrote Mattingly, 'when revenues were rarely adequate to expenditure, an age of rising prices and extravagant courts, obsolete fiscal methods and haphazard emergency financing, there was never enough public money to go round.'[1] And Chapuys had written that he thought Henry would not long be able to continue the wars 'as there was less money in the Treasury *than had been thought*'. In January Chancellor Wriothesley had revived an old exaction, illegal since the time of Richard III, termed, ironically, a 'benevolence'. When two London aldermen had refused to pay, the government put one of them in the Fleet prison till he did, and ordered the other, Richard Reid, to the Scots wars, with a 'following' at his own expense. When he got captured and had to pay ransom to the Scots, it was widely thought a good joke. The 'benevolences' raised a considerable sum, and were again exacted in the next year.

Another expedient, already begun, was carried further. The debasement of the coinage was a usual expedient of governments; but now the English went too far. More and more alloy was put into the money, until the Antwerp bankers refused repayment in English coin. The £1 at Antwerp, merchants complained, fluctuated between 24 and 27 florins, and the Government was so panicked by the shortage of gold that the Privy Council even discussed the loss of gold ore in tin; how 'by negligence of the tinners, and unawares, it was being conveyed into foreign parts to the great lucre of strangers'.[2]

[1] *Renaissance Diplomacy*, p. 231.
[2] Acts of the Privy Council, VII, p. 174.

Henry now turned on the chantries and certain colleges, and in that year the former were officially dissolved; since no survey could be made until 1546, he got little benefit, though his successor did. 'The Act ... implied that as others were already dispoiling the chantries the King would nationalize the plunder, and use it to finance his foreign wars and the schools.'[1] Yet, in spite of the crisis in revenue, Henry continued the grand capital designs that made him the greatest patron of learning among all the rulers of England. In 1546, the last year of his life, he founded the most splendid colleges in both universities; Christ Church at Oxford, Trinity at Cambridge. To this day, his formidable portrait dominates the dais of their great halls—in Trinity, with sinister force, alone.

Wolsey's Cardinal's College at Oxford, in which he had taken so much pride, had been built, as already described, at a great pace; he had employed the architect who had designed Hampton Court and Lupton's Tower at Eton, and already the immense hall, the kitchen, and the west front including the present gate house, since embellished by Wren's Tom Tower, were in being. After his fall, the college had reverted to the crown and Henry had kept it going, on a small scale. Now he replaced it with a direct royal foundation, the only one in Oxford, combining Oxford Cathedral, with Dean and Chapter, and a college whose 'Students' remained subordinate to the establishment until the reforms of 1867—hence their deceptively humble name. Henry did not live to devise the statutes, or extend Wolsey's buildings, but the royal foundation continued and flourished, the reigning sovereign, as the founder's representative, still its head.

At Cambridge in 1546, Henry also founded the largest college in the University; he amalgamated King's Hall, founded by Edward II and Edward III and closely connected with the Court, with the college of Michaelhouse, and quadrupled their joint endowment. Over the outer gate of Trinity still stands a rather truculent statue of Henry VIII.[2]

Though war and bankruptcy threatened, king and Council had the usual small business to attend to. The Mayor of Oxford, for example, had disputed the university's right to the assize of bread, wine and ale: Henry 'marvelled not a little at such wilfullness in so plain a matter', and backed the university, telling the mayor to yield, on pain of his high displeasure. In London, some of the populace, further demoralized by the war, were drunken, riotous and immoral; 'certain lewd fellows' had even hewed down the lanterns on London Bridge, carried a fish

---

[1] A. C. F. Beales, *Education under Penalty*, University of London Press, 1963, p. 18.

[2] Grasping the chair-leg long substituted for his sceptre.

upon a sword and 'did clappe the same in the faces of prentices and men of the country going by';[1] and people still insisted on hunting and hawking in the vicinity of Westminster. The London bawdy houses, too, were becoming such an intolerable nuisance, making youth 'more than ever addicted to fleshly lusts', that in the following year the Council decreed that 'all persons who have been accustomed to abuse their bodies' should depart 'with bag and baggage', an order difficult to enforce.

There were the usual mutterings of local political discontent, not always taken too seriously. John Wyot, a carpenter, had his ear nailed to the pillory in Essex for 'lewd words', 'the same to remain until he should either [appropriately] cut it off or pull it off'; but a lunatic who denounced the king in his frenzy was let off as there 'appeared no malice in him'. Down in Wiltshire, William Weston had talked at Mr Mempesson's house of 'bills, bows, herrings and harness', and asked if his majesty were 'the last of the six Kings Merlin had prophesied to be?'

> '*Tote about and take heed.*'
> One Hunloke had said,
> '*At Midsomer cometh a new moon,*
> *Between* (15)43 *and' Six*
> *All shall be doon.*'

IV

The deep-rooted cause of disturbance, as the king knew well, was not politics but religion. By attacking the Church he had stirred deep waters; he was still trying, without obvious success but better than most rulers on the continent, to calm them.

In June 1544, before leaving for France, Henry had finally commissioned Cranmer to produce a Litany in English; a project begun in the autumn of 1543, after a bad harvest had demanded 'processions'. 'In accordance with Your Highness's commandment,' the archbishop had then written, he had 'translated into the English tongue, so well as I could in so short a time, certain processions [the Litany] to be used upon festival days, if, after any correction and amendment of this, your Highness shall think so convenient.' He had sometimes been constrained, he had said, to use more than the liberty of a translation . . . 'the judgement whereof I refer wholly unto your Majesty; and after your Highness hath corrected it, if your Grace[2] command some de-

[1] Acts of Privy Council, VII, pp. 172-3.
[2] The styles seem interchangeable.

voute and solemn note to be made thereunto (as is to the procession which your Majesty hath already set forth in English), I trust it will much excitate and stir the hearts of all men unto devotion and Godliness.' Thus, by 1545, appeared the famous Anglican Litany, to serve so many generations in cathedrals and minsters and village churches up and down the land: out of the blood, rancour, and cruelty of Tudor politics, that survived.

It was lucky for Cranmer that the king still appreciated and backed him; in 1544 he had again been attacked for heresy; this time, his most malignant enemy, Sir John Gostewycke, Member of Parliament for Bedfordshire, who had himself purchased vast church lands. The matter had come to the king's ears: 'Tell that varlett Gostwycke,' he had exclaimed, 'that if he do not acknowledge his fault unto my lord of Canterbury . . . I will sure make him a poor Gostewycke.'

Now, in 1545, came the most dangerous of these attacks, on a higher level; and, this time, Henry made an end of them. Cranmer's enemies on the Council itself, Gardiner in particular, were involved, and they insisted that the archbishop should be committed to the Tower: since he was a Councillor, they said, no one could freely give evidence against him unless he were under arrest. But Henry saw through their game: he demurred; let them, he said, take the evidence the next morning, then, if necessary commit the accused. And that night Cranmer was fetched to the king's gallery at Westminster. 'I have granted their request,' said Henry, quizzically, 'but whether I have done well or no, what say you, my lord?' And when Cranmer merely thanked him for the warning, the king broke out, 'Oh lord God, what fond symplicity have you, so to permit yourself to be imprisoned that every enemy of yours may take advantage against you! Do you not think that, if they have you once in prison, three or four false knaves will soon be procured to witness against and condemn you, which else dare not open their lips to appear before your face? No, no, my lord, I have better regard unto you. . . .'[1] And he gave the archbishop a ring in token that, if they tried to imprison him, the king would take the case into his own hands.

Next morning, Dr Buttes told his master that he had seen Cranmer kept waiting, with serving men, outside the Council Chamber door. 'What,' exclaimed Henry, 'have they served me so? . . . I shall talk to them by and by.' And he did. For Cranmer had to produce the ring: 'I am sorry, my lords,' he said quietly, 'that you drive me to this exi-

---

[1] *Narratives*, op. cit., pp. 255–6. This account is based on *Morice's Anecdotes*, not on the distorted version in Foxe's *Memorials*.

gent to appeal from you to the King's Majesty.' Whereat politic Russell swore a great oath: 'Did I not tell you, my lords,' he said, 'what would come of this matter?'

The Councillors were summoned before the king: 'How have ye handled here my Lord of Canterbury?' he demanded, 'shutting him out of the Council Chamber among serving men? Would you be so handled yourselves? . . . I would you should well understand that I account my lord of Canterbury as faithful a man towards me as ever was prelate in this realm, and one to whom I am in many ways beholden. By the faith I owe to God,' he swore, laying his hand on his breast, '. . . whoso loveth me will so regard him hereafter.' Nor was the king content with Norfolk's hypocrisy that they had meant no harm: 'Well,' he concluded, 'I pray you not to use my friends so . . . I perceive now well enough how the world goes among you. . . .' So Henry left them, 'and the lords shook hands every man with my Lord Cranmer, among whom nevermore after no man durst spurn during the King Henry's life'.[1]

In no uncertain terms the King thus showed his respect for Cranmer, whose detachment from worldly ambitions he admired; he even made him take three pelicans for his coat of arms instead of the three cranes of his family. He would shed his blood, Henry observed, for the young brought up in the faith; and warned him that he would be 'severely tested' if he 'stood to his tackling'.[2]

This episode may have in part inspired the resounding denunciation of religious strife in Henry's last and most eloquent speech to Parliament. As reported by Hall, it is a masterpiece of English, and shows the king grappling with a perennial problem of authoritarian governments. Having opened the flood-gates of religious speculation for reasons which seemed good to himself, the king was now infuriated at the consequences; so monumental now was his egotism and dynastic arrogance that it seemed to him monstrous that the papal authority, now vested in him, should be contested at all.

The scene of this fine performance on Christmas Eve, 1545, was impressive: the archbishops and bishops were there, and the great peers—though battered, spade-bearded, Suffolk had died that year: the Commons were standing respectfully beyond. As some may then have realized, this was the last time that the monarch still, on occasion, in full and formidable vigour, would speak, in the plentitude of his power, to the Estates of his Realm.

[1] Op. cit., p. 258.
[2] Pollard, *Cranmer*, p. 159.

An old political hand, Henry began by taking them into his confidence and buttering them up. Since, he said, the Lord Chancellor could not set forth the secrets of his heart 'in so plain and ample a manner as I myself can do', he would thank them himself for praising his 'qualities and gifts', of which he felt he were both bare and barren; he then thanked God for such virtues as they had alleged he had 'incorporate in his person'. He thanked them, too, for the subsidies they had voted for the war, and the trust they had shown in committing the chantries and the colleges to his care: 'Doubt not, I pray you,' he said, 'but that your expectation shall be served more Godly and goodly than your will or desire.'

Having got them to a good mind, Henry then roundly denounced them all. 'No prince in the world,' he told them, 'more loves and favours his subjects than I do you . . . for whose defence my treasure shall not be hidden, nor, if necessity requires, my person shall not be unadventured'; but 'unless you, my lords temporal, and you, my lords spiritual, and you my loving subjects, study and take pains to mend one thing which surely is amiss and far out of order,' his affections could but change. Religious strife was disrupting the commonwealth: 'Charity and concord,' he went on, 'are not among you, but discord and dissension beareth rule in every place.' The old lionine tyrant, hardened in craft and cruelty, lust and lies, now, with genuine feeling, quoted St Paul on charity. 'Behold, then, what love and charity is among you, where one calleth another heretic and Anabaptist, and he calleth him again Papist, hypocrite and Pharisee! Be these tokens,' he asked, 'of charity among you?' Were these the sign of fraternal love? 'No! No!' If this strife went on, he warned them, it would 'hinder the fervent love between us'.

The clergy were deeply to blame, for they daily preached one against the other, enveighing without charity or discretion; 'Some too stiff,' he said, in one of his phrases, long remembered, that endeared him to his people, 'in their old mumpsimus'; others 'too busy and curious in their new sumpsimus.' 'Shall I judge you charitably,' he demanded, '. . . no, no, I cannot so do. . . . Amend these crimes, I exhort you, and set forth God's word; or else,' and here his small eyes darted about him, 'as God's vicar and High Minister, I will see these divisions extinct'.

In the ensuing silence, Henry turned on the laymen. He rated them, too, for their malice, envy, and disrespect; they railed on bishops and slandered priests; they put about stupid ideas. Let them bring these high matters to the Council, 'or to us . . . and be not judges yourselves of your own phantastical opinions, for in such high causes ye may lightly [easily] err'. They might use the Bible to instruct their families, but not to 'rail and taunt' at the clergy. He was disgusted to hear how 'that most precious jewel the word of God' was 'disputed, rhymed, sung and jangled in every ale house and tavern'. Such presumption had got to stop. 'Love, dread and serve God,' he concluded, 'to which I, as your supreme Head and sovereign Lord, exhort and require you.'

In their conscious minds most of his audience probably agreed and accorded their prince the arrogant authority he claimed; subconsciously, for some of them, his words were water off ducks' backs. With salvation or damnation at stake, what were order or government? And the politicians watched coldly to exploit the shifts of opinion. The Henrician Anglican Church was still catholic in creed, if the king was its pope; but, as Wolsey and Tunstall had feared, the tides of continental Protestantism had long been seeping into England; the price of order would in time be total schism. Henry was making a politically sound claim, but it was not for a century and a half, following persecution and civil war, that his subjects were to take his advice, and let civil authority decide the undecidable.

V

The war in France dragged on. Henry had renewed his contacts with the German Protestants, blackmailing Charles V, and in the new year, in January 1546, Gardiner and the representatives of the empire signed a Treaty at Utrecht. Henry had long marked down the infant Mary Queen of Scots for Prince Edward's bride: but he now, in March, considered, or pretended to consider, the emperor's daughter Mary of Castile; remarking that 'he was not so light as to negotiate with two persons at once to the same end, like people he knew'. Charles put him off, saying she was pledged to the Prince of Portugal, and offered the hand of one of his nieces, a daughter of Ferdinand of Austria, King of the Romans. The dowry suggested proved disappointing, so that Henry was enraged and 'it was high time to go away and not irritate him further'.

Behind this screen of negotiation, the king was again contemplating a *volte face*: 'I stand amazed,' he remarked, 'after which deer to run.' The French war was mutually unprofitable, and Francis I unlikely long to live. That spring, Paget was writing that it would be wise to attempt negotiations over Boulogne. He cited the tale of a man condemned to die by Louis XI, who had undertaken, if his sentence was postponed for a year, to make the king's donkey speak. 'What?' they said, 'it is impossible!' 'Hold your peace,' he had answered, *'Car ou le Roy mourira, ou l'asne mourira, ou l'asne parlera, ou je mourira.'*[1] Then the pope, the momentous Council of Trent his main concern—it was to last intermittently till 1563 and launch the counter-Reformation—even approached Henry for a settlement. Henry parried, saying it was not the pope's fault that the King of England was not ruined, as he had tried to incite both Francis I and Charles V against him. But he would now 'consider' the authority of a Council, provided it was not held in France.

In fact, his main object was to disrupt the Council of Trent, suspended in June of that year, while the emperor was involved in war against the Protestant League of Smalkalden in Germany. The bankers, it was reported from Antwerp, were too doubtful of his success to lend him more money. Determined to undermine the papacy, Henry was even suggesting that the French might conciliate their Protestants by substituting Communion for the Mass, an extraordinary lapse from orthodoxy. They might then force Charles V, anxious for peace in Germany, to do the same, leaving Rome a mere Italian bishopric. In continental politics, as internal affairs, Henry, with his supreme self-confidence, was ready to switch doctrines to the needs of power.

Against Rome he would go all lengths. That May, Cardinal Beaton, in Scotland, was assassinated by Scots Protestant fanatics with whom the King of England had connived; his body, salted, was hung over a wall for all to see. 'It is half a wonder here,' wrote an English bishop to Paget from Ratisbon, 'that ye dare be so bold as to kill a Cardinal.'

As intended, the death of the pugnacious Beaton furthered negotiations with the French. Through the spring the dismal campaign had continued round Boulogne and Montreuil, and, at last, on June 7, 1546, a peace was signed near Ardres which included Scotland. The English were bought off; but, after eight years, Boulogne was to revert to France, in return for the huge sum of two million crowns. Meanwhile, pensions of 50,000 would be paid to England 'in perpetuity', and of nearly 100,000 during the king's lifetime.

VI

The French may have signed to the Treaty more readily since in March the king had suffered another seizure; had not Lord Montague,

---

[1] Either the King will die, or the donkey will die, or the donkey will speak, or I shall die.

ten years before, remarked 'his leg will kill him, and we shall have jolly stirrings'? and been executed for his temerity? He had a fever, the king had admitted, in his leg, but had said that his robust constitution helped him. He had passed the time playing cards with his intimates, and taken care that his condition should not be known. But his 'visage', an observer reported, 'showed it was worse than he pretended'. Henry's last illness had begun.

CHAPTER XX

LIVID SUNSET

'OPINIONATE and wilfull,' wrote Herbert of Cherbury, 'inasmuch as the impressions privately given him by any court whisperer were hardly or never effaced. . . . Besides, this wilfullness had a most dangerous quality annexed to it (especially towards his later end), being an intense jealousy of all persons and affairs, which predisposed him to think the worst.' Sunk in egotism hard as iron, the old king was at last finished: he met his fate clear headed, fighting to the last to guard his son and preserve the dynasty.

He was never, as often alleged, utterly incapacitated: he had always, indeed, 'had a great deal of the true and appalling hypochondria with which only really selfish men are gifted',[1] and his gouty ulcerated leg and high blood pressure had long been aggravated by the diet and remedies of the day; but his illness had not made him the 'mass of loathesome infirmities' that sensationalist writers depict. 'So unwieldy of body that he could not pass through any ordinary door,' reads the worst of these travesties, 'and could be moved from one room to another only by the help of machinery and a number of attendants . . . his sufferings made his temper like that of a wild beast.'[2] The description is a caricature: Henry was a huge man, unwieldy and immensely stout, and his temper may well have been intermittently frightful, but, only the year before, he had been inspecting forts and the flagship at Portsmouth, as well as 'hawking for pheasants'; and, less than six months before he died, he had made his customary early autumn progress in August, and in September had been watching driven stags pursued by greyhounds. The 'machinery', according to a surviving inventory, amounted to two chairs called 'trammers' for 'the King's Majesty to sit in to be carried to and fro in the galleries and chambers'—no more than a kind of sedan chair.[3] And when Norfolk said 'the King could

---

[1] G. R. Elton, op. cit., p. 68.
[2] *British Medical Journal*, 1910, Vol. I, p. 1303, already cited.
[3] Even Mackie writes 'borne in a wheeled chair or some such machine': Pollard has its e *is said* (italics mine) to have become so unwieldy that he could neither walk nor stand

not go up and down stairs and was let up and down by a device and could not long endure', he was only describing a primitive lift.

The expenses for the king's horses in August 1546 show that, once in the saddle, he could still ride, a fact confirmed by a payment for 'a new stool of walnotry for the King to light upon horseback'. This contraption, with 'a pair of double hinges and four tennaunts and four shuttings and five cross bars and six vyces with forty one revetts', enabled the enormous man to mount.

Though never an addict of state business, even in his prime ('Nay, by my so[ul], that will not be; for this is my removing day sone at New[hall], I will rede the remenaunt at night'),[1] he went on signing warrants and reading and noting dispatches to the end. If he looks senile in the not very skilful portrait of him harping, while his fool tries, it seems, to think of a new joke, his effigy on a medal of that time is majestic and formidable, with the regal Plantagenet profile, now more aquiline, as in his daughter Elizabeth I in her later years, above his thick neck and shoulders.

II

He well knew the weakness of the regime; all depended on the prince. Though his close dynastic rivals had been killed off, the religious settlement had been clamped down on a nation already assimilating Protestant ideas from the continent, where religious strife was now raging, in this, the year of Luther's death. On the Privy Council, the Catholic party led by Norfolk, Gardiner, and Chancellor Wriothesley were faced with Hertford, Prince Edward's uncle, and the Seymour interest, backed by Lisle, the Lord Admiral, and discreetly by the queen, who had been pledged to Sir Thomas Seymour before the king took her, and was to marry him and die, at Studley Priory in Gloucestershire, bearing his child. The last, darkening year of the king's life was dominated by the Norfolk-Gardiner party's attempt to oust this Hertford-Lisle interest and even, it seems, the queen; then by their failure to do so and overthrow.

They failed because the king decided that the boy's uncle would be his best guardian, and perhaps because he assessed Protestant opinion as stronger: certainly the tactical shifts of foreign affairs now favoured a pro-Protestant line. Hertford, unlike Norfolk, had no dynastic claims,

---

and mechanical contrivances were used at Windsor and his other palaces for moving the royal person from room to room', p. 337. Hackett, with less to lose, plumps for 'being moved by block and tackle', *Henry the Eighth*, p. 523.

[1] Quoted G. R. Elton, op. cit., p. 69.

and he was the brother of the only queen who had borne a male heir. Edward's upbringing and entourage—and, indeed, his short life—were dominated by his uncle and by Lisle, afterwards Northumberland.

Chapuys in the closing weeks of the reign illuminated the picture. Queen Catherine, he reported, was infected with heresy; Lord Hertford dominated all and exhortations only made the king more obstinate to show his absolute power. 'This malady,' he told Charles V, 'is incurable and they are all confirmed in it by their plans to control the Prince. . . . To gain a party they drag the whole country into this damnable (Protestant) error.' Not even Parliament, which in former times 'enjoyed its ancient liberties when it met to punish Kings', could stop the rot. 'If St Peter and St Paul were to return to earth, the King would not allow them to enter the Kingdom'; no man could open his mouth against the king and Council. Nor could the country be coerced: the people feared neither French nor Scots 'because of the natural hatred of Englishmen for them'. The king's death, he concluded, would be more inopportune for us now than twenty years ago.[1]

This situation Norfolk and Gardiner had tried to prevent when they attacked the queen. Their approach was insidious, and it began in February 1546, when a rumour was put about that Henry had 'been so addicted to changing queens' that Catherine would have to make way for a seventh consort 'because of her sterility'. Then Gardiner and Lord Chancellor Wriothesley got on the track of a heretic, intimate with Lady Hertford, and known to the queen. Anne Askew, *née* Kyme, a person of substance, had already been arraigned for heresy the year before.[2] Now, in June 1546, she was again brought before the Council and sent to Newgate 'as very obstinate and heady'.

The redoubtable woman, an early example of the nonconformist conscience, at once appealed to the king; when he refused to hear her, she cited Solomon, the wisest king that ever lived, who had 'misliked not to hear two common women'. And when one examiner said 'he would speak with her familiarly', 'so did Judas', she replied; threatened with the stake, she pointed out, reasonably enough, that she had 'searched all the scriptures and never found that Christ or his disciples had put anyone to death'; then, getting into her stride, she told Gardiner—already in Old Testament, non-conformist, idiom—that she 'would not sing a new song in a strange land'. So Gardiner called her a

---

[1] L. and P., XXI, II, 756.

[2] And already made a fool of the Lord Mayor. Asked by that worthy 'what if a mouse shall eat it [the consecrated sacrament], what shall become of that mouse?' 'What say you, My Lord?', she had parried: 'I say that mouse is damned.' 'Alas,' replied Anne Askew, '*poor mouse*.'

'parrot', and when the Bishop of Salisbury told her to recant, she told him it would have 'been good for him never to have been born'. They pronounced her an heretic, and she answered, 'And what do ye call your God? It is a piece of bread.'[1]

Not unnaturally condemned, she was now tortured, contrary to the law, in the hope that she would implicate the queen. 'Anne Askew', wrote Lord Chancellor Wriothesley, 'alias Kyme, was had to the Tower of London and there set on the rack, where she was long tormented, but she would not convert for all her pain.' But it was not conversion they wanted; the king had been informed, they told her, that 'she could name many of her sect'; they even cited Lady Hertford. She refused to implicate her; 'My lord chancellor and Master Riche,' she told her supporters, 'took pains to rack me with their own hands, till I was nigh dead.' The Lieutenant of the Tower, who had refused to do it, now ordered her to be loosed: so, recovering from her swoon, the indomitable woman sat for two hours arguing with the Lord Chancellor 'on the bare floor'. She refused to implicate anyone, and on July 16th died at Smithfield in the flames, her last words 'your mass is the most abominable idol in the world'.

So Catherine's enemies now made a direct attack. The trial of Anne Askew and other heretics had raised some nice theological points, and the queen, excited, dared to contradict her husband. The king was suddenly furious: 'A good hearing it is,' he said, 'when women become such clerks, and a thing much to my comfort to come to me in mine old days, to be taught by my wife.' Gardiner and Wriothesley pounced; they listed, precisely, the heretical views she had expressed, and they brought the document to the king who authorized the queen's arrest.

Warned of what was coming, the queen was appalled; she wept, lapsed into hysterical tears. But told of her condition, Henry, too, softened; went to her room, soothed her down with an experienced touch. When, with Lady Herbert, she ventured to his bedchamber, and apologized in the fulsome, abject idiom of the day, Henry was already mollified. From anger he turned to chaff: 'Ye are become a Doctor, Kate, to instruct us . . .' She had spoken, she assured him, rather to pass away the time and the pain of his infirmity, than to hold argument. Then, turning serious, and laying the flattery on with a trowel, she concluded, 'I had hoped by hearing your Majesty's learned discourse to receive some profit thereby.' 'And is it even so, sweetheart?' said her husband, genially, 'then we are perfect friends again.' He felt better: they went out into the garden.

[1] L. and P., XXI, I, 1181.

Suddenly but belatedly came the tramp of armed men; Chancellor Wriothesley marched into the garden armed with the warrant for the queen's arrest. Henry turned on him like a tiger: beast, he yelled, fool, knave! Hastily the Lord Chancellor took himself off. And when Catherine, always an appeaser, spoke up for him, 'You poor soul', the king answered, 'you little know how evil he deserves grace at your hands.' After that, the queen, like Cranmer, was safe.

III

During the late summer Henry made a diminished progress in Surrey and the complex, pleasant life of the royal palaces went on. They were mowing the lawns at Greenwich, weeding the strawberry beds, taking rose cuttings; a new case was acquired for carrying the king's cross bows; the hawks still cost a great deal—they were given 'horehound water and sugar candy'; a bill survives, too, 'for the king's bird, a bottle of beyond-sea wheat'; they bought 'a new cloth to rub the Spaniels with'.[1] There were the usual heavy bills for books and book-binding, and the king's clocks had to be mended and wound; the one with a great square dial that showed the movement of the sun and moon; a great clock gilt with an alarum standing within a great crystal garnished with rubies and diamonds; one 'like a heart' which struck; one square, one round; a clock which went without plummets; two little clocks 'like books'. The musicians and choristers of the Court and the royal foundations continued to practise and perform; the king now had a 'virginal that goeth without being played' to add to the enormous repertoire of instruments.

But the centre of it all was stricken. By November, as the autumn died, he was at Oatlands Park, in Surrey; then he came up to Whitehall for the last time, 'to the long gallery and the secret jewel house, the garde robe and the secret study and the little study called the new library'. In seclusion, he moved to Ely Place; then back to Whitehall. Henry was now terribly ill, but he had a new, fascinating, deadly matter to attend to: Norfolk and his son Surrey, it appeared, had been dabbling in treason. He must strike them down.

The affair, engineered, of course, by Hertford and Lisle, had begun when, true to sixteenth-century form, Sir Richard Southwell, a member of the Howard household, had denounced his master Surrey, obviously the more vulnerable victim, and Surrey had retorted by offering to fight him 'in his shirt'. For, Southwell had alleged that,

[1] L. and P., XXI, II, 769.

reviving the old Howard gambit, he had incited his young sister, the Dowager of Richmond, widow of Henry Fitzroy, to insinuate herself with the king, though she had said she would 'rather have her throat cut than consent to such villainy'.

Worse technically, Surrey had infringed the Treasons Act. He had revived the arms of Edward the Confessor, depicted on his own with three labels silver which belonged to the Prince as Heir Apparent. He had also quartered the arms of England, not, as he was entitled to do, in the second quarter, but in the first. And his father, it was falsely alleged, had connived. Early in December an official of the Council had arrived in Thetford on the Howard estates in Norfolk, and he had examined the Dowager of Richmond himself. 'Trembling so that she could scarcely stand,' she had vindicated her father; she had always, she declared, 'believed him a true man, though she knew her brother to be a rash one.' But Elizabeth Holland, the duke's mistress—he had for years been estranged from his own Duchess, Surrey's mother—admitted the duke saying that 'none of the Council loved him because they were not noblemen themselves'.[1]

Further, they disliked him, he had said, because he 'believed too truly in the sacrament of the altar', and 'the king loved him not because he was too much loved in his country' (East Anglia). He had also complained that he was not in 'the most secret, or *as it was there termed,* the Privy Council'.[2] None of this was criminal; Norfolk had been far too old a soldier to connive at his son's dangerous heraldic follies, and had told Bess Holland that he 'liked not his son's arms'; she was 'to take no more patterns of them to work with her needle in his house, but as he gave them'. There was really not much evidence against the duke.

Henry Howard, Earl of Surrey, was easier game: cupbearer to the king, companion to Richmond, as will be recalled, at Windsor—they had both afterwards visited the French court; familiar with Italy, a sophisticated poet, he had been made Knight of the Garter in 1540; Cromwell, to him, it will be recalled, had been a 'foul churl'. A rash but gallant defender of Boulogne, he was at once an Italianate scholar who had translated Virgil, and a mad fighting fellow, proud as Lucifer.

On December 12th Norfolk and Surrey were arrested and sent to the Tower. On the same day, the king was drawing up and assessing the evidence with minute professional scrutiny. In a shaky hand, he under-

---

[1] He was not far wrong: Hertford came of north Wiltshire gentry, not nobility; Lisle was the son of Dudley, an upstart civil servant; Russell of mercantile gentry from Dorset; Wriothesley was the son of a Herald called Wryth; Paget of a sergeant at arms to the City; Gardiner of a clothmaker at Bury St Edmunds.

[2] Italics mine; an interesting sidelight on the fluctuating division.

lined the main evidence which might point to his last dynastic and
judicial murder.

'If a man coming of the *collateral line* to the heir of the throne, who
ought *not*,' he emphasized, 'to bear the arms of England but on the
second quarter, with the difference of *their* ancestry, do *Presume to*
change his right place and bear them in the first quarter, leaving out the
true difference of ancestry, and, in lieu thereof, use the *very place* only of
the Heir male apparent, *How this man's intent is to be judged*; and
whether this imports any danger, peril or slander to the title of the
Prince or very Heir apparent, and how it weigheth in our cause?'

That was the first count. Next, he emphasized, 'if a man *Presume to*
take unto his arms an old coat of the crown, *which his ancestors never
bore nor he of right ought to bear*, can use it without offense?' Next, 'if a
man compassing *with himself to govern the realm*, do actually go about
to rule the King and should for this purpose advise his daughter, or sister
to become his (the King's) harlot *thinking thereby to bring it to pass and so
would rule both father and son. What this importeth?*' It imported no good.

On January 7th Norfolk and Surrey were both indicted for high
treason at Norwich in their own East Anglia; and, on 13th, Surrey was
tried on the indictment at Guildhall. All his old escapades were brought
up; three years earlier he had been in prison for breaking windows in
London with a catapult ('stonebow'); he had collogued with Italians—
kept one 'Pasquil' as a jester, more likely as a spy; indeed, 'he had loved
to converse with strangers and conform his behaviour to theirs'. Taxed
with malice to certain officials, he had answered: 'No, no, Cousin
Knyvvet, my malice climbs higher.' But on the main charges he stood
adamant: he had the right, he said, through the Mowbrays, to the arms
of the Confessor, and it was admitted that he could quarter the arms of
England on the second quarter.

But not on the first. It was enough: in spite of a brilliant defence, a
note from the king decided the jury and Surrey was sentenced to
'simple decapitation on Tower Hill within a week'. Norfolk, grilled by
his old colleagues on the Council for 'concealed High Treason', was
attainted: fortunately for him, the procedure took longer; it was not
until January 27th that he was deemed a High Traitor by Act of Parliament, and condemned to suffer the next morning. And by that
morning, Henry VIII was dead.

IV

In the foggy London winter the king had grown worse. Dr Buttes was dead, but the others did what they could; rose water, 'eyebright' water; mouthwashes, fomentations, liquorice; *unguentem pro emeroyd, unguentem ad ventrem*;[1] *saculus pro splene*—a plaster for the stomach; '*Manus Christi*' ('Christ's hands'), a soothing powder—all were applied. There were also cinnamon comfits, and green ginger. The surgeons regularly sponged the great bulk of the king down; the air of the stuffy rooms was heavy with the wood fires, with musk and expensive scents.[2]

So passed Christmas, and on December 29th Henry was better; able to read a dispatch from the Council in the North and attend to business; on the 30th he revised his long and elaborate will of 1544, laying down finally the succession of the Imperial Crown of England and Ireland, 'without title to France'. First, to Prince Edward and his descendants; then to those of Queen Catherine Parr; then to Mary and her heirs, provided she married 'with the consent of the Privy Council or of the most part of them in writing'; then to Elizabeth and her heirs; finally, to Lady Frances Brandon, daughter of his sister Mary, by the Duke of Suffolk. The Scots claimants, through his sister Margaret, were ignored, though, in the third generation, the great prize would fall to them.

The king appointed many executors, spreading his net widely to win support for his son: Cranmer, of course; Hertford; Lisle; Tunstall; Paget; Russell; Herbert; Sir Anthony Denny, chief gentleman of the chamber; Wriothesley, who had now ditched Gardiner and Norfolk. He appointed sixteen councillors for the Regency; he left out Gardiner, saying he knew his temper well enough, and though *he* could govern him, yet none of them would be able to do so. Henry was still confident, in his superb egotism, that his commands would be carried out.

For his body, the king declared, he would for himself be content that it were buried in any place accustomed for Christian folk, but for the reputation of the dignity to which he had been called, it was to be laid in the choir of the college at Windsor, midway between the stalls and the high altar, in a tomb which was almost finished and in which lay the body of Queen Jane. He left large endowments for celebrating four solemn obits a year, and for the saying of masses 'so long as the world shall endure'.[3]

Through January the king grew worse: he sent for the Lady Mary. 'Oh daughter,' he said, 'fortune hath been hard against thee; and I grieve that I did not have thee married as I wished. Try to be a mother

---

[1] Ointment for piles, ointment for the belly.
[2] Apothecaries bills, August–January 1546–7. L. and P., XXI, II, 768.
[3] L. and P., XXI, II, 634.

to thy little brother, for, look, he is very little yet.'[1] Speechless, he signed to her to go, and they both wept.

He sent for the queen: 'It is God's will,' he said, 'that we should part, and I order all these gentlemen to treat you as if I were living still.' She broke down and he ordered her to leave him. Prince Edward, aged nine, was at Ashridge, amid the leafless beech woods of the Chiltern hills; Elizabeth, aged thirteen and a half, was at Enfield Palace: neither saw the king in his last hours.

Practical to the end, he showed minute care over money; the queen must have £7,000 a year; the principal officials suitable and generous annuities. By Thursday, the 27th, he was obviously dying, but since it was high treason to prophesy the king's demise, no one dared tell him so. Then Sir Anthony Denny dared to approach him; telling him he was 'in man's judgement not like to live', and should prepare himself for death. The king remained confident. 'The mercy of Christ,' he said, 'could pardon all his sins, though they were greater than they be.' Asked if he wanted to see a priest, he replied: 'Only Cranmer, but he not yet.' He still refused to accept his fate; self sufficient, taking his own decision to the end, he said, 'I will take a little sleep, then, as I feel myself, I will advise upon the matter.'

But he had miscalculated; when he awoke he could hardly speak, and when near midnight the Archbishop arrived, Henry was past words. All he could do was to press Cranmer's hand in token of faith and repentance; and by two in the morning he was dead. He had dominated England for nearly thirty-eight years.

Early that morning of January 28th, Hertford rode down to Ashridge to break the news to the boy-king, Edward VI, and bring him to Enfield to join his half-sister, Elizabeth. Not till they were together did he tell them of their father's death; the two pale reddish-haired children wept bitterly, in a long passion of grief, clinging to one another, 'the most iron eyes drawn thereby into the society of their tears'. On the 30th the child-king rode to London, and, on the following day, Hertford and Paget induced the Council to admit Hertford as Lord Protector, at once entirely subverting the late king's commands.

Embalmed, cased in lead and chested, the chest covered in blue velvet, the king's huge body was set upon trestles under a pall of cloth of gold in the Privy Chamber. 'Of your charity,' intoned Norroy King at Arms, 'pray for the soul of the Most High and Mighty Prince, our late Sovereign Lord, King Henry VIII.'[2]

---

[1] *Spanish Chronicle of Henry VIII*, op. cit.
[2] See Strype, Ecc: Mem: I. Appendix 1–16 on which this account is based.

On February 8th, in all the churches in England, the bells tolled for the passing of the king. On February 14th, at eight o'clock, in very fair weather, a west wind stirring with a hint of spring, the immense procession started for Sion House, by the Thames, on its way to Windsor. First the bishops, praying, two and two, in order; then, between torches borne by sixteen yeomen of the guard, and under a rich blue canopy fringed with gold, came a goodly image, 'like to the King's person in all respects', and upon the bed the Crown Imperial, the collar of the Garter, the Garter in Gold; then, in the morning sunlight, the standard of the Dragon, the standard of the Greyhound, the standard of the Lion.

Next came twelve Aldermen of London, the lords of the Privy Council, the archbishops, the great lords and lesser barons of the kingdom; after them the Heralds with their banners, Norroy with the Targe, and Garter King at Arms with the King's Cognizance, followed by twelve banners of descent of the king and Queen Jane, and the king and Catherine Parr. Only two queens were officially acknowledged.

Seven great horses, 'wholly trapped in Black Velvet down to the pasterns', ridden by children of honour in black, drew the great chariot in which the coffin lay, sixty ranked torches burning about it, followed by the chief mourners, and the banners of pre-Conquest Kings; of 'Brute, Belin, Arthur, Kadwallader, Athelstane, Edmund, Edward Exile and the Confessor'. Last, halberds reversed, marched the ranks of the King's guard in black.

On February 15th, they came from Sion through Eton. 'Along the churchyard wall', waited provost, fellows and headmaster in copes, with the king's scholars in white surplices, bare headed, holding in one hand tapers, in the other books, all kneeling as the long procession went by. By one o'clock it had come up the hill to Windsor and the Chapel of St George; in the closet made for Catherine of Aragon, stood Queen Catherine, while again Norroy cried out: 'Of your charity, pray for the soul of the Most High and Mighty Prince, our late Sovereign Lord, King Henry VIII.'

February 16th saw the final scene. '*Beati mortui qui in Domine moriuntur*,' intoned Winchester. 'Blessed are they that die in the Lord.' The vault was uncovered, the great coffin lowered with a device by sixteen tall yeomen of the guard; and, while the vault was being closed, the choir sang *de profundis*. Henry VIII had gone to his account.

Shrill under the splendid roof the trumpets rang out: 'Vive le Noble Roy, Edouard!' Garter Herald cried, and two days after, up in London, a little boy, taken for safety to the Tower, was crowned King of England.

'*Sing up Heart, Sing up Heart, and Sing no more down,*'
the crowds were soon singing,
'*But joy in King Edward that weareth the Crown.*'

NOTE ON SOURCES

🞱

I

THE present volume is based mainly on printed sources, in particular upon the multi-volume *Letters and Papers of Henry VIII*, edited by J. S. Brewer and James Gairdner, and upon the chronicles and letters cited below and in the notes.

So well did nineteenth and early twentieth century scholars do their work that the great accumulation has not yet been fully interpreted, and relatively little can be used directly in a book of medium size: vast riches remain, apart from the potential of new discoveries.

The *Calendars of State Papers*, Spanish and Venetian, are also packed with evidence. The *Letters and Papers Illustrative of the Reigns of Richard III and Henry VII*, ed. James Gairdner, Rolls Series, 2 vols., 1861, are also essential for Henry's youth and background.

For the whole range of original and secondary sources and interpretations Conyers Read's *The Bibliography of British History, Tudor Period, 1485–1603* (1933), is the standard work, and there is a valuable bibliography in J. D. Mackie, *The Earlier Tudors*, Oxford, Clarendon Press (1957 ed.).

II

Since for many readers the chronicles and letters of the time are too little known, the following note may be useful, supplementing the references in the footnotes.

Polydore Vergil's *Anglica Historia*, edited with a translation by Denys Hay, Camden Society, LXXIV–V, 1950, is the first chronicle of English history by a Renaissance humanist. It appeared in 1534; a second edition in 1546, and a third in 1555; it is important for the reigns of Henry VII and of Henry VIII up to 1537. Hall was influenced by it, though its outlook is cosmopolitan and catholic, while Hall was militantly English and Protestant. It glorifies the Tudors and is hostile to Wolsey.

The author was already well known for his *de inventoribus rerum* (Of the First Begetters of Things), 1499, and his *Adagia*. He was born at

Urbino in 1470, and came to England in 1503 in the household of Castelli, Bishop of Hereford, as Deputy Collector of Peter's Pence. When Castelli became a cardinal and Bishop of Bath and Wells, Polydore Vergil became archdeacon of Wells and a prebendary of St Paul's, an appointment which brought him into the thick of affairs. He helped secure the Papal Bull for the foundation of St John's College, Cambridge, and to obtain the Cardinalate for Wolsey, whom he came to detest. He returned to Urbino in 1553 and died there in 1555.

Edward Hall's *The Union of the two noble and Illustre Famelies of Lancastre and Yorke*, etc., first appeared in 1542, and was continued and republished by Richard Grafton in 1548 and '50. Sir Henry Ellis edited it in six volumes in 1809. C. A. Whibley edited the part concerned with the 'triumphant' reign of Henry VIII in two volumes in 1904. This is the richest and most comprehensive narrative; robust, detailed and picturesque. It glorifies the king and vindicates the Reformation. A modern edition or selection is much needed. Hall came of Shropshire gentry and was educated at Eton and King's College, Cambridge (1514–18), and at Gray's Inn. He became M.P. for Bridgnorth in 1542, a lawyer and a Londoner, with a flair for detail and dialogue; an eyewitness of many events he describes. He wrote his *Chronicle* up to 1532, and died in 1547.

John Stow's Elizabethan *Annals* were originally entitled *The Chronicles of England from Brutus unto the present Year of Christ* (1580). The version of 1592 became the *Annales of England*. His *A Survey of London* appeared in 1598. John Stow, *Antiquarius Angliae* (1525–1605), was a London tailor, 'a wonder', it was said, that 'the very best that has penned our history in English should be a pour Taylor, honest John Stow'. He 'made no gain by his travails'. Though he was only a young man when Henry VIII died, his *Annals* are full and reliable.

A Chronicle of England . . . from 1485 to 1559, by C. Wriothesley, Windsor Herald, becomes fuller where Hall becomes thin in Grafton's continuation. It was edited by W. D. Hamilton, Camden Society, 1875. The *Irish Chronicle* (1509–1547), ed. R. Stonyhurst, makes good reading.

For contemporary correspondence, Sir Henry Ellis's *Original Letters Illustrative of English History* contain fascinating material. There are three Series (1835–46); the first in three volumes, the others in four. They cover a much wider field than the reign of Henry VIII, but are particularly illuminating for it.

The first biography of the King is Lord Herbert of Cherbury's *The Life and Reign of Henry VIII* (1649). Francis Bacon's *The Life of Henry*

VII (1622), is a great interest, and George Cavendish's life of Cardinal Wolsey, as described in the notes, is a masterpiece of its kind.

All this contemporary, or near-contemporary, material is filled out by the many publications of the Camden Society, some of which are cited in the text. The reader will find the study of these sources and interpretations, which are widely available, very well worth while: they form the next level of study after the current text books which provide an introduction to the age, and an essential background to the particular problems with which modern scholars, on the frontiers of knowledge, are now mainly, and often controversially, concerned. It is the letters and papers and chronicles which most vividly recall what the Tudor English were like; how they wrote and spoke and thought, and how history looked to contemporaries as it was being made.

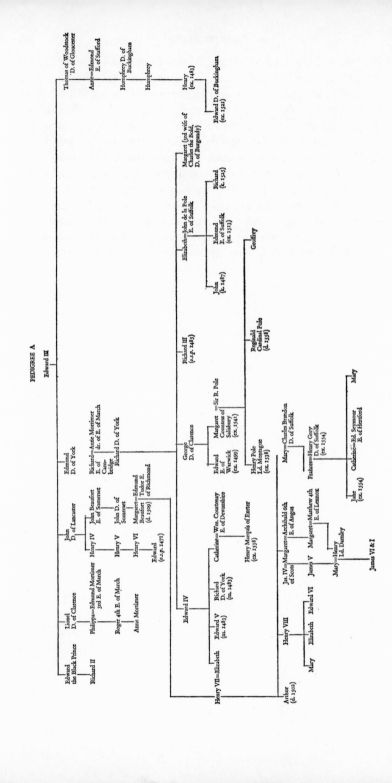

PEDIGREE A

PEDIGREE B

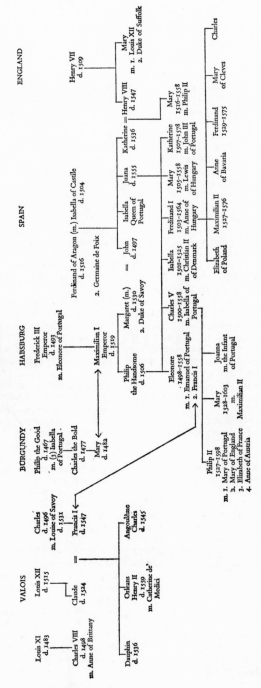

VALOIS   BURGUNDY   HABSBURG   SPAIN   ENGLAND

Louis XI
d. 1483

Charles VIII
d. 1498
m. Anne of Brittany

Louis XII
d. 1515

Claude
d. 1524

Angoulême
Charles
d. 1545

Orleans
Henry II
d. 1559
m. Catherine de'
Medici

Dauphin
d. 1536

Charles
d. 1496
m. Louise of Savoy
d. 1531

Francis I
d. 1547

Philip the Good
d. 1467
m. (3) Isabella
of Portugal

Charles the Bold
d. 1477

Mary
d. 1482

Frederick III
Emperor
d. 1493
m. Eleonore of Portugal

Maximilian I
Emperor
d. 1519

Philip
the Handsome
d. 1506

Margaret (m.)
d. 1530
2. Duke of Savoy

Charles V
1500–1558
m. Isabella of
Portugal

Eleonore
1498–1558
m. 1. Emmanuel of Portugal
2. Francis I

Mary
1528–1603
m.
Maximilian II

Philip II
1527–1598
m. 1. Mary of Portugal
2. Mary of England
3. Elizabeth of France
4. Anne of Austria

Joanna
m. the Infant
of Portugal

Ferdinand of Aragon (m.) Isabella of Castile
d. 1516   d. 1504

=
2. Germaine de Foix

Isabella
Queen of
Portugal

John
d. 1497

Juana
d. 1555

Katherine
d. 1536

Isabella
1501–1525
m. Christian II
of Denmark

Ferdinand I
1503–1564
m. Anne of
Hungary

Mary
1505–1558
m. Lewis
of Hungary

Katherine
1507–1578
m. John III
of Portugal

Maximilian II
1527–1576

Elizabeth
of Poland

Anne
of Bavaria

Ferdinand
1529–1575

Henry VII
d. 1509

Mary
m. 1. Louis XII
2. Duke of Suffolk

Katherine = Henry VIII
d. 1536   d. 1547

Mary
1516–1558
m. Philip II

Mary
of Cleves

Charles

INDEX

Abbeys, *see under* Monasteries
Adrian VI, Pope, 106–7, 117, 119
Advancement of True Religion, Act for, 260
Agnadello, battle of, 53
Aigues Mortes, Pact at, 223
Albany, Duke of, 73, 112–13
Albuquerque Duke of, 270, 272
Ancrum Moor, battle of, 277
Anglican Litany, 283–4
Angus, Earl of, 73, 112, 247, 277
Annates, Act of Restraint of, 164, 175
Appeals Act, 166–7, 175
Aragon, Catherine of, Queen of England: marriage to Prince Arthur, 31–2; widowhood, 34–5; marriage to Henry, 38–9; coronation, 39–40; married life, 41; on French victories, 59; Regent during battle of Flodden, 60–1; achieves meeting with Charles V, 96–7; and Princess Mary's match with Charles V, 129; her divorce, 134–5, 138, 143–6, 162–3, 167–8; her medical case history, 44, 159, 160; banished, 176, 197; death 197–8; funeral, 201
Ardres, Peace of, 288
Arran, Lord, Protector of Scotland, 255, 263, 267, 277
Arthur, Prince of Wales, 26, 31–2, 32; and Catherine of Aragon's trial, 144, 146
Ascham, Roger, 48n., 275
Aske, Robert, 210–12
Askew, Anne, case of, 292–3
Assertio Septem Sacramentorum adversus Martinus Lutherus, 91–2
Attainder, Act of, 229
Aubrey, John, 47; on family life, 49; on Wolsey, 55; on 'convent bells', 222; on William Herbert, 258n.
Audley, Thomas, Speaker, 150; as Lord Chancellor, 166; and Thomas More's trial, 182
Augmentation of the Revenues, Court of, 200

Bacon, Francis, 22, 35, 37
Bainbridge, Cardinal, 29, 54, 63
Bangor, Bishop of, 180–1
Barcelona, Treaty of, 146
Barnes, Dr, 204, 227, 231

'Barriers', game of, 41, 71–2
Baskerville, Geoffrey: on Henry, 17; on dissolutions, 189, 190, 191, 221; on Lincolnshire rising, 209
'Battle of Spurs', 59
Beales, A. C. F., on dissolution of chantries, 282
Beaton, Cardinal David, 247, 256, 263, 267, 276, 277, 288
Beaufort, Lady Margaret, 22, 26, 40
Bellay, Jean du: on Catherine of Aragon's trial, 145; on Wolsey's disgrace, 149; unpopularity of in England, 171–2
'Benevolences', revival of, 281
Bernard André of Toulouse, Friar, 30
Bible, 'Great' or 'Cranmer's', 259
Bindoff, Prof., on the JP 44; on blood sports, 46n.
Bishoprics, new creations of, 234
Bishops, election of, 175–6
'Bishop's book', the, revised, 260
Blunt, Elizabeth, 101
Boleyn, Anne, 32; affair with Henry, 136–8, 140–2, 144; made Marchioness of Pembroke, 165; in France, 166; her marriage, 166–7; her triumph, 168–9; her coronation as Queen, 169–70; her unpopularity, 176–7; pregnancies, 166–7, 179, 200; her power over Henry, 196, and its waning, 198, 200; and Jane Seymour, 200; her fall, 201–4
Boleyn family, 201, 243, *et passim*
Boleyn, Mary, afterwards Lady Carey, 136, 191, 205
Boleyn, Sir Thomas (later Viscount Rochford and Earl of Wiltshire), 137–8, 144, 162–3, 203
Bologna, meeting at, 162–3; university of, 163
Bonner, Bishop of London, 231
Bosworth, battle of, 24
Boulogne, 270, 271, 272, 281, 288
Bourbon, Charles, Duc de, Constable of France, 117–18, 120, 121, 132, 138
Bowes, Sir Robert, 250, 256
Brandi, Karl, on Emperor Maximilian, 59n
Brandon, Sir Charles, *see* Suffolk, Duke of
Brandon, Lady Frances, 297
Brewer, J. S., on Henry, 15; on Duke of